Flame and Crimson

A History of Sword-and-Sorcery

Brian Murphy

Pulp Hero Press
The Most Dangerous Books on Earth
www.PulpHeroPress.com

Editor: Bob McLain
Layout: Artisanal Text
ISBN 978-1-68390-244-7
Printed in the United States of America

Pulp Hero Press | www.PulpHeroPress.com
Address queries to bob@pulpheropress.com

Contents

Introduction

Let me tell you of the days of high adventure...

As a boy I could sit for hours drawing pitched battles between medieval armies. One Halloween I fashioned a complete suit of cardboard armor and wooden sword, the next a fur-clad barbarian costume with (tinfoil) horned helmet. I read the stories of King Arthur and Robin Hood, consumed a steady diet of films like *The Beastmaster* and *Legend*, and spent countless afternoons gathered around the kitchen table rolling dice with a group of friends, vicariously living the lives of mighty warriors and mystical wizards during marathon games of *Dungeons and Dragons*. I was also dimly aware from an early age that a schism lay at the heart of this fantastic genre I loved—or, perhaps more accurately, a battle-line. Arrayed on one side were the wonders of authors like J.R.R. Tolkien, who wrote epic-length novels about brave but domestic hobbits dreaming of home even as they valiantly fought to preserve Middle-Earth. On the other were stories of black-clad, dagger-wielding rogues plying their craft in dirty alleyways for a sack of coin, or the favors of a comely wench. And of barbarian heroes, muscled and bare-chested, awash in blood atop a mound of corpses. Always barbarians.

My preference for this tougher, more muscular brand of fantasy was ignited by a fortuitous find circa 1984–85. While making the rounds at a favorite used bookstore, I noticed an unmarked cardboard box on the floor containing a few rows of what looked like magazines. I lifted out an issue and was immediately arrested by its cover, which in bright colors depicted a muscular hero wielding a bloodied axe against a horde of ghouls, skeletons, pirates, and a wizard. A scantily-clad, voluptuous blonde female looked on in amazement (and desire). Standing stock-still in this dusty bookstore at the edge of town, I found myself overcome with a feeling the same as the blonde damsel—mouth agape, astonished to look upon this miraculous tableaux of mayhem, muscle, and glory.

It was *Savage Sword of Conan*, issue no. 16 to be exact. I knew the name Conan from the movies and from references in popular

culture, but this was something different: A magazine both dangerous and adult, with unfathomable alien articles and lots of text to
go with stunning black and white interior artwork. When I got home
with my new purchase (for the princely sum of $2) I was treated to
the first part of "The People of the Black Circle," hooked and reeled
in by its deliciously perfect synopsis: "In the vast, mysterious sub-
continent that is Vendhya, Conan the Cimmerian battles to save an
ancient throne from the most fearsome wizards of the Hyborian
Age." Next to the splash art was an evocative page with which
I'd soon become intimately familiar, and one that still evokes an
incredible feeling of excitement and a call to adventure—the famous
excerpt from the Nemedian Chronicles:

> Know, O prince, that between the years when the oceans drank
> Atlantis and the gleaming cities, and the years of the rise of the sons
> of Aryas, there was an age undreamed of...

Accompanying this bit of evocative text was a map of the
Hyborian Age of Conan, circa 10,000 B.C. Also in the issue were "A
Probable Outline of Conan's Career" (*appearing by popular demand!*);
"A Portfolio of Robert E. Howard," including illustrations of Conan,
Kull, and Red Sonja; "Fire and Slaughter," the fifth chapter of
Howard's saga of prehistoric civilization (circa 9,500 B.C.); "Worms
of the Earth" (*at last!*), a story of Bran Mak Morn, fearless king of the
Picts, who battles against the invading Romans with the hordes of
Hell on his side; and "Swords and Scrolls," the letters page, featuring
a lengthy letter from Yasmina, flower of the dawn and thief in the
night, a comely belly dancer who attended a comic-book convention
dressed as Conan's love-interest.

Needless to say I was hooked, drawn into a world in which all the
men were mighty of limb; the women full of hip and breast; where
magic was wild and unpredictable and to be feared; where ancient,
vine-choked cities lay in the heart of foreboding forests, to be
plundered only by those foolish or brave enough and trained in the
art of the sword. Conan was my guide in this wondrous Hyborian
Age, and over the next several months I lived a heroic, adventurous
existence, vicariously, through his adventures.

It would be years before I learned the differences between
high fantasy and sword-and-sorcery, but at the time I could feel
it. Although I had not discovered the name by which this brisker,
more visceral style of fantasy had come to be known, I knew that it
existed. I had tasted its purest draught, adaptations of the stories
published in the magazine *Weird Tales* in the 1920s and 30s that
marked the beginnings of the subgenre now known as sword-and-
sorcery. I had discovered the originator and greatest practitioner of
the sword-and-sorcery tale, Robert E. Howard.

Savage Sword of Conan started me down a path of discovery. At the time I was reading books like *The Sword of Shannara* and the *Dragonlance Chronicles*, and while these epic-length, Tolkien-inspired fantasies were okay, they didn't scratch the dark, violent, weird horror-infused itch I got from reading Howard and his ilk. I might have been too young to articulate the difference when I first held *SSOC* #16, but I could feel it, and I knew in my heart that one man's fantasy was not another's, and that sword-and-sorcery was a thing apart from the likes of Terry Brooks, Margaret Weis, and Tracy Hickman.

Fortunately it was the 1980s and I had options. Barbarian heroes were everywhere. Cover blurbs of slim novels promising that "the ghost of Robert E. Howard's Conan moves through the pages" led me to the freewheeling adventures of Fritz Leiber's Fafhrd and the Gray Mouser, the displaced wanderings of the drug dependent albino sorcerer Prince Elric, and the titillating romps of Vakar of Lorsk, hero of L. Sprague de Camp's *The Tritonian Ring*. *Conan the Barbarian* had thundered its way through the theatre and onto endless reruns on HBO and, later, video cassette. Saturday morning cartoons featured the adventures of Thundaar the Barbarian and his companions Princess Ariel and Ookla the Mok. British heavy metal group Iron Maiden, a colossal international phenomenon, was singing sword-and-sorcery-inspired stories like "Sun and Steel," and bands like Manowar turned barbaric fantasy up to 11 with albums like *Sign of the Hammer* and *Fighting the World*. Publishers were turning out S&S anthologies at a white heat, including the likes of *Thieves World*, *Sword and Sorceress*, *Barbarians*, and *Echoes of Valor*.

Little did I know that I was living at the tail-end of the subgenre's revival and renaissance. A bubble was about to burst. Sword-and-sorcery was not much longer for the mainstream. Publishers had eyes for lucrative fantasy trilogies, and lean-and-mean standalone sword-and-sorcery stories could not compete against the likes of the unending cash-cow *The Wheel of Time*. The subgenre was also its worst enemy. A glut of bad novels and beefcake, and B-grade movies of muscled men in loincloths, spelled its doom, driving it underground.

But just as the love of adventure stories and the romance of the sword is still with us, today sword-and-sorcery lives on, transformed and resurgent. Authors like Richard Morgan and Joe Abercrombie are writing stories that straddle the line of high fantasy of sword-and-sorcery, but owe a far greater debt to the latter. James Enge (*Blood of Ambrose*, *The Wolf Age*) and Howard Andrew Jones (*The Desert of Souls*) belong solidly in the sword-and-sorcery tradition. Many of the genre's classics have enjoyed a recent reprint in Planet Stories, a handsome trade paperback collection by Paizo, and in the recent *Sword and Sorcery Anthology* (2012, Tachyon Publications).

The genre is, after a period of frail half-life in distant corners of the internet, clawing itself out of a shallow grave, and bearing with it a bright blade of vengeance.

Sword-and-sorcery's influence extends far beyond the printed page. The subgenre has scaled the walls of a literary Venarium and into music, tabletop role playing games, video games, television shows, and movies, converting new fans who may never have read the source material. World of Warcraft enthusiasts who spend their nights looting and pillaging in the gritty fantasy realms of Azeroth may not have heard of sword-and-sorcery, but in their own way are as devoted to the subgenre as any die-hard reader of the Lancer Conan Saga paperbacks of the 1960s. Long-haired, tattooed fans of the bands Manowar, Blind Guardian and Cauldron Born might never have picked up a an Elric novel, but the powerful riffs and muscular, martial lyrics of heavy metal deliver sword-and-sorcery's invigorating message as purely as any tale of the doomed (and rather metal) albino swordsman.

Flame and Crimson: A History of Sword-and-Sorcery attempts to provide a comprehensive analysis of a still misunderstood and ill-defined subgenre. It traces sword-and-sorcery's glorious rise and ignominious fall, asks the "why" behind why it arose, and makes a case for its greatest works and authors as worthy of exploration and study. Sword-and-sorcery offers escape for its readers, but the best of the subgenre offers more. Like all good literature it not only withstands but demands critical attention and analysis. This book also examines some of the ways in which sword-and-sorcery has permeated the broader culture.

The book is dedicated to the fans who, like the author, have not in life but through its stories known the rich juices of red meat and stinging wine on their palate, the hot embrace of white arms, the mad exultation of battle when the blue blades flame and crimson. And are content.

And it is dedicated to Robert E. Howard, who made it all possible.

CHAPTER ONE
What is Sword-and-Sorcery?

We can give you clues to what it is—and what it is not. It is not high fantasy. High fantasy dresses up life and offers comfort; it is romantic. Our fiction is dark, often very dark, in the same way that unsettling dreams are never far from nightmares, and not at all comforting.

—David C. Smith, "Introduction," *Swords of Steel*

Propelled by the commercial successes of J.R.R. Tolkien's *The Lord of the Rings* in the mid-20th century and JK Rowling's *Harry Potter* in the new millennium, the literary genre broadly known as fantasy has grown to epic proportions. Fantasy and its close cousin science fiction together comprise the world's fourth largest literary genre ("Leading book genres worldwide as of January 2014, by revenue"). The public hunger for fantasy continues to grow without abatement: *Harry Potter* recently became the best-selling series in history with a reported 450 million copies sold, and new volumes of George R.R. Martin's grim and gritty *A Song of Ice and Fire* regularly appear atop the bestseller lists, reaching ever-greater audiences now that they've been adapted as a wildly popular cable TV miniseries.

Fantasy is also an enormously broad genre, encompassing numerous modes, subgenres, and a number of unclassifiable, idiosyncratic works. In the last half century "fantasy" has been used to describe such diverse works as Joe Abercrombie's "grimdark" military fantasy *The Heroes*, C.S. Lewis' Christian apologetic *The Chronicles of Narnia*, and Ursula LeGuin's *Earthsea* series. Fantasy enjoys a multigenerational appeal: Lloyd Alexander's *The Chronicles of Prydain* and Susan Cooper's *The Dark is Rising* sequence ignited a young adult fantasy market in the 1960s, and today *Harry Potter* and Christopher Paolini's *Eragon* have solidified the genre as one enjoyed by both adolescents and adults.

"Fantasy" as a publishing term and structured, codified genre is a relatively modern concept, but its roots are very old, dating back to 2,000 BC and the Sumerian *Epic of Gilgamesh*. In the ancient world the fantastic enjoyed a close relationship with reality, and works like *The Iliad*, *The Odyssey*, and *Beowulf* were not viewed as escapist, but important stories with meaning and truth, both symbolic and literal. Dismissed in the late 19ᵗʰ century as the stuff of moralistic children's stories and bedtime fairy tales,[1] fantasy today enjoys broad appeal, and a measure of critical respect. It is written for adult audiences, with complex plots, political intrigue, and multiple viewpoint characters. Often that leads to intimidating page counts and fantasy series requiring more than one book—or three or five or even seven or more. Fantasy introduces its readers to the geography and geopolitics of secondary worlds and continent-shaking wars. These require complex, multi-threaded plots, or the support of navigation tools including appendices of family trees and detailed maps. Fantasy literature takes not just its characters, but its *readers,* on literary journeys that span years, even decades, of real time. Robert Jordan's *The Wheel of Time* is perhaps the most iconic example, spanning 14 bookshelf-groaning volumes in a series so long its final three books had to be finished posthumously.

This mode of multi-volume, world-shaking fantasy is today known as "epic" or more commonly "high" fantasy. A hallmark of this style of fiction is classic battles of good vs. evil, troupes of heroes engaged in a quest opposed by a Dark Lord, a trope established by J.R.R. Tolkien's *The Lord of the Rings* and continued by authors such as Stephen Donaldson (*The Chronicles of Thomas Covenant*) and Terry Brooks (the *Shannara* series). High fantasy often features ordinary, run-of-the-mill protagonists thrust unwillingly into adventures beyond their control (Frodo Baggins in *The Lord of the Rings,* the assistant pig-keeper Taran in *The Chronicles of Prydain*), or involves seemingly run-of-the-mill characters with great but latent magical powers (Harry Potter, the Pevensie children of the *Narnia* series). High fantasy's roots include Norse, Celtic, Greco-Roman and Christian myth, Arthurian myth, and oral epics like *Beowulf.* Its pioneers are Victorian Age authors Lord Dunsany, George MacDonald, and William Morris. Robert Boyer and Kenneth Zahorski describe high fantasy as possessing other-worldly settings, populated with "a generous number of imposing figures who, with their magical or supernatural power, inspire wonder or fear or often both." High fantasy's subject matter is equally portentous, "deal(ing) with recognizably archetypal themes and motifs such as the initiation into manhood, death and rebirth, and most frequently with the courage an individual needs to undertake the fateful quest." To match its quasi-medieval settings and high-stakes bombast and add to the

---

[1] Fantasy's most visible and acerbic critic in this era was William Dean Howells (1837–1920), editor of *The Atlantic Monthly* from 1871–1881 and an originator of the post-modern literary establishment. Howells championed realistic tales of the common man and denounced stories with exotic settings and heroic protagonists, including H. Rider Haggard's She.

readers' sense of displacement, high fantasy authors often employ an archaic and/or elevated writing style. "The dialogue must befit the stature of the speakers; descriptive passages must be in an elevated style that necessarily works through imagery and comparison to create the imaginary worlds" (Tymn, Zahorski, Boyer 9).

As the most commercially successful and popularly known subgenre of fantasy fiction, high fantasy has become synonymous with "fantasy." Much of the reading public—and even many fantasy critics and scholars—consider fantasy a uniform, homogenous genre. Tolkien scholar Michael Drout in his survey of the fantasy genre *Rings, Swords, and Monsters: Exploring Fantasy Literature* says that fantasy's earth-shaking/universe-hanging-in-the-balance plots—a quest to destroy a magic ruling ring lest it fall into the hands of a dark lord and plunge the world into eternal darkness, for example—are overdone to the point of cliché. "Fantasy ends up playing for very, very high stakes, almost impossibly high stakes. And that's one of the weaknesses of fantasy. Because every fantasy book you pick up—at least just about every fantasy book you pick up—is about the fate of the world hangs upon this small thing someone does. ... it's problematic because the world seems about to end every day if you read enough fantasy" (Drout, lecture 9).

But fantasy fiction is mutable and varied. It did not emerge from a single wellspring, and its many forms, variations, and permutations cannot be easily summarized with a single label. At the turn of the 20th century a new subgenre of fantasy was birthed in the pages of pulp magazines, its authors inspired not by medieval epics, but masculine, two-fisted historical adventure and interplanetary romance. It featured stories of mercenary and often morally compromised "heroes" in search of plunder and wealth, trying to save their own skins as they plunged headlong from one fast-paced adventure to the next. Its plots were set not in ethereal "once upon a time" lands of faerie, but grounded, quasi-historical and/or impossibly ancient pre-historical settings, peopled with scheming kings, dark sorcerers, and scantily clad, nubile women. These stories lacked the epic length of Morris' *The Well at the World's End* or Tolkien's *The Lord of the Rings*. Short and episodic in nature, they matched the editorial requirements and limitations of the pulp magazine medium in which their authors worked.

In the 1920s and 1930s televisions were rare and the printed page was the primary medium by which entertainment was delivered and consumed by an increasingly hungry consumer base, one with more idle time than any previous generation in which to enjoy it. Publishers met the demand with mass-produced short-fiction magazines printed on cheap paper known as the "pulps." Titles like *Argosy, Adventure*, and *Black Mask* published genre fiction ranging from westerns, to boxing, to mystery and detective stories. Much of it was formulaic, written to meet the demands of expectant subscribers, but a handful of imaginative authors began to experiment with genre mixing. Working in one of the more permissive and experimental pulps of the age, a young writer from Cross Plains, Texas, named Robert E. Howard conceived of a barbaric outsider striding like a steel-springed panther through soft, corrupt, civilized lands. Howard was inspired by the adventure stories of Harold Lamb, Jack London, and Edgar Rice Burroughs. His otherworldly stories were watered and fertilized from his native soil, having encountered similar rough-and-tumble, hard-living men in the oil fields and storefronts of rural early 20th century Texas. Into this base material he poured the influence of the weird—strange, otherworldly horrors as seen in the stories of *Weird Tales* contemporaries H.P. Lovecraft and Clark Ashton Smith. In so doing he created a fantasy subgenre apart from the medieval romance inspired works of Morris or the childlike fancies of Lewis Carroll.

Howard's art—a product of his unique upbringing and personal circumstances, intensity of emotion, and idiosyncratic writing talent—birthed a subgenre entirely different aesthetically and thematically from its fantasy ancestors. When Howard died in 1936 it lacked a name. Some writers in Howard's wake carried on the tradition by writing barbaric and savage fantasy fiction of their own, some with new and innovative touches, others with slavish devotion to Howard's originals. These included the likes of C.L. Moore, Clark Ashton Smith, Henry Kuttner, and Fritz Leiber. For more than 20 years this new subgenre remained a vital but marginal force, exalted by a small handful of writers and readers, but trapped in the pages of the swiftly yellowing pulps, largely inaccessible to a wider readership.

Twenty-five years after Howard's death this new style of fantasy was at last given a name. "Sword-and-sorcery" was born in 1961 out of conversations percolating in the pages of the fanzines *Ancalagon* and *Amra*.[2] Coined by Fritz Leiber, author of the Fafhrd and the Gray Mouser stories, two years later it became a permanent part of the parlance, stamped across the cover of the L. Sprague de Camp edited anthology *Swords & Sorcery* (1963, Pyramid Books), one of the earliest and most important sword-and-sorcery titles in a popular new medium replacing the void left by the pulps—the pocket-sized paperback. By the late 1960s sword-and-sorcery was in full bloom. Dozens of new titles by John Jakes, L. Sprague de Camp, Poul Anderson, Jack Vance, and Lin Carter, and reissues of classic

---

[2] This book prefers the hyphenated, lower-case "sword-and-sorcery" as first used by Leiber, though Sword-and-Sorcery, Sword & Sorcery, and other permutations are common.

works by the likes of Howard and Leiber, flooded the marketplace throughout the 60s and 70s, most with evocative covers featuring muscled, sword- and axe-wielding warriors and damsels in distress. Many of these appeared in anthologies with muscular-sounding titles: *Flashing Swords, Swords Against Darkness*, and *Echoes of Valor*.

A few among this new wave of authors turned their attention to aesthetic explorations of the subgenre, including its origins, tropes, and themes. One of the most colorful, easy-to-grasp definitions of sword-and-sorcery can be found in the introduction to *Conan of the Isles*, a 1968 anthology by L. Sprague de Camp and Lin Carter, two important figures in the preservation and popularization of Howard's stories. Writes de Camp:

> There is a kind of story laid, not in the world as it is or was, but as—to an armchair adventurer—it ought to have been. It is an adventure-fantasy, laid in an imaginary prehistoric or medieval world, where magic works and the scientific revolution has not taken place. Or perhaps it is in some parallel universe, or in this world as it will be in the distant future, when science has been forgotten and magic has revived.
>
> In such a world, gleaming cities raise their shining spires against the stars; sorcerers cast sinister spells from subterranean lairs; baleful spirits stalk crumbling ruins; primeval monsters crash through jungle thickets; and the fate of kingdoms is balanced on bloody broadswords brandished by heroes of preternatural might and valor. In such a world, men are mighty, women are beautiful, life is adventurous, and problems are simple. Nobody even mentions the income tax or the dropout problem or socialized medicine. Such a story is called "heroic fantasy" or, sometimes, sword-and-sorcery" (de Camp, *Conan of the Isles* 9).

In 1973 Carter expanded and further codified the definition in the first volume of his *Flashing Swords* anthologies. Here he identified a critical ancestral thread to sword-and-sorcery, "the traditions of the pulp magazine adventure story":

> What does Sword & Sorcery mean? A succinct definition follows:
>
> We call a story Sword & Sorcery when it is an action tale, derived from the traditions of the pulp magazine adventure story, set in a land, age or world of the author's invention–a milieu in which magic actually works and the gods are real—a story, moreover, which pits a stalwart warrior in direct conflict with the forces of supernatural evil (Carter, *Flashing Swords!* #1 13–14).

Editor of the critically acclaimed Ballantine Books Adult Fantasy series, or BAFS (1969–74), Carter was deeply versed in fantasy's literary origins and recognized that sword-and-sorcery represented a divergent path, with largely distinct and separate roots from the high fantasy stories of Tolkien, Lewis, and Ursula LeGuin. As part of the BAFS, Carter wrote and published one of the first literary studies of the fantasy genre, *Imaginary Worlds* (1973). This work, along with the likes of de Camp's *Literary Swordsmen and Sorcerers: The Makers of Heroic Fantasy* (1976), marked the first critical awakenings of sword-and-sorcery, outside of the fanzines.

Even after Leiber and Moorcock's meeting of the minds, and Carter and De Camp's first attempts at exploration and codification, "sword-and-sorcery" remained a diffuse and ill-understood term, its meaning disputed even as the publishing mill ground on in the 1960s and 70s. It didn't help that a few critical/biographical works published in the heyday of the subgenre added more murk than enlightenment. Unauthorized versions of *The Lord of the Rings* published by Ace Books in 1965 described Tolkien's novel as sword-and-sorcery. In *Literary Swordsmen and Sorcerers: The Makers of Heroic Fantasy*, de Camp called the faerie and enchantment-laced *The King of Elfland's Daughter* "the most swordly and sorcerous of [Lord] Dunsany's works" (de Camp, *Literary Swordsmen and Sorcerers* 60). Today, sword and sorcery remains a widely misapplied label. In *Conan the Phenomenon: The Legacy of Robert E. Howard's Fantasy Icon* (2007), author Paul Sammon declared Peter Jackson's *The Lord of the Rings* film trilogy as "the most successful S&S films of all time" (23), grouping Tolkien's high fantasy masterpiece with the historically gritty, violently and sexually graphic, and in all ways tonally opposite *Conan the Barbarian*. More recently Steve Drew, moderator of one of the largest online science fiction and fantasy fan communities, *reddit.com/r/fantasy*, indirectly equated Margaret Weiss and Tracy Hickman's Dragonlance Chronicles—an adolescent-oriented high fantasy trilogy—with sword-and-sorcery. "If you enjoyed reading *Dragonlance* books, that's fantastic, then let's go shift you over to some sword-and-sorcery. ... If you're a certain age maybe that's what you want, you want a Drow elf that spins in circles with scimitars, that's great, I really enjoyed it when I was at that age and there is even people that still enjoy it today" (Drew).

Adding further murk, authors and editors of sword-and-sorcery have disputed and some continue to question the efficacy of the term. Karl Edward Wagner, author of iconic sword-and-sorcery character Kane and editor of the *Echoes of Valor* anthologies and the acclaimed Berkley Medallion reissues of the Conan stories, argued for the term "epic fantasy" or "heroic fantasy." Author Andrew Offutt, editor of the seminal five-volume *Swords Against Darkness* series, rejected the term in favor of the more expansive "heroic fantasy," or no label at all. "As to 'sword & sorcery'—sometimes the tale contains no sword—or no sorcery! Or, more rarely, neither. (Sword and supernatural might come closer, if we're to discuss, haggle, or bicker" (*Swords Against Darkness II* 9). In an essay appearing in a new Wandering Star/Del Rey reprint of the classic Conan stories, Howard scholar Patrice Louinet acknowledges Howard's role in creating the sword-and-sorcery subgenre while simultaneously expressing his dissatisfaction with the term. "What Howard was unaware of ... was that he had given birth to a new subgenre of literature, since dubbed "Heroic Fantasy," "Epic Fantasy," or "Swords and Sorcery"—denominations as unsatisfying as they are reductive" (Louinet 288). Louniet prefers the term "realistic fantasy tales." Moorcock himself is critical of the term, employing it with derision throughout his non-fiction treatise *Wizardry and Wild Romance*.[3]

Yet "sword-and-sorcery" has survived the pedantry of critics and the objections of editors and authors. Recently, it received the blessing and reinforcement of two anthologies published in the new millennium. *The Sword & Sorcery Anthology* (2012, Tachyon Publications) bears its name on its cover and is the subject of an introductory essay by co-editor and sword-and-sorcery author David Drake. A second anthology, *Swords and Dark Magic* (Eos/HarperCollins Publishers, 2010), also embraces the term. Alliterative, elegant, and functional as a descriptive as much as a proscriptive label, sword-and-sorcery has stuck. To paraphrase Leiber in his Fafhrd and the Gray Mouser tale "The Lords of Quarmall," the time has come for sword-and-sorcery. The nomenclature war is over.

Yet even while achieving a degree of critical consensus and some positive critical reappraisal, today sword-and-sorcery is marginalized and often treated with derision, associated with oiled and muscled loincloth-clad barbarians wielding outsized broadswords and battleaxes. The 1982 film *Conan the Barbarian*—painstakingly detailed, stirringly well-made, and widely regarded as one of the finest fantasy films ever made—launched an unfortunate slew of terrible sequels and derivative sword-and-sorcery films. Critics panning sword-and-sorcery as the dumb jock/black sheep brother of its respectable high fantasy sibling have ample cause. B-grade schlock like *The Barbarians* and *The Beastmaster* have become synonymous with sword-and-sorcery, dragging its literary forebears into the mire. Not without some cause sword-and-sorcery has been tarred with the unpleasant brushes of misogyny and racism. Some of these charges can be explained by the time and place in which its chief architect, Howard, wrote. Others, however, claim that racism and sexism are a part of its ethos, and treat the entire subgenre with suspicion.

---

[3] Perhaps a bit hypocritical on the part of Moorcock, who offered up the term "epic fantasy" for the tradition in which he placed his Elric stories, and freely uses "urban fantasy" to promote a style of fantasy fiction he prefers over pastoral fantasy (*Wizardry and Wild Romance* 143).

But sword-and-sorcery also has its champions, a handful of defenders who redirect the conversation toward the gems which continue to shine brightly among the not-inconsiderable chaff. Some few have recognized that sword-and-sorcery fills an important thematic void left by high fantasy. Author and critic Don Herron in his groundbreaking essay "The Dark Barbarian" argues that Howard's sword-and-sorcery contributions are not their surface elements—barbarians, broadswords, sorcerers, and damsels in distress—but their content, a singular "mood and philosophy" that speaks of political overthrow, chaos, and disunion:

> Burroughs' Tarzan is a respectable pillar of civilization as an English lord, and preserves the twentieth-century American sense of the status quo even when adventuring naked in time-lost cities and primeval forests. ... In Howard the unquiet surge of barbarism ever threatens to sweep the works of civilization under, the status quo is at best shaky—even when Howard's barbarians use their swords to put themselves on the thrones of the ruling class (150).

Karl Edward Wagner recognized that sword-and-sorcery offers a space for alternative heroes, giving voice to morally compromised protagonists unwelcome in high fantasy. "As a genre, epic fantasy (or heroic fantasy, as it is also designated) is a fascinating synthesis of horror, adventure, and imagination. While there are as many different concepts and approaches to epic fantasy as with any major genre, the common motif is a universe in which magic works and an individual may kill according to his personal code" (Wagner, *Conan: Red Nails* 1). Sword-and-sorcery provided authors with free rein to tell stories of morally compromised protagonists not seen since the likes of Egil and Njal in the Icelandic sagas, to which it owes a considerable debt.

Riding the momentum of a stunningly successful reissue of Howard's Conan stories in a popular new paperback format, sword-and-sorcery enjoyed a stay in the limelight, roughly 1966–1988, before fading back to its accustomed place on the margins of publishing. Yet even as it faded from the bookshelves sword-and-sorcery did not die, but morphed into a popular new subgenre, with a label befitting its unrelentingly bleak and cynical outlook: grimdark. Pioneered by the likes of Glen Cook, George R.R. Martin, and Joe Abercrombie, this new ultra-gritty, low magic, and often violently and sexually graphic brand of popular fantasy owes its origins to the sword-and-sorcery boom of the 1960s and 70s, and further back, to the pulps of the 1930s.

Even as it evolves and takes exciting new directions, sword-and-sorcery continues to be written and celebrated in fanzines and websites. With 90 years of history under its sword belt, it has a tradition, an ethos, and a style all its own.

Sword-and-Sorcery: The Base Elements

Anyone who has seen the Frank Frazetta painting *Death Dealer*, or watched *Conan the Barbarian*, has a good starting visual for sword-and-sorcery. Harder to define are its literary, stylistic, and thematic elements and characteristics. This next section offers a working, ground-floor definition. While placing rigid borders around anything as malleable as literature inevitably results in exceptions and contradictions, sword-and-sorcery fiction has a distinctive aesthetic and conventions. While no story is likely to contain all these elements, it typically features men (and occasionally women) of action, pitted against enemies wielding dark and dangerous magic, in pursuit of personal and/or mercenary aims. Story and page-turning adventure is privileged over in-depth characterization or world-building. Sword-and-sorcery is rooted in pulp adventure stories and weird horror, a legacy of its *Weird Tales* ancestry and the formidable influence of H.P. Lovecraft. It is inspired by history, and in particular owes much to historical fiction, adventure fiction, and Icelandic saga. Typically it is short, more at home in short stories or novella-length works. Finally, its "heroes" are often outsiders, uncomfortable in positions of great authority and ill-fitted to the civilized mores of the lands through which they adventure. When they do they find themselves in leadership positions, sword-and-sorcery heroes often find the crown heavy and wearying, apt to swap it out for coin to fuel their next binge of drinking and wenching. They are ever attuned to the siren call of dangerous but lucrative adventure—a call to which they frequently answer.

Following is a closer look at these elements, citing examples from representative sword-and-sorcery fiction from approximately 1929 through 1988. This period coincides with the subgenre's beginning (defined as the publication of Robert E. Howard's "The Shadow Kingdom") and its approximate "fall." The latter date is subjective and somewhat arbitrary as sword-and-sorcery never utterly collapsed or vanished, but by the late 1980s it had largely ceased to be handled by mainstream publishers.

Not every sword-and-sorcery story contains each of the following elements, nor in some set proportion or formula. These are intended as broad strokes to help provide a working definition, and will be found in varying degrees in the literature. In recent years authors working in the tradition have deliberately set out to break sword-and-sorcery's conventions, forging new ground as they challenge the reader's expectations and push the subgenre into new and interesting territory.

MEN (AND WOMEN) OF ACTION

These are men of mighty thews, strong passions, indomitable wills, and keen minds, who dominate the stories through which they stride.

—*L. Sprague De Camp, Warlocks and Warriors*

Perhaps the most salient feature of the sword-and-sorcery genre— and the one element from which it can least afford to be separated, lest it lose something so fundamental it can no longer be recognized as such—is its adventure-seeking heroes. Sword-and-sorcery typically features a single protagonist, with some notable exceptions including Fritz Leiber's iconic duo of Fafhrd and the Gray Mouser. Most of these heroes are male and are often powerfully built, walking visions of strength and vitality. Here is a typical description of Conan, from Howard's "The Devil in Iron":

> As the first tinge of dawn reddened the sea, a small boat with a solitary occupant approached the cliffs. The man in the boat was a picturesque figure. A crimson scarf was knotted about his head; his wide silk breeches, of flaming hue, were upheld by a broad sash which likewise supported a scimitar in a shagreen scabbard. His gilt-worked leather boots suggested the horseman rather than the seaman, but he handled his boat with skill. Through his widely open silk shirt showed his broad muscular breast, burned brown by the sun.
>
> The muscles of his heavy bronzed arms rippled as he pulled the oars with an almost feline ease of motion. A fierce vitality that was evident in each feature and motion set him apart from common men; yet his expression was neither savage nor somber; though the smoldering blue eyes hinted at ferocity easily wakened.

Here is another typical description, of Karl Edward Wagner's Kane:

> His visitor was not a reassuring figure. At rather more than twice the thin man's bulk, he sprawled half out of the room's single chair. His massive frame exuded an aura of almost bestial strength. The figure might have been that of some great ape, clad in black leather trousers and sleeveless vest. Ruthless intelligence showed in the brutal face, framed by nape-length red hair and a beard like rust. A red silk scarf encircled his thick neck, and belted across the barrel chest, the hilt of a Carsultyal sword protruded over his right shoulder. The savage blue eyes held a note in their stare that promised sudden carnage should that huge left hand reach for the hilt.

Although the genre is largely dominated by male writers and male protagonists, sword-and-sorcery is not without a few notable heroines. C.L. Moore, a contemporary of Howard's, wrote the first (and some would argue, best) sword-and-sorcery heroine, Jirel of Joiry. Jirel, too, is a whirlwind of power, a match for any man in hand-to-hand combat. Howard populated his Conan stories with a handful of strong women, including Valeria of the Red Brotherhood, leader of a cutthroat band of pirates. Wagner's *Bloodstone* features Teres, a fierce, brash swordswoman whose face bears the scars of battles in which she has slain dozens of adversaries. In the mid-1980s fantasy author and editor Marion Zimmer Bradley began a long-running anthology series appropriately entitled *Sword and Sorceress,* featuring strong female sword-and-sorcery protagonists. With a fair share of female protagonists possessed of stereotypically masculine traits—physical strength, skill at arms, fierce individuality and agency, and implacable determination—some critics and scholars have painted the subgenre as not only accepting of heroines, but feminist in nature (Emmelhainz, "Sword-Edge").

Not all sword-and-sorcery heroes are overwhelming physical specimens. A notable departure from the muscled barbarian stereotype is Moorcock's Elric of Melnibone, a sickly, slight-framed albino dependent on a daily cocktail of drugs to maintain his strength. Elric, however, was written as a deliberate anti-hero, and moreover is an excellent swordsman and formidable opponent in combat. What sword-and-sorcery heroes are uniformly not, is powerless. They are not the hollow men of so many modern and postmodern novels, emasculated and passive, victims of time and circumstance, constantly second-guessing themselves or agonizing over their next course of action. "They are not antiheroes—those pathetic little twerps with neither brains nor brawn nor character who have cringed through the pages of so many stories in recent decades" (de Camp, *Warlocks and Warriors* 8). Often their strength is derived from life outside the walls of the civilized city, a romanticized view of the pure, uncorrupted barbarian owing much to the "Noble Savage" archetype attributed to Jean-Jacques Rousseau. Sword-and-sorcery heroes are typically skilled in hand-to-hand combat, often peerless in the art or so powerful and savage that they can overcome more skilled foes. This differentiates them from many of the iconic heroes of high fantasy—Samwise Gamgee, Thomas Covenant, Harry Potter, and the like—who while possessed of a heroic spirit are incapable of standing toe to toe with fearsome opponents in the press of the battlefield.

The tech level of sword-and-sorcery is typically medieval or Iron Age equivalent, with its protagonists wielding hand-held arms (frequently swords, though axes, maces, poniards, scimitars, and the like are acceptable implements of mayhem, too). Sword-and-sorcery stories are set in ancient and/or pre-historical eras prior to the invention of firearms and gunpowder, in post-apocalyptic or distant futures where magic has replaced technology, or in imaginary worlds where firearms do not exist. This provision excludes the Robert E. Howard creation Solomon Kane, whom some classify as the first sword-and-sorcery hero.[4] It also excludes Tarzan and John Carter of Mars, creations of sword-and-sorcery progenitor Edgar Rice Burroughs. Carter belongs to a separate but related genre, sword-and-planet and/or planetary romance, which involve adventures set on other planets often possessing advanced technology. Leigh Brackett's *The Sword of Rhiannon* (1949) is rightly classified as sword-and-planet for this reason, although many fans of the sword-and-sorcery genre wouldn't put up a fight if you classified it as s&s, so purely does Brackett tap into the heroic spirit of the genre. Likewise, Otis Adelbert Kline's *The Swordsman of Mars* (1929) is probably best classified as sword-and-planet, though one could without much trouble slide it over into sword-and-sorcery.[5]

Despite their immense physical strength and vitality, sword and sorcery heroes are not godlike. They struggle not only with their opponents, but with harsh environments and unforgiving landscapes. Most sword-and-sorcery heroes fall squarely in the middle of Northrop Frye's five-tier heroic scale as described in his *Anatomy of Criticism: Four Essays*. Frye's scale includes 1) heroes of *myth*, the tales of divine godlike beings, 2) heroes of *romance*, superior in degree to other men and to their environment, 3) heroes of the *high mimetic* mode, superior in degree to other men but not to their natural environment, 4) heroes of the *low mimetic* mode, superior neither to other men nor to their environment, i.e., "one of us"; and 5) heroes of the *ironic* mode, inferior in power or intelligence to ourselves (33–34). While you can find a few examples of sword and sorcery heroes edging into categories 2 and 4, most fall squarely in camp 3; they are powerful and capable of heroic feats of arms, surviving battle after battle and often against seemingly impossible odds, but they can die in a desert or a wasteland. They are not

---

[4] Though he predates Kull of Valusia and Conan of Cimmeria, the flintlock-wielding Puritan swordsman is very much of his time—the Elizabethan era, roughly late 16th-early 17th century—and therefore belongs to adventure fiction or historical fantasy.

[5] Why the emphasis on low-tech weaponry as an essential component of the subgenre, other than the obvious modifier of "sword" without which there would simply be "sorcery"? The greater the technology, the less the import of the individual physical skill of the protagonist. It is easier to kill impersonally, on a mass scale, with rapid-firing projectile weapons (to say nothing of guided missiles and laser weapons), than with the muscle and sinew dependent, hand-to-hand implements of the ancient and medieval era. Sword-and-sorcery is in some ways a reaction to modernity and the dehumanizing weapons of mass-slaughter introduced during World War I. The more modern the setting, the less hero-dependent the plot, particularly from a physical sense. Sufficiently advanced technology typically subverts the need for sorcery; spell-casting wizards are passe in a universe permitting marvels like interstellar transport. Conan with an Atlantean blade speaks to a certain reader; Conan with a Barsoomian radium pistol is something else altogether—a mighty hero, still, but not a sword-and-sorcery hero.

divinely fated for some great, legendary destiny, but can meet their end, ingloriously, in dirty back alleys. Many often do.

DARK AND DANGEROUS MAGIC

Those cuts were enough to kill any common beast—or man—but a wizard has a dozen lives. Wound one, and he writhes away like a crippled snake to soak up fresh venom from some source of sorcery.

—Robert E. Howard, "People of the Black Circle"

Unable to get his stories of the Atlantean King Kull published with any regularity in *Weird Tales*, Howard introduced magical elements into a previously rejected story ("By this Axe I Rule"), renamed the character, and managed to sell it to editor Farnsworth Wright (Holmes, "Gothic to Cosmic" 67). This otherwise minor commercial footnote of weird-fiction history helped to solidify magic as an integral element of sword-and-sorcery. Each of the first four Robert E. Howard Conan stories featured the Cimmerian pitting his wits, muscle, and steel against the dark designs and black magic of twisted sorcerers, establishing a powerful template that helped give the subgenre its name.

The magic of high fantasy often follows defined physical laws, features a "light" or good magic that opposes the evil, or is sufficiently ingrained in the narrative of the story to be a routine, safe, even predictable force operating in the universe. The protagonist of Ursula Le Guin's high fantasy classic *A Wizard of Earthsea*, Ged, is born with an innate magical ability which he uses to save his village from a horde of invaders. Magic is inextricably linked to the moral center of Earthsea's universe, tied to an overarching theme that one can become whole only through knowing ourselves, fully and completely. Magic is a mystery whose truth is to be uncovered, disentangled, and ultimately embraced. In contrast, sword-and-sorcery magic does not follow logical rules or rational trains of thought. It is the stuff of chaos and duplicity, disunion and entropy, at the fringes of control, and quite often destroys its user. It is the stuff of romance, representing the irrational, unpredictable, indefinable. Play with magic in a sword-and-sorcery tale and you are likely to get (literally) burned, driven insane, or both. In Howard's "The Phoenix on the Sword" the dark Stygian sorcerer Thoth-amon is in the employ of the scheming Ascalante, who covets the Aquilonian crown on the brow of Conan. Though he's a powerful sorcerer—one of the most powerful of his age—Thoth-amon fears Ascalante, as the latter holds him in thrall with a powerful insurance policy—should Asalante die by treachery, a hermit priest in the southern desert will break the seal of a scroll and read it.

"And having read, a word will be whispered in Stygia, and a wind will creep up from the south by midnight. And where will you hide your head, Thoth-amon?"

The slave shuddered and his dusky face went ashen.

As the direct descendants of adventure stories, sword-and-sorcery heroes' worth is affirmed by their speed, skill, and prowess with a blade. Magic violates the rules which govern their physical universe and threatens their sovereignty, much like the introduction of firearms to the battlefield. "In Howard's stories, the supernatural element is often portrayed as unnatural, intruding into the story world and threatening the existing paradigm. ... The defining characteristic of Howard's sword and sorcery that sets it apart from classical fantasy may therefore be said to be the resolution, through the agency of a heroic protagonist, of the conflict resulting from irrational forces intruding upon the rational empirical world" (Shanks, "History, Horror, and Heroic Fantasy" 13–14, 15–16). Sword-and-sorcery magic is in some ways equivalent to dehumanizing technology, with humanity struggling for relevance and autonomy. Says the sword-maiden Teres of Karl Edward Wagner's *Bloodstone*, "There's little joy in a battle where black sorcery and alien science struggle like giants in the dark sky and brave men become no more than scurrying ants who die unnoticed beneath their tread" (243).

Correspondingly, sword-and-sorcery magic is associated with danger and menace. Pentagrams, cauldrons, and human skulls are its emblems. It is occult; learned by the study of dangerous and arcane arts and texts. A typical trope is the sorcerer who summons demons and monsters from the underworld barely within his or her control, or effects powerful curses and pronouncements of doom.[6] In Wagner's *Darkness Weaves*, the sorceress Efrel summons a demon to reveal to her the name of the man who will lead her forces to victory in a war of bloody vengeance. Efrel rips a heart from the breast of a virgin and offers it to a demon "from the world beyond night," and spends her nights "poring over cryptic lines paged on human skin" to learn her craft. In Leiber's Fafhrd and the Gray Mouser stories,

---

[6] Although they acknowledge the sword-and-sorcery subgenre, Marshall Tymn, Kenneth Zahorski, and Robert Boyer introduce the term "Gothic Fantasy" in *Fantasy Literature*, described as fantasy distinguished by "what we consider to be the very essence of Gothicism—that is, humankind's archetypal fascination with, and fear of, the unknown and the unnatural." Effective ambiance, mysterious settings and characters, and Gothic devices and paraphernalia including "forbidden books of black magic, evil potions and spells, moldering skeletons, dark and forbidding castles" and the like are frequently employed in these types of stories. Authors of Gothic Fantasy include H. Rider Haggard, H.P. Lovecraft, Robert E. Howard, C.L. Moore, Clark Ashton Smith, Fritz Leiber, and Poul Anderson (Tymn, Zahorski, Boyer 15–17). Thus, Gothic Fantasy is certainly bedfellows with sword-and-sorcery.

the protagonists are often pawns of the good-natured and aloof, but opaque and manipulative wizards Sheelba of the Eyeless Face and Ningauble of the Seven Eyes. They rarely see the wizard's ends, but serve as the means of forces beyond their control. Mouser himself is an amateur sorcerer who dabbles in the dark arts, but this aspect of his persona is depicted by Leiber as unsavory, adding to the Mouser's general moral ambiguity.

Perhaps the most innovative depiction of dark sorcery can be found in Michael Moorcock's Elric of Melnibone series. The albino swordsmen frequently summons demons and elemental elder gods to his aid in times of crisis, most notably Arioch, a Lord of Chaos and Duke of Hell. In "While the Gods Laugh," Elric summons the earth elemental King Grome to swallow up a horde of the living dead, eliciting a shudder from his companions:

> Suddenly, a whole area of the surrounding hillside split into cracks, and yawning crannies appeared in the surface. Elric and his companions swung themselves on to their horses as, with a frightful multivoiced scream, the dead lords were swallowed by the earth, returning to the depths from which they had been summoned.
>
> A deep unholy chuckle arose from the shattered pit. It was the mocking laughter of the earth elemental King Grome, taking his rightful subjects back into his keeping. Whining, the devil-dogs slunk towards the edge of the pit, sniffing around it. Then, with one accord, the black pack hurled itself down into the chasm, followed its masters to whatever unholy doom awaited it (67).

Elric's magic sword Stormbringer feeds upon the doomed souls of those it slays. It betrays Elric again and again, twisting in his hands to slay those whom he loves. It can be viewed as a symbol of Elric's own uncontrollable violent predilections from his inhuman/Melnibonean half, whose inexorable pull against which Elric struggles in vain comprises the main action of the saga. In a brief biographical letter written in 1964 in which he explains the origins of the Elric stories, Moorcock describes Stormbringer as a symbol of "my own and others' tendency to rely on mental and physical crutches rather than cure the weakness at source" (Moorcock, "The Secret Life of Elric of Melnibone" 447).

PERSONAL AND/OR MERCENARY MOTIVATIONS

Black Kessak and royal-blooded Paldridian would draw their swords together this night; and who for the better reason, the body of a flame-haired temptress, or the stomach of a hungry man?

— Geo W. Proctor, "The Smile of Oisia"

In J.R.R. Tolkien's *The Lord of the Rings*, the fate of Middle-Earth hangs by a thread—a near-suicidal mission into the heart of Mordor to destroy the One Ring. In Margaret Weiss and Tracy Hickman's *Dragonlance Chronicles* trilogy, a group of mismatched, disparate heroes must unite to defend the world of Krynn from Takhisis the Queen of Darkness and her evil minions, else darkness will consume its fair and green lands. The eponymous hero of *The Chronicles of Thomas Covenant, the Unbeliever* must save the Land (with a capital L) from the ravages of the evil corruptor Lord Foul. High fantasy is the stuff of dark lords striving with virtuous heroes, often with the fate of mankind hanging in the balance. The stakes are incredibly high. The souls of its protagonists are often put to the test—self-doubt and terrible temptations strive with their better angels to corrupt and drag them into the dark. "Good and evil are clearly manifest in fantasy literature ordinarily. The fantasy takes place in a world wherein moral coordinates are clear and distinct, in a moral landscape wherein moral qualities are most often embodied in major characters other than the central character (who is usually at first portrayed as an everyman, a fairly ordinary person of no particular consequence in the world. But the central character becomes a crucial figure in a struggle between good and evil" (Hartwell xiv). In the 20–30 years following Tolkien and C.S. Lewis' *Chronicles of Narnia*, high fantasy followed a "recovery, escape, and consolation" formula promulgated in Tolkien's influential "On Fairy Stories" essay, with the comfort and security of an all-knowing, all-loving God watching over the struggle. More than one critic expected all of fantasy literature to conform to Christianity's moral coordinates. "We should demand that all will be well in the end. It is the Christian expectation" (Lochhead 105).

In contrast, sword-and-sorcery protagonists are driven by personal and immediate goals, often mercenary. "Where epic fantasy celebrates heroic virtue, S&S prefers moderate virtue allied with good sense and a capacity to compromise" ("Sword and Sorcery"). Many of the "heroes" of sword-and-sorcery operate out of far less than heroic motives, and in some instances are no better than the forces against which they fight. Declares Wagner's most famous creation, the immortal warrior Kane, "Ethics! Your moral scruples are a senseless wasteland of contradictions and stupidity!" he exploded. "I serve Kane, and no other gods or obscure values!" (*Bloodstone* 183). Gods populate sword-and-sorcery stories, but they are pagan, flawed, and often indifferent to the struggles of their heroes.

Sword-and-sorcery typically operates on a small scale, with its stories told from the perspective of an individual hero in personal, day-to-day or minute-to-minute struggles of life and death. In the introduction to *Swords & Dark Magic: The New Swords and Sorcery*, editors Lou Anders and Jonathan Strahan boil this critical difference of scope down to a snappy comparison: sword and sorcery is a product of the *Odyssey*, high fantasy a child of the *Iliad*. "If high fantasy is about vast armies divided along lines of obvious good versus ultimate evil, epic struggles to vanquish dark lords bent on world domination, then sword and sorcery is its antithesis. Smaller-scale character pieces, often starring morally compromised protagonists, whose heroism involves little more than trying to save their own skins from a trap they themselves blundered into in search of spoils" (xi). High fantasy favors heroes like Hector, fighting to protect his city from outside invaders for a larger cause; sword-and-sorcery heroes are akin to Achilles, whose preoccupation with personal wealth and feminine beauty, and the death of his friend Patrocles finally motivating him to action, are familiar to fans of the subgenre.

Sword-and-sorcery stories are occasionally set against vast back-drops. The centerpiece of David Gemmell's sword-and-sorcery classic *Legend* is a sprawling, endurance-testing battle that evokes the Trojans holding out against a besieging army of Achaeans. Robert E. Howard's epic *The Hour of the Dragon* sees Conan reclaim his throne of Aquilonia after an epic battle of armies in the Valley of Lions, and Karl Edward Wagner's Kane employs alien science and a devolved race of frog-men to carve out an empire in *Bloodstone*. Yet these great struggles are secondary to the mercenary and the personal—Druss, the aging but still mighty eponymous hero of *Legend*, agrees to fight on the walls of Dros Delnoch not to save a country but for his own self-interest, in order to die a good death, not the straw-death of the aged warrior. The ransom Conan asks of the defeated king Tarascus in *The Hour of the Dragon* is a comely Nemedian slave girl, whom he vows to make queen of Aquilonia. Kane pursues power and conquest solely out of personal boredom, centuries of lonely immortality driving him to search for new experiences lest he succumb to despair or ennui. The stories of Moorcock's albino hero Elric include elements typical to high fantasy, including the downfall of the ancient city of Imryyr and the return of the High Ones to earth. But Elric's motiva-tions are intensely personal: solace for his tumultuous and conflicted heart and mind. The fate of the world rates a distant second, if at all.

Sword-and-sorcery has an uneasy relationship with kingship. It typically portrays kings as unfit hereditary dynastic rulers, sloth-ful, corrupt, and in need of overthrow. Warns the hero of Gardner Fox's *Kyrik: Warlock Warrior*, "By Illis! Kingship corrupts a man. Its power goes to his head. Don't let it go to yours. Or I'll come back to take it away from you" (145). Sword-and-sorcery protagonists are ill-suited for positions of leadership. Though he eventually attains the throne of Aquilonia, Conan spends much of his days as a pirate, raider on horseback, and a thief. While kingship is among his objectives, it is not his end-game. When Conan does find a crown on his head in "The Phoenix on the Sword" it rests on a troubled brow, assailed by subtle doubts within and threats from without: "When I was a fighting-man, the kettle-drums they beat, the people scattered gold-dust before my horse's feet; but now I am a great king, the people hound my track, with poison in my wine cup, and daggers at my back." Conan longs for the freedom offered by the deck of a ship or a horseback on the open steppes. As for the fate of the Hyborian Age, Conan never gives it a thought; tomorrow's cares are not his. His philosophy is spelled out clearest in "Queen of the Black Coast":

> I seek not beyond death. It may be the blackness averred by the Nemedian skeptics, or Crom's realm of ice and cloud, or the snowy plains and vaulted halls of the Nordheimer's Valhalla. I know not, nor do I care. Let me live deep while I live; let me know the rich juices of red meat and stinging wine on my palate, the hot embrace of white arms, the mad exultation of battle when the blue blades flame and crimson, and I am content. Let teachers and priests and philosophers brood over questions of reality and illusion. I know this: if life is illusion, then I am no less an illusion, and being thus, the illusion is real to me. I live, I burn with life, I love, I slay, and am content.

Proto sword-and-sorcery writer Lord Dunsany helped create the template for a grimy, street-level scale as fantasy setting. In his "Distressing Tale of Thangobrind the Jeweller, and of the Doom that Befel Him" (1912), Thangobrind agrees to steal a great jewel in exchange for the soul of a young girl (Dunsany presents this morally objectionable arrangement without comment). While it sounds apocryphal, Leiber drew inspiration for his Fafhrd and the Gray Mouser stories from a real-world party attended by booze-soaked celebrities and politicians. Watching the revelers with a combination of bemusement and repulsion, Leiber later admitted that the escape served as inspiration for the "intrigue-ridden, pleasure-sated, sorcery-working, thief-ruled city of Lankhmar, its fat merchants and cutthroats, rogues, and its linkages to a certain city in our world." In a letter written to his friend and literary collaborator Harry Fischer, Leiber sums up the sordid business: "This would be a fine place for you, Gray Mouser. Everyone and everything is so confused; in short, there is so much of chaos out here, chaos built on fear, suspicion, too much and too little bureaucracy, that a person with a knowledge of the whims and pettishnesses of the blind God Azathoth would have the upper hand" (Leiber, "Fafhrd and Me" 136–137). In the Nebula and Hugo award-winning story *Ill Met in Lankhmar*, Fafhrd and the Gray Mouser meet in a happenstance joint ambush to steal jewels from a pair of rogues in a Lankhmarian Thieves' Guild. The two ultimately split the loot, capping their profitable night back at the Gray Mouser's apartment drinking and carousing with their girlfriends and forging a lifelong friendship in the process. And in Karl Edward Wagner's *Darkness Weaves*, Kane joins a coup attempt by the horribly deformed, black-hearted demon-sired sorceress Efrel solely because she has coin to offer him; "right" and "wrong" does not enter his thinking.

Glen Cook's *The Black Company* is the quintessential example of sword-and-sorcery's mercenary outlook. It and its sequels feature a group of hard-bitten warriors fighting for whichever side offers it the best deal. The Black Company is bound and operates solely by the provisions of its contracts; abstract concepts like "good" and "evil" are meaningless. The captain of the Black Company continually reminds the titular "hero" Croaker that the Black Company always fulfills its contracts. Morality never enters into the equation.

Sword-and-sorcery stories are often set in cities and urban settings rather than the idyllic pastoral landscapes common to high fantasy. Cities are where the action is at: intrigue, double-crosses, women, and coin. Sword-and-sorcery heroes are continually drawn to cities; Fafhrd and Gray Mouser flee Lankhmar for the wilderness, but return again and again to sample its dangers and pleasures. Set against the black-roofed city of Lankhmar with its excitingly dangerous Plaza of Dark Delights, two sorcerers enlist the barbarian Fafhrd to confront an insidious threat that threatens to consume Lankhmar and its (only slightly less corrupt) business and trade in "Bazaar of the Bizarre." Here is no glittering, white-spired Minas Tirith, but a grimy city where "the vendors of drugs and the peddlers of curiosa and the hawkers of assignations light their stalls and crouching places with foxfire, glowworms, and firepots with tiny single windows, and they conduct their business almost as silently as the stars conduct theirs."

HORROR/LOVECRAFTIAN INFLUENCE

The rattle of dry bones, journeys into dark pits and ghost-haunted towers, and confrontations with nameless horrors, are all hallmarks of the sword-and-sorcery genre. While monsters and wizards are ubiquitous in fantasy fiction, the invocation of stark fear and use of Gothic tropes and trappings is largely unique to sword-and-sorcery. Sword-and-sorcery was born in the horror-suffused pages of *Weird Tales,* and the pulp's influence is evident from the subgenre's beginning. C.L. Moore's "Hellsgarde" (1939, first appearance in "Weird Tales") is horror masquerading as sword-and-sorcery, a terrifying tale of a revenant-haunted, hell-guarded castle that can only be come upon at night. The red-haired heroine Jirel, alone, must overcome her fears and enter:

> But—the mists between her and the castle had thickened, and her eyes might be playing her false—but were not those the shapes of men drawn up in a double row before the doorway of Hellsgarde? Hellsgarde, that had stood empty and haunted these two hundred years? Blinking through the dazzle of sun on water and the thickening of the mists, she rode on toward the gateway. She could feel the horse trembling between her knees, and with every step he grew more and more reluctant to go on. She set her teeth and forced him ahead resolutely, swallowing her own terror.

Many classic sword-and-sorcery authors also wrote horror fiction. One of Howard's highest-regarded stories, "Pigeons from Hell," is a southern gothic tale of horror set in the 20th century. Leiber is perhaps best known for his horror novels *Conjure Wife* and *Our Lady of Darkness*. Henry Kuttner cut his teeth in *Weird Tales* with tales like "The Salem Horror" and "The Graveyard Rats." Wagner edited the annual *Year's Best Horror and Fantasy Series* and also wrote several short horror classics of his own including "Sticks", ".220 Swift," and "Where the Summer Ends." Many of his Kane stories are quasi-horror, featuring chilling descriptions of vampires, werewolves, and cities of the dead:

> The twilight deepened and was swallowed up by the night. Across dead Demornte settled the blackness of the tomb. No lights shone in the empty towns and abandoned homes, and a velvet curtain was drawn over the plague scarred corpse of the stricken land. Starlight and gibbous moon looked down on dead Demornte, their soft illumination no more than shading the night to gray. Their glow was like candles burning at a wake, sculpturing the face of the deceased with stark angles and shadowed hollows. ["Cold Light"]

Of all of these, Clark Ashton Smith is a master of horror and dread, and today he is largely known as a writer of weird horror rather than sword-and-sorcery. In tales such as "The Return of the Sorcerer" and "The Double Shadow," Smith evokes creeping, relentless doom with a mastery rarely surpassed. In "The Dark Eidolon," the strange appearance of a black and white fortress, mummies of dead kings, and the panicked reactions of the populace recall scenes from Edgar Allan Poe's "The Masque of the Red Death."

Sword-and-sorcery fiction would not be the same—certainly it would not exist in its present form—without the influence of H.P. Lovecraft (1890–1937). In addition to his contributions as prolific horror author in *Weird Tales*, Lovecraft was a contemporary and correspondent with Howard, Smith, Moore, Henry Kuttner, and Leiber. Lovecraft and his correspondents created a shared universe of prehistoric legends and monstrous myths in their fiction. These included joint references to vanished cities, half-forgotten tomes, and horrible, crawling monsters of the dark. Lovecraft referred to this shared mythology as "Yog-Sothothery," named after one of his Gods from the outer void. Howard drew directly upon the Cthulhu mythos as inspiration for his Hyborian Age setting of the Conan stories (Solon 143–145). Prior to "The Call of Cthulhu," Howard had not assembled all the elements of a classic sword-and-sorcery story in a single tale. His first published story, "Spear and Fang," was firmly historical, set in prehistoric times, while his Solomon Kane stories borrowed from traditional Gothic horror, including wild beasts, vampires, and werewolves ("Wolfshead," "In the Forest of Villefere"). But post-Lovecraft, Howard's writings were transformed, and took on a decidedly weird bent. "The Shadow Kingdom" features an ancient race of Serpent Men similar to Lovecraft's Old Ones, a group of primordial beings entombed in the mythical city of R'lyeh ("The Call of Cthulhu") and the reptilian, fish-like Deep Ones of "Dagon." Howard's Bran Mak Morn story "The Children of the Night" references Lovecraft's famed book the Necromonicon, while "Worms of the Earth" features a banished race of men living beneath the earth so long that they have reverted to a semi-reptilian state. In the tale Howard mentions Lovecraft's city of R'lyeh and the fish-god Dagon. Lovecraft later returned the favor, referencing Howard's serpent men in "The Haunter of the Dark":

> It was treasured and placed in its curious box by the crinoid things of Antarctica, salvaged from their ruins by the serpent men of Valusia, and peered at eons later in Lemuria by the first human beings. It crossed strange lands and stranger seas, and sank with Atlantis before a Minoan fisher meshed it with his net and sold it to swarthy merchants from nighted Khem (218).

Leiber's first story of Fafhrd and the Gray Mouser, "Adept's Gambit," contains several Lovecraftian motifs including references to elder gods. Lovecraft's influence extended to second generation sword-and-sorcery authors such as Wagner, Lin Carter, and Ramsay Campbell. Wagner's *Darkness Weaves* featured the Scylredi, an ancient "Elder" race who once dwelt in great cities of cyclopean masonry, now largely vanished, but whose discovery awaits those who unlock the secrets contained in books of blasted lore.

But Lovecraft's influence on sword-and-sorcery genre runs deeper than "Yog-Sothothery" and other surface elements. In his "Supernatural Horror in Literature" (first published in 1927), Lovecraft expressed a conviction that the most effective weird horror conveyed a "dread of outer, unknown forces," a trait which would later characterize his best stories:

> The true weird tale has something more than secret murder, bloody bones, or a sheeted form clanking chains according to rule.

A certain atmosphere of breathless and unexplainable dread of
outer, unknown forces must be present; and there must be a hint,
expressed with a seriousness and portentousness becoming its
subject, of that most terrible conception of the human brain—a
malign and particular suspension or defeat of those fixed laws of
Nature which are our only safeguard against the assaults of chaos
and the daemons of unplumbed space.

Howard, Leiber, and Smith incorporated elements of Lovecraft's
cosmic pessimism into their sword-and-sorcery. Despite all of
Conan's heroics, the coming cataclysm will consume the great works
and kingdoms of the age, just as it had the Atlantean age of Kull.
Howard's sorcerers practice foul arts that violate the laws of nature,
and Conan's instinctive fear and distrust of magic is well-earned.
Smith's fantastic stories of Hyperborea, Poseidonis, Averoigne, and
Zothique are heavily concerned with death and decay. Unexplained
forces of chaos irrupt at random, and at best can be held temporar-
ily at bay, as in his "The Beast of Averoigne": "Indeed, it were well
that none should believe the story: for strange abominations pass
evermore between earth and moon and athwart the galaxies; and
the gulf is haunted by that which it were madness for man to know.
Unnameable things have come to us in alien horror, and shall come
again. And the evil of the stars is not as the evil of earth" (296).
Leiber's world of Nehwon is ancient, sentient, and threatens to wake
from an uneasy sleep and overthrow the newcomer man. Moorcock's
Elric stories feature the fall of its greatest shining city and death
of their protagonist, and a black sword whose soul of chaos and
disorder cannot be eradicated. If high fantasy is typically about
restoration and the return of civilized order, sword-and-sorcery is
about red-handed barbarians overrunning the walls, a literature of
decay, entropy, and violent overthrow (Tompkins, "After Aquilonia
and Having Left Lankhmar").

SHORT, EPISODIC STORIES
Sword-and-sorcery was born in the pages of pulp magazines, which
published short stories and the occasional serialized novella.
Following the collapse of the pulp market in the late 1940s and
early 1950s sword-and-sorcery migrated to fanzines and magazines,
which again required its authors to work in the short form. Howard's
lone Conan novel, *The Hour of the Dragon*, is a trim 255 pages. Karl
Edward Wagner's *Darkness Weaves* in less than 300 pages covers the
entirety of a war, including the overthrow of an empire by a sorceress and her rebel forces. Poul Anderson's Icelandic saga-inspired
The Broken Sword, published in the same year as *The Lord of the Rings*
(1954), checks in at a slim 207 pages in paperback, less than one
fifth the length of Tolkien's work.

Market restrictions alone cannot account for the relative brevity of sword-and-sorcery fiction. Even with the advent of the mass-market paperback, sword-and-sorcery stories typically remained confined to a single volume, even as publishers embraced the lucrative model of trilogies and later as many as 10–12 separate volumes to tell a single story. David Eddings' popular high fantasy series *The Belgariad* takes five novels to cover the events of a quest and war against the dark lord Torak. Sword-and-sorcery has no equivalent. The nature of the stories themselves, which typically privilege brisk, action-packed plots, theme, and mood over deep characterization, multi-character viewpoints, and complex world-building, lend themselves to the short story format. In an October 1936 letter to Henry Kuttner, H.P. Lovecraft stated the relative unimportance of characterization to the weird tale. "But after all, the human characters are the least part of weird fiction" (*H.P. Lovecraft: Letters to C.L. Moore and Others* 254). While sword-and-sorcery fiction is populated with memorable heroes, changes in their character are typically revealed across successive stories, not within the confines of a single tale. The emphasis instead is on the immediate life-or-death situation at hand. Brisk storytelling is paramount.

Sword-and-sorcery stories typically involve pursuit of a single, immediate goal, conducted by either a single hero or, as in the Fafhrd and the Gray Mouser stories, a pair of heroes. Absent are the multiple viewpoint cast of characters popularized by the likes of George R.R. Martin in his sprawling *A Song of Ice and Fire* series. As will be demonstrated in Chapter Two, sword-and-sorcery is the direct ancestor of adventure stories, including the historical fiction of Sir Walter Scott and Alexandre Dumas, and the Lost World stories of Edgar Rice Burroughs, Arthur Conan Doyle, and H. Rider Haggard. They are immediate and thrum with urgency, often beginning *in medias res*. In his introduction to the 1963 anthology *Swords & Sorcery*, L. Sprague de Camp contrasted the brisk pacing, raw vitality, and immediacy of sword-and-sorcery with the rambling pace and archaic language of the novels of William Morris (8). Modern high fantasy series like Patrick Rothfuss' *The Kingkiller Chronicles* and J.K. Rowling's Harry Potter layer in complex histories, multiple characters, and mythos and history, often in the form of "Easter Eggs," hints and foreshadowed events to come in later volumes of the series. Sword-and-sorcery is not entirely without such elements, but they are far less frequent.[7]

---

[7] Howard created a rich backdrop for his stories in an elegant, non-intrusive manner. His Hyborian Age was given no detailed exposition in the stories but was hinted at in dialogue, bits of verse, and snatches of "historical" text from the Nemedian Chronicles. Readers did not receive a full treatment until the posthumous publication of his "The Hyborian Age" essay.

Brevity has become an increasingly vestigial trait of sword and sorcery. The further the subgenre has evolved from its pulp roots the longer its stories have become. By the 1960s and 70s Michael Moorcock and Karl Edward Wagner were writing novelized treatments (albeit short) of Elric and Kane. Wagner's later Kane stories including *Darkness Weaves, Dark Crusade,* and *Bloodstone* were published as standalone short novels. In another decade novels became series; Glen Cook's *The Black Company,* published in the 1980s, can each be read as standalone short novels, but readers can follow a group of mercenaries across multiple books. David Gemmell's Drenai series is a loosely connected series of novels featuring various heroes of legend, including the classic sword-and-sorcery protagonist Druss. Today, the short sword-and-sorcery novel is giving way to longer and more complex works. Joe Abercrombie's sword-and-sorcery inspired "grimdark" novels, though not proper doorstoppers, often climb over the 500-page mark. Whether these are truly sword-and-sorcery is a matter of debate, but they demonstrate that sword-and-sorcery has the flexibility and thematic heft to survive and thrive in the longer form.

INSPIRED BY HISTORY

It may sound fantastic to link the term "realism" with Conan; but as a matter of fact—his supernatural adventures aside—he is the most realistic character I ever evolved. He is simply a combination of a number of men I have known, and I think that's why he seemed to step full-grown into my consciousness when I wrote the first yarn of the series. Some mechanism in my sub-consciousness took the dominant characteristics of various prize-fighters, gunmen, bootleggers, oil field bullies, gamblers, and honest workmen I had come in contact with, and combining them all, produced the amalgamation I call Conan the Cimmerian.
—Letter from Robert E. Howard to Clark Ashton Smith, July 23, 1935

To paraphrase Howard, it may seem fantastic to associate sword-and-sorcery fiction—the stuff of demon-summoning wizards, tentacled crawlers of the dark, and muscled heroes at the vanguards of armies that never were—with the real world. But the subgenre is rooted in realism. Sword-and-sorcery is of course a-historical, but its rootedness in history lend the stories a degree of realism not seen in gossamer fairy tales and myth. Fritz Leiber declared this element essential to fantasy if it was to connect with the reader. "... it illustrates a point I firmly hold: Fantasy must be fertilized—yes, watered and manured—from the real world" ("Fafhrd and Me" 137).

Howard preferred historical adventure above other forms of fiction and famously wrote, "There is no literary work, to me, half as zestful as rewriting history in the guise of fiction'" (Knight 118). Howard grew up in rural early 20th century Texas, a time when his home state was undergoing huge transformations, including the recent closure of the frontier and the boom (and bust) of the oil business. These elements underpin and inform his fiction (Finn, *Blood and Thunder* 17). Howard was inspired by the historical fiction writers of the late 19th and early 20th centuries, including Jack London, H. Rider Haggard, Harold Lamb, and Talbot Mundy, and earlier writers James Fenimore Cooper and Alexandre Dumas. Before he created Conan, Howard experienced success in the historical fiction genre writing for the pulp magazine *Oriental Stories* (Holmes, "Gothic to Cosmic" 70). There is little evidence Howard read the early practitioners of high fantasy. In his landmark essay "The Dark Barbarian," Don Herron states flatly, "The importance of the imaginary world tradition has been overrated in defining Howard's place in literature" (154). Howard favored historical fiction authors and adventure stories largely absent fantastic elements. These included Arthur Conan Doyle, H. Rider Haggard, Jack London, Mark Twain, Sax Rohmer, Jeffery Farnol, Talbot Mundy, Harold Lamb, Robert W. Chambers, Rudyard Kipling, Sir Walter Scott, Stanley Lane-Poole, Jim Tully, Ambrose Bierce, Arthur Machen, Edgar Allan Poe, and H.P. Lovecraft. Of that list, only Bierce, Machen, Poe, and Lovecraft are fantasy writers (Knight 118).

Some sword-and-sorcery authors set their tales directly in ancient historical periods and even use quasi-mythical/historical figures as protagonists. Some notable examples include Poul Anderson's use of the Danish hero Hrolf Kraki in *Hrolf Kraki's Saga*; Richard Tierney's stories of Simon of Gitta, set during the brief reign of fourth Roman Caesar Caligula (*Swords Against Darkness* series); and Manly Wade Wellman's tales of the Stone Age warrior Hok (*Amazing Stories* and *Fantastic Adventures*, later reprinted in part in Karl Edward Wagner's *Echoes of Valor II*). These stories are differentiated from historical swashbuckler/adventure fiction with their inclusion of supernatural elements or fantastic/impossible settings (Hok's travels take him to mythic Atlantis and into encounters with surviving pterodactyls, for example).

Most sword-and-sorcery fiction is either set on worlds whose physical laws mirror our own, or is our own world in some remote antediluvian past or distant, post-cataclysmic future. Its material is fantastic, but also familiar, relatable reflections of the present. Howard's Conan stories take place on Earth, albeit during a mythic and pre-cataclysmic "Hyborian Age." The countries in which Conan adventures, exotic as they may seem, have clear analogues with historical countries and geography. So Khitai is clearly China, for example, Kush is located in Africa, Stygia corresponds with historical Egypt, and so on. Charles Saunders' Imaro stories employ a mythic land of monsters and magic and gods that is also a deliberate fantasy version of Africa. Jack Vance's Dying Earth stories are set in a far-flung future when science has "fallen" and magic is on the ascendency, but is still the Earth. Even Leiber's Nehwon is likewise obliquely connected to Earth, and resembles it closely in topography and climate. Leiber hinted that Nehwon might have existed in our own distant past or perhaps post-apocalyptic future. "And while I seem to want the world of Nehwon definitely linked to the real world of today, I don't want to specify exactly where it lies and whether in past or future" ("Fafhrd and Me" 135).

OUTSIDER HEROES

But if S&S is to be distinguishable from epic fantasy, it has to have some distinguishing characteristics. It seems to me (and to many) that the hero has to be some kind of outsider, the genre equivalent of a lone gunman.

—James Enge, SF Signal Podcast

At the outset of "The Shadow Kingdom," Kull sits uneasily on his newly won Valusian throne, barbaric spirit coursing through his veins. Though he has fought and shed blood to achieve his kingship, he does not find victory in the prize. Like a modern man who has sacrificed freedom for the security of the office, Kull finds that his crown has come with a steep price. "Kull reflected long upon the strange state of affairs that made him ally of ancient foes and foe of ancient friends. ... Chains of friendship, tribe and tradition had he broken to satisfy that ambition." Fighting battles and leading men on the battlefield are second-nature to Kull, but the art of statecraft is not. The council chamber is a "social palace," where Kull is regaled with formal and laudatory phrases of lords and ladies, ultimately hollow. The courtly goings-on and carefully protected, half-feigned speeches are a "dim maze," concealing truth and plain conversation. "All was like a masquerade, where men and women hid their real thoughts with a smooth mask."

All of the iconic figures of sword-and-sorcery are outsiders. Conan is a wandering barbarian from the crags and piney woods of Cimmeria, which borders the Pictish wilderness and the frozen wastes of Vanaheim and Aesgaard. A mysterious figure out of the depths of time, Wagner's Kane is homeless, an outcast and a tormented loner who finds solace in a series of shallow encounters with women. He is also ageless, unable to die from means other than violence, and utterly alienated from humanity. Michael Moorcock's Elric, though a member of the ancient privileged race of Melnibone, is uneasy in his own skin and at odds with the depravity of his race. The last of the line of Melnibonean emperors, Elric is so disgusted with their decadent slide into amorality that he leads an invasion of barbarians on a secret raid to its destroy its capital city. Fafhrd and the Gray Mouser are outsiders, too. While listening to the celebrations of nobles from the cold empty streets of Lankhmar outside the castle walls, the Gray Mouser asks his barbarian friend why they aren't part of the privileged class. "We are not dukes because we're no man's man," explains Fafhrd. "Even a duke must butter up a king, and demigods the gods. We butter no one. We go our own way, choosing our own adventures—and our own follies! Better freedom and a chilly road than a warm hearth and servitude" (Leiber, "The Cloud of Hate" 13).

Charles' Saunders Imaro is another memorable outsider. Imaro's mysterious origins lie outside the fierce, proud, and insular group of warriors known as the Ilyassai, and he is allowed to live among the tribe begrudgingly. Bullied mercilessly as a youth, Imaro reaches prodigious size and strength as a young man. But his physical gifts only serve to isolate him further from the other young warriors. Consumed by loneliness even when among his tribesmen, Imaro experiences freedom when walking alone among the tall grasses of the Tamburure. "It was then that he felt he belonged in the Tamburure, at one with the vast herds of impala, zebra, kudu, gazelle, and countless other creatures that roamed where there will guided them. Even more did the youth identify with the predators" (Saunders, "Turkhana Knives" 17–18). Eventually Imaro is betrayed by his greatest rival, whom he kills in a duel to the death, and is forced to flee, an outcast.

Many of sword-and-sorcery's iconic authors were themselves outsiders. A child of the Great Depression, Leiber hit upon the idea for Lankhmar after attending a cocktail party and watching in detached, bemused disgust the privileged behaviors of a group of Hollywood actors, directors, and producers. Leiber ultimately opted to shelve a budding career as an actor to pursue the solitary craft of writing. Wagner became disillusioned of the field of psychiatry and dropped out of the medical establishment to write fiction. His lifelong struggle with alcohol was an attempted coping mechanism. Wrote friend and fellow horror author Paula Guran, "Dissatisfied by coping with the mundane and incapable of finding happiness in dull routine, he could find no rational way to deal with the irrationality of one's emotions, or creativity. As a man, he was a fount of common sense ... rarely applied to himself." Unwilling and unable to conform to the norms of early 20th century society, Howard considered menial jobs and the classroom anathema. He believed that civilization was a whim of circumstance, an unnatural event in mankind's long and bloody history of barbarism. Howard opted out of the 9-to-5 round and turned to writing larger than life heroes, a career that proved empowering in a disempowering and often bewildering age of rapid technological change. "As it did with Lovecraft, writing gave Howard a chance to control his own destiny in a fundamentally flawed world" (Nyikos 43).

Mercenary, outsider heroes pitted against dark sorcery. A subgenre born in the pages of *Weird Tales*, suffused with horror, informed by historical adventure and coated with the grit of history. Today these traits are recognized as hallmarks of sword-and-sorcery and have come to define the subgenre. But prior to its coalescing and long before it had a name, a handful of authors working inside and outside the fantasy tradition were writing proto sword-and-sorcery of their own, seeding the ground for the subgenre's birth.

Sword-and-Sorcery: Helpful or Harmful Label?

Sword-and-sorcery. High fantasy. Sword-and-planet. Sword-and-sandal. Does anyone really care about labels and categories? Probably not your average reader, to whom a book with a warrior fighting a dragon on the cover = fantasy, regardless of whether it's Conan plunging a poisoned spear into the mouth of a dinosaur outside the walls of Xuchotl, or Bard shooting a black arrow into the hollow of Smaug's left breast.

For most of its existence genre fiction has been the object of scorn, surpassed only by genre fiction studies. Says Michael Moorcock, author of the Elric series, "I've long held the view that category definitions in the arts are destructive both of the thing they try to describe and of the aspiration of the artist. They produce an unnecessary self-consciousness. They are convenient only to over-formalized stock systems and third rate academic discussion" (*Wizardry and Wild Romance* 116). Genre authors sacrifice creativity in order to fit an expected set of criteria, critics argue, resulting in stale, formulaic writing and genre ghettos. E.R. Eddison's *The Worm Ouroboros* is a great novel for many reasons, among which may be the fact that it was written pre-genre. Genre allegiances can breed elitism and in-fighting among fans. Some Tolkien fans dismiss Howard's tales as low-brow pulp, while some in Howard's camp deride high fantasy as pretentious and boring.

But after weighing the arguments for and against, I decidedly like drawing distinctions in my fantasy—and believe that subcategorizing is a helpful exercise. As the fantasy genre has grown, subgenres have become a tool in the arsenal of critical and commercial discussion. Here's a few arguments in my defense.

1. **Subgenres allow fantasy readers to make meaningful recommendations.** If I know someone who adores Leiber and Howard I'm not going to push *The Belgariad* or *Dragons of Autumn Twilight* on him; I'll steer him towards Joe Abercrombie or David Gemmell instead. If

someone gravitates toward Conan and Fafhrd and Brak, and you hand them a Harry Potter novel, don't be surprised if they react with skepticism. There are real, aesthetic differences between Patrick Rothfuss' *The Name of the Wind* and Karl Edward Wagner's *Dark Crusade*, and one way to talk about them is to note that the latter is sword-and-sorcery, and the former is not. A reader can examine a cover depicting John Carter, Prince of Helium, gazing into the eyes of Dejah Thoris against a Barsoomian background, and make a somewhat educated guess at whether it's a book they want to read, or a publisher can make it easy and call it sword-and-planet. *Black Gate* and *Heroic Fantasy Quarterly* publish very different types of stories than the rosewater *Realms of Fantasy*; self-identifying as heroic fantasy or sword-and-sorcery prevents misleading rabid fans of *The Mists of Avalon*.

2. **Subgenre restrictions can lead to creative breakthroughs for artists.** Genres and subgenre instill expectations in readers that, when tweaked or broken, create frisson in an expectant reader and an experience only subgenre insiders can appreciate. Writers chafing from genre boundaries can paradoxically experience creative breakthroughs that elevate their art. In grappling with the long shadow cast by Conan, Moorcock opted for deliberate opposition, and in so doing created a lasting character in Elric.

3. **Engaging in pedantry is fun.** Many readers enjoy mental book-shelving exercises and arguing about the finer points of genre classifications (Fritz Leiber's Fafhrd and the Gray Mouser series has two protagonists: Does that mean it's not sword-and-sorcery? Is L. Sprague de Camp's *The Tritonian Ring* sword-and-sandal?). *The Hobbit* director Guillermo del Toro called Tolkien's body of work sword-and-sorcery, a near-unforgiveable gaffe if you take this stuff seriously.

So in the end, for all their exceptions, conflations, and geeky slap-fights, give me my steampunk, my historical fantasy, and my dying earth. And especially my sword-and-sorcery. Plain old "fantasy" just doesn't cut it.

CHAPTER TWO
Origins

The raw elements of Sword & Sorcery are as old as written literature itself.
  —Lin Carter, "Swordsmen and Sorcerers at Play," *The Spell of Conan*

The roots of fantasy run deep. The earliest stories ever told—myth, legend, and saga—are its wellsprings. Likewise, sword-and-sorcery has in some respects always been with us. In poems shared around the hall-fires of the cold pagan north by traveling skalds, the heroic verse of the anonymous poem Beowulf, and Homer's *Iliad* and *Odyssey*, exist the prototypes for Conan, Kull, and Kane.

Fantasy—as widely understood today—is a type of literature characterized by tales of adventure and quest in realms of faerie, populated by wizards, warriors, and monsters, in which magic works. Modern fantasy got its start with works such as Sara Coleridge's *Phantasmion* (1837), George MacDonald's *Phantastes* (1858), and Lewis Carroll's *Alice in Wonderland* (1865). Readers enjoyed these works with the implicit understanding that they were fiction, with no pretense of historical accuracy. This dividing line separates modern fantasy from the ancient epics. In *The Evolution of Modern Fantasy*, Jamie Williamson postulates that fantasy—which he calls "literary fantasy"—began with a group of writers directly engaging with and remaking ancient myth and legend. These included William Morris, Lord Dunsany, James Branch Cabell, E.R. Eddison, and J.R.R. Tolkien. These authors were literary mavericks, working independently and not as part of a conscious tradition or within a defined genre. In this tradition Morris and Tolkien created secondary worlds, the latter with staggering levels of detail. The fantasy genre was codified in the 1960s with the publication of the Lin Carter-edited Ballantine Adult Fantasy Series, which stitched together the works of disparate authors into a canon of fantasy literature. Its hallmarks include maps, formulated background "mythologies" or "historical" appendices, and so on (Williamson 16–19).

In contrast, sword-and-sorcery authors wrote for specific, narrow audiences, starting with the pulps and later for small-press collections marketed to specific types of readers. "When the literary writers published in periodicals, it was in *Harper's* rather than *Weird Tales*; when the popular writers published books, they were published by Arkham House rather than Houghton Mifflin Co" (Williamson 13). Sword-and-sorcery is not, as is high fantasy, an update of the ancient heroics for a 20th century audience, but incorporates a number of diverse, relatively modern influences. These include historical adventure fiction, including the works of Sir Walter Scott (1771–1832) Alexandre Dumas (1802–1870), Rafael Sabatini (1875–1950), Talbot Mundy (1879–1940), and Harold Lamb (1892–1962). From these swashbuckling, action-oriented authors sword-and-sorcery inherited its fast-paced plots and modern, muscular prose style. Sword-and-sorcery also draws its inspiration from the fantastic "Lost World" genre pioneered by writers H. Rider Haggard (1856–1925), Edgar Rice Burroughs (1875–1950), Rudyard Kipling (1865–1936), and Arthur Conan Doyle (1859–1930). These authors lent sword-and-sorcery an air of unexpected strangeness—lost cities, atavistic races, surviving dinosaurs at the earth's core—that provided a template for connecting the fantastic worlds of sword-and-sorcery to our own. The planetary romances of Burroughs, and the weird extraplanetary horror of H.P. Lovecraft (1890–1937), add important color, atmosphere, and flavor to the subgenre—fearsome beasts and eldritch horrors that can only be vanquished by muscular, sword-wielding protagonists.

Yet for all its departures from high fantasy, sword-and-sorcery shares with it some common ancestors, including "pre-genre" fantasy authors E.R. Eddison, Lord Dunsany, Abraham Merritt, H. Rider Haggard, and James Branch Cabell. And as this chapter argues, it has a similar northern-ness of spirit, which can be traced directly to a shared affinity for Nordic mythology, and in particular Icelandic saga.

Icelandic Saga and Nordic myth

William Morris (1834–1896) is generally regarded as the first author of the imaginary world novel (Carter, *Imaginary Worlds* 8). An eclectic polymath, Morris was an artist, poet, prose author, and translator, perhaps most famous for his lavish and faithful reproductions of medieval art, which he sought to re-introduce to a contemporary world (Hartwell, *Masterpieces of Fantasy and Enchantment* 532). Later Morris turned his attention to writing long, serious works of fantastic fiction inspired by medieval romances, including the likes of Spencer's *The Faerie Queene* and Thomas Malory's *Le Morte D'Arthur*. Morris reached back in time to engage these old stories and myths, but added the great imaginative leap of placing his novels in wholly invented fantastic secondary worlds. *The Wood Beyond the World* (1894) and *The Well at the World's End* (1896) are completely divorced from earth and without foothold in history or earthly geography, arguably the first novel-length works to employ this conceit. Many subsequent authors would follow Morris' lead and create their own secondary worlds even more perilous and fair, most notably J.R.R. Tolkien.

Morris' fantasies, crucial as they are to the development of modern fantasy, have a tenuous connection to sword-and-sorcery. There is no evidence that sword-and-sorcery originator Robert E. Howard ever read them, for example. But Morris influenced the subgenre in his more than 30 translations of Icelandic saga, including the likes of *Grettis Saga: The Story of Grettir the Strong* and *The Saga of Gunnlaug the Worm-Tongue and Rafn the Skald* (1869). Late 19th/early 20th century novelists H. Rider Haggard and E.R. Eddison read the sagas in Morris and collaborator Eiríkr Magnússon's translations and transmogrified them into Norse-flavored fantasy works of their own (P.E. Thomas 263-264). Eddison translated "Egil's Saga" (1930) and his modern reimagining of a Norse saga, *Styrbiorn the Strong* (1926), and Haggard's popular romance *Eric Brighteyes* (1890) provided modern readers with access to the sagas by adapting them as palatable modern novels, constructing a Bifrost bridge between the old heroics and a 20th century reading audience. In turn these works influenced, directly or indirectly, some of the seminal authors of sword-and-sorcery.

The Icelandic sagas tell stories of larger-than-life heroes grappling with raw human emotions and failings: vice, lust, revenge, tragedy, cruelty, loyalty, and ambitions sated and thwarted. Eddison observed that the sagas possessed "the quality of vivid, unstaled and undauntable life … replete with individual character and action" (*Hrolf Kraki's Saga* ix-x). Originally chanted aloud by skalds as a means to transmit history, values, and customs in an oral culture, the Icelandic sagas were committed to paper circa 1200–1400, some 200-400 years after the Viking age. The sagas are semi-historical and often concern real personages, but are heavily mythologized. Historians today largely ignore much of their purported "facts" and instead view them as important windows into the culture of the Viking age. Despite some archaisms of style and form they remain largely accessible and rewarding to the modern reader, offering stories of red-blooded and red-handed men (and women) of a heroic bent, with a particular focus on the triumphs and tragedies of individuals. They are "written with such immediacy and forthrightness and they concern such basic human dilemmas that for the most part they are readily accessible and seductive" (Smiley ix). Adds Eddison, "There is no "Keltic Twilight" here, no barbaric exaggerations, no embroidery, no weaving of words or fancies, no boggling at truth: there is much shrewd insight into character and the springs of action, a power of direct and vivid narrative rarely matched in any other literature, much deep-seated humor and philosophy of hard and manly life" (*Styrbiorn the Strong* 260).

Eddison's description of the sagas is a rough approximation of sword-and-sorcery. If high fantasy is the stuff of myth and fable, inspired by the Eddas and their tales of gods striving against giants with the ending of the world in the balance, sword-and-sorcery is the material of saga, of earthly heroes with personal ambitions and mercenary motivations striving against like-minded foes. Its pages are littered with muscular, violent "barbarians from the north" plundering their way through adventures worthy of the wildest saga. While sword-and-sorcery is often guilty of "barbaric exaggeration," this is no hard-and-fast rule. Nor are the sagas themselves guiltless in this regard. The hero Skallagrim of "Egil's Saga" takes a boat out at night to retrieve a stone from the shallow waters to serve as a forge for his iron; today the rock remains "still there with a pile of slag beside ... four men today could not lift it" (Scudders 50). Skallagrim passes on his otherworldly strength to his son Egil, who wins a series of pitched battles fighting alone against as many as half a score of men.

Sword-and-sorcery is perhaps closest to saga literature in its use of the outsider archetype. In the introduction to *The Sagas of Icelanders*, Robert Kellogg notes that "saga heroes occupy a social space on the edges of society," adding that three of the major heroes of the sagas (*The Saga of Grettir the Strong, Gisli Sursson's Saga*, and *The Saga of Hord and the People of Holm*) are outlaws (xviii). Saga heroes were thorns in the side of historical Danish kings. Their age-old personal systems of justice—oath-taking and vengeance for broken oaths, settled in death-duels known as *holmgangs*—clashed with Danish kings' codified laws. Many were banished as outlaws. Around this time organized religion was pushing out the old pagan beliefs with Christian virtues of charity and mercy, often at the point of a sword. Coupled with the rise of a prospering class of land-holding farmers increasingly intolerant of the Vikings' culture of heroic individualism, the Vikings were forced westward and seaward, to the likes of Iceland and Greenland. Though the sagas are written impartially, and their heroes often terribly flawed, readers can sympathize with their loss of individuality and the slow death of their heroic culture. "Most of the saga heroes are just barely on one side or the other of the law, but it also seems to be true that the law itself is being tested along with the finest men" (Kellogg xviii).[1]

---

[1] Coincidentally, the "Inklings," an influential social and literary circle that included the likes of J.R.R. Tolkien, C.S. Lewis, and Charles Williams, also drew upon Icelandic Saga and Norse myth to inform their own stories, albeit through the lens of their Christian faith. In a review of *The Lord of the Rings*, C.S. Lewis described the quality of Catholic-underlaid Northernness in Tolkien's tale as "hammer-strokes but with

Sword-and-sorcery authors would employ this simple, timeless tension—the individual striving against society—to lend their stories additional resonance and relevance. Michael Moorcock states that "from a very early age I was reading Norse legends and any books I could find about Norse stories" ("Moorcock's Miscellany Forums"), and "outlaw" certainly applies to Elric. It also describes the majority of the careers of Fafhrd and the Gray Mouser, the latter of which wind up finding a measure of peace on Rime Isle, a rough equivalent for Greenland. At the same time Fritz Leiber and collaborator Harry Otto Fischer were dreaming up the characters of Fafhrd and the Gray Mouser and exchanging ideas via letters they were reading Norse myth; Leiber says both were "steeped" in it. This influence can be seen in the Gray Mouser, who expresses many of the same qualities as the Norse trickster god Loki (Leiber, "Fafhrd and Me" 129–130).

As early as 1926 Howard was writing of his great admiration of G.K. Chesterton's "The Ballad of the White Horse" and the saga era of Iron/Middle Age Europe in letters to his friends (*The Collected Letters* 77). In an October 1930 letter to his friend Harold Preece, Howard wrote stirringly of the pull of an ancient Norse strain in his ancestry:

> All that is deep and gloomy and Norse in me rises in my blood. I would go east into the sunshine and the nodding palm trees, but I bide and the dream of the twilight of the gods is on me, and the dreams of cold and misty lands and the ancient pessimism of the Vikings. It seems to me, especially in the autumn, that that one vagrant Danish strain that is mine, predominates above all my Gaelic blood (Connors, "Twilight of the Gods" 99).

In an August 1931 letter to H.P. Lovecraft, Howard wrote of the resentment he felt toward Charlemagne and his draconian repression of Nordic paganism, which included execution for non-converts to Christianity:

> Like you, the Sagas of Norse gods and heroes fascinate me. Their mythology seems more characteristically Nordic than any other—naturally, of course. I still feel a deep resentment toward Charlemagne for his bloody conversion of the Nordic pagans—and while I do not consider that it was in revenge for his ruthless crusade that sent the more remote Norsemen sweeping down to ravage the south—it was more likely a natural result of growth and expansion and press of population—still I can appreciate the feelings of those Odin-worshippers who destroyed shrine and monastery and burned the priests in the ruins of their altars.

In a March 1933 letter to Lovecraft, Howard buttressed his argument for preferring barbarism over civilization by drawing on the examples of saga heroes:

---

compassion" (Lewis 89); in contrast, sword-and-sorcery employed a hammer to crush its enemies with impunity.

You say the attractions of a barbaric life could not exist without the perspective of civilization. Yet (if we call the Vikings barbarians) do you not think that they found their life good without that perspective? The sagas hum with self-glorification, with praise of "the whale path," and the glory of the foray. Dull, mindless clods, mere hulks of inert, dead matter? I can not agree there. Such men as Eric the Red, Leif the Lucky, Hrolf the Ganger, Hengist—they could not have been feeble jelly-like organisms groping blindly through the scum of primordial night. They were alive; they stung, burned, tingled with Life—life raw and crude and violent doubtless; but Life, just the same, and worthy to be classed with the best effort of the intellectual side of man (Howard, *A Means to Freedom* 547-548).

In a subsequent July 1935 letter to Lovecraft, Howard sang the praises of the *Heimskringla*, a collection of sagas about the Norwegian kings written circa 1230 featuring stories of heroic deeds by larger-than-life heroes from a bygone era, yet told in a convincing historical style amid familiar settings:

By the way, I recently got hold of a book that ought to be read by all writers who strive after realism, and by every man with a drop of Nordic blood in his veins—the "Heimskringla" of Snorre Sturlason. Reading of his sagas of the Norse people, I felt more strongly than ever my instinctive kinship with them, and the kinship between them and the frontier people of America. In many ways the Norsemen figuring in his history more resemble the American pioneers of the West more than any European people I have ever read about (*A Means to Freedom* 881-882).

Howard dipped into Icelandic saga and Norse myth as inspiration for his own fiction. The very first story he wrote was of the adventures of a young Dane Viking, when he was age nine or ten (Howard, *A Means to Freedom* 171). At least as early as March 1926, the same year he began work on the Kull story "The Shadow Kingdom," Howard evinced a profound influence from *The Saga of Grettir the Outlaw/Grettir the Strong*, recommending it and the broader field of Icelandic saga for a series of reprints in a letter to *Weird Tales* (Roehm). Later he wrote several historical fiction stories set in the Viking age, including "Spears of Clontarf," a dramatized account of the historical Battle of Clontarf in 1014; "Swords of the Northern Sea," originally published in *Tigers of The Sea* (1974); and the stories of the Gaelic hero Cormac Mac Art and his adventures with Wulfhere the Skull-splitter and his Viking crew ("The Night of the Wolf", published in *Bran Mak Morn* (1969). He also wrote several poems featuring Northmen including "The Song of Horsa's Galley," "Singing Hemp," "Viking's Trail," and "The Outgoing of Sigurd the Jerusalem-Farer" (Eng 34).

Conan himself is an echo of the heroes of the *Heimskringla*. In a review of Poul Anderson's *The Last Viking* trilogy, L. Sprague de

Camp draws parallels between the Viking heroes of history and Howard's most fantastic creation:

> The nearest thing in real history to Conan was Harald Sigurdson (Anderson uses the more archaic spelling Sigurdharson), king of Norway, 1046-66. Seven feet tall, with a lifetime of wild adventure behind him when he became king, including a stint as captain of the Byzantine Emperor's Varangian Guard, he resembled Conan in other ways. Like Conan he was even-tempered: always aggressive, irascible, and dangerous. He became known as Harald Hardrede (or Hardraadhi; there are several spellings), translatable as "Hard-counsel," or perhaps "Hard-boiled." The resemblances between Conan and Harald, however, are still so striking that, if Howard had read the Heimskringla earlier, it would not have caused any material change in his concept of Conan the Cimmerian (de Camp, "Scroll").

Howard did not merely update the sagas as did Eddison and Haggard, but infused Icelandic saga-age realism into his stories of fantasy. This historical vividness separated his fiction from the relatively removed, medieval romance-fantasies of MacDonald and Morris. "The Frost-Giant's Daughter" is set during a battle of Viking-like Aesir and Vanir on the snowy steppes of a pre-historic/quasi-mythological Northern Europe (Nordheim). Howard writes into the story frost giants and the ensorcellments of the beautiful waifish daughter of the God Ymir, who lures Conan into a desperate foot chase deep into the wastes. Other notable Nordic-inspired Howard stories include "Cairn of the Headland" and "The Grey God Passes," which feature historical battles and settings interspersed with fantasy and weird horror, including an appearance by the Norse god Odin.

Sword-and-sorcery publishers seized on these similarities at the height of sword-and-sorcery's renaissance in the 1960s and 70s. *Eric Brighteyes* enjoyed a pair of paperback re-releases, once as part of the Newcastle Forgotten Fantasy Library in 1974 and again with Zebra Books in 1978.[2] The latter was reprinted with an introduction by Lin Carter and "Zebra Sword and Sorcery" on its spine, proclaiming itself as a member of a subgenre now very much in the critical discourse. The cover of the 1978 release is an interesting time capsule into what was selling at that time and the great lengths to which a publisher would stretch to put "sword-and-sorcery" on its cover: Eric holding what is presumably his sword Whitefire; in the novel his blade is described as a brightly gleaming brand but on the Zebra reprint it could pass for a lightsaber. In his arms Eric cradles a scantily clad

---

[2] Many of Haggard's most popular works were re-released by Dover Publishers in the early 1950s, including *Eric Brighteyes* as part of the collection *Lost Civilizations: Three Adventure Novels* (1953). Heralded in the September 1953 edition of The Magazine of Fantasy and Science Fiction to which Anderson was a regular contributor, it is likely Anderson had read Haggard's novel prior to writing *The Broken Sword* (1954).

and utterly limp and defenseless woman—presumably Gudruda, although in the story she is strong willed and hardly a clinging waif, more than once putting the somewhat cloddish Brighteyes in his place. A blurb "His sword shone with magic might—and his heart burned with ardent lust!" and the purple back-cover copy significantly distorts and dumbs down the content, turning a relatively straight-laced story of heroism and tragedy into a tale of barbaric lust, a titillating love triangle far removed from the facts of Haggard's tale. A weird greenish castle that looks like something out of Edgar Rice Burroughs' Barsoom looms in the background, completing the misleading but wonderfully 1970s tableaux.

While not sword-and-sorcery, *Eric Brighteyes* serves as a bridge between sword-and-sorcery and saga, an example of how one seemingly disparate genre can slip into the other—and vice-versa. Little imaginative leap is needed to connect the dots from a saga hero "going a Viking" for plunder with Conan plundering merchant vessels on the Vilayet sea. The sagas at their heart share a bleakness of vision—a belief that fate is unchangeable, and that all roads end in darkness. In *Eric Brighteyes* fate is depicted as a tapestry woven by the Three Fates, or the Norns. Human lives are threads in this grand but finite pattern, shorn off by a weaver at the Norns' appointed time. This same pagan conception of fate or "wyrd" would be used by Moorcock in his sword-and-sorcery tales of Elric of Melnibone. Arguably the greatest novel-length work today that could be classified as sword-and-sorcery, Poul Anderson's *The Broken Sword* (1954), is utterly northern in its Ragnarok spirit and character, though written in a modern style and featuring a heavier quotient of monsters and magic than the Icelandic originals.[3] It proved hugely influential to a handful of later authors including Moorcock, Wagner, and Richard Morgan, author of the sword-and-sorcery trilogy *A Land Fit for Heroes*. Anderson later penned a second Viking novel *Hrolf Kraki's Saga* based off the fragments of an authentic saga, transforming a fragmentary tale of the historical Danish king Hrolf Kraki into a full-blown Norse saga for the modern age. Anderson's "The Tale of Hauk" (first appearance in *Swords Against Darkness* 1) is another Icelandic saga-inspired sword-and-sorcery story.

Subsequent sword-and-sorcery authors continued to dip into Northern saga and myth for inspiration. David Drake employed an effective northern setting and the historical "berserk" in his dark, moody, horror-infused s&s tale "The Barrow Troll" (1975), inspired by his youthful readings of Norse myth in Bulfinch, translations of the Eddas, and later, the Icelandic sagas themselves:

---

[3] Anderson's parents were of Scandinavian descent, and as a youth he spent a few formulative years in Denmark prior to the outbreak of World War II.

> And finally I came to the Icelandic sagas. I found their style and
> outlook very similar to my own. The narration is terse. Although the
> tales are fiction or at least fictionalized, there's a real attempt to keep
> the action realistic: even supernatural events are described in a realis-
> tic fashion. ... "The Barrow Troll" was an attempt to turn the elements
> I found in saga narration into a modern fantasy short story (Drake).

Robert Holdstock, writing under the pseudonym "Chris Carlsen,"
set the first book of his Berserker trilogy, *Shadow of the Wolf* (1977),
in eighth-century Norway. The main character, Harald, is possessed
with the savage spirit of Odin and against his will becomes a red-
handed berserker. As sword-and-sorcery was passing its peak and
sliding into self-parody, the first book of the *Haakon* trilogy by Eric
Neilson debuted in 1984. Though perhaps more accurately classified
as historical adventure, these series bear many of the hallmarks of
sword-and-sorcery, from cover blurbs/packaging to content.

Historical Adventure and "Lost World" Fiction

Icelandic saga and Norse myth are its distant forebear and spiritual ancestor, but sword-and-sorcery owes a larger debt to younger
branches of literature from a comparatively modern age. Historical
fiction first appeared in the early/mid-19th century with the likes
of Sir Walter Scott's *Ivanhoe* (1820) and James Fenimore Cooper's
The Last of the Mohicans (1826). By the end of the late 19th and
early 20th century, it and a related genre, adventure fiction, were
in full flower, with such titles as Robert Louis Stevenson's *Treasure
Island* (1883), Rudyard Kipling's *Kim* (1901), and Jack London's *The
Call of the Wild* (1903). Howard devoured these and other works,
including Alexandre Dumas' *The Count of Monte Cristo* and possibly
Rafael Sabatini's *Scaramouche*.[4] He also consumed a heavy diet of
Talbot Mundy and Harold Lamb in the pages of the pulp magazine
Adventure (de Camp, "Robert E. Howard's Fiction" 24). Lamb, Mundy,
H. Rider Haggard, and London influenced Howard's style and
inspired the themes he would later incorporate into his sword-and-
sorcery. Haggard and Mundy were also formative influences on Fritz
Leiber and Harry Otto Fischer, who incorporated these influences
into Fafhrd and the Gray Mouser (Leiber, "Fafhrd and Me" 127).

Historian and historical fiction writer Harold Lamb (1892–1962)
inspired a young Howard with his colorful tales of cossacks, cru-
saders, Vikings, and Mongols in the pages of *Adventure*. Lamb was
also a prolific historian with many colorful works of biography

---

[4] Howard had at least one Sabatini volume on his bookshelf at the time of his death:
The Snare (1925). Scaramouche was perhaps Sabatini's most popular work and Howard
may well have read it.

and non-fiction to his credit, including *Genghis Khan: The Emperor of All Men, The Crusades, Charlemagne: The Legend and the Man,* and *Hannibal*. But his histories and biographies are written with the blood and verve of rousing adventure fiction. From *Hannibal*:

> He threw back his black mantle to display the jewels in his sword, and pointed around him, smiling. *These,* he told the leaders, *are the walls not only of Italy but of Rome. You have surmounted them. There,* he pointed down, *are the cities of wealth with many women. You have only to ride down to reach them* (66).

Howard was an admirer of *Adventure* and even though he failed to place a story in its pages, he considered himself a historical fiction writer first and foremost and maintained a fierce loyalty to the magazine (Finn, *Blood and Thunder* 51). From Lamb, Howard incorporated into his sword-and-sorcery historically accurate descriptions of military campaigning, battle-tactics, gear, and military leadership. But he also drew inspiration for his barbaric heroes' wild strength and rough codes of honor. The parallels with Conan are plain. Lamb's "The Three Palladins," originally published in *Adventure* in 1923, traces the rise of Temujin, aka Genghis Khan, from ambitious youth to chief of the Mongol hordes. Lamb conveys the wild strength, endurance, and fighting skill of the Hun plainsman, but also romanticizes reality. In place of the historic Khan who sired numerous children with multiple wives, and ordered the slaughter of countless women and children, Temujin is portrayed by Lamb as monogamous, and fierce but fair on the battlefield. Temujin is strong, half-wild, and a natural leader of men, but is also ruthlessly driven. Though he's of a race of barbaric nomads, his sights are set on conquest of the greatest civilized kingdom of the age—Cathay, today known as China. "The Three Palladins" contrasts the barbaric strength of the Mongols with the soft opulence of the Cathayans. In one scene Temujin holds captive a civilized princeling by circling both his wrists with the fingers of one hand. The story vividly paints several apocryphal feats of strength by Temjuin, including a wrestling match to the death against a monstrous Turk, a test of Temujin's ongoing fitness to rule: "O my cousin," spoke up Jamuka coldly, "have you sat so long on the carpet of the council that you fear to set your feet on the wrestling rug? It was not so with Yesukai, your father. Show us, as aforetime, your strength and skill" (Lamb, "The Three Palladins" 118). Though he lacks the Turk's imposing size, Temujin draws on his reservoir of barbaric strength and shatters the man's skull against a tent pole. Later Temujin exacts revenge on the traitorous Jamuka with another feat of barbaric strength, lifting him bodily and throwing him to his death from a high castle wall, a scene that Howard later borrowed for the Conan story "The Scarlet Citadel."

"The Three Palladins" culminates with a seemingly irreducible crux: When barbarism triumphs and overthrows civilization, what is next for the victors, and what will take civilization's place? Standing in the palace of the overthrown Cathay, gazing at its empty throne while a dying palace slave breathes his last, Temujin reaches the conclusion that he is a "wild boar of the steppe" and unfit to rule a civilized kingdom. "You have conquered an empire in the saddle; you cannot govern it so," advises his friend, the Cathayan prince Mingan. Even barbarians must practice diplomacy and statesmanship if they are to rule the kingdoms they conquer, ironically resulting in new cycles of complacency, decay, and decadence. Temujin understands the limitations of barbarism but sidesteps the ultimate question (What happens when Ghengis Khan has conquered all the world?) by turning over the rule of Cathay to Mingan, leaving him with the freedom to continue his conquests in the west.

Fellow *Adventure* writer Talbot Mundy placed many of his stories in the modern age but also added in magical elements. These light supernatural touches to otherwise historical adventure helped give sword-and-sorcery its sorcerous proportions. Mundy's writing style, "boast(ing) the considerable virtues of well-built plots, fast pace, abundant quiet humor, and clear, brisk, literate, unaffected prose" (de Camp, "Mundy's Vendhya" 187) are hallmarks of Howard's prose. Mundy's most popular creation, Tros of Samothrace, first appeared in *Adventure* and later was collected and reprinted in various hardcover and paperback editions beginning in the 1930s through the 1960s. Tros was an enormous influence on several of the major early writers of sword-and-sorcery. C.L. Moore, author of the iconic swordswoman Jirel of Joiry, professed her enjoyment of the Tros stories in a January 1936 letter to H.P. Lovecraft (*H.P. Lovecraft: Letters to C.L. Moore and Others* 98), while Fritz Leiber once stated that Tros of Samothrace was in influence akin to his generation's *The Lord the Rings* (Schweitzer, "Fritz Leiber, Critical Essays"). Mundy's most swordly and sorcerous character was later repackaged and rebranded for genre audience by Zebra in the late 1970s. In an amusing twist, the publisher blurbed the cover as "in the tradition of Robert E. Howard's Conan," despite being published well before Howard's earliest tales (Herron 179). But the comparison is otherwise apt. Here is Mundy's description of Tros:

> He looked a giant compared to the others, although he was not much taller than they. His clothing was magnificent, but travel-stained. His black hair, hanging nearly to his shoulders, was bound by a heavy gold band across his forehead...his forearm was a Titan's, and the muscles on his calves were like the roots of trees; but it was his face that held attention: Force, under control with immense stores in reserve; youth unconquerable, yet peculiarly aged before its time; cunning of the sort that is entirely separate from cowardice;

imagination undivorced from concrete fact; an iron will and great
good humor, that looked capable of blazing into wrath (12).

Tros is an outsider, son of a prince from the mysterious Grecian
island of Samothrace at the edges of the sprawling Roman empire.
Although Tros possesses all the traits of a leader—natural charisma,
inner strength and conviction, and an ability to make shrewd decisions under fire—he has no use for courtly life or kingship, "for he
would rather journey into unknown lands than be the emperor of
all the known ones" (Mundy 134). He spends most of his time as
an adventuring seafarer on the coasts of Gaul and Britain where his
speedy ship allows him to stay one step ahead of the hated Romans.
Like Conan's commandeering of a pirate ship at the conclusion of
"Iron Shadows in the Moon," Tros' sheer force of will allows him
to take command of a ship crewed by reluctant Britons who could
otherwise overrun and kill him by sheer weight of numbers.
Offered the opportunity to raise and command an army of
Britons, he refuses:

> "You, who have lost all except your manhood and the clothes you
> wear!" she said at last, and her voice was bold and stirring, "what is
> your ambition?"
>
> "To possess a ship," he answered, so promptly that he startled her.
>
> "A ship? Is that all?"
>
> "Aye, and enough. A man is master on his own poop. A swift ship, a
> crew well chosen, and a man may laugh at Caesars" (31).

The Tros stories depict the Roman empire as a rapacious conqueror
and Caius Julius Caesar as a cruel, vain, amoral lover of torture, his
ambition trumping any sense of honor. "Civilization" of the kind
brought by the Roman occupiers is an evil, and the fierce natives of
Gaul and Briton, though clad in wolf-skins and their skins dyed a barbaric shade of blue, are oppressed peoples fighting for their freedom.
Mundy's portrayals likely colored Howard's sympathy for the barbarian and antipathy for the Roman empire, as well as his general belief
that civilization would ultimately collapse under its own gluttony
and rottenness. Tros, however, is hardly the unbridled savage that
Howard would pioneer with Kull and Conan; he abhors killing and in
one scene chastises his sidekick Conops for knifing to death a couple
legionnaires instead of bludgeoning them unconscious.

With his rousing tale of a lost civilization set in the deeps of Africa,
King Solomon's Mines (1885), H.R. Haggard pioneered what is today
known as the "Lost World" genre. A wildly popular and influential
writer of the Victorian Age, Haggard's influence on sword-and-
sorcery is formidable. Haggard influenced not only the first wave

of sword-and-sorcery authors—Robert E. Howard, Clark Ashton
Smith, C.L. Moore, and Henry Kuttner—but also second generation sword-and-sorcery authors Poul Anderson, Fritz Leiber, and
Michael Moorcock. Haggard is today credited as the inventor of
exotic adventure fiction, inserting fantastic elements into otherwise
historical tales of treasure hunters, adventurers, Vikings, and the
like to create page-turning tales of rousing action, strangeness, and
wonder. "When it comes to the literary movers and shakers who
influenced sword and sorcery, Haggard towers above all as a colossus, a titan, if not the outright supreme deity thereof" (Richardson,
"Forefathers of Sword and Sorcery: H. Rider Haggard"). Haggard's
blood-and-thunder action sequences could be inserted directly into
sword-and-sorcery without alteration. Here is 210-pound fair-haired
Sir Henry Curtis of *King Solomon's Mines* in the press of combat:

> And yet more gallant was the vision of Sir Henry, whose ostrich plumes
> had been shorn off by a spear-stroke, so that his long yellow hair
> streamed out in the breeze behind him. There he stood, the great Dane,
> for he was nothing else, his hands, his axe, and his armor all red with
> blood, and none could live before his stroke. Time after time I saw it
> come sweeping down, as some great warrior ventured to give him battle,
> and as he struck he shouted, "Oh-hoy! Oh-hoy!" like his berserker fore-
> fathers, and the blow went crashing through shield and spear, through
> head-dress, hair, and skull, till at last none would of their own will come
> near the great white "tagati" (wizard), who killed and failed not (367).

Though today fallen out of fashion, Haggard remains a singular
influence on fantasy fiction. He not only directly influenced the development of sword-and-sorcery, but also the more popular strain of
high fantasy popularized by J.R.R. Tolkien. In Haggard's *She* (1887),
three Europeans embark on a quest to the deepest reaches of Africa
in search of a rumored lost civilization, home to the beautiful, ageless
goddess Ayesha, rumored to have power over life and death. Tolkien
acknowledged a boyhood infatuation with the novel. Scholars have
written extensively about Ayesha as an inspiration for his Elf-queen
Galadriel, and Tolkien also drew inspiration from the book's great,
ancient lost city, which served as the subject of his 1915 poem "Kor:
In a City Lost and Dead" (Garth 80). Heavy with a portentous *fin de
siècle* atmosphere, *She* and its forgotten city of Kor may have reinforced Howard's conviction that civilization was prone to entropy and
decay and eventual barbaric overthrow. Ayesha has clear analogues
in Howard's works, including the immortal princess Tascela, wicked
ruler of the Tecuhltli tribe of "Red Nails." Ayesha and Tasclea discover
the secret of immortality under mysterious circumstances, including
death of the men whom they charmed into revealing its source.

She, King Solomon's Mines, and works like Arthur Conan Doyle's *The
Lost World* (1912) are sources for the lost civilizations that Howard

would employ in works like "Red Nails" and "The Slithering Shadow." The joy of adventure and wonders of exploration expressed in these and other lost world novels are mirrored in sword-and-sorcery. Says the narrator of Conan Doyle's *The Lost World*, "for it is only when a man goes out into the world with the thought that there are heroisms all round him, and with the desire all alive in his heart to follow any which may come within sight of him, that he breaks away as I did from the life he knows, and ventures forth into the wonderful mystic twilight land where lie the great adventures and the great rewards."

Haggard may be unique in claiming direct influence on the two major authors at work on opposite ends of the fantasy spectrum. But sword-and-sorcery in its present form might not have existed without Edgar Rice Burroughs (1875–1950). Burroughs grew up a fan of the pulp magazines but thought he could do better than their sometimes hackneyed, clunky contents. His judgment proved correct, as his first published story, "Under the Moons of Mars," (1912, *The All Story* magazine) attests. Burroughs looked to the stars—the romance of the mysterious red planet Mars—and to the deep and still largely uncharted jungles of Africa for inspiration for his stories. Against the backdrop of these evocative settings he created and placed memorable, powerful heroes John Carter and Tarzan, as well as lost world stories including *At the Earth's Core* (1914) and *The Land that Time Forgot* (1918).

The John Carter stories, though technically sword-and-planet, are told with such swashbuckling, pulp sensibility that they are essentially sword-and-sorcery with radium pistols and hovercraft, lacking magic and horror. Burroughs' Barsoom (i.e., Mars) stories depict savage hand-to-hand fighting with a heavily stylized pulp sensibility. When Carter leaps into battle to fight a pack of ferocious plant-men, he does so with a barbaric gusto the equal of Conan, Kane, or Brak: "I grasped a mighty long-sword in my hand and in my heart was the old blood lust of the fighting-man, and a red mist swam before my eyes and I felt my lips respond to my heart in the old smile that has ever marked me in the midst of the joy of battle" (Burroughs, *The Gods of Mars* 262-263). Carter is able to prevail against hordes of opponents due to his earthly muscles, honed and developed in the gravitational pull of our own planet and capable of generating prodigious leaps and powerful sword-strokes in the thin Martian atmosphere. Carter is possessed of a primal lust for combat, "the fighting blood of (his) Virginian sires" and "the fierce blood lust and the joy of battle." His combination of muscular strength, skill with a blade, and utter fearlessness in the thick of the melee became a hallmark of sword-and-sorcery protagonists. While Mundy's relatively subdued Tros represents the beginning of the arc of the larger-than-life heroes of sword-and-sorcery, Carter is the first of this near-superhuman kind, a forerunner of the subsequent over-the-top heroics of the likes of Kyrik, Imaro, and Brak. Carter is also possessed of an inherent nobility, including a hatred of injustice and cruelty, although the Barsoomian rulers consider him an uncouth barbarian from a lesser species.

Burroughs was a natural storyteller, and if his stories lack sophistication or elevated style, they make up for it with narrative drive, inventiveness, and ideas. Moorcock described Burroughs' muscular, clipped style of page turning prose as profoundly influential to fantasy writers of the 20th century. "This laconic as opposed to lyrical romanticism, with admiration for the native outsider, the primitive—the unrepressed wish-fulfillment 'noble savage' of Victorian fiction—was to be the dominant voice in science fiction and fantasy until relatively recently" (Moorcock, *Wizardry and Wild Romance* 52).[5] Though principally a writer of sharply plotted action stories, Burroughs occasionally engages with deeper themes. "The Gods of Mars" offers an extended critique of organized religion and its "stupid infatuation for impossible superstitions" and also takes aim at blind Barsoomian nationalism. The latter may be a critique of the same forces that plunged Europe into the butchery of World War I ("The Gods of Mars" was published just before the outbreak of hostilities as a five-part serial in *All-Story* from January-May 1913, and later as a complete novel in September 1918). Writing in the immediate aftermath of the Victorian age, Burroughs grappled with the same loss of faith wrought by modernity and scientific progress. "Heaven" in "The Gods of Mars" is revealed as a sham, a place of exploitation and cruel death. A hollow-voiced intonation greets Carter and his companion Tars Tarkas with the grim message, "There is no hope, there is no hope; the dead return not, the dead return not; nor is there any resurrection" (Burroughs, *The Gods of Mars* 285-286). The Holy Therns of "The Gods of Mars" are reputedly of an advanced, ancient culture, but are possessed with a narrow fanaticism and self-worship, leading to their degradation and the "eradication of all the broader humanitarian instincts that the race might have once possessed" (369). Burroughs' original Martian trilogy, *The Warlord of Mars*, concludes with John Carter creating an enlightened, multi-cultural society shorn of its religious superstitions, false beliefs, and dead-end hopes.

Burroughs' most famous novel, *Tarzan of the Apes*, depicts civilization as a flawed endeavor, analogous though perhaps not as dark as Howard's portrayal in the Conan stories. Howard wrote in "Beyond the Black River" that "Barbarism is the natural state of mankind. Civilization is unnatural. It is a whim of circumstance.

---

[5] Moorcock was so taken with Burroughs that he started his own fanzine, *Burroughsania* (published circa 1956–58), in homage to the likes of Tarzan and John Carter of Mars.

And barbarism must always ultimately triumph." In Burroughs' universe, being raised among the animals trumps a civilized upbringing. Tarzan is not only far physically superior to civilized men but morally and spiritually superior as well, and judges with clarity man's capacity for capricious, wasteful, sub-animal behavior ("for it has remained for man alone among all creatures to kill senselessly and wantonly for the pleasure of inflicting suffering and death").

Sword-and-sorcery owes a substantial debt to Burroughs' liberal use of exotic settings, including lost cities, forgotten treasures, and lost races (Holmes 65). Fritz Leiber's "The Jewels in the Forest," Howard's "Red Nails," and Karl Edward Wagner's *Bloodstone* are a few representative examples. As the Tarzan series progressed, Burroughs layered in additional fantastic "lost world" elements including miniature races, remnants of vanished Roman legions, and intelligent apes and dinosaurs. In Burroughs' Pellucidar series (1914's *At the Earth's Core*, 1937's *Back to the Stone Age*), explorers discover that the earth is hollow and its interior is home to prehistoric monsters and cave men. *The Land that Time Forgot* (1918) is one of Burroughs' more famous examples of this style of lost world fiction. A German World War I U-boat lands at the forgotten isle of Caprona, where the hero must save a damsel in distress from the clutches of lusty Neanderthals.

Burroughs' Lost World books were repackaged and republished at the height of the sword-and-sorcery renaissance and accompanying "Tarzan boom" of the 1960s and 70s (Mandel). Their liberal use of cover art featuring muscular barbaric figures as painted by Conan artist Frank Frazetta—an odd dissonance with the average physiques of the modern, scientific explorer heroes featured in the works themselves—attest to the popularity of sword-and-sorcery at the time, and the degree to which publishers would stretch to get a piece of the burgeoning s&s market.[6][7]

[6] See *Back to the Stone Age* and *At the Earth's Core* (Ace publishing, 1978) for representative examples.

[7] With Burroughs' close thematic ties to sword-and-sorcery and the latter's indebtedness to Tarzan and John Carter of Mars, some critics have made the claim that sword-and-sorcery is a subgenre of science fiction (Williamson, 5). But this is inaccurate. Sword-and-sorcery's relationship with saga, and its roots in adventure fiction and weird, Gothic horror, are alien to SF. Howard's anthropologic approach to world-building is tenuous "science" at best, based on romantic notions of race and evolution (and infused with inexplicable sorcery and fell beasts without evolutionary record). Works like Karl Edward Wagner's *Bloodstone* and Jack Vance's *The Dying Earth* may contain advanced technology, but these elements are subsumed by heavy doses of magic, monsters, and gods. The Mars' stories use of technology and space-travel place them in the adjacent sword-and-planet subgenre, or as Lester Del Rey preferred, "science romance"—science fiction infused with "fighting and love" (Del Rey, *The World of Science Fiction* 26). That these somewhat pedantic definitions exclude the likes of Burroughs and Leigh Brackett from the ranks of sword-and-sorcery is regrettable, but in genre studies, lines must be drawn somewhere.

Early Fantasy / Proto-Sword-and-Sorcery

Yet in the blood of man there is a tide, an old sea-current rather, that is somehow akin to the twilight, which brings him rumours of beauty from however far away, as driftwood is found at sea from islands not yet discovered; and this spring-tide or current that visits the blood of man comes from the fabulous quarter of his lineage, from the legendary, of old; it takes him out to the woodlands, out to the hills; he listens to ancient song.
—Lord Dunsany, "The Bride of the Man-Horse"

Despite its affinity to adventure fiction and the Lost World genre, sword-and-sorcery is a subgenre of fantasy, and not just for its liberal use of demon-summoning sorcerers, magic rings, and monsters. Early fantasists Lord Dunsany, A. Merritt, James Branch Cabell, E.R. Eddison, and H.P. Lovecraft all played a hand in its shaping. Of these Lovecraft arguably cast the widest net, influencing all of sword-and-sorcery's major first generation writers including Howard, Leiber, Moore, Kuttner, and Clark Ashton Smith. Prior to his tales of cosmic horror for which he is best known, Lovecraft wrote several fantasy stories set in fabled lands, known as his "Dream Cycle series. The most notable of these is "The Doom That Came to Sarnath" (1920). "Sarnath" is a mix of horror and the weird, and with a liberal definition can be classified as proto-sword-and-sorcery. It tells the story of a semi-barbaric shepherd folk who settle in the land of Mnar and build the city of Sarnath, located adjacent to the ancient city of Ib. Ib is populated by voiceless toad-like beings with "bulging eyes, pouting, flabby lips, and curious ears," and it is rumored that they are not of Mnar. "It is also written that they descended one night from the moon in a mist; they and the vast still lake and grey stone city Ib." Sickened by the alien appearance of their neighbors, the young warriors of Sarnarth take up their spears and bows and march against Ib "and slew all the inhabitants thereof, pushing the queer bodies into the lake with long spears, because they did not wish to touch them." But the denizens of Ib once worshipped a sea-green stone idol chiseled in the likeness of Bokrug, a great water-lizard and an ancient god. Bokrug ultimately takes his vengeance, summoning his followers when the stars are right to complete Sarnath's doom.

It is largely from Lovecraft that sword-and-sorcery derives its elements of weird horror—tentacled monsters, blasted books of lore, and demon-summoning sorceries. "Sarnath" also provided an early template for the trope of the decadent, over-civilized city, with the residents of Sarnath building ostentatious towers to the sky and flaunting their prosperity and wealth, fueling the city's righteous destruction. But Lovecraft himself was inspired by an early fantasy author who wrote several fantasies of a singular style independent of the pulps and largely bereft of any pulp sensibility. Though lesser

known today, Edward Plunkett, 18th Baron of Dunsany, most commonly
known as Lord Dunsany (1878–1957), was a highly influential writer
of the fantastic in his heyday—"perhaps the strongest single influence
in the development of fantasy fiction in the (20th) century" (de Camp,
The Fantastic Swordsmen 21). Dunsany was so influential to the young
Lovecraft that in a March 1929 letter he classified his early fantasy
efforts as his "Dunsany" pieces (*Lovecraft: A Look Behind the Cthulhu
Mythos*). "The Doom that Came to Sarnath" is thoroughly Dunsanian
in style, including its opening of a brief window to a secondary world,
in *media res*, populated with odd races, beautiful cities, and alien
gods and religions, told in short, deft sketches of detail and ornate
language. Dunsany influenced several of sword-and-sorcery's earliest
practitioners including Clark Ashton Smith, C.L. Moore, and to a lesser
degree, Robert E. Howard. While there is no extant evidence that
Howard read Dunsany's prose fiction, in a 1930 letter to Lovecraft, he
admitted that he had read "some" Dunsany (*A Means to Freedom* 81) and
in a followup 1932 letter he lists Dunsany as one of his favorite poets,
but tellingly in the paragraph prior in a long list of his favorite writers
both of prose and verse, Dunsany does not appear (*A Means to Freedom*
510). Moore's debt to Dunsany is far greater. She wrote in a 1936 letter
to Lovecraft that "no one can imitate Dunsany, and probably anyone
who's ever read him has tried" (Moore, *Lord Dunsany: In the Land of Time
and Other Fantasy Tales* ix), and her stories contain many Dunsanian
flourishes and motifs—dreamlike landscapes, gothic castles—as well
as a preference for moody, atmospheric stories over action-driven plots.
Dunsany remained an influential figure to second generation sword-
and-sorcery/science fiction writers working in the 1960s renaissance;
Jack Vance in particular shows the heavy influence of Dunsany in his
"Dying Earth" series of stories, set in a post-apocalyptic age of earth in
which magic has returned to supplant technology.

Dunsany helped pioneer an innocuous but important element
in the development of the sword-and-sorcery tale: brevity. Prior to
Dunsany, fantasy fiction was the stuff of full-length novels popularized by Morris and MacDonald. Dunsany, however, preferred to
work in the short form and a handful of his short stories approximate sword-and-sorcery, including "The Fortress Unvanquishable,
Save for Sacnoth," "The Sword of Welleran," "The Horde of the
Gibbelins," and "The Distressing Tale of Thangobrind the Jeweller,
and of the Doom that Befel Him." Of all these stories, "Sacnoth"
is perhaps the most swordly and sorcerous. In it, the young hero
Leothric embarks on a mission to slay the fell sorcerer Gaznak.
Gaznak is invulnerable to all weapons save for the legendary sword
Sacnoth, a weapon that must be forged from the metallic hide of the
fearsome dragon Tharagavverug. Leothric must therefore slay the

dragon before he can confront the wizard. This he does (curiously by causing the creature to starve), and with reforged blade in hand bulls his way through Sacnoth's fortress, hacking at beasts and turning aside sorcerous spells before engaging in a desperate final duel with the sorcerer. Although the dialogue is quasi-medieval and somewhat akin to the high fantasy of Tolkien, and Leothric is a civilized noble, in the end "Sacnoth" is a lone hero pitting his sword against sorcery and falls into the ranks of sword-and-sorcery (for a detailed look at why "Sacnoth" may be the first sword-and-sorcery story but is generally not credited for launching the subgenre, see the sidebar).

Another candidate in the running for first sword-and-sorcery story is A. Merritt's *The Ship of Ishtar* (1924). Published as a serial in *Argosy All-Story Weekly* five years prior to Howard's "The Shadow Kingdom," Merritt's novel is the essence of the genre: swashbuckling adventure, voluptuous women in need of rescue, and strong men with swords pitted against evil sorcery. Merritt's contributions to sword-and-sorcery are, like Dunsany's, today often overlooked; Ray Capella, in "Hyborians, Be Seated," originally published in *Amra* #19 (1962), noted that although he rarely garnered any attention in the pages of the fanzine, Merritt was a sword-and-sorcery writer of the first rank, selecting his stories *The Ship of Ishtar, The Moon Pool* (1918), and *The Dwellers in the Mirage* (1932) as belonging firmly to the subgenre (Capella, 178). Though little-read today, Merritt influenced Lovecraft, as well as second generation sword-and-sorcery author Michael Moorcock.

Merritt was in his heyday a staple in *Argosy All-Story Weekly* magazine. He collaborated with Lovecraft, Howard, C.L. Moore, and Frank Belknap Long on "The Challenge from Beyond," a round-robin story commissioned by *Fantasy* magazine in 1935 in which the authors all contributed to a jointly-written story, picking up the narrative thread and continuing the tale where the other left off. Though not a particularly great story and worthwhile only as a curious pulp artifact, "The Challenge from Beyond" demonstrates that the editors of *Fantasy* once considered Merritt as in the same hierarchy of fantasy and science fiction's biggest stars.

The protagonist of *The Ship of Ishtar*, John Kenton, is an archeologist whose zest for life has been sapped by his experiences in World War I. Wounded at the battle of Belleau Wood, he loses his sense of wonder. "The war had turned the present to quicksand beneath his feet; worse, it had destroyed that bridge to the past over which his soul had been gay to tread." Kenton is roused from his torpor by the arrival of a great and mysterious block, inscribed with the names of gods from ancient Babylon. The block splits apart, revealing to Kenton a detailed toy ship, an ancient galleon of half ivory, half black, divided in color neatly at midships. While closely observing

the craft Kenton is sucked into some unexplained time-space con-
tinuum and swept 6,000 years into the past in which a war of gods
is played out on the deck of the ship. On the side of the light is
Sharane, a gorgeous, red-haired priestess of Ishtar; on the side of
the dark is Klaneth, priest of Nergal, Babylonian God of Death.

Merritt's techniques of displacement are superb. The room in
which Kenton first examines the block (and to which the story continually returns) is drab and prosaic; the ship of Ishtar on which
Kenton's otherworldly adventures unfold is bursting with color and
vividly detailed. The sea is azure, Sharane has fiery red hair and a
curvaceous body that can't be contained by her wispy outfits, and so
on. Kenton is transformed inside and out by the experience: he grows
muscles under the strain of the oars, but also rediscovers a purpose.
Soon he becomes a hero cut from the cloth of a Robert E. Howard
story, freed from the societal restrictions of the modern world. "All
that had been modern had fallen from him," writes Merritt.

Freed from his literal and symbolic bondage, Kenton (and the
reader) are taken on a vivid, memorable passage of nostalgia for the
heroic life, and the dread of the banal evils of modernity:

> On and on they had sailed. And ever as they slipped through the
> azure seas, memory of that other life of his had dwindled and sunk
> beneath the horizon of consciousness, as the land sinks behind the
> watcher on an outward bound ship. He thought of it, when at all,
> with numbing fear that he might be thrust back into it again—that
> old life of his (Merritt, *The Ship of Ishtar* 87)

During a calm in the action, Kenton describes the modern world
to his companions. They recoil from his descriptions of its savage,
anti-heroic wars, its pale customs, and its ineffectual gods. Says the
Persian: "For a man of taste such as I, it seems no world at all to live
in. And I like not your way of waging wars, nor could I learn to like
it—I who seem to be a soldier of an old school, indeed."

As Tim Powers notes in an introduction, *The Ship of Ishtar* taps
into the spirit of a pagan, pre-Christian era. Life and death are
treated very differently in this world. A clean death on the battlefield is a gift, freeing the hero from world-weariness. When Zubran
the Persian turns at bay to slow the pursuit of oncoming enemies, a
sacrifice that allows Kenton, Sharane, Gigi, and Sigurd to escape, he
does so knowing he will die, and no god—certainly not the Christian
god—will rescue him, nor even comfort him in his final moments.
But he does so with a swelling Ragnarok spirit, and a smile on his
face, because his death has a purpose, and his life meaning:

> "By all the Daevas!" swore Zubran, "never have I known such feeling of
> freedom as now! Lo—I am all alone—the last man in the world! None
> can help me, none can counsel me, none weary me! Life is simple at

last—all there is to it is for me to slay until I am slain. By Ormuzd—
how my spirit stands on tiptoe—" (Merritt, *The Ship of Ishtar* 156)

As the book ends, we're left with many unanswered questions.
Was it all a dream, or is this world—our world—a dream within a
dream? From whence does the look of fulfillment on Kenton's dead
face come? Has he found recovery from the horrors of Belleau Wood
and modernity in a heroic dream, or in death? Kenton's time on the
ship takes only nine hours of real time, the amount of time it might
require a reader to spend with such a book, wrapped up in a tale.

Ishtar perhaps fails to qualify as sword-and-sorcery as it keeps a
foothold in the modern world. But it is nascent sword-and-sorcery.
Merritt's other best-known works including *The Moon Pool*, *The Face in
the Abyss*, and *Dwellers in the Mirage* use this same framing device of
modern men discovering ancient races in remote corners of the earth,
and are perhaps more accurately classified as science fantasy or portal
fantasy. But their influence on sword-and-sorcery is considerable.
Dwellers in the Mirage acknowledges a barbaric spirit and atavistic urge
that lies dormant in the hearts of men, via ancestral memory, which
under the right circumstances may be rekindled. While it's not quite
in alignment with Howard's conception of barbarism, its influence
on the Conan stories is undeniable. *Dwellers in the Mirage* was originally published in serialized form in *Argosy* beginning in January
1932, mere months prior to Conan's first appearance in *Weird Tales*,
and its protagonist Leif Langdon likely served as a template for the
Cimmerian. Compare Langdon's declaration in *Dwellers*:

> By Zarda! But it was as it was of old—enemies to slay, a city to
> sack, a nation to war with and a woman's soft arms around me. I
> was well content!

With Conan's famous proclamation on the meaning of life from
"Queen of the Black Coast":

> I know this: If life is illusion, then I am no less an illusion, and being
> thus, the illusion is real to me. I live, I burn with life, I love, I slay,
> and am content.

Like Haggard, Merritt cast a spell of influence on a host of sword-
and-sorcery authors, including Howard, Smith, Moore, Kuttner,
Anderson, Andre Norton, Gardner Fox, Moorcock, Lin Carter, Ray
Capella, Karl Edward Wagner, Gary Gygax, and Keith Taylor, among
others (Richardson, "Forefathers of Sword and Sorcery: A. Merritt").

Among early/pre-sword-and-sorcery fantasists, James Branch
Cabell (1879–1958) is perhaps second in influence, lagging only
Dunsany. Fritz Leiber acknowledged Cabell as a chief early influence; it is from Cabell that Leiber derives much of his irony and
playful censor-skirting sexuality (although Shakespeare is another
likely source). Clark Ashton Smith and Michael Moorcock were also

Cabell admirers and adherents. Howard perhaps shows the least direct influence, but he too read Cabell; among the works donated to the Howard Payne library following Howard's death is Cabell's *The Cream of the Jest; A Comedy of Evasions* (1917). Howard also admired Cabell's novel *Something About Eve* (1927) and claimed Cabell "... writes with a diamond pen" (de Camp, *Dark Valley Destiny* 221).

Cabell's most famous work of fantasy is *Jurgen, A Comedy of Justice* (1919). On the surface it bears little resemblance to traditional sword-and-sorcery. The tone is wildly different, comic and light-hearted save for a few moments of introspection. Jurgen is no muscular hero that cleaves through his enemies. Its most memorable battle is an early sword-duel in which Jurgen suffers a humiliating defeat—and then exacts an even more humiliating and cowardly revenge upon his opponent. Later he embarrasses himself in a failed attempt to rip in half a tough piece of parchment. He takes multiple lovers, but each brings with them complications and baggage, resulting in a series of awkward exits. The tale is a classic heroes' journey common to high fantasy, but shorn of any ponderous Campbellian overtones. By stories' end, Jurgen arrives at his destination with a greater depth of self-awareness and maturity, having literally passed through the fires of hell. Overall it seems to share more in common with the works of Jonathan Swift, as *Jurgen* mercilessly satirizes religion, politics, and relationships.

Jurgen falls into a camp of the cynical, anti-heroic literature that followed World War I. Its broad influence—it enjoyed several printings and gained greater public attention after winning an eventual misbegotten obscenity trial (*Virginia Commonwealth Library*)—helped pave the way for heroic revival. Jurgen is a helpless modern male who "had lost the most of [him]self; and there was left only a brain which played with ideas, and a body that went delicately down pleasant ways." He has "lost the faith in the importance of [his] own actions," drowned in a thousand compromises. In mid-life he surrenders his calling as a poet, trading it in for the prosaic banalities of a pawnbroker, and setting down into unhappy marriage. It is a sad exchange; as Jurgen admits in a rare moments of unguarded honesty, "poetry is man's rebellion against being what he is." Jurgen suffers a fate familiar to middle-aged men everywhere—the surrender and the loss of vigor and passion, replaced with compromise: "For we who are tax-payers as well as immortal souls must live by politic evasions and formulae and catchwords that fret away our lives as moths waste a garment; we fall insensibly to common-sense as to drug; and it dulls and kills whatever in us is rebellious and fine and unreasonable." A decade later the same bitter war of art vs. commerce raged in Howard's breast.

Jurgen's influence on sword-and-sorcery is plain in the series of picaresque adventures Jurgen undertakes for self-gain, glutting himself on pleasures of the flesh. The unrelenting cynicism, irony, and humor of the story are a hallmark of the Fafhrd and the Gray Mouser tales, albeit muted; we also see the same characteristics (minus the humor) in Moorcock's Elric series. In Jurgen too is the outsider. "But for all his laughter, he could not understand his fellows, nor could he love them, nor could he detect anything in aught they said or did save their exceeding folly."

Still another early/pre-modern fantasy genre influence on sword-and-sorcery is E.R. Eddison (1882–1945). An "unabashed romantic," Eddison had little love for the advances of the twentieth century, and his published fiction reflected the same values (de Camp, "E.R. Eddison" 119). His greatest work, the fantasy novel *The Worm Ouroboros* (1922), belongs to an era prior to the commercial fantasy genre. It straddles the line of high fantasy and sword-and-sorcery, but is of the same heart-material as the latter. The *Worm*'s central heroes, including Juss, Goldry Bluszco, and Brandoch Daha, are larger-than-life lovers of adventure and battle, at their most content when "the blue blades flame and crimson." "Pagan these warriors may be and semi-barbarous, but they are not oppressed by weasel-faced doubts and whining uncertainties" (Prescott xvi). Their opponents include the fearsome Corinius, more or less a well-groomed Viking chieftain, and the demon-summoning sorcerer-king Gorice XII, who summons dark forces to the aid of the witches. Eddison's direct influence on early sword-and-sorcery is slight; we have no evidence that the likes of Howard, Smith, or Moore ever read him, although Fritz Leiber was among *The Worm*'s adherents (Leiber, "Author's Note" 2). Its archaic vocabulary and ornate, highly styled prose resembles nothing in sword-and-sorcery, save perhaps the work of Clark Ashton Smith. In the ensuing decades, however, the novel enjoyed subsequent reprints and literary acclaim, and second-generation sword-and-sorcery authors and editors Karl Edward Wagner and Avram Davidson acknowledged its influence (Mayer).

Even as newer authors began to integrate fantasy influences into sword-and-sorcery, the subgenre retained its early adventure and historical fiction influences. One part historical and adventure fiction, one part pre-genre fantasy and Lost World stories, and with one Odinic eye fixed on the ancient northern heroics and saga, this heady mix was to be poured into the bubbling cauldron of a weird-pulp receptacle. The elements were in place, the medium primed for its flowering. But it would take the right writer in the right place at the right time to pull it together and add his unique stamp to this wild brew of barbaric warriors, dark sorcerers conjuring black magic, and lost worlds of adventure.

That writer was just about to burst onto the scene.

"Sacnoth" or "Shadow"?

What was the first sword-and-sorcery story? When the dust has settled from this hundred-years war, and swords returned to their uneasy scabbards, Lord Dunsany's "The Fortress Unvanquishable, Save for Sacnoth" (1908) seems the obvious choice. Published when Robert E. Howard was just two years old, and the precocious Clark Ashton Smith had not yet written his first story, "Sacnoth" pits steel against magic and a hero against a dark wizard—all the required elements of a sword-and-sorcery tale. Historian and critic S.T. Joshi says that Dunsany "could be said to have initiated the subgenre of 'sword and sorcery,'" in which heroic battles in fantastic lands are the focus" (*Lord Dunsany: In the Land of Time* xii).

Yet the story most often credited for launching the subgenre (a claim advanced by this author, as well as many other genre fans and observers), is Howard's "The Shadow Kingdom" (1929). So how can a story which appeared some two decades after "Sacnoth," and five years after another strong candidate in A. Merritt's *The Ship of Ishtar*, be considered its origin?

To help clarify this concept, let's draw an analogy with heavy metal.

Debate rages over who recorded the first heavy metal song. Some make the case for The Kinks' 1964 hit "You Really Got Me," which included one of the first instances of distorted, power-riffed guitar playing. Blue Cheer is often trotted out as another candidate, given the nature of the hard-edged guitar work in their cover of "Summertime Blues." Others argue convincingly for Led Zeppelin, and their hard, fast-driving "Communication Breakdown" (1969). If that song doesn't check enough boxes, certainly Zeppelin's "The Immigrant Song" (1970) is heavy metal by all but the strictest definitions (listen to that opening scream, chugging guitar and bass, and lyrics of invasion and war, and try to claim otherwise). But these songs are isolated examples from Zeppelin's expansive catalog. When you consider their wider oeuvre, Led Zeppelin is basically a blues-influenced rock-and-roll band, with a hard (and occasionally metal) edge.

While heavy metal was cooking and formulating in the 1960s, and occasionally announcing itself in songs like Steppenwolf's "Born to be Wild," the first band to coalesce all its classic elements is Black Sabbath. Sabbath's self-titled debut album contains iconic riffs that are still among the heaviest the genre has ever produced. Other metal bands sprang up in the wake of *Black Sabbath*, including Judas Priest and Iron Maiden, who arguably perfected the template Sabbath began, but today Black Sabbath is recognized as metal's flash point. So while Led Zeppelin technically beat Black Sabbath to the starting line, and the Kinks and Blue Cheer performed songs you could reasonably categorize as early heavy metal and not be entirely incorrect, the question of which album and band started the heavy metal genre is inarguable. With apologies to Judas Priest fans everywhere.

"Sacnoth" is to sword-and-sorcery as Zeppelin's "The Immigrant Song" is to metal. Sacnoth may be sword-and-sorcery, but it is a single tale that did not start a movement. Fantasy critic Darrell Schweitzer argues against "Sacnoth's" inclusion in sword-and-sorcery altogether, noting that "there is something very different in Dunsany's tone and approach, his irony, his cynical and civilized heroes, and his undertones of black, cosmic comedy" ("King Kull as a Prototype of Conan" 127). Schweitzer also makes the argument that the story lacks an integral component of the sword-and-sorcery story, "the figure of the barbarian," which Howard first introduced with Kull of Valusia and later immortalized in Conan the Cimmerian. Others disagree. Editor and sword-and-sorcery author Karl Edward Wagner notes that Dunsany pioneered the genre's mercenary, anti-heroic sensibility with "The Distressing Tale of Thangobrind the Jeweller," featuring a morally ambiguous master jeweller and thief on a mission entirely to further his own wealth and satisfy his lusts. Thangobrind's sexual proclivities and detached, ironic bearing harken greatly to Fritz Leiber's Gray Mouser (*Echoes of Valor* 114).

But even if he was first to the starting line, the more compelling question is, did Dunsany truly *launch* sword and sorcery as a subgenre? That claim seems far less tenable. "Sacnoth" and "Thangobrind" arrived in the first decade of the 20th century without fanfare, and did not launch a wave of imitators. Dunsany enjoyed commercial success and critical acceptance during his lifetime, but mainly in his latter years, as a widely traveled lecturer and popular playwright. His early material, including the *Gods of Pegana*, *Time and the Gods*, and *The Book of Wonder*, though influential, highly inventive, and arguably superior to his later works, was not the chief source of his popularity. Dunsany's stories are gossamer and ethereal, his heroes dreamlike phantoms striding through the lands of Faerie, closer to the likes of Tolkien and Morris than Lamb and London. His stories do not feature recurring, archetypal protagonists resembling the earthly, grounded, muscular heroes that would typify the next 60 years of sword-and-sorcery. The case can be made that "Sacnoth" failed to break new ground, as it was too grounded in what came before. "[A]dmiring readers are hard-pressed to say what wouldn't exist right now had 'Sacnoth' never been written. No new genre label was deemed necessary because of 'Sacnoth,' no clamor for similar fare was heard, no groundswell of imitation followed its publication. 'Sacnoth' and Dunsany both deserve better than they've got in recent years, but as it stands the story is a minor curio for fantasy fans" (Grin, "The Fortress Unvanquishable, Even for Sacnoth").

In his introduction to *Kull: Exile of Atlantis*, Steve Tompkins makes the case that no Conan or Kull ever strode from the pages of a Dunsany story or *The Ship of Ishtar* into mass assimilation, nor were any subsequent Hyborian Ages charted from their example. "The Shadow Kingdom" had a markedly different impact. "But the Howard tale jumps out at us as not only the first American sword-and-sorcery story but the first to summon a series into being by offering a setting, an arena, greater than was required for just a single adventure, a setting the depth and detail of which all but demanded sequels" (xix). That is why Howard's "The Shadow Kingdom," while perhaps not the first sword-and-sorcery story, is the subgenre's true north.

CHAPTER THREE

Robert E. Howard and the Birth of Sword-and-Sorcery

"A wizard is a hard man to beat, Kull," said this man. "In this game or in the real red game of battle—Well, there was once when my life hung on the balance of power between a Pictland wizard and me—he had his charms and I had a well forged blade—"
—Robert E. Howard, "Untitled Fragment", *Kull: Exile of Atlantis*

On a sweltering August day in 1926, 23-year-old Robert E. Howard hunched over his black Underwood typewriter in the heat of Cross Plains, Texas, banging out heavy key strokes with a staccato rhythm. Howard shouted passages as he wrote, and a passer-by of the white clapboard house at the junction of Texas State Highway 36 and Avenue J might have heard something like this:

> Valusia—land of dreams and nightmares—a kingdom of the shadows, ruled by phantoms who glided back and forth behind the painted curtains, mocking the futile king who sat upon the throne—himself a shadow.

Not satisfied with the story, Howard put it away in his writer's trunk. But unlike many of his unfinished manuscripts and fragments, Howard returned to the draft the following year, rewriting it and finally submitting it to *Weird Tales*. It was rejected. But Howard did not give up so easily: gritting his teeth, he kept at the story, revising it and submitting it yet again to meet the demands of finicky editor Farnsworth Wright.

We don't know the source of Howard's dogged determination with this particular tale. Perhaps it was a mercenary reality that drove him on, refusing to let so much effort and word count go to waste. Each page of a manuscript represented precious coin at a time when he needed it. But perhaps Howard felt some power in the tale, a sense that he was on the verge of something new and different with this story of the impossibly ancient, antediluvian Kull of Atlantis—a character that would transcend the Puritan avenger Solomon Kane and the Pictish King Bran Mak Morn, who were of history and bound to the eras in which they lived. Kull was something more, a figure out of the deeps of time.

Wright accepted the "The Shadow Kingdom" for publication in September 1927, and it finally saw print in the August 1929 issue of *Weird Tales*.

And with that, sword-and-sorcery was born.

It is tempting to affix the label "mad genius" to Howard (1906–1936). Biographer L. Sprague de Camp described the Texan pulp author as "a fatally flawed personality. He suffered from pathological dependence on his mother, from delusions of persecution, from a fascination with suicide" (de Camp, *Dark Valley Destiny* 366). As the only full-length biography of Howard for more than 25 years, the label of unhinged visionary stuck, dogging Howard in the years subsequent to his untimely death in 1936. In de Camp's defense, however, how else could a young, largely self-educated young man, living in Great Depression-era rural Texas, create an entirely new genre that influenced countless subsequent authors, generated dozens of imitators and pastiches of his work, and even today continues to spawn films, TV series, and video games?

Part of the blame for this legend must fall to Howard, a self-mythologizer. Howard claimed that he felt a strange magic in the creation of the Conan stories, describing his writing process as something akin to alchemy, ancient voices speaking to him from a dim and remote past. In a December 14, 1933, letter to fellow sword-and-sorcery writer and *Weird Tales* contributor Clark Ashton Smith, he wrote: "I have sometimes wondered if it were possible that unrecognized forces of the past or present—or even the future—work through the thoughts and actions of living men. This occurred to me when I was writing the first stories of the Conan series especially. I know that for months I had been absolutely barren of ideas, completely unable to work up anything sellable. Then the man Conan seemed suddenly to grow up in my mind without much labor on my part and immediately a stream of stories flowed off my pen—or rather off my type-writer—almost without effort on my part. I did not seem to be creating, but rather relating events that had occurred" (Wagner, *Conan: The Hour of the Dragon* 4).

With the perspective of time and distance, and scholarly research, we now know that the Conan stories and Howard's broader literary corpus were the product of something more than divine inspiration. Despite the formidable obstacles he faced in his personal life in rural Texas—isolation from like-minded peers, skepticism of his writing profession, and suspicion by the local populace—Howard had a ready medium in which to place his stories, and a creative, permissive playground in which he could stretch his talents. The pulp magazine *Weird Tales* was not only a paying market (though chronically late with its reimbursements during critical stretches of Howard's life), but also a community. In its pages, like-minded authors could compare their works, test their ideas, and receive commentary and criticism from magazine editor Farnsworth Wright, a stable of creative peers, and a loyal, actively involved fan base of readers (Everett and Shanks, ix). *Weird Tales* was, in its own unique way, both internet message board, blog, and email server for writers like Howard. It served as a conduit for the likes of Clark Ashton Smith, C.L. Moore, H.P. Lovecraft, and Fritz Leiber to "meet" and later begin corresponding in personal letters. Their discussions on matters of genre and the craft of writing were critical to the development of weird fiction and the burgeoning sword-and-sorcery genre.

Howard relished literary experimentation and genre-mixing, and *Weird Tales*, under the editorship of Wright and his non-patronizing view of pulp literature, provided a flexible and accepting sandbox in which Howard could stretch his creative muscles. "The larger context of the pulp magazine culture, too, is also important to note in the establishment of sword-and-sorcery, in providing a creative space in which Howard could play with genre, to experiment so freely and perhaps wildly, and in what would become culturally significant ways" (Emmelhainz, "Strange Collaborations" 59). Howard also had a tradition in which to work, albeit a rough and largely amorphous one. Authors such as Lord Dunsany and A. Merritt were already writing proto-sword-and-sorcery, although as described in Chapter Two, these stories lacked some of the distinctive elements that Howard would pioneer with his stories of Conan and Kull. They had proven that fantastic fiction could be written for and enjoyed by adults. Howard was part of a nascent fantasy movement, even though it lacked shape and a dedicated publisher outside of the pulps.

But Howard's success is not merely the result of a ready marketplace or fortuitous timing. He was also a first-rate talent, a natural storyteller who worked with an effortless, muscular prose style that propelled the reader along. Howard honed and perfected his craft over the course of more than 300 stories, but his natural talents are evident from his earliest days. His first professional sale, "Spear and Fang" (1924), a story of the clash of Neanderthal and Cro-Magnon, may lack the sophistication, plot development, and polish of his later efforts, but as Mark Finn notes in his Howard biography *Blood and Thunder*, "It stood out in one important aspect; the story is practically all action, galloping along at breakneck pace" (Finn, *Blood and Thunder* 88). The vitality of Howard's prose is something apart from the gossamer fantasies of Dunsany.[1] Wrote Howard's first significant

---

[1] A. Merritt, especially his The Ship of Ishtar, exhibited some of the "blood and

biographer, L. Sprague de Camp, "Howard's passionate intensity carries the reader along on a galloping steed. Conan's gigantic angers and consuming hates recreate for us the tangled emotions that surged through Howard's own soul" (*Dark Valley Destiny* 17).

With the illumination afforded by the publication of his collected letters, we now know that Howard's statement that the Conan stories "seemed suddenly to grow up in my mind without much labor on my part" stems from self-deprecation and perhaps a deliberately inculcated mysticism than from fact. Howard had a voracious appetite for stories and tall tales, and he honed his storytelling craft by telling his own tall tales, first aloud with playmates and then with his typewriter (Finn, *Blood and Thunder* 38). Howard was widely read and had a curious mind. He was a student of world and local history and a voracious reader of historical fiction, which he admired for its melding of dramatic real events and larger-than-life personages with the art of taut plotting, vivid action scenes, and propulsive dialogue. He once claimed that were not it not for the time required to produce it, and the vagaries of the market, historical fiction would have been his preferred mode. In a 1933 letter to H.P. Lovecraft, Howard wrote, "There is no literary work, to me, half as zestful as rewriting history in the guise of fiction. I wish I was able to devote the rest of my life to that kind of work ... A single paragraph may be packed with action and drama enough to fill a whole volume of fiction work" (*A Means to Freedom* 651).

Howard could not find a steady market for historical fiction, nor could he afford to take the time to perform the research that the genre and its often pedantic readers demanded. So he struck a brilliant compromise. He took a creative leap—or, rather, a series of small inspired jumps—that moved his stories out of the historical and into the realms of fantasy, while still maintaining a foothold in the real world. Howard's first Kull story—unpublished, though later included as "Exile of Atlantis" in the posthumous collection *King Kull*—includes an unnamed character loosely of Cro-Magnon and "historical" Atlantean heritage.[2] Within the tale Howard switches the lens from this character to Kull of Valusia, the latter an utterly fantastic country without historical ties. This moment marks the conception of sword-and-sorcery, claims Howard scholar Patrice Louinet. "When Howard dropped Atlantis for Valusia, he dropped Am-ra for Kull. In a nutshell, he stopped writing 'historical' tales in favor of fantasy tales" (Louinet 292-293). Kull eventually suffered a

---

thunder" gallop of Howard, but it was not so pronounced nor distinctively styled.

[2] Many historians in Howard's era believed that Atlantis once existed (Shanks, "Hyborian Age Archaeology" 17).

similar fate as the unnamed Cro-magnon of the story after Howard dropped the Valusian king for Conan. But the Thurian Age became a yet deeper "prehistoric era" on which Howard built the Hyborian Age of Conan, and thus Kull continued to live on in a half-life (289).

Howard's development of a fictional universe in which he could place his Kull and Conan stories is a feat of imagination comparable to J.R.R. Tolkien's creation of Middle-Earth. In fact his "The Hyborian Age" essay—a mythic account of earth's pre-history—accomplished what Tolkien did decades later with *The Silmarillion*. Tolkien is often mistakenly credited as the first fantasist to provide a rigorous historical grounding for his stories, but "The Hyborian Age" saw print in its entirety in 1938, some four decades prior to the 1977 publication of *The Silmarillion*.[3] Although unpublished during Howard's lifetime, "The Hyborian Age" served as the underpinning for both his Conan stories and the earlier Thurian Age of King Kull. It is one of the first examples of a "shared universe" in the annals of fantasy literature, in which fictional characters published in separate stories inhabit the same imaginary world, whose actions might influence another character operating in a later timeline, and in the right circumstances could theoretically "meet."

But even as he turned from history to fantasy Howard continued to weave historical elements into his fantastic tales. In "Kings of the Night," Kull is transported millennia forward in time to help the Pictish king Bran Mak Morn defeat an invading army of Romans, taking up arms in a Viking shield wall. The countries of Howard's invented Hyborian Age correspond with Europe, parts of Asia, and northern Africa, and their fictional cultures are recognizably fictional representations of actual countries.[4] This was Howard's intent; the Hyborian Age is intended to be an age of earth, prior to a great cataclysm. This melding of the real and the unreal lent Howard's fantastic stories a firm grounding in reality, a verisimilitude that sets them apart from his predecessors and their stories of gossamer fantasy. "In doing so, he created a fictional setting that was steeped in realism unprecedented within the genre of speculative literature up to that point" (Shanks, "Hyborian Age Archaeology" 14).

Howard's fantasy tales are not the ethereal fantasies of Dunsany or MacDonald, nor the measured epics of Morris, but are historical in feel, grounded in dirt and blood, and written with a pulp sensibility. They are the outgrowth of his unique influences, principally two-fisted historical adventure stories. Though his writings

---

[3] Tolkien started chronicling the mythology and history of Middle-Earth perhaps as early as 1914.

[4] For example, Howard's Afghulistan=Afganistan, Vendhya=India, Stygia=Egypt, etc.

contain a wide breadth of influences including Shakespeare, the noted Theosophist Helena Blavatsky, and the works of British folklorist Lewis Spence (Shanks, "Hyborian Age Archaeology" 20-22), Howard's principal sources of inspiration were the colorful historical fiction tales of Harold Lamb and Talbot Mundy in the pages of the pulp magazines *Argosy* and *Adventure* (Finn, *Blood and Thunder* 51), as well as the adventure fiction of Jack London (see sidebar). Howard also drew upon the rich history of the state in which he lived. Texas offered veins of inspiration: floods and famines, Indian raids, and bloody range wars fought among cattlemen. The boom and bust of oil towns and their influx of calloused workmen and reckless fortune seekers offered ample inspiration to Howard, and instilled in him a rather dim view of the "progress" wrought by civilization (Finn, *Blood and Thunder* 17).

Howard's stories are also uniquely and intensely Howard, reflecting his beliefs and biases. Perhaps the most astute insight of the curious power of Howard's fiction came from the pen of his longtime correspondent H.P. Lovecraft, who in a September 1936 letter published in *Fantasy Magazine* wrote, "It is hard to describe precisely what made his stories stand out so—but the real secret is that he was in every one of them, whether they were ostensibly commercial or not." Howard projected his insecurities, hates, and seething passions into his stories. Conan and Kull were outsiders because Howard himself was an outsider. While some colorful biographers and editors have perhaps overplayed this aspect of his personality, as a pulp fiction writer in early 20th century working-class Texas, Howard had chosen a solitary—and to many residents of the town a questionable, even suspicious—vocation. Although Howard possessed a handful of steadfast friends with whom he corresponded and occasionally traveled and caroused, he felt misunderstood by most of his Cross Plains neighbors—and for good reason. In a June 1933 letter to Lovecraft, he expressed a feeling of being a stranger in his home town: "The people among which I lived—and yet live, mainly—made their living from cotton, wheat, cattle, oil, with the usual percentage of business men and professional men ... but the idea of a man making his living by writing seemed, in that hardy environment, so fantastic that even today I am sometimes assailed by a feeling of unreality" (*A Means to Freedom* 604-605). Assessed de Camp of Howard's intellectual isolation: "So alien, indeed, was his profession that few people in Cross Plains ever tried to understand the lone young man who lived among them. They chose, rather, to ignore him or to dismiss him as merely eccentric" (DeCamp, DeCamp and Griffin 11).

Conan is an outsider in the lands through which he adventures, and the kingdoms which he eventually rules. Unlike a recent film adaptation of his most famous creation, Howard opted not to portray Conan living amidst his fellow Cimmerians. He is a man apart. A handful of acquaintances accompany Conan on some of his adventures—Valeria in "Red Nails," Balthus in "Beyond the Black River," and Taurus in "Tower of the Elephant," among others—but none remain with him from story to story. Outside of an intense but brief love affair with the she-pirate Bêlit in "Queen of the Black Coast," none of these relationships can be considered anything other than brief acquaintances. Almost all these characters fundamentally misunderstand Conan, or cannot identify with his barbaric mien, save Bêlit. The same is true of Conan's predecessor. In "Exile of Atlantis" a young Kull spares a young girl a painful death with a merciful throw of his dagger, but the fateful cast renders him a permanent outcast from his own clan.

"The Shadow Kingdom" is the first story in which Howard assembled all the elements that would constitute classic sword-and-sorcery: a barbaric hero on the civilized throne of Valusia, beset by a race of serpent-men plotting overthrow, disguised and masked by dark sorcery. Kull's antediluvian world is pre-historical but feels grounded in history, and it is, a pre-cataclysmic age of earth millennia prior to the Hyborian Age of Conan. The story contains surprising depths, including philosophic ruminations on reality. The masks with which the serpent-men disguise themselves are symbolic of mankind's duplicity; no one can really be trusted, particularly the ultra-civilized courtiers and nobility that are akin to the wealthy oil tycoons whom Howard despised.

In the subgenre's literal birth, "The Shadow Kingdom" demonstrated that sword-and-sorcery could aspire to more than boyish adventure and escape. The Kull stories are noteworthy for a relative lack of action and an emphasis on introspection. "The Screaming Skull of Silence" and "The Striking of the Gong" are philosophical examinations of the nature of life and illusion, echoing Howard's own psychological and philosophical delvings. Kull's introspective nature and intellectual leanings may have led to the character's commercial demise. *Weird Tales* editor Farnsworth Wright criticized the young Howard for over-writing and over-intellectualizing, and rejected all of his Kull stories save two: "The Shadow Kingdom" and "The Mirrors of Tuzun Thune" (Louinet 299). Later, Howard rewrote the Kull story "By this Axe I Rule" with some calculated changes: he swapped out the moody, introspective Atlantean king for the more extroverted and action-oriented Conan, whose briskly paced tales enjoyed a far higher acceptance rate in *Weird Tales*.

If Kull was the memorable ur-sword-and-sorcery figure, Conan was his more commercially acceptable and popular younger brother.

Howard would eventually write twenty-one tales of Conan of Cimmeria, eighteen of which were published in his lifetime. All but one were printed in *Weird Tales*—a very respectable success ratio for the unpredictable Wright. What would later become known as "sword-and-sorcery" is on full display in the first four Conan stories in order of publication ("The Phoenix on the Sword," "The Scarlet Citadel," "The Tower of the Elephant," "Black Colossus"). Each of these stories features an evil sorcerer pitting his magic against Conan's sword. The Conan stories created a commercial template for a new kind of fantasy, a radical departure from the earlier fantasies of William Hope Hodgson, Lord Dunsany, and E.R. Eddison. Howard's fantasy stories were fast-paced and cinematic, told with a no-frills prose style borrowed from the likes of Jack London, Harold Lamb, and Edgar Rice Burroughs. "Howard ... wrote in direct language. He eschewed the arty toying about with elves, enchanted princesses, and magical dragons and cut loose with stories about thick-armed warriors, harem girls, and flesh-eating apes" (Knight 118).

In addition to innovations of style, Howard also experimented thematically. Into the briskly plotted adventure stories pioneered by the likes of H. Rider Haggard, Rudyard Kipling, Mundy, Lamb, and Burroughs, Howard wove a dark undercurrent of mankind's fruitless but fierce struggle against fate. As he wrote in a June 1931 letter to H.P. Lovecraft:

> I lack your universal and cosmic scope and comprehension ... it is the individual mainly which draws me—the struggling, blundering, passionate insect vainly striving against the river of Life and seeking to divert the channel of events to suit himself—breaking his fangs on the iron collar of Fate and sinking into final defeat with the froth of a curse on his lips (*A Means to Freedom* 169).

Unlike the horrible ends suffered by the protagonists of Clark Ashton Smith and H.P. Lovecraft, Howard's heroes valiantly fought back, and mostly win—or at least live to fight another day. They will ultimately lose, lost in time beneath floods or sweeping barbaric hordes, or robbed of their vitality by age and infirmity. But they struggle mightily. Howard's protagonists are not helplessly swept along by the tide of fate, withdrawn brooders, or the scuttling, crab-like hollow men of a T.S. Eliot poem. They plunge into life and initiate action, even in the face of impossible odds or stark, living fear. "His important characters were 'doers' who put themselves in control of their fate, whose moments of fear of the unknown, if any, passed quickly into action" (Rickard 68). Howard cherished traditional masculinity and male-ness, and his heroes were men (and occasionally women) with the strength and will to make a stand. The phrase "true man" is found throughout the Kull stories. In "The Cat and the Skull" Kull demands of an ancient lake-king, "Swear not by gods or devils ... give your word as a true man." When the lake-king gives his word, Kull reciprocates, vowing never to molest the under-sea kingdom again. (Howard, "The Cat and the Skull" 107–108). Howard valued integrity, honor, and transparent, honest motives. He sought to hold on to the fading vestiges of an honorable yester-year which he saw as under assault from encroaching civilization. He longed for a time when men could make a difference; when Kull shatters the ancient Valusian laws in literal fashion, smashing them with his axe and roaring "I am the law!", it is the roar of frustration at the byzantine laws and customs of hyper-civilized society, and a clarion call for a return to clear-eyed fairness.[5]

Howard was a self-described agnostic, skeptical of the existence of a higher power. His stories are populated with characters sharing a similar worldview. In "Kings of the Night," the Pictish king Bran Mak Morn describes a priest's portents as "mummery" in which he places no faith, save in the boost of fighting morale it lends to his men (Howard, "Kings of the Night" 218). Howard shied from atheism and hinted that the weird workings of the world could possibly be ascribed to some type of divine being, or greater spiritual forces. This may have been partially due to the high esteem in which he held his father, with whom he shared a belief in reincarnation (de Camp, *Dark Valley Destiny* 87). Howard was also heavily influenced by Jack London's *The Star Rover*, which posited that man's soul was immortal, reborn time and again over thousands of years and able to survive the destruction of the body (see sidebar).

Kull and Conan triumph in adversity due to their savage, barbaric upbringing, one that proves itself superior to the training of softer, civilized men. Howard's introduction of the figure of the barbarian to fantasy literature is among his most notable accomplishments (Moorcock, *Wizardry & Wild Romance* 82). Prior to Howard, fantasy heroes were typically sons of nobles, knights, or civilized men trans-ported back from our own era. For example, Leothric, hero of Lord Dunsany's "The Fortress Unvanquishable, Save for Sacnoth," is son of a lord. The hero of A. Merritt's *The Ship of Ishtar*, John Kenton, is an affluent archeologist who assumes heroic form through magical means. Edgar Rice Burroughs' John Carter of Mars is a southern

---

[5] And yet these stories contain surprising depth and moral complexity: "True men" do not always fight on the side of good. In "Swords of the Purple Kingdom" enemy soldiers are arrayed against Kull under a false flag, swept up in machinations beyond their con-trol, but still "died like men" on the battlefield. True men may be tricked and corrupted by "the hands of the usurers," perhaps an unconscious (or conscious) commentary on the catastrophic bank failures of the Great Depression through which Howard lived and wrote. Kull's trusted adviser and right-hand man Brule the Pict shrewdly observes, "Want will make a rogue of any man" (Howard, "Swords of the Purple Kingdom" 208).

gentleman and Civil War captain who accumulated his wealth in the antebellum south. Talbot Mundy's Tros of Samothrace appears to be a homeless wanderer, but is a prince. Howard aimed for something very different with his barbarian heroes, who were wild and uncivilized, outsiders in the lands through which they strode. Coming from nothing, they claimed everything with their sword arm and naked will. When Howard's barbaric heroes do attain the throne of civilized countries they rule restlessly. After taking the throne of Valusia with blood-drenched axe in hand, "an hour of weariness" falls upon Kull, who experiences "a longing in him for things beyond himself and beyond the Valusian court" (Howard, "The Mirrors of Tuzun Thune" 55). Kull finds kingship a form of slavery, a maddening maze of illusions. Seizing power proves far less difficult than holding it; what can be accomplished in a sweeping act of swordplay and brute strength requires subtlety and diplomacy to manage, and an outsider will never truly be a man of the people. "Valusia overlooked the fact that I was a foreigner—now she cannot forgive me," acknowledges Kull, who also shrewdly realizes that "a great poet is greater than any king. ... I will be forgotten, his songs will live forever" (Howard, "By this Axe I Rule" 162).

Howard today stands as a counterweight to high fantasy with its restoration of kings and the return of order, as popularized in the fantasies of J.R.R. Tolkien and C.S. Lewis. In his stories, civilization is a veneer papering over mankind's true savage state. Civilization is not only artificial, but unnatural: Stifling bureaucracy and custom replacing healthy skepticism and inquiry, leading to a decline in morality and decency. Civilization ultimately breeds indolence, decay, and corruption, leading to violent overthrow from within or destruction at the hands of barbarians from without. Howard could no more write of the virtues of advanced civilizations than he could imagine a Roman empire that didn't rot from within and fall, or a Texas frontier unsullied by "progress." In one story Kull is petitioned by lovers who wish to marry, but are forbidden by old laws preventing the sons and daughters of nobles from marrying into lower classes. Notes Kull, "Here is a great to-do—custom and tradition! I have heard little else since I first pressed the throne of Valusia—in my land women mate with whom they will and with whom they choose." Kull's advisor Tu replies, "Aye Kull ... but this is Valusia—not Atlantis. There all men, aye, and all women are free and unhindered but civilization is a network and a maze of precedence and custom" (Howard, "Untitled Draft" 67).

Because civilizations are corrupt and decadent, Howard's barbaric heroes needed open space to roam and alternatives to explore. When Howard's worlds became too developed and crowded with humanity, cataclysms offered a fresh start. After the apocalypse arose wild frontiers to explore and to conquer. Here Howard introduced into his burgeoning new subgenre a staple of the western, though rarely employed in fantasy—the concept of the frontier. The Conan story "Beyond the Black River," in which a small group of settlers struggle to make a living on the edge of a vast, dark Pictish wilderness, is essentially a western masquerading as a weird tale. Howard, who loved westerns and turned to the form later in his writing career after he ceased writing Conan, consciously or unconsciously allowed the west to creep into his fantasy, which lent them much of their unique character. "It was this fusion of Old World myth and Old West legend that directed the emergence of a new approach to epic fantasy in Howard's writing" (Wagner, "Editors Introduction to 'The Black Stranger'" 11).

Howard's sympathies were ever with the barbarians, whom he thought would one day overrun their would-be civilizers. But he also believed that barbarism was not something to be celebrated, or held up as a mythical standard of excellence. It was merely the natural state of man that, over the objections of all his civilized trappings and traditions, would inevitably rise, red-handed and roaring, to the surface.

It is in this timeless tension of civilization vs. barbarism that Howard made his greatest literary contribution. And that contribution is due in no small part to a remarkable exchange in letters with another *Weird Tales* author, Howard Phillips Lovecraft.

Flashpoint: Civilization vs. Barbarism in *Letters*

From 1930 through 1936 Howard and Lovecraft engaged in a remarkable exchange of letters. Spanning more than 900 printed pages, their correspondence covers a vast depth and breadth of each man's personal interests, paints a vivid picture of the landscape and architecture of 1930s Texas and the northeast United States, and spans each man's thoughts on history, literature, and politics. The exchange also provides a revealing look into the sociopolitical atmosphere of the first third of the 20th century.

The letters reach their crescendo in a spirited philosophical and political debate that included a heated discussion on the merits of civilization vs. barbarism. This spar of thoughts helped spur the development of sword-and-sorcery (Emmelhainz, "Strange Collaborations" 58). Howard had already launched his first forays into sword-and-sorcery prior ("The Shadow Kingdom" was written in 1926-27 and published in 1929; Howard and Lovecraft did not begin corresponding until 1930), but his correspondence with Lovecraft crystalized his beliefs on civilization vs. barbarism. While Lovecraft astutely observed of Howard's stories "the real secret is that he himself is in every one of them," less acknowledged is Lovecraft's role in fomenting Howard's beliefs. Lovecraft challenged Howard in this exchange of letters and pushed him to reach new heights in passionate, sustained arguments of deepening subtlety and complexity.

In 2009 Hippocampus Press released this exchange (remarkably, most of the letters were preserved, and only a few of Lovecraft's are missing) in a two-volume set entitled *A Means to Freedom: The Letters of H.P. Lovecraft and Robert E. Howard*. What the letters demonstrate, broadly, is the clash of the rationalist/skeptic, abstract/theoretical mind of Lovecraft vs. the romantically inclined, parochial/personal-oriented mind of Howard. Lovecraft is revealed as a skeptic, an atheist, and a materialist. Using historical trends and evolutionary concepts to buttress his arguments, he argues for a form of fascistic socialism as the ideal form of government. Howard meanwhile is revealed as an agnostic, but also a romantic. In the letters he relies on his intuition and a combination of personal experience and emotional truths to argue his personal preference for a type of frontier libertarianism.

The letters not only contrast the differences between the two men, but illuminate the philosophical and moral underpinnings of the mind that gave birth to sword-and-sorcery. Howard's nostalgia for a somewhat romanticized version of frontier barbarism informs not only his own sword-and-sorcery, but that of the authors he influenced. In particular, the palpable tension between the harsh freedoms of the barbaric frontier vs. the decadent pleasures of the civilized city would later be used to great effect in the sword-and-sorcery of Fritz Leiber.

This remarkable exchange of two authors of weird fiction— Howard with an eye fixed on a distant, fantastic era populated by dark sorcerers and larger-than-life heroes, Lovecraft firmly on the present, the illimitable expanse of a dark universe, and the powerlessness of humanity—caught Howard's mind afire, providing potent fuel for the best of his Conan stories and the development of the sword-and-sorcery subgenre.

The HPL-REH correspondence began with a series of pleasant exchanges on historical matters, mainly the pre-history of Britain. The two men expressed a common love of history and languages. Howard, just 24 in 1930, is in these early exchanges deferential and at times a bit in awe of the elder (then 38-year-old) Lovecraft, who at the time was a well-established writer in the pulps. But over the next six years the exchange deepened and sharp differences emerged,

largely tied to Howard's romantic vs. Lovecraft's rationalist leanings. For example, Howard attributed a personal preference for
Danes over Saxons as a latent racial memory inherited through the
blood; Lovecraft dismisses Howard's theory as bunk, rendering the
likelihood of distant ancestral inheritance a mathematical impossi-
bility (*A Means to Freedom* 184). Lovecraft wrote of his admiration of
Hellenic Greece and Imperial Rome—the former for its exaltation
of scientific thought and philosophy and rationalism, the latter for
its organizational and political brilliance (332). Howard unerringly
expressed sympathy for barbaric cultures. By early January 1932,
he made his first reference to the Picts, an aboriginal confederation
of tribes who once dwelled in ancient northern Scotland. Howard
mythologized and transformed them in his fiction into a warlike
race of painted, half-savage barbarians led by the great king Bran
Mak Morn. His love for this barbaric race is so strong it even trumps
his own mixed Irish/Danish/Scottish/Germanic ancestry. "Yet, in
reading of the Picts, I mentally took their side against the invading Celts and Teutons, whom I knew to be my type and indeed,
my ancestors" (255). In December 1932, Howard summed up their
diametrically opposed outlooks: "Your impartial viewpoint is admi-
rable. For myself, I must admit that I am motivated more often by
emotion and sentiment than by cold logic" (501).

But Lovecraft continued to press the issue. In a letter dated
January 1933, Lovecraft launched a blistering salvo at the supposed
merits of barbarism. "Naturally, there are primitive, retarded, and
atavistic types to whom barbarism would be better suited than
civilization," Lovecraft wrote. "Behind every argument in favor of
barbarism, it seems to me, there lurks a fatally fallacious romanticism and sentimentality, and a fatally reckless disregard of the actual
facts and values involved" (530). Not without cause Howard assumed
Lovecraft's belittling words were an affront to his own character,
and counterpunched by implicating Lovecraft of romanticizing civilization. "But civilization is full of hideous things, too ... that was
part of the [barbarian's] life, just as grinding men and women to dust
and crushing their souls into ashes is part of the civilized system"
(547). The decade in which Howard lived provided ample evidence
for civilization's shortfalls, both home and abroad. "What consti-
tutes human suffering?" Howard asks. "The German barbarians had
their feuds and tribal wars; we have strikes, child labor, sweat shops,
unemployment, gang-rule" (597). Of the unrest in Europe circa 1934
and its steady drumbeat portending a second world war, he echoed
Lovecraft in describing it a "stewing cauldron." "I'm not surprised at
the massacre of helpless people, the torturing and abuse of women
and children. It's what I expect of cultured Europeans. It's what

I'll expect of the people of this country when they get sufficiently imbued with European culture and civilization" (817).

Howard's antipathy of civilization was fueled by recent events in his native Texas. In 1890 the United States officially listed the frontier as closed, and by the early 20th century it had been exploited by business interests, first by huge beef syndicates and later big oil companies. The latter also brought an influx of roughneck workers with a penchant for violence and criminality. In the boom and bust cycles of oil drilling, towns sprang up overnight and disappeared just as quickly, bringing with them corruption, unrest, and exploitation. "Capital with its ruthless practices came to stay. And with it came all the riff-raff that follows in the wake of whole-sale exploitation. A few corrupt politicians sold us out, and we've been fighting for our rights ever since," Howard wrote to Lovecraft (775). Howard's political views aligned with the New Deal democracy of Franklin Roosevelt. He attacked the fashionable fascism of the era of which Lovecraft was an adherent, painting the Republican politics of Herbert Hoover with the same broad brush. "You can not prove that Fascism is anything but a sordid, retrogressive despotism, which crushes the individual liberty and strangles the intellectual life of every country it inflicts with its slimy presence ... and Fascism is nothing but a new fad-name for industrial tyranny ... the Fascist movement in America is nothing but a move on the part of the money-barons to establish themselves more firmly than ever, to stamp out the last vestige of freedom in the people beneath them" (808).

Howard employed a rather sophisticated form of cultural relativism to buttress his preference for barbarism and barbaric cultures. "Where does barbarism leave off and civilization begin?" he asked Lovecraft. "We can hardly conceive ourselves to be the sole possessors of the only true civilization that the world has ever known" (547). Howard offered as evidence the great accomplishments of "barbaric" cultures such as the Vikings, which built the best ships the world had ever known, and wrote "poetic sagas that have never been surpassed for strength and beauty." Later he juxtaposd the inhumanity of modern warfare with the violent but small-scale parochial raids of barbaric cultures. "When the primitive German or Gaul went on the war path he went with more enthusiasm, with more reason, and with more assurance of personal, material gain, than the modern soldier goes to war" (642). Howard endorsed a form of local, regional rule, and customs of "courtesy and decency" that could include settling of private feuds with lethal but limited duels. "I certainly don't consider a man a criminal just because he kills a personal enemy in a fair stand-up fight. Some of these killings are a result of blood-feuds going back thirty or forty years" (646).

Howard believed that honor still had a place in the 20th century: men could boast all they wanted but ought to be ready for the consequences, to "back up [their] words with his fists or his guns" (704). A government that imposed a uniform set of rules and regulations across a land as vast and diverse as the United States was to Howard crude and overreaching. He instead advocated for a broad tolerance of different cultures and individuals; this extended to personal values such as the right to value the physical life over the mental, the boxer and football player over the artist or scientist: "With regard to things of 'real value' in life, I don't recognize the right or ability of any man to lay down arbitrary rules as what are and what are not of value; the best any man can do is define what things make life worth living for himself, while realizing that his indifference to or contempt for certain other things doesn't keep those things from being highly valued by other types of humans. The only intelligent attitude in this manner is one of broad tolerance" (650).

Lovecraft, ostensibly the more erudite of the two men, argued that only cultures steeped in western concepts of rationality and scientific progress were worth preserving. Lovecraft's qualitative standard by which he judges all cultures and individuals is how far they are removed from protozoa, or the "degree of biological advancement from amorphous protoplasm toward complex specialization" (557). Lovecraft believed his valuation to be a universal truth, an absolute standard of quality regardless of culture. He believed in a strong, centralized government whose role should include applying and enforcing these standards with an all-encompassing policy, in contrast to the local, regionalized government favored by Howard. Although he found warfare highly objectionable, Lovecraft also wrote that warfare in the advancement and development of civilization was a necessary evil, and in some cases, just. "The evils in question of course accompany all warfare, and warfare is sometimes waged in the defense of civilization—or in the extension of it" (886). Although colonization and subjugation of indigenous races were an "evil," they were in Lovecraft's view necessary steps in the progress of the human race. Lovecraft openly stratified various races and their cultures, placing third-world countries at a plane below that of Europeans and North Americans (924). He deemed such races as in need of conquering. "Many technically 'unjust' wars are waged against races so low or degraded or mutually murderous that the conquered people are actually benefited in the end by the change" (929).

In contrast Howard greatly admired native North American Indians and his approximately equivalent fictional race of Picts, and felt a kinship with the barbaric northern European races. He answered Lovecraft's belief in the civilized nations' right to "extend" itself with a savage rebuttal, denouncing Lovecraft's claims of "protecting and extending" civilization as doublespeak for looting, butchering, and plundering. "People claiming to possess superior civilization have always veneered their rapaciousness by such claims" (896). Howard had an easy target in Mussolini, the Italian dictator who garnered Lovecraft's sympathies yet by this time had invaded Ethiopia, kicking off the ill-fated Italo-Ethiopian war. "Your friend Mussolini is a striking example," Howard wrote. "In that speech of his I heard translated he spoke feelingly of the expansion of civilization. From time to time he has announced: 'The sword and civilization go hand in hand!' ... You say that 'the fruits of civilization must be preserved at all costs.' Just who is trying to loot these fruits? The Ethiopians?" (897) Howard pressed the attack, calling for abolition of any policy that would give a more powerful nation a free hand to subjugate a weaker. In a 1936 letter, Howard noted that such a policy could easily justify a war of first-world nations, with a civilized country declaring a neighbor less civilized, requiring violent "correction":

> But you may say, let us consider that the "civilized" countries and regions held by the civilized countries are sacred and inviolate, and give the plunderers a free hand with the uncivilized regions. All right. What regions are these? Who's to judge? The people who do the looting? These folks always consider their victims as uncivilized (919).

Howard's claim proved prescient when Germany invaded Poland three years later.

Howard also offered as evidence of civilization's ill civility the ruthless and destructive actions of private business. He took aim at the cattle and oil industries in his native Texas, and skewered a utilities company that attempted to build a hydroelectric dam on the Colorado River, impoverishing thousands of people of their rightful water supply. "Every corporation that has ever come into the Southwest bent solely on looting the region's people and resources has waved a banner of 'progress and civilization!'" (899). Lovecraft agreed that commercial greed was a lamentable byproduct of burgeoning civilized nations, and hoped that it would lessen as governments grew more socialistic (927).

In retrospect, Howard held up quite well in his debates against an (ostensibly) more educated Lovecraft. How Lovecraft's "evolutionary degree" can be the only metric humanity uses to measure value is not immediately clear, and seems to make allowance for ethnic cleansing and other retrograde beliefs; his insistence of a hierarchical order and "superior" races is today highly dated and distasteful to the modern reader. Howard largely emerges as the more tolerant and egalitarian of the two men.

Howard and Lovecraft shared a common skepticism of an afterlife, and a general acknowledgement for the horrors of material existence. But whereas Lovecraft used his writings to expose the realities of an indifferent mechanical universe—as symbolized by half-shadowed glimpses of the tentacled, terrible Old Ones who would one day reclaim the earth and lay waste to humanity when the stars were right—Howard's heroes raged against the dying of the light, drinking and feasting and reveling in the pleasures of the flesh while they still had the strength of their sword-arms. In the short term at least, Howard's heroes conquered the monsters. Howard acknowledged he lacked Lovecraft's "universal and cosmic scope" and instead placed his focus on the individual hero struggling to overcome an impersonal universe. "It is the individual mainly which draws me—the struggling, blundering, passionate insect vainly striving against the river of Life and seeking to divert the channel of events to suit himself—breaking his fangs on the iron collar of Fate and sinking into final defeat with the froth of a curse on his lips" (169).

Howard's barbaric heroes, though prone to violence and quick to draw swords, operated with a code of ethics, a sort of natural chivalry that Howard himself shared. Anything less was beneath contempt, behavior typical of sub-barbaric degenerates or hyper-civilized, amoral intellectuals. Howard described this natural chivalry as a trait common to historical frontiersmen. He recalled the epic story of endurance by James W. Parker, who, escaping with a group of women and children from Fort Parker after its pillaging by a group of Comanches, dragged his starved and bleeding body 35 miles through briar thickets to summon help: "Doubtless this seems inexplicable and a bit ridiculous to that school of moderns which sneer at 'chivalry' as artificial, and at self-sacrifice and heroism as mere romantic poses" (848). Lovecraft countered that chivalry did once serve a noble purpose, but its continuance in modern times was archaic, even dangerous "if the sacrifice entails harm to the whole community." He also stridently noted that "chivalry and barbarism don't agree!" (854), indirectly accusing Howard of perpetuating the myth of the "noble savage" (a charge which Howard vehemently denied, but one which doesn't hold up in a close examination of his fictional barbaric heroes).

Lovecraft could not grasp Howard's preference for barbarism over civilization. Time and again in their letters he expresses a disbelief, bordering on incredulity. "I can't see why the half-life of barbarism is preferable to the full, mentally active, and beauty-filled life typical of the Antonines in Rome or the 1890s and 1900s in pre-war England and France" (359). Howard was not blind to the advances offered by civilization, including modern medicine and greater access to goods and services. But he also recognized the equivocal nature of "progress," which brought with it great compromises in individual freedom. Unlike Lovecraft, he did not believe that humanity was headed on a clear path of upwards progression; in fact he believed that by the 1930s humanity's best days already lay in the past, in the rapidly fading and all but extinct frontier age. "I believe that our modern civilization has passed its peak already (except in the mechanical way) and is receding from, rather than advancing toward, a higher plane of life. I believe many modern trends are retrogressive rather than progressive" (828).

Howard acknowledged barbarism's weaknesses, including its absence of modern medicine, but noted that "civilized" modern medicine embraced repulsive scientific theories like eugenics, which was taking firm root in Nazi Germany in the early to mid-1930s and also had proponents in the United States. Howard did not whitewash the savage raping, butchering, and plundering done by barbaric tribes, but accused Lovecraft of hypocrisy for defending the same activities committed by technologically advanced first-world nations as unfortunate steps on the road to progress. Lovecraft wrote that "nothing which is lost in [civilization's] acquisition can possibly be compared with what is gained," (747), but Howard stridently disagreed, noting that the loss of moral certitude, and purpose, and freedom—in short, much of what we consider to be fundamental to humanity—was a steep price to be paid.

Both scored points in the debates, and because both largely presented personal preferences in their arguments, the issue of who "won" is somewhat of a moot point. Howard advocated for a high degree of personal freedom, Lovecraft for a subsuming of some degree of freedom in favor of an ordered society. Howard's views are largely incompatible with living in a settled modern country, even for the early 20th century. But his beliefs in cultural toleration are more in line with modern thinking than Lovecraft's quasi-fascist brand of politics.

Howard and the Frontier Myth

Howard was born in a region of Texas where the frontier age had only recently passed and whose heritage could still be felt. It was a land "that had suffered Indian raids less than 30 years before my birth, and range-wars less than ten; a region of whose population a large percent still consisted of the original settlers" (812). From his birth, Howard wrote, he had been "listening to first-hand narrations and descriptions of the pioneering era by the people who made that era." He frequently described himself as a man born out of his time, and again and again in his correspondence declares that he wished he could have lived in the early days of the Texas frontier: "I was born about a hundred years too late; that's not my fault; it's my misfortune" (542).

Howard believed that civilization bred graft and corruption, in time leading to a rigged game in which average men were bound to lives of servitude to wealthy businessmen. "A big shot can get away with anything while ordinary men are ruthlessly trodden into the mire," he wrote. Frontier life, on the other hand, did not allow slick-talking lawyers to spin gossamer lies into truth. The frontier not only permitted but encouraged rough vigilante justice, including honor killings and feuds settled not in the courtroom but on the open plains or in dusty main streets of clapboard towns, man-to-man and gun-to-gun. One of Howard's heroes was the notorious outlaw John Wesley Hardin (1853–1895), a gunfighter who spent most of his life on the run from the law for a murder committed when he was just 15 years old, allegedly in self-defense. Howard idolized Hardin's flagrant disregard for the judicial system and for the way in which he carried out his own personal brand of rough frontier justice. "All the vaunted power of civilization could not shake him. In him the individual was never subjected to the advantage of the mass" (451).

Howard believed that morality was integral to frontier living. Although not blind to its quick-to-ignite violence, and regrettable massacres of Native Americans, Howard believed that the main of the men who forged the frontier were inherently honorable, even altruistic.

"Beyond the Black River" depicts a group of Aquilonian settlers striving to carve out a living on the borders of the Pictish wilderness. In the story, the settler Balthus and his dog Slasher sacrifice their lives to hold off a band of invading Picts; Conan drinks to Balthus' shade, and toasts his sacrifice with as high a compliment as the Cimmerian would ever deliver: "He was a man." Men living in these harsh frontier environments required mutual cooperation to survive, and so developed a code of ethics to match. "Why didn't the Texans go to the extremes you say are natural results of war and colonization?" Howard asked Lovecraft in a letter. "They had a code and they lived up to it. They didn't abandon it with emotional hysteria when they found the going rough" (917).

Above all its virtues, Howard valued the freedom afforded by the frontier, and its absence of settled and stifling custom and restrictive laws. Open territory could be claimed by men possessed of sufficient strength and resolve to take it. "In the last analysis, I reckon, I have but a single conviction or ideal, or whateverthehell it might be called: individual liberty. It's the only thing that matters a damn. I'd rather be a naked savage, shivering, starving, freezing, hunted by wild beasts and enemies, but free to go and come, with the range of the earth to roam, than the fattest, richest, most bedecked slave in a golden palace with the crystal fountains, silken divans, and ivory-bosomed dancing girls of Haroun al Raschid" (501). The frontier afforded men the opportunity to live unchained from the encumbrances of loans and taxes, a point acutely important to Howard, frequently denied payment by the vagaries of publishers and the modern economy. "Freedom from the tyranny of money—that's the one thing I mean by the freedom of the old days. Freedom of new, fresh, fertile land," he wrote (709). Although Howard enjoyed a far greater degree of freedom as a writer than he did in his other menial jobs, he felt acutely the greater opportunities afforded his frontier ancestors, who were not subject to serfdom by the "soulless machine" of the mechanized, capitalist age. "And just as I have struggled for a maximum amount of freedom in my own life, I look back with envy at the greater freedom known by my ancestors on the frontier. Hard work? Certainly they worked hard. But they were building something; making the most of opportunities; working for themselves, not merely cogs grinding in a soulless machine, as is the modern working man, whose life is a constant round of barren toil infinitely more monotonous and crushing than the toil on the frontier" (698).

Howard believed modern civilization limited his opportunities and was unfit for a man of his interests and temperament. He looked wistfully upon the vanished frontier as a time when life was visceral and palpable and worth living. If he did love the frontier, he loved it for all its struggles and bitter toil. His wish to live in the frontier age stemmed from a reasonably informed personal choice, not one based on sensationalized western novels or rosy daydreaming. "There's nothing really scandalous or romantic or incredible about a westerner expressing the wish that he had lived when land was cheap and cattle plenty and the range was open and men bulked bigger than the dollar" (813). The charge of romanticism seemed to be a particularly sore spot to Howard, who later in the debate wrote, "There is no reason under God's sun why I should have a romantic or idealized conception of the frontier" (940). Yet much of what Howard wrote in his fiction and in his letters revealed otherwise. For example, in waxing poetically to Lovecraft of a road trip he and good friend Truett Vinson took to the wild and isolated frontier village of Lincoln, home to the infamous and bloody Lincoln County War, Howard described his arrival as stepping into an elder age where old ghosts stalked its dusty, haunted streets, and of catching a glimpse of the once limitless frontier in the open desert plains west of the Pecos River: "The world seems suddenly to expand—the horizons roll back illimitably. What has been a dreary and monotonous waste suddenly takes on the somber grandeur and magnificence of a primal desert. Man seems small and insignificant, his works mere scratches ignored by the slumbering titan and soon to be forgotten—and yet there a man is conscious of an individuality, a dignity, and a vitalness not be realized or recognized in any city or swarming bee-hive of humanity" (814). Howard projected his own internal dissatisfactions with modern life onto 20th century humanity, claiming that, "People enjoyed their simple pleasures a damn sight more than any modern enjoys anything he does. Even now many of the survivors of that epoch, at greatly advanced ages, show much more zest for living, enthusiasm and ability to enjoy life than any of their descendants, or their descendants' contemporaries." Howard also erroneously claimed that in the days of the frontier "there were no neuroses or psychological phobias. People were healthy and hearty and wholesome" (941). These are surely broad-strokes of romantic feeling, unsupported by scientific data. But Howard also admitted that his preference for frontier life was merely that, a personal preference, and not an indication of its inherent superiority. "I do not, and have never advocated, the perpetuation of the frontier as a permanent condition, nor have I advocated the solving of modern problems after the fashion of the frontier. I have merely said that I wished I had lived in those times instead of now, and pointed out certain things that modern temperaments would consider advantages that life has over the modern, mechanized life" (707).

Howard took his preference for the frontier life and its freedoms, and his knowledge of its history and stories, and spun it into a new myth of the frontier. The Hyborian Age is Howard's impossibly ancient re-creation of the western, when the entire world was still a frontier to be explored, great plains and vistas of wild lands to be traveled and settled, forgotten cities and their riches waiting to be discovered and plundered, and decadent cities and civilizations ripe for treading under the sandaled feet of the barbaric races.

Howard's brand of barbarism is ahistorical and romantic. His sword-and-sorcery incorporated real elements of the United States frontier era of the 1800s and blended it with history and pseudo history to create a barbaric ideal, creating in Conan a figure of muscle and steel, fierce and free, unencumbered by the mechanistic punch-clock of the 9-5 job and artifice required of urban living. It was Howard's attempt to restore manhood to men who lost their way. This underpinning imbues his sword-and-sorcery stories with an earnest, human connection. "There seems to be both a happiness and a sadness in the character of Conan ... as Howard himself seems to acknowledge over the course of years of letters both the benefits of civilization at the same time lamenting the loss of frontier, hard work, and being alive through physical activity" (Emmelhainz,

"Strange Collaborations" 60). This partially explains why Howard's Conan stories were never duplicated or even successfully imitated by subsequent generations of pastichers. Slightly romanticized though this frontier history was, it was emotionally true to Howard.

Rage Against the Machine

While the 1920s and 1930s may seem quaint, even archaic to 21st century eyes, to Howard and Lovecraft these decades were a shock to the senses. Both men were born in a largely pre-industrial era in which material goods were still largely hand-produced, and in Howard's case food and fuel were grown and produced on small farms. Twenty years later widespread industrial mechanization— the assembly-line production of automobiles, clothing, food, and household devices like refrigerators and dishwashers—had transformed the nation. Mass production removed individual craftsmanship from the equation, transforming men and their labor into dispensable parts of a machine.

Though largely opposed to the machine age, Lovecraft expressed a degree of ambivalence about its arrival. Like many prominent thinkers he believed that mechanization and large-scale industry was impossible to check in the face of overwhelming economic and political pressures, and viewed it as an unfortunate but inevitable by-product of progress. "It is a pity that we cannot manage machinery instead of having it manage us," he wrote. "If we were more truly civilized—with a keener sense of values—we would undoubtedly try to restrict its use to the supplying of genuine needs" (*A Means to Freedom* 686). Lovecraft expressed a degree of optimism that mechanization would free up time for worthy artistic pursuits. "The one redeeming point in the new order is its increased leisure—and the big fight will be for the right to spend that leisure as one pleases" (211).

Howard, a champion of hard labor and an admirer of the physical, had no such hopes. He disliked both machines and machine-work, and thought the fate of the men who worked on machinery was to become machines themselves: "Standardization is crushing the heart and soul, the blood and the guts, out of humanity and the eventual result will be either complete and unrelieved slavery or the destruction of civilization and return to barbarism. Once men sang the praises of ephemeral gods carved out of ivory and wood. Now they sing equally senseless praises to equally ephemeral and vain gods of Science and Commerce and Progress. Hell" (225).

Unlike the slightly more optimistic Lovecraft, Howard saw the dawning machine as a portent of doom for humanity. "In a system where men are protected by hired forces, and waited on by machines, how can any real self-confidence and self-reliance be induced, or long-sustained?" (595) This is the foundation of Howard's philosophy, and by extension, one of sword-and-sorcery's central themes. The modern age, in which big government and social conformity rounds the sharp edges off life, has no room for martial heroes. An age in which physical labor and hardships are supplanted by machines is an age in which Howard saw no point in living. Because frontier life allowed men to live like men, "by the sweat of his hands unharried by taxes, crowds, noise, unemployment, bank-failures, gang-extortions, laws, and all the other wearisome things of civilization" (595), it would always be superior in Howard's eyes to modernity. Although an outsider, Howard believed he was not alone in this thinking, but part of a burgeoning zeitgeist of hot-blooded young men dissatisfied with the progress of the modern age and mechanized living (596).

Howard would not live to see the full horrors of science unleashed—fire-bombed cities like Dresden laid to waste, and the ultimate atomic hell of Nagasaki and Hiroshima—but was acutely aware of the dehumanizing effect of the technological advances in weaponry. A fan of the works of war poet Siegfried Sassoon, Howard referenced in his letters the inhumanities inflicted by mustard gas and the machine gun on the battlefields of World War I. His predictions of mass aerial bombings and impersonal, distant killing proved prescient: "Though I'm far from war-like, yet I've always felt that with the proper training, I could learn to be fairly annoying to the enemy with a bayonet or a rifle butt, but this new-fangled chemical warfare would make me a total loss. What's the glory in pushing a button and slaughtering men fifty miles away, or flying over a city and spraying the combatants with liquid hell? When they traded the warhorse for a submarine, they ruined the blasted business as far as I'm concerned" (252). Sword-and-sorcery, in contrast, restored man-to-man and sword-to-sword conflicts, up close and personal.

Unsatisfied with his world, dreaming of not-so-distant frontier times when rough but honorable men could and did make a difference, and fueled with outrages and pent up frustrations endemic to 20th century life, Howard turned to tales of sword-and-sorcery, churning them out in a white heat of creativity. He pioneered the figure of the barbarian hero—an outsider as the protagonist—and imbued his stories with powerful themes of the inevitable corruption and fall of civilization, the opportunity of the frontier, and the triumph of barbarism. Sword-and-sorcery emerged, powerful and vital and wholly formed, in no small part from his exchange of letters with Lovecraft.

JACK LONDON AND *THE STAR-ROVER*:
A SINGULAR INFLUENCE

Robert E. Howard once referred to Jack London as "this Texan's favorite writer," and boasted that London "stands head and shoulders above all other American writers" (*A Means to Freedom* 550). A spinner of rugged wilderness adventure fiction, London did not write sword-and-sorcery, but the thematic material of *The Call of the Wild, The Sea-Wolf,* and *The Star-Rover* are evident in Howard's stories.

Howard was particularly attracted to London's depiction of life as survival of the fittest. In *The Call of the Wild* (1903), the protagonist—a great St. Bernard/Scotch shepherd crossbreed named Buck—learns a series of brutal lessons as he transitions from domestic life to sled dog. City living breeds softness, and the wilderness—if it doesn't kill—toughens the mind, hardens the body, and restores both man and beast to their natural, primal state. Buck appears to have had at least some influence on Howard's most famous creation. Although Conan is a barbarian born, and Buck is introduced at the outset of the story as a domesticated and city-bred animal, his civilized veneer is purely illusory. Within his powerful breast dwells "the dominant primordial beast," dormant until brought out by the stark, unforgiving Yukon country:

> All that stirring of old instincts which at stated periods drives men out from the sounding cities to forest and plain to kill things by chemically propelled leaden pellets, the blood lust, the joy to kill—all this was Buck's, only it was infinitely more intimate. He was ranging at the head of the pack, running the wild thing down, the living meat, to kill with his own teeth and wash his muzzle to the eyes in warm blood.

London's disdain of soft, city-bred effetes is apparent in his depiction of Hal, Charles, and Mercedes, a pathetic trio wildly ill-prepared and out of their depth in the unforgiving Yukon. After killing most of their dog-team through incompetence and ignorance, the three are swallowed up in literal fashion by the wilderness, a fate common to the pampered city-dwelling nobles of Howard's Hyborian Age of Conan.

Fritz Leiber described *The Star-Rover* (1915) as sword-and-sorcery, save that "only the sorcery is lacking. ... There is the same preoccupation with feats of physical prowess, with the strong man of fixed purpose whom nothing daunts, with a savagely Darwinian view of life (battle for survival, Nature bloody in tooth and claw, civilization a false fleeting dream in the reality of barbarism" (Leiber, "Howard's Style" 31). Howard was particularly enamored with the story, noting in a letter that "I've read and read [it] for years, and that generally goes to my head like wine." Compare this passage from *The Star-Rover*:

> I speak with authority—I say that matter is the only illusion. ... It is life that is the reality and the mystery. Life is vastly different from mere chemic matter fluxing in high modes of notion. Life persists. Life is the thread of fire that persists through all the modes of matter. I know. I am life. ... I am the unquenched spark ever flashing and astonishing the face of time, ever working my will and wreaking my passion on the cloddy aggregates of matter, called bodies, which I have transiently inhabited.

With this, from Howard's "Queen of the Black Coast" (1934):

> I have known many gods. He who denies them is as blind as he who trusts them too deeply. I seek not beyond death. It may be the blackness averred by the Nemedian skeptics, or Crom's realm of ice and cloud, or the snowy plains and vaulted halls of the Nordheimer's Valhalla. I know not, nor do I care. Let me live deep while I live; let me know the rich juices of red meat and stinging wine on my palate, the hot embrace of white arms, the mad exultation of battle when the blue blades flame and crimson, and I am content. Let teachers and priests and philosophers brood over questions of reality and illusion. I know this: if life is illusion, then I am no less an illusion, and being thus, the illusion is real to me. I live, I burn with life, I love, I slay, and am content.

The Star-Rover tells the story of Darrell Standing, a University of California professor serving a life sentence in prison for killing a colleague "in a surge of anger, obsessed by that catastrophic red wrath that has cursed me down the ages." Standing is powerless to quell his primitive urges, "for the red wrath is my disastrous catastrophic heritage from the time of the slimy things ere the world was prime." He complains of an "iron collar" about his neck, a metaphor for the galling restrictions of modern life. Howard would use the same imagery in a letter to H.P. Lovecraft: "It is the individual mainly which draws me—the struggling, blundering, passionate insect vainly striving against the river of Life and seeking to divert the channel of events to suit himself—breaking his fangs on the iron collar of Fate and sinking into final defeat with the froth of a curse on his lips" (*A Means to Freedom* 169).

This passage from *The Star-Rover* may as well be Conan's love song to Bêlit on the deck of her pirate ship, so closely does it resemble the Cimmerian's philosophy and idiom:

> We are man and woman, you and I. Our life is of this world. Of these other worlds is all a madness. Let these mad dreamers go the way of their dreaming. Deny them not what they desire above all things, above meat and wine, above song and battle, even above

> love of woman. Deny them not their hearts' desires that draw
> them across the dark of the grave to their dreams of lives beyond
> this world. Let them pass. But you and I abide here in all the sweet
> we have discovered of each other. Quickly enough will come the
> dark, and you depart for your coasts of sun and flowers, and I for
> the roaring table of Valhalla.

Standing "escapes" his cell through a self-induced trance.
Though his body is strait-jacketed, his mind roams the stars. At
one point he inherits the body of a Viking:

> My first memories are of Tostig Lodbrog's beaked ships and fighting
> men, and of the feast hall at Brunanbuhr when our boats lay beached
> beside the frozen fjord. For I was made drink-boy, and amongst
> my earliest recollections are toddling with the wine-filled skull of
> Guthlaf to the head of the table where Tostig bellowed to the rafters.

Central to the Star-Rover are reincarnation and the transmission
of ancestral memory. The book opens with the line, "All my life I
have had an awareness of other times and places. I have been aware
of other persons in me—Oh, and trust me, so have you, my reader
that is to be." Standing asserts that every person has been reincar-
nated thousands of times over thousands of years of history, and
the past lives in us all. "Truly do we carry in us, each human of us
alive on the planet to-day, the incorruptible history of life from life's
beginning. This history is written in our tissues and our bones, in
our functions and our organs, in our brain cells and in our spirits,
and in all sorts of physical and psychic atavistic urgencies and
compulsions." In an introduction to the anthology *Tigers of the Sea*,
editor Richard L. Tierney claims that Howard employed the idea of
reincarnation in his stories without taking much stock in it himself,
"and probably used it for its poetic effect only" (10). But Howard's
letters reveal otherwise. In a 1931 letter to H.P. Lovecraft, Howard
stated that his preference for Danes over Saxons was due to a latent
racial memory inherited through the blood. "My sense of placement,
as I've mentioned, is always with the barbarians outside the walls.
In my dreams of old times, I am always a light eyed, yellow haired
barbarian, resembling myself but little" (*A Means to Freedom* 170).
Howard explored the theme of reincarnation throughout his fiction.
His poem "Cimmeria" reflects on an age of axes and flint-tipped
spears, a heritage which leaves its protagonist wrapped "in the grey
apparel of ghosts." James Allison is a crippled Texan who remembers
his adventurous past life as an Aryan tribesman in "The Valley of the
Worm," "The Garden of Fear," and "Marchers of Valhalla." And in his
weird horror tale "The Children of the Night" the narrator, struck
on the head and knocked unconscious, awakens to find himself a
member of the Aryan tribe that conquered Britain from the Picts.

CHAPTER FOUR

Weird Tales:
Howard's Sword-and-Sorcery
Contemporaries

Some of the stories now being published in Weird Tales will live forever. Men in the progressive ages to come will wonder how it was possible that writers of the crude and uncivilized age known as the Twentieth Century could have had foreknowledge of the things that will have, by that time, come to pass. They will marvel, as they marvel even now at the writings of Poe and Verne.

—Otis Adelbert Kline, "Why Weird Tales"

Robert E. Howard's weird brew of barbaric, sword-swinging men of action pitted against sorcerous foes and sanity-blasting monsters created an intoxicating literary template. *Weird Tales* subscribers devoured his stories with relish, and Howard's peers had a compelling new subgenre in which they could tell their own tales. Some were contemporaries who were already writing proto- sword-and-sorcery and other related weird fiction concurrent to Howard. Others were inspired to pick up a pen and try their hand at Conan and Kull-inspired stories.

Unlike some of Howard's more slavishly devoted successors, C.L. Moore and Clark Ashton Smith were innovators who employed unique writing styles and thematic concerns to stories that are unquestionably sword-and-sorcery. Both were working concurrent to Howard, and his influence on them is less overt than on his later imitators and pastichers. A case can be made that sword-and-sorcery was evolving organically, and had Howard not been first to the starting line, either Smith or Moore may have laid claim as the subgenre's originator—Smith with "The Tale of Satampra Zeiros" (*Weird Tales*, November 1931; written in late 1929) or Moore with her first and most famous sword-and-sorcery tale, "Black God's Kiss" (*Weird Tales*, October 1934).

While the 1929 publication of "The Shadow Kingdom" marks the origin of sword-and-sorcery, Smith and Moore's efforts indicate that other influences and external factors must be considered in the subgenre's genesis. The most logical explanation is the medium in which all three were working. Even as it later migrated to standard magazines and paperbacks, sword-and-sorcery retained a style and a form traceable to pulp magazines, and principally *Weird Tales*. *Weird Tales* broadly published two types of stories: traditional horror (further specified as "psychic phenomena" or the "occult story") and weird fiction, or "highly imaginative stories" (Kline 569). These two types of tales were far from exclusive. Many bled over into each other, blending elements of horror and fantasy.

Weird Tales was a cauldron of creativity. It served as an accommodating, liberal sandbox for its authors, allowing them not only creative freedom to mix and match various influences, but also provided a forum in which they could comment on each other's articles, and even borrow elements of one another's fictions and fictional mythologies. The editorship of Farnsworth Wright and Edwin Baird and the letters column "The Eyrie" offered stewardship, encouragement, and pruning for the magazine's contributors. Although the "Roaring Twenties" is associated with Prohibition-defying bootleggers and fashion-defying flappers, publishers of the era were relatively conservative.[1] Occult horror and sword-swinging fantasy were not considered respectable material for the newsstands. "Up to the day the first issue of *Weird Tales* was placed on the stands, stories of the sort you read between these covers each month were taboo in the publishing world" (Kline 568). Wright's and Baird's willingness to publish a wide range of weird fiction gave artists the medium and the leeway to engage in genre-bending experimentation, unbound from the strictures of the typical detective, western, sport, and adventure fiction genres that served as the fodder for most pulp magazines of the era. *Weird Tales* not only took a chance on this "taboo fiction," it nurtured and grew it. It also shaped and informed its writers' craft by exposing them to a broader circle of creative minds, a creative community that fed off itself and drove one another to new heights of imagination.

Today, scholars recognize the impact of *Weird Tales* as greater than any single artist's contributions. The magazine is now recognized as a cultural touchstone and nexus of creative expression that helped foster new subgenres. "In considering the broader impact of a cultural phenomenon such as *Weird Tales*, it is clear that the community, editorial process, and medium of the pulp magazine interacted in a unique way, contributing to an explosion in new American literary forms, such as the hard-boiled detective yarn, sword-and-sorcery, the Cthulhu mythos, and so forth" (Shovlin

---

[1] James Joyce's *Ulysses*, for example, was (in)famously banned in 1921, after charges of obscenity were brought by the New York Society for the Suppression of Vice.

202). *Weird Tales* was not a uniformly positive force in the development of sword-and-sorcery. The magazine fostered a few of its less-praiseworthy stereotypes, including cover art depicting nubile, scantily-dressed women in need of rescue. Often these women are depicted as helplessly bound and in the process of receiving a stinging lashing from a whip-wielding woman, the inclusion of which in a story was more likely to get its author accepted in the magazine and splashed on the cover in a Margaret Brundage illustration (Helland 189). But *Weird Tales* was the fecund platform that allowed sword-and-sorcery to take root.

At the nexus of this community was Providence, Rhode Island, native H.P. Lovecraft (1890–1937). Early in his career, Lovecraft was published in a wide range of amateur journals, but starting in 1923 he began making regular appearances in *Weird Tales*. He quickly became a fan favorite. Lovecraft's bleak cosmic horror with its materialist/atheist thematic underpinnings represented a sharp break from the Victorian writers of the generation prior. Lovecraft introduced *Weird Tales* readers to a universe in which "the black planets roll without aim; where they roll in their horror unheeded, without knowledge or lustre or name" (Lovecraft, "Nemesis"). While today he is popularly known for Cthulhu ephemera—tentacled monsters, weird interstellar fungi, blasted books of ancient lore—Lovecraft's particular genius lay in the dark, unsettling mood he created in his works, an unsettling dread rooted in the utter meaninglessness and fragility of human existence. Lovecraft was intensely critical of common "commercial pulp" which forsook its ties to humanity in favor of flashy commercial elements, "glibly piling on extravagant marvels without the least relation to mankind's natural myth-making tendencies" (*H.P. Lovecraft: Letters to C.L. Moore and Others* 267). "Seriously artistic" weird stories don't describe monsters or ghosts as their principal function," Lovecraft wrote, but "present a powerful & subjectively realizable picture of man's deeply ingrained emotions—largely a fascinated fear—concerning the unknown, or of man's persistent illusions of a circumambient world of unreality … the first law of weird fiction is that *the emotional atmosphere must overshadow the weird events*" (*H.P. Lovecraft: Letters to C.L. Moore and Others* 350). He recognized in Howard's fiction deeper and more substantive connections to the primal and primitive in man, traits which raised them above other common *Weird Tales* fare.

In addition to writing fiction, Lovecraft was an indefatigable author of letters. One estimate places the number of letters Lovecraft wrote over his lifetime at 100,000 (Loucks). Lovecraft's correspondents included all the major founders of sword-and-sorcery. This group—whose ranks included Howard, Smith, Moore, and

Leiber, as well as non-sword-and-sorcery authors including August
Derleth, Frank Belknap Long, and Robert Bloch—later came to be
known as "the Lovecraft circle." The group was not a cult following
of Lovecraft sycophants and imitators, but created something new,
inspired by Lovecraft's singular influence. "In their letters and in
the pages of the magazine they wrote for, these writers consciously
developed their own separate literary tradition." This included a
deliberate departure from mainstream literature and the production
of displacement and sublime thrills in their readers (Nyikos 29-30).

More so than his published stories, in which his influence is
extant but tenuous, Lovecraft's exerted an enormous influence on
sword-and-sorcery behind the scenes. In personal correspondence
Lovecraft challenged its writers to develop their thought and art, all
while providing sanguine encouragement as a fellow enthusiast of
the weird. In addition to his lengthy correspondence with Howard
as described in Chapter Three, Lovecraft was an enormous influence
on the likes of Leiber, Smith, and Kuttner, and to a lesser but not
insubstantial degree C.L. Moore. Upon his discovery of Lovecraft's
"The Colour out of Space," "The Shadow out of Time," and "At the
Mountains of Madness" in *Amazing Stories* and *Astounding Stories*, a
young Leiber experienced "a wonder, mystery, and delightful terror
I found in no other writing" (Leiber, "My Correspondence with
Lovecraft" 374). Leiber credited his later lamentably short correspondence with Lovecraft for developing his own first attempts at
published fiction, providing as they did encouragement to the then
young, unpublished author. "I came to think of myself as at least
potentially a professional author," wrote Leiber ("My Correspondence
with Lovecraft" 376). As for Smith, Will Murray (editor of Smith's
The Book of Hyperborea) claims that "if Clark Ashton Smith had not
come into contact with Howard Phillips Lovecraft and fallen under
his mesmeric literary influence, he would probably not have written
his legendary *Weird Tales* stories. And he certainly would never have
written the Hyperborean tales that comprise this volume." Moore
meanwhile confessed to Derleth that she collected nearly 200 pages
of letters from Lovecraft. Lovecraft considered Moore in the upper
tier of *Weird Tales* contributors along with Smith and Howard, and
described her fiction as possessing the qualities of "outsideness &
cosmic dread" which he so prized in weird fiction (*H.P. Lovecraft:
Letters to C.L. Moore and Others* 10–11).

Starting in 1929 and over the next seven years, stories like
Howard's "The Tower of the Elephant" and "People of the Black
Circle," Smith's "The Tale of Satampra Zeiros" and "The Empire of
the Necromancers," and Moore's "Black God's Kiss" and "Jirel Meets
Magic" laid the foundations of sword-and-sorcery. But in June 1936

the burgeoning subgenre suffered a near death-blow. Howard was waiting on several checks from *Weird Tales,* which had run into financial troubles. When late payments did wend their long way to Cross Plains, Howard had to pay them back out to cover mounting medical bills. His mother, Hester, was in the end stages of a long battle with tuberculosis, and her dutiful son waited on her day and night, changing her soaked bedclothes and administering what little comfort there was for the then-incurable disease in rural Texas. Howard was strung out from a loss of sleep, and the ceaseless demands placed on him for his mother's constant care meant he could not find time to write. This meant much more than a loss of income—cutting off Howard from writing was akin to severing his lifeline, the one place in his confined, constricted world that he could find solace. Sword-and-sorcery allowed for worlds that made sense in which the rich struggle was worth it; real life afforded no such consolations. On the evening of June 10, 1936, Howard kept an all-night vigil at his mother's bedside. When told she would never regain consciousness, he went outside, sat in his car, and shot himself in the head with a pistol.

Howard's death rocked the *Weird Tales* community. Letters to *The Eyrie* poured in from all corners. H.P. Lovecraft summed up Howard's accomplishments best in a tribute published in the September 1936 issue of *Fantasy Magazine*:

> The character and attainments of Mr. Howard were wholly unique. He was, above everything else, a lover of the simpler, older world of barbarian and pioneer days, when courage and strength took the place of subtlety and stratagem, and when a hardy, fearless race battled and bled and asked no quarter from hostile Nature.

Howard's stories reinvigorated fantasy with a blood-and-thunder gallop, bright splashes of color and setting, and unsettling philosophical underpinnings. With Kull and Conan he had created something entirely new. Said later sword-and-sorcery author Michael Moorcock, "He brought a brash, tough element to the epic fantasy which did much to change the course of the American school away from precious writing and static imagery, just as Hammett, Chandler, and the *Black Mask* pulp writers were to change the course of American detective fiction" (*Wizardry & Wild Romance* 57). The Kull and Conan stories were indeed something entirely new and original, although it would take decades before a critical apparatus would catch up to Howard's powerful, visceral fantasy aesthetic. But his death created a heroic fiction void that begged to be filled, a barbaric template too powerful and intoxicating to be left to history.

Readers did not have to wait long. The May 1937 issue of *Weird Tales* featured "Duar the Accursed" by Clifford Ball, a Howard/Conan inspired tale that won a write-in poll by readers for best story in the issue ("The Eyrie" 128). The July 1937 *Weird Tales* featured more Ball with "The Thief of Forthe" in the principal position, leading off the issue and commanding the cover with a painting by Virgil Finlay. Ball's story of the thief Rald "who coveted a kingdom, and the appalling secret of an old magician," is workmanlike, and did not make many readers forget Howard. Ball wrote one more story of Rald with "The Goddess Awakes" (*Weird Tales*, February 1938) before disappearing from the sword-and-sorcery scene.

Sword-and-sorcery eventually managed to spread beyond the pages of *Weird Tales*. In 1939, the short-lived pulp magazine *Unknown* published a short novel by Norvell Page called *Flame Winds*, featuring the Scythian gladiator Wan Tengri, aka., Hurricane John/Prester John. Page followed *Flame Winds* with another Hurricane John short novel, *Sons of the Bear God*, also published in *Unknown*.[2] While containing some novel points, Page's story is an unremarkable Conan pastiche.[3]

Other writers began to work in sword-and-sorcery with greater faculty and conviction. Starting in 1938 with the aptly titled "Thunder in the Dawn," Henry Kuttner's sharply drawn and invigorating stories of Elak of Atlantis were a welcome shot of adrenaline to readers who only two years prior had read the breathless last installment of Howard's grim Conan story, "Red Nails." Though Howard-inspired and in places perhaps too imitative, Kuttner's tales contain improvisational touches on the familiar barbarian-king stories of Conan and Kull. Kuttner's work resulted in the cementing of a sword-and-sorcery template that endured for decades—and whose powerful echoes can still be felt today.

Clark Ashton Smith

Cosmic horror, fantasy, science fiction, and weird fiction have all been used to describe the works of Clark Ashton Smith (1893–1961). Today, Smith is regarded as one of *Weird Tales*' "holy trinity" along with Lovecraft and Howard. Of these three, Smith was the superior stylist, writing with a lush, decadent prose few authors in or outside of fantasy can match. His short stories, penned largely in a flurry of creativity from 1930–1935,[4] defy easy description or genre labels. Fantasy critic Ryan Harvey calls Smith "a one man

---

[2] The August 1939 issue of *Unknown* also published a story by Fritz Leiber, "Two Sought Adventure." This noteworthy event is covered in chapter five.

[3] In later years, at the height of the sword-and-sorcery boom, these works would be republished by Berkeley, with the cover blurb "Heroic Fantasy in the great Conan tradition."

[4] Smith holds the distinction of most appearances in *Weird Tales* during this period, beating out even prolific fan favorites Seabury Quinn, August Derleth, and Howard (Connors and Hilger xi).

literary movement, an alpha and omega unto himself … who seems to have borrowed his style from almost no one" (Harvey). Smith's style is simultaneously baroque and lyrical. Studded with a far-flung vocabulary and suffused with poetic meter and sensibility, some have likened it to "prose-poetry, or even incantation" (Dirda vii). Describing Smith to a young C.L. Moore, Lovecraft extolled, "But for sustained magic & subtle colour it is hard to touch Klarkash-Ton, High-Priest of nighted Tsathoggua. Poet—artist—fantaisiste— nobody else has yet produced such an exhaustless & exuberant stream of rich, maturely polished fantasy of every sort" (*H.P. Lovecraft: Letters to C.L. Moore and Others* 33).

Smith regarded himself first and foremost as a poet, and was once acclaimed as one of America's foremost living poets (de Camp, *Literary Swordsmen and Sorcerers* 195). His influences include the 19th century French poet Charles Pierre Baudelaire, the novelist Gustave Flaubert (in particular his *Salammbo* and *The Temptation of Saint Anthony* ("Clark Ashton Smith"), and the artists of the 19th century Decadent movement. Smith's wide-ranging literary influences, and the bohemian lifestyle he inculcated while living in an isolated cabin in northern California, converged to create a writing style and an esthetic far different from the prevailing muscular style common to most sword-and-sorcery.

Smith holds an important albeit tenuous connection to the sub-genre. Most of his work falls into the category of weird horror or Gothic fantasy, ghoulish and unsetting tales of dark realms alien to our own. His best works displace the reader with a jarring, out-of-body experience—an effect for which he was precisely aiming. Smith considered "mind-flight" the principal calling of weird fiction and poetry, fomenting rebellion against "mechanized imaginations" and uniformity of thought" (Connors, "Pegasus Unbridled" 156). Literary critics often dismiss fantastic fiction as lightweight and escapist, but Smith embraced that charge. He saw escape as a means to broaden the mind, extending the experience of readers otherwise hemmed in by the circumstances of their experiential, cultural, and temporal circumstances. In a letter to Lovecraft, Smith stated that there is "no justification for literature unless it serves to release the imagination from the bounds of every-day life" (156). Smith's stories often offer no explanation or apparent meaning other than displacement and weirdness. Some are loosely allegorical, but most simply *are*, opening windows to worlds and civilizations and experiences utterly alien to our own. Readers return from stories like "The City of Singing Flame" unsettled but also enriched; eyes that have looked upon Smith's alien landscapes and terrible fates are not blasted, but opened.

Included in Smith's far-flung, wide-ranging corpus is a small but importance slice of sword-and-sorcery. Sword-and-sorcery historian Morgan Holmes describes Smith as the second most important author of sword-and-sorcery ever to appear in *Weird Tales*—a considerable claim, given that of Smith's more than 100 published tales, most fall squarely into the camp of weird horror. But with just a few sword-and-sorcery tales Smith carved out an enormously important legacy in the subgenre, in influence lagging only Howard, Fritz Leiber, and Michael Moorcock.

Smith set many of his stories in worlds on the brink of extinction. He introduced readers to mythic Atlantis prior to its sinking (his "Poseidonis" cycle) and the earth in a far-flung future in which the weakening sun is on the verge of burning out and plunging the earth into eternal blackness (his "Zothique" stories). Smith's stories did not feature recurring characters; no Conan, Kane, or Elric lived to fight another day in his lands of Hyperborea (with a few exceptions, including the one-handed thief Satampra Zeiros who appeared in two stories). Smith's protagonists at best meet with muted success, and often suffer failure or death (see sidebar). Heroism is of little to no avail against universal forces of destruction and the inevitable decay wrought by the passage of time. "Howard used sword-and-sorcery as a means for telling adventure tales, while Smith created stories of irony, nostalgia, and doom within a fantasy context" (Holmes, "Gothic to Cosmic" 71).

Howard was a fan of Smith's style and expressed an intense admiration for Smith's poetry collection *Ebony and Crystal*. In a signed copy of the volume sent to Howard, Smith referred to Howard as like a brother (Eng 19-20). But their co-influence is otherwise non-existent. Smith quickly tired of Howard's brand of sword-and-sorcery, even as he realized it was more commercially viable than his own grim, downbeat fantasies. In a September 1931 letter to Lovecraft, he wrote, "Robert E. Howard's omnipresent gore-spattering is surely getting monotonous, but I fear it will prove a hard fault to eradicate" (*H.P. Lovecraft: Letters to C.L. Moore and Others* 32). Smith's grim tales stemmed in part from his own "jaundiced view of human nature" (Reiter 176). A few representative examples of Smith's cynicism include "Empire of the Necromancers" and "Isle of the Torturers." In the former, a pair of dark necromancers, driven out of their homeland for recklessly practicing their black art, carve themselves out a new empire by reanimating corpses—a darkly comic critique of the fitness of kings, and the state of mind of their repressed subjects. Says one of the sorcerers, "None living shall dispute us here; and those that we have summoned from the tomb shall move and breathe only at our dictation, and may not rebel against us." In "Isle of the Torturers," a young king flees a plague-ridden city only to find himself in worse straits, shipwrecked on the shores of an island inhabited by cruel beings whose chief pleasure is inflicting creative tortures upon unlucky outsiders. The hideous manner in which the isle's populace has "evolved" leaves them fit only for extinction, fully deserving of the coming contagion.

Smith's brand of sword-and-sorcery belongs to a protean period before the genre had taken its classic Howardian shape. It offers an alternative template, based not on the triumphs of muscular warriors but figures struggling vainly in lands of strange and often terrifying otherworldliness, and provides a glimpse into how the genre might have developed in the ensuing decades had it hewed closer to the moody horror and bleak philosophy of Poe and Lovecraft. In Smith's "The Dark Eidolon" (*Weird Tales*, January 1935), the mighty sorcerer Namirrha exacts revenge on Zotulla, King of Zylac, who maimed Namirrha when the latter was a powerless street urchin. Years later Namirrha returns to the city as a dread necromancer with an understandable thirst for vengeance, but not as a hero worthy of our sympathy. Zotulla is so utterly unlikeable (he tortures a woman in horrible fashion and wantonly destroys innocent inhabitants of the city) that the story plays out as a gorgeously choreographed car wreck.

Smiths' anti-heroic stance reached its zenith in "The Seven Geases" (*Weird Tales*, October 1934). Lord Ralibar Vooz, high magistrate of Commoriom and a mighty-thewed warrior, embarks on a hunting expedition to the Eiglophian Mountains with a score of retainers. The object of his hunt are the cave-dwelling Voormis, a dwindling, half bestial race rumored to be the offspring of men and primal beasts. In another writer's hands, "The Seven Geases" might have resembled a fantastic safari expedition with a desperate struggle between Vooz's men and a monstrous race of humanoids, ending with gold and riches plundered. But not in Smith's. Vooz falls under the powerful geas of the sorcerer Ezdagor in a chance and unfortunate encounter. Helplessly cursed, Vooz endures a series of encounters with increasingly dangerous and subhuman demigods of the underworld. Each in turn lays a powerful geas of their own upon the hapless warrior. Vooz never gets to swing his sword and eventually meets a grim and decidedly un-heroic end, alone and unsung, far beneath the earth.

"The Colossus of Ylourgne" (*Weird Tales*, June 1934) can be classified as sword-and-sorcery, pitting a hero against a demonic giant made of the flesh and bones of animated corpses. Weapons are useless against the monster, so Gaspard du Nord crafts a powerful spell to stop the monster on its destructive path of vengeance: "The formula, which called for the cooperation of Alastor and other evil spirits, he used with unwillingness. But he knew that there was no alternative: sorcery could be fought only with sorcery." Another story, "The Tale of Satampra Zeiros" (*Weird Tales*, November 1931), features two thieves that could have been plucked from Howard's Maul or Leiber's Lankmar. Infused with liquid courage, the two men seek to despoil the deserted city of Commoriom and its rumored riches but meet with horror beyond all reckoning. The story introduces Smith's Hyperborean cycle, a series of stories set in the prehistoric arctic continent of Hyperborea. Lovecraft and Howard both dipped into Smith's creation, borrowing Smith's monstrous and ravenous god Tsathoggua for their own stories (Lai).

The closest Smith came to traditional sword-and-sorcery might have been "The Beast of Averoigne" (*Weird Tales*, May 1933). It contains most of the subgenre's classic trappings, including a medieval setting, horror, and monsters pitted against sorcery and steel. A portentous red comet passes near Averogine—Smith's fantastic stand-in for medieval France—and deposits an amorphous, shadowy beast that wreaks havoc by night. The monster kills and partially consumes beasts, then eventually men, women, and children. A local abbot enlists a sorcerer and two men-at-arms to summon a demon and put an end to the creature. Yet it ends with a note of Lovecraftian unsettledness; the "hero" of the tale, the sorcerer Messire le Chaudronnier, conceals the fact that the monster used the body of the abbot to commit its atrocities. An unknowing populace unwittingly canonizes a mass-murderer, and the reader is left with a sense of foreboding that the cycle will repeat itself. Chaos can never be conquered, for it lives beyond the stars, a symptom of an uncaring universe.

C.L. Moore

Catherine Lucille Moore (1911–1987) was not the first, nor the most prolific, female writer to appear in the pages of *Weird Tales*. It's not quite accurate to proclaim her "the first lady of fantasy," as does the Paizo Planet Stories line in which her work was recently re-issued; to do so overlooks the prior fantastic efforts of authors like Mary Wollstonecraft Shelley, author of *Frankenstein*, and Sara Coleridge, author of *Phantasmion*. But in sword-and-sorcery circles, Moore is a pioneer, the first female writer to work in the subgenre. And she did so with a style that while Howard inspired also greatly departs from the Howardian sword-and-sorcery template.

Moore developed a love for adventure stories from reading pulp magazines *Adventure* and *Amazing Stories*. Like Howard, Moore greatly enjoyed the stories of Edgar Rice Burroughs and early adventure writer Talbot Mundy of *Adventure* fame (Lovecraft, *Letters to C.L.*

Moore and Others 8-9), as well as A. Merritt. In 1934, she became the first female to try her hand in the new and still nascent subgenre with "Black God's Kiss." From 1934–1939 Moore wrote five stories (and later collaborated with author and future husband Henry Kuttner on a sixth) of Jirel of Joiry, sword-and-sorcery's first and arguably most memorable female protagonist. Jirel is a beautiful, fiery, red-haired and yellow-eyed French noblewoman and warrior-knight living at the turn of the 16th century. But the stories quickly move the reader from a pseudo-historical setting and into weird, fantastic horror, with Jirel embarking on quests and adventurers in worlds beyond our own.

The publication of "Black God's Kiss" coincided with the height of the Conan stories, and Howard's influence on Moore is apparent. Jirel fights with a white-hot barbaric fury. Her skill and strength render her more than a match for almost any man. She is ambitious and lusty, a woman who has enjoyed the pleasures of male embrace without thought of commitment. Moore admitted readily to Howard's influence during her correspondence with Lovecraft. She extolled Howard's Bran Mak Morn story "Worms of the Earth" for its "lusty vitality" (Lovecraft, *Letters to C.L. Moore and Others* 31) and expressed a sympathy with Howard's romanticism over Lovecraft's grinding materialism. Moore shared Howard's optimism that mankind could prevail with valor, courage, and willpower (88-89, 11). A mild-mannered bank secretary, Moore had a love for outdoor sports that echoed Howard's obsessions with football and boxing. Moore corresponded with Howard in his last days and expressed profound shock at the news of his death. Of his influence she wrote, "As you [Lovecraft] say, he seemed to live in every story he wrote, breathing life and color and vitality in the pages until sometimes it was a little surprising the paper itself was not sodden and bright with blood and vocal with bugles and the sounds of battle. The end of every story was like the slamming of a door in one's face upon such a world of color and vividness and peril as never existed anywhere else" (131).

But Jirel is not a female equivalent of Conan, and the similarities between Moore and Howard are superficial and soon fade.[5] The world in which Jirel inhabits is the equivalent of medieval France, far different than the pre-historical Hyborian Age of Conan or Smith's imaginary continents. This skillful blend of fantasy and history was one of Moore's masterstrokes. "[Moore's] particular genius lay in a transposition of the likes of Conan from a brutish warrior-figure of a European version of the Australian Dreamtime to an equally

---

[5] Despite the claims of sword-and-sorcery historian Lin Carter, who called Moore's "Black God's Kiss" "pure Howardian heroica" and Jirel a "gal Conan" (*Realms of Wizardry* 205).

savage and athletic woman, a fully armored, strong young woman wielding broadsword and dagger in another, more recent Dark Age" (Charnas 14). Though stronger than an average man and three times the fighter, Jirel is not the physical equal of the most powerful of her male adversaries. But she is possessed of another kind of strength—an iron, unconquerable will.

Tonally and thematically, Moore and Howard's stories are very different. Whereas Howard's stories grip the reader with visceral action and the clash of civilization vs. barbarism, the Jirel stories are about mood. These moods, internal to Jirel, are reflected and amplified by her external environment through Moore's skillful use of symbolism. Her ability to create an atmosphere of the strange that utterly displaces the reader is arguably without parallel, and perhaps second only to Smith. Moore was also a Smith devotee and described his writings as "exquisite and fantastic ... he is another writer whose work it is a pleasure to read, and for almost opposite reasons from those that make R.E. Howard's writing so good" (Lovecraft, *Letters to C.L. Moore and Others* 31). Moore's early influences include *Alice in Wonderland* and the Oz books, and her ability to effortlessly transport readers into weird parallel universes rivals these works. Moore was also influenced by Lord Dunsany (in particular his atmospheric *King of Elfland's Daughter*) and the Robert Browning poem "Childe Roland to the Dark Tower Came." While Moore modestly wrote that "I must blushingly admit knowing nothing whatever about Childe Roland save a fragment of unidentified verse" (Lovecraft, *Letters to C.L. Moore and Others* 39), echoes of the dark, haunted, symbolic landscapes of Browning's poem are evident in the haunted underworld of "Black God's Kiss." Moore also counted among her influences the fantastic and heroic poems of Lord Alfred Tennyson and the tales of King Arthur in all its various forms, citing a particular affection for poetry evoking "the horns of Elfland" (Lovecraft, *Letters to C.L. Moore and Others* 103).

Moore got her start as a writer of science fiction with the likes of "Shambleau" (*Weird Tales*, November 1933) and "Black Thirst." These caught the attention of publisher Lester Del Rey, who described her ability to convey mood and theme a genuine revelation in a science-fiction scene then dominated by dry, clinical descriptions of technological gadgetry and two-dimensional, square-jawed heroes (Del Rey, "Forty Years of C.L. Moore" xiv). The Jirel stories are works of moody strangeness in which the supernatural works on a literal level as well as the symbolic. The gray heights of Castle Joiry are solid and imposingly real, as is the cold edge of the wicked two-handed sword Jirel wields with deadly skill while riding at the van of her forces. But these stories also involve a strange journey through a portal into other worlds. The effects are dizzying; Jirel loses her firm footing, as does the reader.

Jirel may be a warlord with a will of steel, but she finds herself compromised by human desires and emotions. Unlike Howard, Moore explored the then taboo subject of female wants and desires, infusing her stories with "a background thrum of erotic energy, so markedly absent from most of this type of writing by her fellow male authors" (Charnas 17). The dreamy, out-of-body sequences typical of the Jirel stories are battlegrounds of traditional gender roles. Jirel's quests of vengeance represent the struggle to find her way in a man's world while simultaneously reconciling her feminine wants and desires. In "Shambleau," Moore displays an intense interest in traditional female roles, and society's expectations of women vs. their personal desires for power and sex—desires often at odds with the expectations of male readers of the era. According to scholar Jonathan Helland, "'The Black God's Kiss,' taken by itself, is a work that challenges patriarchy and undermines traditional gender constructs" (187).

Moore explored the precarious position of women, both in the artificial constructs of sword-and- sorcery and in the medieval age in which her stories are set. Moore herself opted to conceal her gender from *Weird Tales*' majority male readership, opting for the asexual "C.L." over her birth name Catherine Lucille.[6] Jirel is under constant threat of men who seek to take her by force. They eye her curvaceous form with lustful gazes and plant kisses on her against her will. This may explain her ever-present rage and anger, and why she has difficulty experiencing and expressing genuine love and affection when it does come upon her, unbidden.

Jirel is an intimate partner with pain and death. Her life is a series of one martial challenge after the next, with the constant onslaught of obstacle-conflict-reward consuming her energies and attention, resulting in little time for self-reflection. But in "Black God's Kiss," the first and arguably greatest of Jirel of Joiry stories, Jirel confronts the darkness, meaninglessness, and despair underlying the polished steel veneer of a life of unchecked ambition, leading to a surprising and very personal revelation. Castle Joiry has been overrun by the forces of the warlord Guillaume and the story opens with Jirel captive and standing before her gloating conqueror. Guillaume plants a hot kiss on Jirel's mouth, an act that offends her on levels she cannot articulate. Though bound with rope, Jirel bites Guillaume's neck, drawing blood. He strikes her, knocking her

---

[6] Others theorize that Moore assumed the initials "C.L." to hide her career as a pulp writer from her employers at the bank, a job she could not jeopardize during the throes of the Great Depression (Sargent 191).

unconscious. Jirel comes to as a prisoner in a turret of a tower of her own castle. When she awakes her first thought is not just retaking Castle Joiry, but plotting a dreadful personal revenge on her captor.

With her forces scattered and no hope of retaking Joiry by main strength, Jirel descends into the basement of the castle to enlist supernatural aid. There she enters a strange wormhole. The tunnel through which she travels and its otherworldly landscape can be viewed as an inner journey, Jirel's struggle to reconcile her confused, jumbled motivations and feelings with the rigid mask of strength she's forced to wear (one clue that this strange land is intended as symbolic is that when Jirel enters the same weird dimension a second time, and by the same route she had previously traversed, the landscape is entirely different, mirroring her own uncertain, tumultuous moods). The stones she forces aside and the heavy steel lid she strains to lift are inner walls Jirel has erected to cope with an unforgiving, male-dominated world. The strange, Childe Roland-like land through which Jirel travels is full of startling imagery. Blinded snow-white horses and a beautiful nude woman in the grips of madness are symbolic of purity and sexuality damaged and corrupted; perhaps externalized representations of Jirel's tormented wants and desires. These marred traditional symbols of purity can also be viewed as a loss of innocence. Jirel must drop a cross around her neck to clearly observe this strange landscape; finding her way in a new world of sexuality and human desires is incompatible with Christianity.

Moore ends "Black God's Kiss" with an exquisite touch that skillfully reconciles and bridges traditional male and female roles. Jirel exacts her vengeance on Guillaume, but does so with a unique feminine power—a kiss, amplified by the sorcerous power of a black god. The poisonous kiss spreads throughout Guillaume and he drops, lifeless, to the flagstones. But Jirel's revenge is followed by swift shock, as she realizes that the man she deeply hated is a man she can't live without. She spends the next installment of the series ("Black Gods Shadow") in a desperate quest to bring Guillaume back from the dead.

Jirel's revelation that she loves Guillaume may disappoint some readers, as it seems to reinforce and re-establish the primacy of the weepy, emotional female stereotype. But some critics place "Black God's Kiss" in the camp of feminist literature for its fully rounded representation of Jirel. Nicole Emmelhainz, for example, notes that Moore describes Jirel using masculine imagery. She does not exhibit stereotypical feminine traits, such as passivity and domesticity ("A Sword-Edge Beauty" 123). Jirel acts with agency, unconstrained by gender, and is possessed of conflicted desires and all-too-human wants that render her fully three-dimensional.

The remainder of the Jirel of Joiry stories are uniformly good, though they lack the psychological depths of "Black God's Kiss." Moore later collaborated with husband Henry Kuttner on "Quest of the Starstone" (1937), a tale of time-travel in which Jirel forges a temporary alliance with a group of smugglers to recover a powerful talisman. Joiry is paired with Northwest Smith, a swashbuckling interstellar hero and early archetype for Han Solo of *Star Wars*. "Hellsgarde," the sixth and final story in the series, is horror masquerading as sword-and-sorcery, a terrifying tale of a revenant-haunted, hell-guarded castle that can only be entered by those who come upon it at night. Jirel, alone, must enter.

Although Moore made a very favorable impression on *Weird Tales* readers of the 1930s, Jirel of Joiry did not enjoy the same level of notoriety or staying power as Conan, nor that of later sword-and-sorcery protagonists Elric or Fafhrd and the Gray Mouser. Moore's relative anonymity as a sword-and-sorcery writer may be due to the fact that her heroine is ultimately a bit too one-note: Conan, a man of "gigantic melancholies and a gigantic mirth," was at various times a reaver and a thief, a pirate and a king; Jirel is rather one-dimensional in comparison, all rage and unchecked white-hot anger save for brief moments of humanity and femininity. More likely it's because Moore simply wrote too few tales of the fiery red-headed swordswoman, with six stories not enough to convey a full character arc. Moore's last story of Jirel appeared in 1939. She declined to write further stories, reportedly because "both she and the public taste had changed" (de Camp, "Conan's Compeers" 274). Moore returned to science fiction, then out of the print game altogether, applying her talents to screenplays and television scripts (Del Rey, "Forty Years of C.L. Moore" xiv). Sword-and-sorcery was the poorer for her decision. Although tough heroines are now common in modern novels and cinema, Moore deserves credit for penning the first female with a starring role in sword-and-sorcery, as well as for developing a unique style that bridged Howard's propulsive heroics with Smith's moody strangeness.

Henry Kuttner

Along with innumerable *Weird Tales* readers, Henry Kuttner (1915–1958) was enthralled with the stories of Lovecraft and Howard. Inspired by the duo, the young Kuttner began his own writing career in the 1930s. Kuttner wrote a short fan letter to Lovecraft in February 1936, sparking a brief correspondence in which Lovecraft freely shared his thoughts on weird fiction and encouraged the budding young author to borrow the mythical elements from his writings for use in his own tales of horror (Lovecraft, *Letters to C.L. Moore and Others*

13–14). The awe-struck Kuttner—who described Lovecraft as his "literary idol"—accepted the invitation with gusto. Kuttner managed to crack *Weird Tales* in March 1936 with the Lovecraft-inspired "The Graveyard Rats," and went on to write several "Lovecraft mythos" stories including "The Eater of Souls" and "The Salem Horror."

Although his early efforts chiefly consisted of horror, Kuttner soon set out to fill the considerable void left in heroic fiction by Howard's death. The product was Elak of Atlantis, a blonde, semi-barbaric (of royal blood, albeit distant) hero who adventures alongside his drunken, comedic sidekick Lycon. Between 1938 and 1941, Henry Kuttner wrote four Elak stories, all published in *Weird Tales*. The Elak stories owe an obvious debt to Howard's Conan. Although he is the rightful inheritor of half the throne of Cyrena, the northernmost kingdom of Atlantis, like Conan, Elak is a wanderer and an outsider who prefers the freedom of the road over the crown of responsibility. Three of the four stories begin with Elak in pursuit of women and gold. The last of the four Elak stories, "Dragon Moon," opens with Elak carousing in a tavern with a rare full purse and nearly meeting his end in a barroom brawl. He's rescued by the druid Dalan, who issues a plea for Elak to reclaim his ancestral seat on the Dragon Throne. Elak agrees, but reluctantly.

Elak wrestles with responsibility throughout the stories. With a purse full of coins and a brimming horn of mead Elak is happy, and wealthy beyond measure in his own way. But unanswered questions linger: Are revelry, pleasure-seeking, and unencumbered freedom all there is to life? Do we have the right to expect more than the pursuit of happiness in anyone? Must we eventually accept the mantle of responsibility?

In "Thunder in the Dawn," Elak attempts to free his brother, Orander, from the mind-control of the wizard Elf. But we're unsure whether Orander desires his freedom. Elf has made the Cyrenian king the ruler of a glorious kingdom, albeit within his own mind. "Would you rob a god of his worlds? I put no enchantment on Orander. The king asked me to grant him this boon, and with my magic I did so—made worlds over which your brother rules. Would you drag him back to Cyrena—a place from which he fled?" Elf asks. Elak is forced to confront the same uncomfortable question within himself. "I don't want to rule. ... I seek no crowns" (Kuttner, "Thunder in the Dawn" 74-75).

In "Dragon Moon," a dark eldritch god threatens Cyrena and the Atlantean continent, and slays Orander. Dalan tells Elak he has no choice but to ascend the throne:

> "Blood of kings is in your veins, Elak. It is not yours to deny. You must obey."

> "Must?" Elak asked. "The decision is mine, Druid. By Mider! The throne of Cyrena means much to me. Therefore I shall not sit in it!" (Kuttner, "Dragon Moon" 127).

When Elak reluctantly takes his place on the throne it's no soaring coronation, but a dirge for what is lost, the exchange of passionate living for the sedate rule of order:

> He did not see the triumphant banners of the dragon tossing in the wind, nor did he envision the throne of Cyrena that waited. He was remembering a low, rippling voice that spoke with longing of the fields and hearth-fires of earth, a slim, inhuman hand that had reached through a curtain—a sea-witch who had died to save a world to which she had never belonged (163).

Today, Kuttner's reputation as a writer is mixed. Some criticize him for a lack of originality and for following too closely in Howard's and Lovecraft's footsteps.[7] In addition to their debt to Howard, the Elak series contain overt homages to Lovecraft, including a cult of tentacle fish-men who worship the malignant sea god Dagon, and the god Baal-Yagoth, who looks and sounds suspiciously like Lovecraft's globular creation Yog-Sothoth. But Kuttner was not a hack, or rank imitator. Although certainly Conan-inspired, the Elak stories contain small but important variations on the Howardian sword-and-sorcery template. Kuttner ups the magic quotient considerably. In "Beyond the Phoenix," Elak channels the power of a god to beat back another god and slay a powerful priest. Elak's royal blood allows him to survive a test of flames of the dragon throne of Cyrena which consumes a pretender.[8] Fritz Leiber is often credited with introducing two protagonists to sword-and-sorcery, but Kuttner beat Fafhrd and the Gray Mouser to the starting line by a year with "Thunder in the Dawn" (May/June 1938 *Weird Tales*). Kuttner's Elak stories are more humorous than Howard's, foreshadowing the wit Leiber would employ to great effect in his sword-and-sorcery. With their mashup of Nordic elements (particularly in "Thunder in the Dawn"), the Elak stories appear to have at least partially influenced Poul Anderson, who in 1954 wrote perhaps the greatest sword-and-sorcery novel ever, *The Broken Sword*.

Elak has demonstrated some lasting power and Kuttner's

---

[7] L. Sprague de Camp, for example, said of Kuttner, "Another quirk was a tendency to imitate whatever other writer had recently achieved fame. … This fact, together with his lavish use of pen-names, suggests a deeply-rooted lack of self-confidence" (*Literary Swordsmen and Sorcerers* 279).

8 At times this heavy-handed use of magic weakens the Elak series; in "Thunder in the Dawn," Elak is bailed out of trouble time and again by the druid Dalan. Dalan pushes the reluctant Elak toward a fate he seems powerless to avoid, robbing him of the agency that makes Conan such a compelling character.

reputation has improved in recent years. By the tail-end of the sword-and-sorcery renaissance in the 1980s, editor and author Karl Edward Wagner assessed, "While not strictly in the Howard mold— [they] more closely call to mind Michael Moorcock's Elric series of the present day—he was the best of those who sought to fill the gap left by Howard's death" (*Echoes of Valor III* 54). Planet Stories recently republished the four stories of Elak, packaged with a pair of tales of Prince Raynor, in *Elak of Atlantis* (2007). In the volume's forward, Bram Stoker-winning horror author Joe Lansdale wrote glowingly of Kuttner, describing the pulp author as "one of those rare kinds of writers who was a combination story teller, stylist, and thinker" (13). Most recently, author Richard Morgan included an homage to Elak in his "Land Fit for Heroes" sword-and-sorcery trilogy, whose protagonist, Ringil Eskiath, wields a blade made of Kiriath steel (Kiriath lays just south and west of Elak's homeland of Cyrena).

But the most noteworthy contribution of the Elak stories is the way in which they reinforced and strengthened the Howardian template: fast-paced stories of warriors battling sorcery in ancient depths of time, outsider heroes involved in mercenary intrigues and personal entanglements. Kuttner's Elak stories differ from Howard's tales of Conan and Kull but only by a matter of degree and detail. "Kuttner's creation, Elak, was his own thing, and not Howard's Conan, but they certainly were characters who might have crossed paths and gone on a three-day drunk and whoring expedition together. In the end, that ramble might have led to a savage duel due to the fact that they were both in their own way what today would be describe as alpha males" (Lansdale 12).

Kuttner was also an admirer of Moore, whose tales of Jirel of Joiry were a particular favorite. The pair began corresponding at Lovecraft's behest (Carter, *Realms of Wizardry* 206), and in 1938 met in person. Two years later they married, a marriage that lasted until Kuttner's untimely death in 1958. Their relationship went beyond the romantic as the two formed a tag-team writing partnership, and published several joint stories under pseudonyms. Principal authorship of these stories is uncertain and often credited interchangeably to one or the other—or both (Del Rey, "Forty Years of C.L. Moore" xii). Included in their collaboration is a tale of Jirel of Joiry, "Quest for the Starstone," published in 1937, as well as dozens of science-fiction stories. By the early 1940s the pair had ceased any further sword-and-sorcery efforts for the far more popular and lucrative SF genre. But their joint efforts are today regarded as seamless works of excellence, melding Moore's "sensitivity and emotional coloration" with Kuttner's intellectual leanings and structured plotting (Del Rey, "Forty Years of C.L. Moore" xii).

Why did the template begun by Howard, and continued by Kuttner, become the default standard for sword-and-sorcery, instead of one based on the works of Smith and Moore? Perhaps because the former are easier to access for the average reader, and more compelling. Howard told gripping stories of visceral excitement and danger. Smith's stories, while appreciated by some fans and receptive editors, including *Weird Tales* editor Farnsworth Wright, were rejected by the likes of *Wonder Stories*' David Lasser as being not action-oriented enough. Smith refused to bend to market pressures, steadfastly maintaining in a letter to *Amazing Stories* that the action and human-centric view of literature established by Howard was a narrow and limited one (Connors, "Pegasus Unbridled" 162). Moore's stories of Jirel of Joiry, though containing much more blood and thunder than Smith, were more concerned with mood, exploration of strange Oz-like worlds, and displacement, and less with pulse-pounding visceral action. Her comparative lack of influence may also simply be that her corpus of sword-and-sorcery is quite small in comparison to Howard, who churned out three times the number of Conan stories as Jirel and some 300 stories overall in a white-hot frenzy during his brief lifetime.

Howard was, arguably, less driven by high-minded artistry and more by economic reality than the bohemian Smith. Moore had a day job with a reliable paycheck. Married young, she enjoyed a relatively stable income. With an ailing mother to support and medical bills to pay, Howard needed the income, and couldn't afford to embrace the hermetic lifestyle of a literary aesthete like Lovecraft. Thus the introspective, philosophical, but less accessible tales of the brooding Kull of Atlantis gave way to the largely extroverted, colorful adventures of Conan of Cimmeria. The demands of the marketplace and pulp fiction readership, as much as any conscious artistic decision, helped establish the sword-and-sorcery template. With some exceptions, sword-and-sorcery post-Howard and Kuttner emphasized action and plot over atmosphere and the experience of bizarre events found in the work of Smith which Lovecraft so valued (Lovecraft, *Letters to C.L. Moore and Others* 238). It's hard to imagine sword-and-sorcery without Howard, and the subgenre surely would have been much the lesser without his two-fisted, heroic, high-energy stamp. But through the works of his peers we can imagine such a universe. A Smithian-based sword-and-sorcery tradition would perhaps have given us something equally wonderful—worlds of mind-bending displacement, soul-destroying cosmic horror, and ironic, bitter endings for would-be heroes—while a subgenre with Moore as its progenitor may have featured heroes torn by as much inner strife as outer, embarking on weird symbolic journeys of psychological self-discovery.

But even though Smith's and Moore's sword-and-sorcery stories fall within Howard's long shadow, the two played a crucial role in the early days of the subgenre. Amid the din of the keystrokes of Howard's Underwood typewriter, Smith and Moore added a quieter but undeniably potent, sustaining force and legitimacy to a burgeoning new genre. By the time of Henry Kuttner and the Elak of Atlantis stories in the late 1930s and early 1940s, the mold of sword-and-sorcery was beginning to take shape, the trope of outsider swordsman pitted against monsters and magic in fast moving, narrative tales firmly ensconced—or so it seemed.

Although the time seemed right for a sword-and-sorcery explosion, it did not occur. In the late 1930s and into the 1940s the long-term prognosis for the subgenre remained uncertain. Howard was buried in Greenleaf Cemetery in Brownwood, Texas, on June 14, 1936, laid to rest alongside his mother, Hester. Mourned by his grieving father, his friends and acquaintances, and a sizable contingent of Cross Plains residents, Howard's legacy in the broader literary circles was negligible. Although feted in *The Eyrie* letters column by Lovecraft as well as his fans, Howard seemed destined to become little more than a pleasant memory shared among a handful of loyal heroic fantasy and pulp aficionados, his stirring tales of muscular adventure and dark sorcery forgotten.

Weird Tales in little more than a year was to lose its three most talented practitioners. Lovecraft died in 1937 from stomach cancer. Aggrieved by the losses of his literary peers and the death of his parents, Clark Ashton Smith all but ceased writing weird fiction by the end of 1937, retreating to a secluded existence as a sculptor and painter in rural California. In rapid succession the three writers chiefly responsible for the magazine's golden age had vanished from the scene. A handful of popular old stalwarts including Seabury Quinn soldiered on in *Weird Tales*, but the sudden departure of so much raw talent began the start of a long decline for the magazine.

Sword-and-sorcery also began to suffer from the rapid explosion of science fiction, which for a time grew unchecked and threatened to overwhelm all other speculative literature. Technological advances spurred by the expediency of World War II—jet engines, radar, self-propelled rocket bombs, and the development of atomic energy— fired the public imagination from the late 1930s into the 1950s. The literary world met the demand with stories of space-traveling rocket ships and colonies on Mars. Magazines like *Amazing Stories* and *Astounding Stories* helped launch what is now regarded today as the golden age of science fiction, publishing the likes of L. Ron Hubbard, Clifford Simak, Lester del Rey, Isaac Asimov, Arthur C. Clarke, and Robert Heinlein. Sword-and-sorcery authors abandoned the genre for greener pastures and began writing in this suddenly much more profitable niche, including Moore, Kuttner, and Leiber. The latter turned his creativity to such works of science fiction as "Gather Darkness" in *Astounding Stories,* even as he continued to soldier on with the occasional Fafhrd and the Gray Mouser story for *Unknown.* Kuttner in 1943 turned to writing for *Astounding* under the pen-name Lewis Padgett to disguise his "unsavory" past in sword-and-sorcery, a genre which the hard-SF readers of *Astounding* treated with derision (Del Rey, *The World of Science Fiction, 1926–1976* 104–105). Few writers were actively producing sword-and-sorcery. It lacked a canonical breadth and depth and the necessary literary invention to ensure its survival and progression. It even lacked a name.

That would all change with the advent of the 1960s, and the emergence of a pair of literary talents who expanded sword-and-sorcery's literary borders in creative directions, and the appearance of a popular new re-packaging of Howard's original tales that would bring the obscure stories of Conan the Cimmerian to a mass-market audience.

HEROIC VS. ANTI-HEROIC SWORD-AND SORCERY

Much classic sword-and-sorcery written circa 1929–1989 is heroic in nature. *Heroic* sword-and-sorcery (not to be confused with "heroic fantasy"*) protagonists perform improbable feats of a physical, martial nature. Heroic sword-and-sorcery characters are active, influence their surroundings, and carve out their own destinies. Typically, their stories end in success, but even when they don't, heroic sword-and-sorcery protagonists often achieve partial successes or at least live to fight another day. In heroic sword-and-sorcery, the barbaric spirit (i.e., man in his natural state, free from civilized corruption) prevails. Though today more commonly associated with sword-and-sorcery and fantasy in general, in Robert E. Howard's day heroic sword-and-sorcery "that valued personal emotionalism over detached cosmicism" was in the minority in *Weird Tales* (Grin, *Barbaric Triumph* 155), which catered to tales of horror or dark fantasy.

Heroic stories, if they are true, must end in darkness, death, and uncertainty. At some point, age and infirmity afflicts even the mightiest of heroes, wasting sword arms and sapping strength. But while a feeble, aged Conan is true to life, it is not the stuff of heroic sword-and-sorcery. Howard was motivated to write about humans and humanity in desperate but not fruitless battles to overcome the forces of time and decay. All of Howard's characters fit more or less into the heroic mode. John Jakes' Brak the Barbarian and Fritz Leiber's Fafhrd and the Gray Mouser are further examples of heroic sword-and-sorcery protagonist.

A related but separate strain is anti-heroic** sword-and-sorcery, also described as dark fantasy (Williamson, 169), Gothic fantasy (Tymn, Zahorski, and Boyer 15), or sardonic sword-and-sorcery (Holmes, "RE: "Smith-ian" or Gothic sword-and-sorcery") in which characters struggle vainly against implacably evil and/or indifferent forces of corruption, death, and decay. Its stories are typically pessimistic, and failure is common. Its characters (and readers) are imbued with a sense of dread. The anti-heroic mode of sword-and-sorcery is best exemplified in the writings of Clark Ashton Smith, and later Jack Vance and Ramsay Campbell. The anti-heroic strain of sword-and-sorcery tells stories of regression and decay, and even death for their protagonist. Its heroes typically fall into category 4 of Northrop Frye's five-tier heroic scale as described in his *Anatomy of Criticism*—a low mimetic mode, superior neither to other men nor to their environment. Anti-heroic stories hew far more closely to sword-and-sorcery's horror roots than its close ancestor adventure fiction. While heroic sword-and-sorcery stories crib Lovecraft's monsters and tentacled menaces, anti-heroic tales leverage Lovecraft's underlying bleakness and cosmic pessimism. An example is Smith's "The Testament of Athammaus," which features a headsman with a terrible ability to unerringly sever the necks of doomed criminals. Called on to behead the outlaw Knygathin Zhaum, Athammaus fails on three consecutive attempts. Each time he is "executed" Zhaum rises from the tomb, less and less human in appearance, until he is a shibboleth of hungry mouths and orifices. Any remaining semblance of order disintegrates, and the stricken populace of Commorium flees the doomed city. Athammaus at the last turns and departs, recognizing the futility of valor. Smith paints a chaotic universe where decay and disunion will ultimately prevail.

Some sword-and-sorcery authors wrote with equal faculty across the heroic and anti-heroic modes. Ramsay Campbell's Ryre stories are heroic, for example, while his story "The Stages of the God" is anti-heroic. *Whispers* magazine featured stories of the anti-heroic mode, including David Drake's "The Barrow Troll" where wealth-seeking warriors are doomed to become paranoid and delusional beasts, reduced to defending their hordes against other "heroes" who would plunder them. Some sword-and-sorcery contains the heroic and the anti-heroic in equal measure. In the 1970s, the clash of heroic and anti-heroic played out in an uneasy but skillful balance in Karl Edward Wagner's Kane stories.

These two forces, heroic and anti-heroic/sardonic, waged war in the early days of sword-and-sorcery. Ultimately, the heroic mode prevailed. Perhaps this strain was more palatable for the majority of readers, with Smith's idiosyncratic tales told in ornate prose too opaque to access (Williamson, 171–172). Recurring heroes offer the possibility of ongoing series, appealing to magazine editors seeking to build fan bases, as well as licensing in comics and movies. But it's arguable whether the victory of the heroic did not ultimately hasten the downfall of sword-and-sorcery, which eventually descended into repetitive, stale formula. Today, the pendulum has swung back, as the novels of Richard Morgan and Joe Abercrombie demonstrate public appetite exists for amoral or morally ambiguous characters and settings and unexpected deaths of its central protagonists.

The uneasy meeting of the heroic and anti-heroic continues, surging back and forth as it always has.

* "Heroic fantasy" is a somewhat ill-defined term, often used interchangeably to describe works of sword-and-sorcery and high fantasy.

** "Anti-heroic" refers here to fantastic literature with a strong horror bent, in which the protagonists, though sometimes of heroic stature, suffer death or decay or defeat. This is not be confused with the term "antihero," a literary term used to describe an ineffectual character who lacks heroic qualities, including strength, bravery, and agency. Author Jamie Williamson advocates for the term "dark fantasy" to describe the fiction of Smith and his predecessor H.P. Lovecraft. Williamson makes the case that Smith's dark fantasy descended from Gothic traditions, in particular William Beckford's novel *Vathek* and the works of Edgar Allen Poe, and were "preoccupied with generating a rich, poetically textured atmosphere," whereas Howard's sword-and-sorcery "was interested in a combination of swashbuckling heroics and quasi-historical verisimilitude" (Williamson, 169–172). This book claims that some of Smith's corpus is sword-and-sorcery, but of a different strain than the Howardian.

CHAPTER FIVE
Revival

The time has come for sorcery and swords!
—Fritz Leiber, "The Lords of Quarmall"

Outside of a few small press collections, sword-and-sorcery was largely inaccessible to the general public in the 1940s and early 1950s, save for those lucky enough to own back issues of the swiftly yellowing *Weird Tales*. Some sword-and-sorcery saw reprint in the Donald A. Wollheim-edited *Avon Fantasy Reader* (1946–1952). The short-lived but influential and beloved pulp magazine *Unknown* (1939–1943) published the first stories of Fritz Leiber's iconic Fafhrd and the Gray Mouser stories, including "Two Sought Adventure" in the August 1939 issue. But the magazine lasted only four years before low circulation and wartime paper shortages ended its run. Leiber managed to place a handful of stories of his iconic sword-and-sorcery duo in the likes of *Suspense, Other Worlds*, and *Fantastic*, but the market for such fiction was drying up. *Weird Tales* ceased publication in September 1954 after a 21-year run, portending the end of the pulp era.[1]

But all was not lost. Laboring to keep heroic fantasy and Howard's legacy alive was the small press fanzine *Amra* (1955–1982) and its loyal "Hyborian Legion" of readers and contributors. Founded in November 1955 by editor George Heap, *Amra* had an abortive, inauspicious start before George Scithers assumed editorship for a lengthy, storied volume-two run in 1956. Named after the sobriquet "Amra the Lion" bestowed on Conan during his days as a corsair in "Queen of the Black Coast," *Amra* sought to preserve Howard's legacy and expand on his creations through the promulgation of "Hyborian scholarship," or scholarly exploration of Howard's invented worlds of Conan and Kull. *Amra* soon expanded its editorial focus to include

---

[1] This would not be the end for *Weird Tales*; publisher Leo Margulies resurrected it for a brief four-issue run in 1973. Seven years after this second run ended, Zebra Books launched *Weird Tales* for a third time, this time in a mass-market paperback format. Four paperback volumes were published under the editorship of Lin Carter between 1980 and 1983. *Weird Tales* saw an aborted fourth revival with two issues published in 1984 and 1985 under two separate editors before another long run began in 1987. A new group published a single issue in 2019, with little fanfare.

other heroic fantasy and science fiction. The second and most famous iteration of the fanzine featured extensive artwork, as well as articles, stories, poems, and letters from the likes of L. Sprague de Camp, Poul Anderson, Fritz Leiber, Michael Moorcock, and Roger Zelazny, among others (Breakiron, "A Lion Among Fanzines"). *Amra* helped connect sword-and-sorcery with the swashbuckling historical romance, with essays and articles on historical personages, battles, and empires, Society for Creative Anachronism tournament reports, and medieval sword-fighting techniques, alongside essays on Howard's fiction, book reviews, fiction, and heroic and weird poetry.

In its early days *Amra* championed a style of fiction that seemed lost to time. Former *Unknown* magazine editor John W. Campbell's column "Heroes Are Out of Date" (*Amra* Vol. 2, No. 2) described the disfavor into which heroic fantasy had fallen with the general reading public. Responding to a column by Arhkam House publisher August Derleth, which predicted a favorable future for heroic/swash-buckling fantasy, Campbell countered:

> Mr. Derleth has, I think, made a significant error of evaluation. He is quite correct in speaking of Gus Elkar bucolic-humor stories going out of date due to changing times and customs ... but quite incorrect in saying that the swashbuckler hasn't gone out of date. The climate of the times has changed, and changed violently, in that regard.
>
> The essence of it is this last generation there still remained a nostalgic feeling for the Hero—for the man who was a Man, and more than ordinary run-of-the-mill people.
>
> Today, the psychological and sociological climate is not merely uninterested—it is very positively oriented *against* such characters...
>
> Swashbuckling is out of fashion—and Psychology, Sociology, and the current philosophy of what-is-good is doing everything possible to deny it ever existed! That's the major reason such stories aren't being published or written (J. Campbell 7).

A subsequent letter from Michael Moorcock in the May 1959 *Amra* supported Campell's assertion about the poor state of "swashbuckling adventure":

> You bet I'll have something to say about the decline in the market for the Conan type tale. Since I got a letter from a publisher saying that—"ye-es, they'd accept my Rackhir story but they didn't want any more really—and we hope you didn't mind if it's held over until we are desperate for material"—I've had a personal grudge (4).

In the early 1960s sword-and-sorcery not only continued to languish, it lacked a name. Several possibilities were bandied about in *Amra*, among them "historical-adventure," "modern mythology," and "nonhistoric adventure-fantasy." A Nov. 1959 editorial column "Blunders" described a humorous muster of *Amra* officiants, gathered to discuss what type of name would suit Conan and other tales "sufficiently like the Conan stories":

> Ye Muster was called to order, in the absence of Ye King of Aquilonia, at the unCromly hour of 11:00 AM, by Ye Royal Chancellor. The principal subject discussed was the question of just what made the Conan stories what they were, as well as the questions what stories are sufficiently like the Conan stories to fit well into AMRA and what would be a good type name for such stories.
>
> After some discussion, it was agreed that at least some of the factors that made the Conan stories effective are the presence of a hero in the old sense of the word exerting his wit and his muscle against magical and mundane opponents, all displayed against a strange and wonderful time and place.
>
> It was pointed out that the economics of putting out AMRA are such that it must seek readers interested in other sagas than Conan's alone; in addition, broadening of AMRA's scope can avoid the problem of running out of purely Conanish material. The problem then was to determine *what* sagas, and what, as a class name, to call them.
>
> Quite a few stories and story cycles were mentioned; Fafhrd & the Gray Mouser fit into the class, in part because their writer, Fritz Leiber, quite frankly admits they were inspired by Conan. Burroughs' John Carter stories, though they are set in a "science fiction" rather than a "fantasy" background, fit into the class, for Barsoom is a strange and wonderful place where the science isn't allowed to get in the way of a good sword fight. Tarzan, though a satisfactory hero, doesn't qualify; the setting for his activities (with the notable exception of the Pellucidar adventure) is merely Africa. Tolkien's Ring trilogy, on the other hand, though its setting is an altogether magnificent work of imagination, seems to some to lack a central figure of sufficient physical prowess, though this point was disputed by a number of Hobbits present. (One of AMRA's editorial board was heard to mutter that he had *extreme* difficulty identifying with a hero, no matter how heroic, who was but four feet tall)
>
> As for names for the class, several were suggested, but no real agreement was reached. "Worlds of Fantasy," "Worlds Beyond," and the like tend to concentrate on the background of the stories, while the term "Heroic Fantasy" tends to concentrate only on the personality of central character.
>
> Whatever the class be called, certain it is that there is interest in it. ... The meeting was closed with the hope that the discussion would be continued in AMRA ("Blunders" 3).

Discussion continued in ensuing issues. In the May 1961 issue of the fanzine, a then 22-year-old Moorcock called for the matter to be settled, and proposed the term "epic fantasy." Moorcock's first story of the moody albino sorcerer Prince Elric, "The Dreaming City," was published in June of that year in *Science Fantasy* #47, and he was seeking a term to match. Moorcock described epic fantasy as "stories of high adventure, generally featuring a central hero very easy to identify oneself with." Epic fantasy was a thing apart from traditional fantasy stories "in which present day heroes enter worlds of legend and myth and don't take the idea together seriously ... In the Epic Fantasy group the author more or less asks you to accept the background and so on as important because his characters consider it important, then take the story from there, respecting the laws and logic which are to be taken for what they are, and taken seriously" ("Putting a Tag on it" 15–18).

Leiber, also a regular contributor to *Amra*, disagreed with Moorcock's rather lofty-sounding "epic" appellation. Leiber was after coinage to match the style, content, and pulp heritage of his Fafhrd and the Gray Mouser stories, and offered a term more suited to the grounded, realistic style of fantasy fiction which Howard had begun and he continued. In a letter in the pages of the Philadelphia Science Fiction Society newsletter *Ancalagon* (issue #2, April 1961), Leiber had suggested for the first time that "sword-and-sorcery" be considered:

> ANCALAGON looks nice, especially the cover (where the art seems nicely gauged to the method of reproduction) and the article on fantasy-adventure—a field which I feel more certain than ever should be called the sword-and-sorcery story. This accurately describes the points of culture-level and supernatural element and also immediately distinguishes it from the cloak-and-sword (historical adventure) story—and (quite incidentally) from the cloak-and-dagger (international espionage) story too! The word sorcery implies something more and other than historical human witchcraft, so even the element of an alien-yet-human world background is hinted at.
>
> At any rate I'll use sword-and-sorcery as a good popular catchphrase for the field. It won't interfere with the use of a more formal designation of the field (such as the "non-historical fantasy adventure" which Sprague once suggested in a review of Smith Abominations of Yondro in AMRA) when one comes along or is finally settled on.
>
> Of course there will always be wide fringes of borderland around a story-area like this, and too-careful efforts at placing any single story or sets of stories may result in a sort of nonsense. For instance Burroughs' John Carter stories have so much the feel of sword-and-sorcery (rather than science fiction) that one immediately wants at least a new category for them—sword-and-superscience? To me, Burroughs' Mars stories are Atlantis-on-Mars and no more science fiction than Smith's [Clark Ashton] stories of Atlantis—or no *less* science fiction. ... Ah well (*Ancalagon* #2 6-7).[2]

---

[2] Leiber does not make the connection, but sword-and-sorcery echoes sword-and-sandal, a niche film genre then at its peak. Sword-and-sandal films featured shirtless, muscular heroes in historical settings (mainly ancient Greece or Rome), and often featured mythological monsters and romance. See the likes of *Hercules* (1958) and *Spartacus* (1960).

Amra bolstered the use of Leiber's new term by reprinting his letter from *Ancalagon* in the July 1961 *Amra*, adding additional parentheticals expressing enthusiasm for the term and its possible application across other subgenres:

> I feel more certain than ever [that this field] should be called the sword-and-sorcery story. This accurately describes the points of culture-level and supernatural element and also immediately distinguishes it from the cloak-and-sword (historical adventure) story—and (quite incidently) from the cloak-and-dagger (international espionage) story too! [There are many possibilities along this line—cloak-and-mask (comic book heroes), cutlass-and-dagger (piracy), rocket-and-ray gun (space opera), and vine-and-loincloth (Tarzan).] *(Amra* Vol. 2, No. 16 21-23)

Thereafter, sword-and-sorcery was quickly adopted in *Amra*, though it was often used interchangeably with "swordplay-and-sorcery." The tagline "The magazine of swordplay-and-sorcery" began making regular appearances on the cover of *Amra*, and the contents page of Vol. 2 No. 46 (April 1968) officially recognized Leiber as the originator of the term ("...swordplay & sorcery is a term thought up by Fritz Leiber to describe the kind of swashbuckling fiction this magazine is all about.")

Leiber added further explanation and color in an author's note to his 1968 Fafhrd and the Gray Mouser novel *The Swords of Lankhmar*, highlighting the aesthetic differences between his roguish pair of heroes and the (relatively) upright and stainless heroes of Tolkien's *The Lord of the Rings*:

> Fafhrd and the Mouser are rogues through and through, though each has in him a lot of humanity and at least a diamond chip of the spirit of true adventure. They drink, they feast, they wench, they brawl, they steal, they gamble, and surely they hire out their swords to powers that are only a shade better, if that, than the villains. It strikes me (and something might be made of this) that Fafhrd and the Gray Mouser are almost at the opposite extreme from the heroes of Tolkien. My stuff is at least equally as fantastic as his, but it's an earthier sort of fantasy with a strong seasoning of "black fantasy"— or of black humor, to use the current phrase for something that was once called gallows humor and goes back a long, long way. Though with their vitality, appetites, warm sympathies and imagination, Fafhrd and the Gray Mouser are anything but "sick" heroes.
>
> One of the original motives for conceiving Fafhrd and the Mouser was to have a couple of fantasy heroes closer to true human stature than supermen like Conan and Tarzan and many another. In a way they're a mixture of Cabell and Eddison, if we must look for literary ancestors. Fafhrd and the Mouser have a touch of Jurgen's cynicism and anti-romanticism, but they go on boldly having adventures—one more roll of the dice with destiny and death. While the characters they most parallel in *The Worm Ouroboros* are Corund and

Gro, yet I don't think they're touched with evil as those two, rather
they're rogues in a decadent world where you have to be a rogue to
survive; perhaps, in legendry, Robin Hood comes closest to them,
though they're certainly a pair of lone-wolf Robin Hoods... (2).

While Leiber greatly admired Howard's Conan stories and readily
admitted to their influence, Moorcock struggled to reconcile his admiration for Howard's earnestness and powerful prose with aspects he
didn't like, including Howard's (supposed) romanticism of barbarism. He later adopted a cynical view of the field of "epic fantasy,"
his all-encompassing term for secondary world fantasy into which he
grouped Howard as well as the likes of J.R.R. Tolkien and C.S. Lewis.
Moorcock deliberately set out to break epic fantasy's "genre ghettos"
by tweaking its conventions in a calculated, deliberate manner.
"Those who learn one particular dialectic find themselves trapped by
it," Moorcock later explained. "Once a movement comes into vogue it
is not unusual for its original adherents to reject it and move into new
territory" (Moorcock, *Wizardry and Wild Romance* 141).[3]

Although their estimations of Howard varied, Moorcock and
Leiber were united in a desire to distance themselves from *The
Lord of the Rings*. Tolkien's work, published in 1954 in hardcover
with moderate success, exploded in popularity in paperback in the
1960s—just as Moorcock was writing his Elric stories and Leiber
was turning out his best Fafhrd and the Gray Mouser material. It
was impossible to avoid Tolkien's influence, and so fantasy writers
were forced to react to it. Leiber and Moorcock responded with
stories and characters in opposition to Tolkien, whom they criticized for a perceived limited moral simplicity. Tolkien's stories told
of heroes who were in essence pure of heart, though tempted by evil.
Arrayed against them were the forces of darkness, a classic struggle
of good and evil. Leiber's explication of sword-and-sorcery as an
"earthier sort of fantasy," populated with characters who "hire out
their swords to powers that are only a shade better, if that, than the
villains," provided him with a framework to tell a different type of
fantasy story. Enflamed with the 1960s spirit of rebellion, Moorcock
found in Howard, Leiber, Poul Anderson, James Branch Cabell, and
Mervyn Peake a malleable blueprint for the stories of his doomed
albino outcast, prince Elric of Melnibone. In the freedom of the
Young Kingdoms, Elric could operate in freewheeling adventures
set in decadent, amoral lands of law and chaos.

Yet even the considerable combined talents of Leiber and
Moorcock were not enough to bring sword-and-sorcery to a mass

---

[3] Eventually Moorcock would find some measure of peace with Howard and admit
to his importance on his development as a writer (*Elric: The Stealer of Souls* xxiii) and
even refer to Howard as a "forgotten master."

audience. In the early 1960s their stories remained largely confined to magazines. It would take a fortuitous publishing deal to revivify the Conan stories of Robert E. Howard and by extension, sword-and-sorcery. Packaged as a chronological, numbered "saga," and published in paperback with arresting covers by the most talented artist ever to work in the subgenre, this convergence of authorial and visual artistry, marketing, and business acumen led to the re-emergence and conscious reawakening of sword-and-sorcery in the subgenre's "silver age," or renaissance.

Fritz Leiber (1910–1992)

Barbarism can match civilization's every stench. Not one move in our frostbit lives but is strictured by a mad god's laws, which we call customs, and by black-handed irrationalities from which there is no escape.

—Fritz Leiber, "The Snow Women"

Struggling financially and spiritually in the throes of the Great Depression, Harry Fischer and Fritz Leiber (1910–1992) longed for a heroic escape valve. In the summer of 1934 Leiber was working as an Episcopalian minister, Fischer as a puppeteer. Neither of their hearts lay in their odd careers. Fischer worried aloud at the decay of his artistic soul, telling his friend "the Gods have laid my soul aside to moulder for a time." But Leiber felt a stirring of an imaginative endeavor, a fuel that merely needed the right spark to set it alight. "But there is much of strong hope," he wrote to Fischer ("Fafhrd and Me" 120–121) who responded to this optimism by creating a pair of fictitious heroes that were both larger than life, and rough approximations of himself and Leiber. In a September 1934 letter to Leiber, Fischer sketched the initial outlines of what would become the Gray Mouser:

> For all do fear the one known as the Gray Mouser. He walks with swagger 'mongst the bravos, though he's but the stature of a child. His costume is all of gray, from gauntlets to boots and spurs of steel. His flat, swart face is shadowed by a peaked cap of mouse-skin and his garments are of silk, strangely soft and coarse of weave. ... He was sly as a wolverine, and while a great cheat and hard to engage in a fair quarrel, yet he did not fear to die and preferred great odds to single combat ("Fafhrd and Me" 121–122).

Fischer next described a barbarian hero, Fafhrd, whose boisterous but warm personality mirrored Leiber's own:

> [T]here strode into the group of laughing bravos a pair of monstrous men. The one who laughed the merrier was full seven feet in height. His light chestnut hair was bound in a ringlet of pure gold, engraved with runes. His eyes, wide-set, were proud and of fearless mien. His wrists between gauntlet and mail were white as milk and thick as a hero's ankle (122).

Leiber had the spark he needed. The son of a Shakespearian actor and himself an actor who later abandoned the profession, Leiber had a natural storyteller's flair and responded with a letter adding more detail, and the beginnings of a story germ. In 1935 he began writing his first tale of Fafhrd and the Gray Mouser, published more than a decade later as "Adept's Gambit" (1947). A fan of the pulps and *Weird Tales*, Leiber had begun corresponding with Lovecraft in the last year of the latter's life and shared with him an early draft of the story (an exchange detailed in *Fritz Leiber and H.P. Lovecraft: Writers of the Dark*). Lovecraft's urgings and constructive feedback pushed the young Leiber to keep writing and submit his stories for publication. Leiber was rejected by *Weird Tales*, but met with acceptance in the new pulp magazine *Unknown*, his first professional sale (de Camp, *Literary Swordsmen and Sorcerers* 282-286). "Two Sought Adventure" (*Unknown*, August 1939) marked the published debut of an unlikely pair of heroes adventuring in the grimy, dangerous, exciting city of Lankhmar in the invented secondary world of Newhon. It would be the beginning of a lifetime of stories. Leiber's writings on the pair spanned seven decades—from the 1930s to the early 1990s—and followed their adventures as they progressed from carefree youths, to calculating mercenaries, to aging legends in (semi) retirement. Although Leiber did almost all the writing, his stories retain Fischer's principal descriptions of the two main heroes in exact detail, down to their clothing, weapons, bearing, and mien.

Leiber's sword-and-sorcery bears Howard's stamp, in particular in its use of outsider heroes participating in picaresque adventures. Leiber's northern barbarian Fafhrd mirrors Conan with his might, mirth, and barbaric upbringing. But Leiber was not a Howard clone and did not slavishly follow the Howardian template. His heroes are less powerful than Howard's: Although Fafhrd and the Gray Mouser, fighting alone, are more than a match for any single foe, two armed opponents becomes an immediate life-or-death struggle; any more than that is cause to flee and live to fight to another day. Perhaps the most fearsome opponent they encounter is the mountain Stardock, a towering, sheer-faced spire of rock and ice the heroes must scale on one of their adventures. Leiber is at the height of his powers in "Stardock" and portrays the climb with an extended episode of palpable tension played out on its dizzying heights and treacherous paths. Leiber skillfully conveys the fear of the climber who is stuck and cannot ascend or descend, battling the steady rise of throat-clenching panic that threatens to freeze him in place.

Leiber's influences included pre-sword-and-sorcery-fantasists James Branch Cabell and E.R. Eddison (Moorcock, *Wizardry & Wild Romance* 59), adventure writers Talbot Mundy and H. Rider Haggard, and the classics of Shakespeare and the 19th century Norwegian playwright Henrik Ibsen ("Fafhrd and Me" 127). This confluence of diverse influences resulted in a style and feel that is uniquely Leiber. If the Conan stories are strongly marked by a feverish intensity and a blood-and-thunder gallop, the hallmark of Fafhrd and the Gray Mouser tales are their irony and sardonic wit. At the apex of "The Lords of Quarmall," the would-be heir to the throne Gwaay marshals his forces for a counter-offensive with a heroic salutation: "The time has come for sorcery and swords!" One would here expect the action to elevate to typical sword-and-sorcery bombast, but Leiber undercuts the moment with a sick bird weakly chirping defiance. At the conclusion of "The Two Best Thieves in Lankhmar," Fafhrd and the Gray Mouser—whom we naturally assume are the "two best thieves" in the city—are outwitted by a pair of the *actual* best thieves, who happen to be a pair of women. Occasional sword-and-sorcery critic S.T. Joshi argues that the subtle, playful tone of the Fafhrd and the Gray Mouser stories place them closer to the postmodern novel than heroic epic. "While the Fafhrd and the Gray Mouser stories might seem like harmless excursions into literary and historical nostalgia, their very lightness of tone—frequently highlighted by sardonic humor and self-parody—betray a modern consciousness that has little in common with the lofty bombast of the heroic fantasy tradition ("Science and Superstition" 117–118).

But the Fafhrd and Gray Mouser stories are not glutted with slapstick humor or self-mockery. Though an admirer of Cabell's *Jurgen*, Leiber maintained a stronger allegiance for full-blooded heroes, like Talbot Mundy's Tros of Samothrace. "Perhaps Cabell wanted to stir us not to give in as easily as Jurgen did. In this he succeeds. For me, give me sword and sorcery, not lancet and disillusionment!" ("Tittivated Romance" 203). Leiber was deeply versed in Norse mythology, including the Elder Edda, as well as Greek mythology and the great Shakespearian tragedies ("Fafhrd and Me" 129). From these wellsprings a dark pessimism occasionally surfaces in his writings. In and amongst their rollicking adventures Fafhrd and the Gray Mouser suffer great tragedies and staggering disillusionment. In the origin story "The Unholy Grail" we're introduced to the Gray Mouser as a young apprentice to the wizard Glavas Rho, a lover of nature and practitioner of white magic. Studying alongside the Mouser is the young girl Ivrian, for whom he feels the first stirrings of a young love. But in a bout of weakness and fear, Ivrian leads a band of executioners to the home of the wizard. Glavas Rho is murdered, his home put to the torch. The Mouser's cheerfully optimistic self is swept away, "burned in one sudden swift holocaust," after which he views life as "the hub of a wheel on which men are broken" ("The Unholy

Grail" 89-90). He embarks on a mission of revenge that leads him
to spurn Glavas Rho's teachings and embrace black sorcery, a power
augmented by the forces of fear and hate. He changes his name
from the playful "Mouse" to the sinister, predatory Gray Mouser,
symbolic of his newly adopted mercenary/amoral outlook on life.
Fafhrd's youth is likewise marked by tragedy: his father is slain
by the women of his own tribe due to his wanderlust, and Fafhrd
flees his homeland, never to return. Perhaps as a consequence of
the absence of family the pair become loners, uncomfortable save
in each other's company, and unable to settle down, galled by the
city and restless amid the lonely stretches of Nehwon's wilderness.
Tragedy continues to dog the pair, who lose their first loves, Vlana
and Ivrian, to a gruesome form of assassination intended for the
men. Gripped by loathing and self-disgust they flee "the great and
glamorous city that was now loathsome to them ... a city of beloved,
unfaceable ghosts" ("Ill Met in Lankhmar" 170).

Swords Against Death opens with the two heroes consumed with
existential despair after the death of their female companions.
Striding out of the gates of the cursed city of Lankhmar to which
they vow never to return, their bitterness and grief is mirrored
by the landscape around them. Leiber displays here a mastery
of metaphor:

> Ahead the sky was bright pink, like the bubbling rim of a great
> crystal goblet brimmed with effervescent red wine for delight of
> the gods, while the paler pink glow rising therefrom drove the last
> stars west. But before the sun could glare one scarlet sliver above the
> horizon, a black storm came racing out of the north over the Inner
> Sea—a sea-squall making landfall. It grew almost as dark again as
> night, except when the lightning stabbed and the thunder shook his
> great iron shield. ("The Circle Curse" 9.)

Leiber used his stories not only to tell entertaining adventures
but to offer social and political commentary and critique. In "Lean
Times in Lankhmar," Fafhrd loses himself in the fringe Lankmarian
god Issek of the Jug, and through devotion and asceticism elevates
the all-but forgotten god to near-canonical status. But in so doing
Fafhrd loses his sense of humor, his subtlety, and ultimately himself.
Religion fails to provide purpose, and instead is just another tool
in the scramble for physical and spiritual capital. At the end of the
series Fafhrd and the Gray Mouser take up residence on Rime Isle,
a peaceful new habitation whose populace is now happily atheist.
In stories like "The Mouser Goes Below," Leiber addresses the mat-
uration and aging of the pair of sword-and-sorcery heroes, who are
now no longer confronted with issues of immediate life and death at
swordpoint, but old grudges held by former adversaries and vengeful

gods, which crop up like chronic diseases. These latter stories lack the headlong dash of Leiber's early material, but are rich with metaphors of aging, the need for family and legacy, and the struggle to find order, purpose, and meaning in the jumble of disparate events that constitute a life. Collected in *Swords and Ice Magic* (1977) and the *Knight and Knave of Swords* (1988), these quieter adventures form the conclusion of the series, written when Leiber himself was much older and nearing the end of his own writing career.

Leiber employs a skillful and deliberate duality/doubling in his stories, driving the action forward with the friction of opposing forces: barbarism vs. civilization, tradition vs. change, religion vs. reason, and life vs. death. In the Fafhrd and the Gray Mouser tales, the struggle of barbarism vs. civilization is more equivocal than in Howard. Whereas the latter declared that "civilization was just a whim of circumstance, and barbarism must ultimately triumph," it's unclear in Leiber which is in the ascendency. Fafhrd and the Gray Mouser experience the simultaneous allure of the decadent city, and repulsion from its more unsavory elements. The wilderness of Newhon offers clean air and a welcome relief from the grimy city streets and corrupt economy of Lankhmar, but also harsh, unforgiving wastes that test the endurance. Newhon's barbaric cultures are burdened with superstition and hidebound tradition, but its civilized city-dwellers engage in duplicity and double-dealings.

Leiber's "The Snow Women" (first publication *Fantastic* magazine, April 1970) is an extended dialectic on the civilization vs. barbarism debate. Here Fafhrd is just 18 years of age, on the cusp of becoming a man. Though he hasn't reached his full physical maturity, he's unnaturally tall, strong, and a spectacular climber, very much like a young Conan. Although a product of an uncouth culture, he's also smart, inquisitive, and intensely interested in civilization and the wider world. But stifling tradition and morality rule his tribe. The Snow Clan is a matriarchal society; men are the warriors and family leaders, but the women are the real power behind the throne and staunch, conservative enforcers of clan rule. Men who break the rules are punished with hard-thrown balls of ice and snow, or worse. Years prior Fafhrd's father was slain by his own wife, Mor, who summoned a deadly ice storm as he strove with the cliffs of the mountain White Fang during a fit of wanderlust. The snow-women symbolize the calcifying customs necessary to maintain these barbaric traditions and social order; their very name implies a cold, hard rigidity, and the ice and snow of the northern wastes serve as metaphor for conservative, custom-bound tribe rule.

Fafhrd chafes under the rule of the matriarchs and longs for the warmer, civilized lands of the south. "A whole world calls and have we eyes only for Cold Corner?" he asks his partner, Mara. Fafhrd's mother is appalled by her son's yearnings to experience the wider world:

> But you have inherited threefold your father's secretiveness along with his urge to neglect his family and indulge himself in useless adventurings. Except that in you the sickness takes a more repulsive form. Cold mountaintops were his mistresses, while you are drawn to civilization, that putrid festering of the hot south, where there is no natural stern cold to punish the foolish and luxurious and to see that the decencies are kept. ("The Snow Women" 52).

Mor blunts Fafhrd's wanderlust with the threat of an icy blast. The corpse of Fafhrd's father, buried in the earth under his family's tent, is a chilling reminder of his fate should he choose to flee, but also foreshadows his eventual end should Fafhrd remain in the cage of custom. Though mated to Mara, Fafhrd develops an obsession for the beautiful dancer Vlana. She represents the Other, a tantalizing glimpse of a world beyond Fafhrd's cold corner of the map. When Fafhrd makes the decision to enter Vlana's tent he encounters a gateway to the exotic in its complicated lashings: "The knot joining the lacings of its doorway was hidden in shadow and felt complex and foreign." The knot foils him and he is forced to enter the tent on this belly like a snake, foreshadowing the dirty compromises that must be made in dealings with the civilized world. Though she welcomes him in, Vlana warns Fafhrd, "As for civilization, it stinks" (56).

As in Howard, Leiber's cities are places of culture and wonder, but beneath the veneer of finery lurks darkness and corruption. If the barbaric villages of the wasteland suppress individuality through isolation and tradition, cities are nests of corruption and decadence in which nothing is sacred. Most of their inhabitants toil in hard labor until they expire, save for those fortunate enough to inherit wealth, or murder or steal to obtain it. In "The Lords of Quarmall," the slave-girl Ivivis tells the Gray Mouser, "Here in the lower levels we are buried before we are born. We live, love, and die buried. Even when we strip, we yet wear a garment of invisible mold." Civilized success "requires a low cunning, a smirching of yourself as civilization is smirched ... a calculated evil." The Mouser realizes that in cities "cash is all-powerful, the idol placed highest, whether one sweat, thieve, grind others down, or scheme for it." Even after surviving a near-death experience in Quarmall the Mouser experiences an overpowering urge to return; only when a fortuitous bend in the road obscures its towers is its powerful spell broken.

> "Up again, Fafhrd, and whip up!" he cried. "This Quarmall is a cunninger witch than I guessed. If we waste time by the way, I fear for our freedom and our souls ("The Lords of Quarmall" 187).

When the duo spend too long in cities they surface like a drowning man, gasping from the reek for the open air and expanse of the wilderness, treacherous though it may be. The mountain Stardock, for all its sheer cliffs and the deadly indifference of its fickle, quick-to-turn weather, is beautiful and pure. After barely surviving its perils, Fafhrd gazes longingly at the mountain and refers to her as a "gallant lady." But the wilderness is no simple restorative balm. Old Nehwon—that which exists outside the cities and the civilizations springing up in Rime Isle and elsewhere—is actively hostile toward man. Its old gods seek to arrest or reverse mankind's "progress." In "The Seven Black Priests," Fafhrd warns the Mouser: "Those who truly worship Nehwon guard its mountain-wounds and wait and pray for the great day of fulfillment when Nehwon shall wake again, this time in man's form, and rid itself of the vermin called men" ("The Seven Black Priests" 168).

And so Fafhrd and the Gray Mouser are at a standstill: civilization balanced against barbarism, tradition against freedom, individuality and progress opposed by conformity and compromise. How can one break free? What is the moral center of Leiber's universe, if not barbarism's stifling traditions, or civilization's decadent freedoms? Perhaps friendship and loyalty. Fafhrd and the Gray Mouser's bonds of friendship endure when other institutions fail. Fafhrd's father instructs his son in the virtues "of courage, of honor, or prudence, of thoughtfulness in giving and punctilio in keeping your word, of following your heart, of setting and unswervingly striving toward a high, romantic goal, of self-honesty in all these things but especially in recognizing your aversions and desires," and his son carries them in his heart. Leiber's writings exalt honor, integrity, and living the examined life.

The ultimate end is death, which robs men of their agency. Death paradoxically gives meaning to existence, and impetus to action. The threat of death is finally the force that sets Fafhrd in motion, allowing him to break away from his clan. "Death no longer stood at his side. Death had stepped inside him. It was Death's feet that were lashed to the skis. ... His skis had thrust, Fafhrd told himself, not he. His skis, that had their own life, Death's life, and were carrying him on a doomful journey" ("The Snow Women" 91). Free from the clan's clutches, Fafhrd exalts at the thought of exploring the eight cities of the North, but Vlana counters that the eight warm-clime cities of the South also await. Life is navigated by straddling its contradictions and playing them off one another in a propulsive Hegelian dialectic, not settling on one source of incorruptible truth.

Along with Fafhrd and the Gray Mouser, Leiber created a distinctive supporting cast of memorable characters, including the garrulous Ningauble of the Seven Eyes and impenetrable Sheelba of the Eyeless Face. His secondary world of Nehwon and its cities, thieves' guilds, diverse cultures, and pantheons and gods and demigods, stands as an enduring work of the imagination. But more than his fantastic creations Leiber's greatest achievement was bringing to sword-and-sorcery a level of literary sophistication not seen before or since. His sharp insights into the human condition produced a high and uncommon art, transcending genre fiction. As Lovecraft wrote to Leiber, then a promising young artist about to set out on what would become a remarkable writing career:

> Certainly, you have produced a remarkably fine & distinctive bit of cosmic fantasy in a vein which is, for all the Cabellian or Beckfordian comparisons, essentially your own. The basic element of allegory, the earthiness & closeness to human nature, & the curious blending of worldly lightness with the strange & the macabre, all harmonise adequately & seem to express a definite mood & personality. The result is an authentic work of art—& I certainly hope it can eventually get published somewhere even though its genre makes it the hardest conceivable sort of thing to place. (*Fritz Leiber and H.P. Lovecraft: Writers of the Dark* 40)

Michael Moorcock (b. 1939)

Not content to stand there, shuffling uneasily beneath its threadbare sword and sorcery banner, Moorcock's prose instead took the whole stagnant genre by its throat and pummeled it into a different shape, transmuted Howard's blustering overcompensation and the relatively tired and bloodless efforts of Howard's competitors into a new form, a delirious romance with different capabilities, delivered in a language that was adequate to all the tumult and upheaval of its times, a voice that we could recognize.
—Alan Moore, "Foreword," *Elric: The Stealer of Souls*

For Michael Moorcock, reading was not an indulgence, but rather a serious pursuit of truth and meaning. Even as a youth he turned over authors' words like a scientist searching for evidence, rejecting those he deemed unsound. Rarely did he treat his omnivorous literary diet—detective thrillers, science fiction, fantasy, and traditional literary fiction—with ambivalence. About as close as he came to unequivocal embrace of an author's works was Edgar Rice Burroughs, whose action-packed stories of interplanetary strangeness and romance would later inform his first attempts at fiction. Moorcock went on to write Burroughs pastiche in a self-published fanzine, *Burrougsania,* as well as the British weekly magazine *Tarzan Adventures* (Moorcock, *Elric: The Stealer of Souls* xxii).

By the early 1960s, Moorcock began a rigorous exploration of fantasy and science fiction, turning a critical eye on its most beloved, bedrock works (Scroggins 16). No authors were sacred cows.

Once deeply taken with Robert E. Howard's raw storytelling talent and exotic landscapes, Moorcock came to see Conan as a brute, and Howard's views on history and humanity, particularly his disdain for civilization, distasteful. "Over a period of time following almost exactly the period in which I was writing the first Elric stories, I was inclined to distance myself from the work of Robert E. Howard, even though he had been an important influence" (*Elric: The Stealer of Souls* xxii–xxiii). As for J.R.R. Tolkien, who by this time was experiencing a meteoric rise to fame with *The Lord of the Rings*, Moorcock developed a feeling of antipathy. Where many readers fell under the spell of Tolkien's powerful secondary world of Middle-Earth, Moorcock was disenchanted with what he perceived as *The Lord of the Rings*' nursery-rhyme language, its embrace of a conservative, backwards-looking political stance, and its artificial cheat of a happy ending. His essay "Epic Pooh," originally published in 1978, skewered Tolkien, C.S. Lewis, and Richard Adams (author of *Watership Down*) for, among other perceived offenses, writing the equivalent of coddling, consolatory, nursery-room tales for grownups, stories that reinforced the paternalism of the establishment:

> I suppose I respond so antipathetically to Lewis and Tolkien because I find this sort of consolatory Christianity distasteful, a fundamentally misanthropic doctrine. ... It is moderation which ruins Tolkien's fantasy and causes it to fail as a genuine romance. ... *The Lord of the Rings* is much more deep-rooted in its infantilism than a good many of the more obviously juvenile books it influenced. It is Winnie-the-Pooh posing as an epic (126–127).

As he entered his late teens and early 20s, even Burroughs' blood-pumping tales of Tarzan and John Carter of Mars began to lose their charm for Moorcock, who was by now distancing himself from pastiche and beginning to write his own original material—and with greater literary aspirations. As the 1960s began, he channeled himself into a new speculative literature fomented by the decade's spirit of rebellion. Already a successful genre fiction and comic-strip writer, Moorcock was hired to edit the British science-fiction magazine *New Worlds* from 1964–1971, and again from 1976–1996. At *New Worlds* he championed a "New Wave" of young science fiction writers who were striving for something much different than the works of the established "Golden Age" authors of the 1930s–1950s. He also applied his authorial talents to fantasy stories that deliberately broke away from the genre's respectable older dons. Moorcock had by this time discovered the works of Fritz Leiber, James Branch Cabell, Fletcher Pratt, and Mervyn Peake, in particular the latter's acclaimed novels *Gormenghast* and *Titus Groan* (Moorcock, *Elric: The Stealer of Souls* xxiv). Their influence began to coalesce in his fiction.

Other influences included the ancient Finnish hero Kullervo of the epic *Kalevala*; Poul Anderson and in particular his *The Broken Sword*; Monseiur Zenith the Albino, a villain from the Sexton Blake detective stories by Anthony Skene; and *The Threepenny Opera* by Bertolt Brecht. Emerging from these diverse influences was the figure of Elric of Melnibone, a sickly, drug-dependent albino warrior/sorcerer, and reluctant emperor of the Ruby Throne. The Elric stories ushered in a fantastic revolution to sword-and-sorcery, the first hero written in deliberate reaction against Howard and his powerful, action-oriented, and sure-of-purpose Conan of Cimmeria. "Elric, to put it simply, is the anti-Conan, the dark underside to the healthy and hygienic barbarism the Cimmerian embodies" (Scroggins 25).

Although a deliberate departure from Conan, Elric is nevertheless of the sword-and-sorcery genre. Published as stand-alone short stories, most appearing in the British magazine *Science Fantasy*, nearly all the Elric stories up to the series-concluding "Stormbringer" are loosely-connected, episodic adventures in which Elric serves as a mercenary, or battles exotic monsters and explores forgotten cities on personal missions of revenge. The stories are told in a swashbuckling, brisk pace, with exotic landscapes and pulpy feel reminiscent of the sword-and-planet stories of Leigh Brackett and Burroughs' Tarzan. With his propensity for dark brooding on the meaninglessness of the universe, and the dead-end of a life spent in wealth and stature-seeking, Elric shares much in common with Kull, Howard's Atlantean king and predecessor to Conan. He is also an outsider, and while he's the latest in a long line of Melnibonean emperors—the 428th, to be exact—he's a reluctant inheritor of the throne, and loathes many of his cultures' inhuman traditions. By 1963 Moorcock was using the term "sword and sorcery" to describe the Elric stories (*Elric: The Stealer of Souls* 437-438).

In the early 1960s a few critics accused Moorcock of creating a Conan clone (Moorcock, *Elric: The Stealer of Souls* 451).[4] But this criticism ignores Moorcock's significant departures and innovations. The Elric stories often blur the lines between sword-and-sorcery and high fantasy, particularly in "Stormbringer," the concluding book of the original six-volume saga. Its events are epic in scale, with the fate of the earth hanging in the balance of a titanic battle of the Lords of Chaos and the Lords of Law. Elric seems to be a pawn in a struggle of larger forces, caught up in a web of fate. Just prior to the events of "Stormbringer," Elric declares to his wife, Zarozinia, "I'm

---

[4] Ironically, Moorcock's impetus for the Elric stories was a request of *Science Fantasy* editor E.J. Carnell for "some Conan-type stuff." Moorcock was relieved to find that that Carnell didn't want actual Conan pastiche, but something in the sword-and-sorcery line (Scroggins 24).

tired of swords and sorcery"—quite possibly a deliberate, metafictional tweak of the subgenre he was about to subvert.

Prior to "The Dreaming City" (*Science Fantasy*, June 1961), most
sword-and-sorcery authors had depicted magic as transgressive,
an alien presence against which its sword-wielding protagonists
must fight. While magic is dark, dangerous, and unpredictable in
the Melnibonean universe and its multiverses, and often incurs a
great physical toll on its caster, Elric harnesses its chaotic energies
and wields it, successfully, against his enemies. Sorcery is typically
of last resort to Elric in the early tales, but as the series progresses
he draws upon it in increasingly larger (and increasingly self-de-
structive) doses, much like a drug addict on a downward spiral
of addiction.

The Elric stories subvert the sword-and-sorcery stereotype of the
muscular, powerful hero. Without access to a regular dose of powerful drugs to replenish his thin blood, Elric is unable to function.
His demonic sword Stormbringer is unpredictable, barely within his
control, and at times acts in opposition to Elric's wishes (or so we
are led to believe), turning on its wielder in terrible and increasingly
unpredictable ways. According to Moorcock, Elric's cursed blade is
a symbol of our species' tendency to rely on physical and mental
crutches and support systems, rather than attacking and curing a
weakness at its source (Moorcock, *Elric: The Stealer of Souls* 447). Elric
is a deliberate echo of the doomed Finnish folk hero Kullervo, who
like Elric wields an intelligent magic sword that ultimately claims
his own life. Moorcock was also greatly taken with Poul Anderson's
sword-and-sorcery novel *The Broken Sword* (1954) in which the hero
Skafloc must undertake a quest to reforge the eponymous broken
sword, a weapon of terrible demonic power that demands blood each
time it is drawn and ultimately turns on its wielder.

The incredibly ancient sorcerer-race of Melnibone is utterly amoral,
living by the maxim "seek pleasure however you would" (Moorcock,
The Elric Saga Part I 73). They take their pleasure in drug-fueled
dream-ventures for knowledge, whetting their sexual appetites with
polyamorous encounters, ruthless martial conquests of the outer
lands, and in the exquisitely drawn-out torture of their enemies.
Though of the Melnibonean race, Elric is an aberration, convicted
with the idea that "mankind's wish-fulfillments" (i.e., its artifices
of culture and religion) are not only lies, but are a dangerous form
of pseudo-knowledge capable of inflicting great damage (Moorcock,
Elric: The Stealer of Souls 450-451). He sits on the throne uneasily, troubled by a conscience which allows him to see his fellow Melniboneans
in all their cruelty, pride, and avarice. His moral compass cries out
for rebellion. Most of his subjects including his cousin Yrkoon view

him as an ineffectual ruler, and he has the same view of himself: Elric despises his "weakness" and conflicted thoughts, and wishes he could serve as a cold, merciless emperor like his forefathers. He agonizes, "What I have done has, in the main, been foolish, destructive, and with little point. Yrkoon was right to despise me, and that was why I hated him so" (Moorcock, *The Elric Saga Part I* 62).

Overarching the war of individual freedoms vs. societal and political order is a larger "eternal struggle" of Law vs. Chaos. These two forces are not the equivalent of good and evil, as each encompasses many shades of gray. "Chaos is disorder, but it is also life-giving change, evolution; Law is boundary and regularity, but it is also enforced conformity, the suppression of vitality and creativity" (Scroggins 29). Each cannot exist without the other, and the eternal struggle ensures that they and the universe remain in balance. Law and Chaos manifest as actual gods and goddesses, but also as concepts warring within the hearts of men. An adherent to Chaos, whose personal deity is the archduke Arioch, Elric nevertheless finds himself fighting on the side of Law, since a total victory for Chaos will mean mayhem, destruction, and the ending of the world. Yet Law without Chaos is not the answer, as society's laws and traditions are often unjust and stultifying. The struggle is bitter, and Elric often questions if it's worth fighting:

> What was thought, he asked himself, what was emotion? What was control and was it worth achieving? Better, maybe, to live by instinct, than to theorize and be wrong; better to remain the puppet of the gods, letting them move you this way and that at their pleasure than to seek control of your own fate, clash with the will of the Lords of the Higher Worlds and perish for your pains (Moorcock, "Stormbringer" 365).

Moorcock wove into Elric's universe the ancient Norse concept of "wyrd," or fate, in which the lives of men are in a sense pre-destined. In the Norse tradition, powerful goddesses known as the Norns weave the fabric of a man's fate, and at some appointed time cut the threads. But being under the umbrella of one's "wyrd" does not assume an absence of free will; mankind maintains some control over his destiny in a complex interplay of fate and self-determination. In "The Sailor on the Seas of Fate," Elric boards a strange ship that moves between the worlds. Its captain is nameless and blind, yet his hand is on the tiller—he both controls fate, yet cannot see its ends. Explains the demigod Sepiriz to Elric, "Fate, as I told you, is our master, and Fate has wrought a fabric for this earth which would be hard to alter. But it *could* be altered and we are entrusted to see that Fate is not cheated" (Moorcock, *Elric: The Stealer of Souls* 256). Elric is able to alter the fate of the world through the exertion of his will, but is also manipulated by the universe's higher powers, and demonstrates an increasing reliance on demons and eventually Arioch himself for aid. The deeper his quests to find his origins and the source of spiritual conflict with his Melnibonean ancestors, the more he is forced to act Melnibonean, and less human. To end the reign of the Chaos Lords, Elric summons the Lords of Law for a final apocalyptic battle that will allow a new age of Law to take root. But Elric's sword, Stormbringer, has other ideas. It lives on after the final battle, a corruption, ensuring that man's baser instincts to possess and dominate will continue into this next age. This is Moorcock's dark, fatally flawed vision of humanity: there is no truth, no golden age (in the past or in the future) whose truths we can discover or whose promise we await, but only the eternal struggle. Moorcock delivers the full measure of tragedy in the concluding pulpy tragedy of the Elric Saga, the short novel "Stormbringer." We are all doomed to die, and this doom is stronger than the will. All that we love— our creations, our friends, and ultimately, ourselves—cannot avoid immolation. The best we can hope for is the rest of equilibrium, to which Moorcock gives tangible form in the elusive city of Tanelorn. "Tanelorn will always exist while men exist," says the hermit at the conclusion of *The Bane of the Black Sword.* "It was not a city you defended today. It was an ideal. That is Tanelorn."

Moorcock admitted that the Elric stories were in some sense a self-examination, a vehicle to work out his own obsessions and problems (*Elric: The Stealer of Souls* 442). For example, the Elric stories have applicability to Moorcock's native land of England. The Melnibonean empire can be seen as an allegory of post World War II Britain, once strong but clearly on the decline and rapidly fading into yesteryear, its footprint on the world significantly diminished and vulnerable to the rise of young kingdoms. Just as many modern Britons question the county's long history of brutal colonialism, Elric is uneasy with Melnibone's long history of conquest and subjugation, and feels ill at ease in its city of spires. The Melnibonean landscape is dotted with ancient, once-proud cities now in decay or in ruins, much like the blasted buildings left by the Nazi blitz through which a young Moorcock wandered in the early 1940s (Moorcock, *Wizardry and Wild Romance,* 205). The chaotic, twisted landscape of Melnibone may also be a homage to Moorcock's love of Gothic fiction, whose crumbling castles and mansions "symboliz(ed) and even explain(ed) the anxiety felt by those who witnessed radical changes in the world they knew" (36). Filling the void left by these failing institutions are the Young Kingdoms, which honor individuality over hierarchical institutions and free thinking over conformity. The Young Kingdoms in a sense represent America, a country to which Moorcock later immigrated (and still lives, in rural Texas).

Moorcock experimented with innovative concepts that today are well-known and well-worn fantasy tropes. These include the pseudo-scientific concept of a "multiverse," or multiple universes existing concurrently on different planes of existence, accessible by sorcerous portals. He also pioneered the concept of the Eternal Champion, a hero who appears in various times, places, and universes in very different physical forms, fighting to restore the cosmic balance between law and chaos. "The Sailor on the Seas of Fate" introduces readers to the three eternal champions Erekose, Corum, and Hawkmoon, while Elric is a fourth. The Eternal Champions are destined for some great end, perhaps preordained.

Moorcock wrote a significant portion of the Elric stories as a young man not yet at the height of his literary powers, and many were written in a white-hot pace for reasons of financial expediency (Scroggins 8). As a result, they suffer stylistically when compared to Leiber's best Fafhrd and the Gray Mouser stories, and Howard's better material. Nevertheless, the imaginative concepts they introduced, their genre-bending elements, and the conflicted, self-loathing, doomed character of Elric, place them in a category above most other sword-and-sorcery published before or since. And they represent only a small sliver of Moorcock's literary output. He would go on to write science fiction, literary fiction, and return to fantasy with his "Eternal Champion" series of books, featuring the likes of Dorian Hawkmoon, Erekose, and Corum. Moorcock is also a critic and essayist of some repute, with his collection *Wizardry and Wild Romance: A Study of Epic Fantasy* perhaps his best known work of non-fiction. But Elric remains Moorcock's greatest creation, and he would return to the character again and again over his lengthy writing career, including an Elric trilogy in the first decade of the 21st century—*The Dreamthief's Daughter* (2001), *The Skrayling Tree* (2003), and *The White Wolf's Son* (2005)—and the short story "Red Pearls" for the 2010 sword-and-sorcery anthology *Swords and Dark Magic*.

A New Saga Begins: Conan and the Lancers

Sword-and-sorcery did not disappear with the demise of *Weird Tales* and the death of the pulp magazines. It continued to be published in the 1950s, principally in digest-sized magazines and in particular *Avon Fantasy Reader* (1946–1952), *The Magazine of Fantasy and Science Fiction* (1949–present), and *Fantastic* (1952–1980). After *Weird Tales*, *Fantastic* is arguably the most important historic vehicle for sword-and-sorcery, publishing writers such as Leiber and Moorcock as well as L. Sprague de Camp, Lin Carter, and John Jakes. Hillman Periodical, Inc. published the first works of a young author who worked effortlessly across the genres of science fiction and fantasy/sword-and-sorcery—Jack Vance (1916–2013), who gained fame with the publication of his collection of "Dying Earth" stories starting in 1950.

Sword-and-sorcery also began to see print in limited hardcover editions. Specialty press Arkham House published the first volume of collected Howard stories with *Skull-Face and Others* in 1946. Arkham House also published a limited collection (some 3,000 copies) of Leiber's fiction, *Night's Black Agents*, in 1947, which included two tales of Fafhrd and the Gray Mouser. A decade later Gnome Press published a great deal more of Leiber with the volume "Two Sought Adventure" (1957), a hardcover edition consisting entirely of Fafhrd and the Gray Mouser stories, limited to approximately 4,000 copies.

In 1950 L. Sprague de Camp, an author of science fiction and cynical, ironic fantasy stories, discovered Howard in the Gnome Press hardcover *Conan the Conqueror* (de Camp, "Editing Conan" 113). It was a relatively late find for the then 43-year-old de Camp, who had not read Howard in the pages of *Weird Tales*. Reading Howard opened de Camp's mind to a new style of fantasy fiction. Howard channeled an earnest, romantic brand of sword-and-sorcery, and de Camp acknowledged their power and appeal even if he could not fully identify with them. De Camp pursued his newfound interest with dogged determination, tracking down old copies of uncollected Howard stories in *Weird Tales* and obtaining unpublished Howard manuscripts (114). De Camp lightly revised these and offered them up for publication in the magazines *Fantasy Fiction* and *Space Science Fiction* in 1952 and 1953 (Carter, *Imaginary Worlds* 135) before setting his sights on loftier goals. Around this time de Camp offered his services as Conan editor to Gnome Press, with whom he was already a contracted author. Over the next five years de Camp edited—and, in a move that would prove controversial and divisive, rewrote four non-Conan Howard stories, which were published as tales of the Cimmerian—for the volume *Tales of Conan*. After Gnome published *Conan the Conquerer* (a retitled version of Howard's novella "Hour of the Dragon") and a second volume, *The Sword of Conan*, Howard's literary agent Oscar Friend approached de Camp to help prepare additional Howard short stories for publication in the series. By the third volume, *King Conan*, de Camp had assumed principal editorship (Sammon, *Conan the Phenomenon* 34) and began to intermingle "posthumous collaborations" and wholesale pastiche among Howard's originals. The sixth volume in the series, *Tales of Conan* (1955), was 100% non-Howard pastiche, and the seventh and final volume, *The Return of Conan* (1957), was a full-length pastiche novel written by little-known author Bjorn Nyberg. The Gnome Press series proved moderately successful from a financial perspective (35).

At this time, the science-fiction and fantasy publishing business was undergoing a profound transformation. Magazines saw a sharp downturn beginning in the early 1950s, as potential readers began to gravitate toward the "glass teat" of the television screen. In June 1957, the largest magazine distributing company, American News Company, ceased operations (Del Rey, *The World of Science Fiction, 1926–1976* 195). Outside of a few western and mysteries, pulp magazines—the principal vehicle for sword-and-sorcery—had vanished from the scene.[5] But in the 1950s and 60s a new, cheap, readily available medium arrived in the U.S. that would return sword-and-sorcery to its previous heights, and even surpass its 1930s heyday: the mass-market paperback. Paperbacks did not require a customer to commit to a subscription. They could be bought cheaply, and saw wide distribution in wire spinning racks in bookstores and drugstores across the United States. Even more than the benefits afforded to the consumer, they were a great business model for publishers, who could produce large print runs for a fraction of the cost of hardcovers. In fantasy and science fiction, the paperback boom began in 1952 when publisher Donald A. Wollheim left Avon to found Ace Books, which found a successful formula packaging two novels together "tete-beche" style, meaning that the "front" of said book would contain the title of one novel and its own artwork, and the reverse side featured a cover for a second title (Liptak, "Donald Wollheim and the Ace Double Novel"). These became known among fans and collectors as the "Ace Double." One of the earliest of the Ace Doubles featured Robert E. Howard's *Conan the Conquerer* and Leigh Brackett's sword and planet romance *The Sword of Rhiannon*, published jointly in a single volume in December 1953. Wollheim would later add to his legacy the distinction of publishing the first-ever stand-alone sword-and-sorcery novel, Lin Carter's *The Wizard of Lemuria*, in 1965 (Richardson).

By the early 1960s, sales of paperback books had eclipsed their hardcover counterparts (Liptak, "The Rise of the Paperback Novel"). Publishers scrambled to meet the demand with genre titles of every category. The likes of Ace, Avon, Ballantine, Bantam, Dell, Macmillan, and others found a winning formula in men's adventure fiction—war novels, spy novels, westerns, and the like—and began to turn them out at a rapid rate, as quickly as authors could write them. Publishers needed to find new niches in an increasingly

---

[5] For an excellent account of the troubles facing magazines and pulps at this time, see *The World of Science Fiction*, 1926–1976, by Lester del Rey.

crowded, competitive marketplace. The dramatic success of Tolkien's *The Lord of the Rings*, published in a mass-market three-volume paperback edition, opened eyes to the possibility of fantasy fiction and sword-and-sorcery.

After Gnome went bankrupt in 1962, de Camp secured the rights to the Conan stories, and in 1964 approached Lancer books with a deal to republish them in paperback form. In 1966, Lancer published the first of an eventual twelve-volume series known as the Conan Saga. Using the blueprint established at Gnome Press, de Camp used notes, aborted story attempts and fragments, and unpublished Howard stories in the possession of Oscar Friend, and repurposed them, creating additional stories of the Cimmerian. De Camp also wrote his own stories to fill in what he considered gaps in Conan's career, and performed whole-cloth conversions of other Howard stories—even ones set in relatively modern times—into tales featuring the Cimmerian. "By means of simple substitution, guns became swords, and so on" (Finn, *Blood & Thunder* 236).

Aiding de Camp in this effort was a young and sword-and-sorcery author just emerging on the scene. Lin Carter had established his sword-and-sorcery credentials when he sent de Camp a draft of a brisk barbarian tale eventually published as *A Wizard of Lemuria* (1965). Carter was later asked to edit some of Howard's unpublished stories and fragments for Lancer, published as *King Kull,* as well as for Dell, published as *Bran Mak Morn*. His successes on these books led to de Camp bringing him on to complete and edit the Lancer Conan Saga. De Camp by then had also managed to acquire additional Howard Conan material, mainly unfinished fragments unearthed by Howard's new literary agent, Glenn Lord. This material would also go into the Lancer books, edited and finished by Carter (Sammon, *Conan the Phenomenon* 43).

While the content of the Lancer Conan Saga had undeniable appeal, the books themselves needed something additional to distinguish them in increasingly crowded wire-spinner racks. Publishers at this time were beginning to use the most garish art imaginable to vie for consumer attention in a sort of paperback cover "arms race."[6] Frank Frazetta (1928–2010) was a fantastic artist of wide renown, with credits ranging from popular and science-fiction, horror, and fantasy magazines (*Mad Magazine, Creepy*, and *Eerie*, among others) to comic books, comic strips, and movie posters. But his work on the Lancer Conans—Frazetta would illustrate eight of the twelve covers—catapulted him into stardom. His cover art for the 1966

---

[6] For an entertaining account and pictorial of this phenomenon, see *Paperbacks from Hell: The Twisted History of 70's and 80's Horror Fiction.*

Lancer *Conan the Adventurer*—featuring a muscular, bare-torsoed Conan atop a pile of corpses and skulls, with a near-nude, curvaceous female clinging to his lower leg—remains the definitive visual representation of Howard's character. Later Frazetta was commissioned to paint covers for reissues of Edgar Rice Burroughs' Tarzan novels, as well as the 1970s sword-and-sorcery works of Karl Edward Wagner. It's hard to overstate the impact Frazetta's art had and continues to have on sword-and-sorcery and the broader fantasy genre. His muscular images turned readers on to more authors than just Howard; Mark Scroggins, author of *Michael Moorcock: Fiction, Fantasy and the World's Pain*, admits to having picked up Moorcock's *The Silver Warriors* (Dell, 1977) while on a Frazetta artwork purchasing spree. This latter cover included an image of a muscular warrior drawn through the snow on a chariot drawn by four polar bears and turned Scroggins into a lifelong reader of Moorcock (5).

The Lancer Conan Saga proved wildly popular. While sales figures are somewhat contradictory, series contributor Lin Carter stated that some three million copies of the Lancer Conans were in circulation by 1972/73 (Carter, *Imaginary Worlds* 141–142). Another source states that the Conan Lancers ultimately sold more than 10 million copies (Sammon, *Conan the Phenomenon* 45). Arguments continue to sway back and forth over whether the author or the visual artist—Howard or Frazetta—deserves the most credit for the series' success, but in either case the Conan Saga was a runaway hit.

Today the Lancer Conan Saga is the source of much critical controversy, mainly for its literary infidelity and disregard of authorial intent. Howard wrote the original Conan stories in no particular order, merely as they came to him (or to Conan; Howard once stated that they were intended to be told from the perspective of an aged Conan later in his career) and without a formal introduction or conclusion. This did not suit the completist de Camp, who wanted a defined timeline. To make his "saga" model work, he needed additional material to fill in gaps in Conan's chronology. The Lancer Conan Saga added a complete arc and an epic air to Conan's life, taking him from youthful barbarian all the way through to aging king sailing off into the sunset in the Carter/de Camp pastiche *Conan of the Isles*. It filled in the "gaps" in Conan's career with either wholly created non-Howard material, or non-Conan Howard stories converted into tales of the Cimmerian.

The editorial alterations and additions proved to be a lightning-rod for Howard fans. Some who grew up on the popular paperbacks defended and still defend them, declaring them the best presentation of Howard's works. Others judged them as needlessly altered, hybrid bastardizations that caused considerable harm to Howard's legacy. Moorcock later described the intermingled pastiche as "mindless, silly stuff which would disgrace even a schoolboy imitator of Conan, let alone one of science fiction's most careful writers (de Camp). ... Conan was never more dead than he is in these travesties of the original stories" (*Wizardry & Wild Romance* 89-90). In *Conan the Avenger* (1968), a repackaging of the Gnome Press Nyberg novel *The Return of Conan*, a middle-aged Conan, now king of Aquilonia, embarks on a mission to save his abducted queen. Readers are treated to a nostalgia trip as he revisits his old stomping grounds as a pirate captain on the Vilayet Sea and desert chieftain of the Zuagirs. The novel is fun, and certainly fills a "gap"—Conan in middle-age, post-kingship—that many readers would have enjoyed had Howard written it. But its heavy-handed "epic" elements, including appearances (in dreamlike visions) by Conan's god Crom, indicates a general lack of understanding of Conan's fundamental character, and Howard's underlying agnosticism and existentialism. At the end of the story Conan is saved by a direct intervention from his typically *in abstentia* god, implying that he is living out some sort of divine destiny:

> "Man of Cimmeria! You are a son of Crom, and he will not let you suffer eternal damnation! You have always been true to him in your heart, and the black arts of the East shall not have your soul!" (Nyberg and de Camp 166).

Today, most serious scholars consider the publication of the Lancer/Ace Conans an important historical event in sword-and-sorcery history, but an unsuitable vehicle for preserving Howard's stories from a standpoint of textual and editorial purity. Alongside his questionable editorial decision to supplement Howard's original tales of Conan with pastiche, de Camp used the introductions to the Lancers to make grand and at times inflammatory or even inaccurate declarations about Conan, sword-and-sorcery fiction in general, and Howard the author. De Camp's curious habit of dismissing Howard as a serious writer of literary merit within the introductions to his works began with the Gnome Press hardcovers. In the introduction to 1950s *Conan the Conqueror*, John D. Clark (best known in Howard circles as the co-author of "A Probable Outline of Conan's Career," which appeared in the pages of REH fanzine *The Hyborian Age* in 1938) wrote of Howard's works, "Don't look for hidden philosophical meanings or intellectual puzzles in these yarns—they aren't there" (Herron 156). De Camp's introductions amplified Clark's dismissals. In the introduction to *Conan* (1967), de Camp infamously summed up Howard: "Although moderately successful in his work and a big, powerful man like his heroes, Howard was maladjusted to the point of psychosis" (de Camp, *Conan* 10). The Lancer Conan Saga implanted in the public mind the idea that the creator of sword-and-sorcery was an unhinged, antisocial loner. As will be demonstrated in Chapter Seven, such summary judgments of Howard and sword-and-sorcery as a whole by the likes of de Camp and Carter contributed to the genre's poor reputation among critics, and possibly served as a factor in its eventual collapse in the mid-1980s.

While the literary merits of the Lancer Conan Saga are open to justifiable debate, its commercial success is not. It created a ready market for sword-and-sorcery and opened the door for an entire generation of sword-and-sorcery authors. If *Weird Tales* was the creative nexus of sword-and-sorcery, the Lancer Conan Saga was the engine that drove it into the public consciousness and popularized it. Its commercial success opened the door to additional collections from publishers seeking to replicate the profitable formula. While this ultimately led to the publication of several derivative and poor quality Howard-inspired heroes, the mass-market paperback also provided a lucrative market for talented original authors to flourish.

The best of these were Leiber and Moorcock. Both were consciously writing in the now established Howardian sword-and-sorcery tradition, but were also original. Each created something new to expand the subgenre while still working within the parameters of sword-and-sorcery. Their works demonstrate a flexibility and malleability to the subgenre that many critics, fans, and adherents have failed to acknowledge. With an injection of terrific stories from two first-rate talents—a reawakening of the old guard in the irrepressible and approachable yet sophisticated stories of Leiber, and a talented, genre-tweaking newcomer in the iconoclastic Moorcock—coupled with the irresistible repackaging of its originator with the Lancer Conan Saga, by the mid-1960s sword-and-sorcery was ripe for a critical and commercial reawakening.

CHAPTER SIX
Renaissance

Stories such as these offer the reader the supernatural thrills of the horror story, the limitless horizons of Science Fiction, the swashbuckling adventure of the historical romance, the gory action of a war story and the savage moral code of the western.
—Eric Pendragon, "Introduction," *Savage Heroes: Tales of Sorcery & Black Magic*

As rock-and-roll reached its full flower in the 1960s and 70s, in parallel arose the halcyon days of sword-and-sorcery—a subgenre as revolutionary to traditional fantasy as Black Sabbath was to the Beatles. It was a true renaissance in every sense of the word: a time of experimentation, artists writing thrilling new stories of high adventure, pushing sword-and-sorcery in surprising new directions. It was a time of rediscovery, with young readers encountering pulp-era authors like Robert E. Howard, Clark Ashton Smith, and C.L. Moore for the first time in mass-market reprints. It was also a time of (moderate) fortune and fame for its artists. A few fortunate writers used to toiling away for rent money in small corners of fandom suddenly found themselves in the spotlight, in demand by opportunistic publishers, and signing relatively lucrative book contracts. Michael Moorcock described the abrupt transition as "something like the feelings experienced by the old black blues-singers of the late fifties who were brought from obscurity in America to England and the Continent to discover that they were heroes to the large audiences waiting to hear them. I went from having a tiny audience primarily of magazine readers to becoming a cult within a few years. Within ten years we saw books originally published in small editions and often remaindered enjoying large sales" (*Wizardry and Wild Romance* 143–144). By 1970 the demand for more sword-and-sorcery forced Moorcock to revive his doomed albino sorcerer-king, whom he had inconveniently killed off in "Stormbringer" in 1965. Death would prove no obstacle. Moorcock began producing Elric prequels, and for the first time directly for book publication, bypassing magazines (*Elric: The Sleeping Sorceress* xv-xvi). Soon Moorcock was calling his own shots, cranking out 180-page manuscripts in less than a week for $1,000 apiece (a tidy sum in 1970's dollars). "I could have asked almost any money I wanted for an Elric book" (*Elric: Duke Elric* xvii).

Lin Carter, author of the *Thongor* series of novels, experienced a similar surge in demand for his stories, driven by publishers—even those with little prior track record in science fiction and fantasy— seeking out sword-and-sorcery authors. In a review of *The Players of Hell* (Belmont Books, 1968) by David Van Arnam, a science-fiction author who hopped on the sword-and-sorcery train, Carter described the scene circa 1970 in breathless, excited tones:

> The Sword and Sorcery Boom, as can be seen here, continues and is beginning to spread rapidly. Ace's revival of Edgar Rice Burroughs and the Ace/Ballantine editions of Tolkien have tapped or developed a truly enormous market for adventure fantasy (you and I always knew it was there, but publishers have to be *shown*!) The first publisher to notice this developing market and reach for it was Lancer, with their well-timed revival of the Conan series. It continues full swing, and Lancer has gone on to bring the Elric and Dorian Hawkmoon stories into print to capitalize on the astounding popularity of Conan.
>
> Other publishers have not lagged very far behind in reaching for this booming market. The next to jump in was Paperback Library, who took over my Thongor the Lemurian series from Ace (now in its fifth volume). Then Belmont began dabbling in borderline S&S, choosing yarns with a slight frosting of science fiction, like my 1967 novel, FLAME OF IRIDAR, a fantasy laid on prehistoric Mars (of all places!). Now they have gone into straight S&S—THE PLAYERS OF HELL has not the slightest taint of Science, and it's the first of a series. At the same time Paperback Library wisely purchased Jane Gaskell's splendid Cija of Atlan trilogy—Ballantine brought the Zimiamvia books of Eddison into print—de Camp's TRITONIAN RING and Pratt's WELL OF THE UNICORN emerged in long overdue paperback editions.
>
> Now Avon has jumped into the act with Brak the Barbarian, Ace has begun printing all Fritz Leiber's Fafhrd & the Gray Mouser stories— and the end is not yet in sight! With new writers like Van Arnam entering the genre and new publishers actively seeking Sword and Sorcery, we are on the verge of an active, healthy, and continuing interest in our favorite reading matter. Evidence of this is that Signet—a publisher of little interest to the science fiction world, except for its Heinlein editions—has just signed a contract with me for a Sword and Sorcery novel. This is particularly significant when you consider that Signet buys very little science fiction, even. For them to seek out and purchase a novel of S&S when they do not have a very lively line of sf in the first place is strong indication of the boom in adventurous fantasy. (*Amra* Vol. 2 No. 52, April 1970)

As demonstrated in Chapter Five, a confluence of talent— Moorcock and Fritz Leiber—and marketing—Robert E. Howard's Conan stories, packaged with irresistible Frank Frazetta covers— set the table for sword-and-sorcery's revival. But other underlying factors, outside the subgenre, aided its rapid and widespread proliferation. One was the general popularity of post-pulp "men's adventure" stories at this time. Starting in the 1950s publishers began to produce spy, war, western, and other "male-oriented" paperbacks, with plenty of sex and violence on and in between the covers. These were often series, featuring strong, lusty, and violent recurrent characters, with titles like "Mack Bolan, The Executioner," "Nick Carter: Killmaster," and Joseph Rosenberger's "Death Merchant" series (Jackson). Sword-and-sorcery was an easy sell for publishers, who recognized in its muscular, provocative cover art a familiar and profitable totem. If publishers had any lingering doubts about the commercial viability of fantasy fiction, *The Lord of the Rings* craze of the mid-1960s put those to rest. Prior to this period, Tolkien's opus had enjoyed modest success in hardcover and had yet to reach the new popular paperback format. Exploiting a loophole in copyright laws, publisher Ace in 1965 brought to market an unauthorized three-volume paperback that quickly sold more than 100,000 copies (Liptak, "The Unauthorized Lord of the Rings"). After Ace withdrew the books under pressure from Tolkien representatives, Ballantine followed with an authorized edition in November 1966 that proved equally popular. By 1968 some three million copies of *The Lord of the Rings* had been sold (Carpenter 233-234). The western world had gone crazy for Middle-Earth and Tolkien's work had sparked a popular demand in fantasy fiction.

On the heels of the Tolkien craze came *Conan the Adventurer* (1966), kicking off the 12-volume Lancer/Ace Conan Saga series. Publishers of all sizes began to turn out their own sword-and-sorcery titles, including Ace, Berkeley Medallion Books, Daw, Dell, Lancer, Pocket Books (Simon and Shuster), Pyramid, Signet, Star, Tor, Warner Books, and Zebra Books. Fritz Leiber's Fafhrd and the Gray Mouser stories went from sporadic magazine appearances in the likes of *Unknown, Suspense, Other Worlds* and *Fantastic,* and limited edition hardcover printings, to widespread distribution in a line of paperbacks by Ace. These included a famous "swords" series *Swords and Deviltry* (1970), *Swords Against Death* (1970), *Swords in the Mist* (1968), *Swords Against Wizardry* (1968), and *The Swords of Lankhmar* (1968), later expanded to include *Swords and Ice Magic* (1977) and *The Knight and Knave of Swords* (1988). Jack Vance, author of a gorgeous series of loosely connected "Dying Earth" stories in the late 1940s, published in a small paperback run by Hillman Periodicals in 1950 and later the *Magazine of Fantasy & Science Fiction*, had several of his stories republished in the Ace paperback *The Eyes of the Overworld* (1966). Lancer republished Vance's *The Dying Earth* in 1962 and again in 1969.

Magazines began to publish more sword-and-sorcery during this period. Stuart David Schiff's *Whispers* specialized in horror but also published several outstanding sword-and-sorcery tales including

David Drake's "The Barrow Troll", Ramsey Campbell's "The Stages of the God" (published under Campbell's pen name Montgomery Comfort), and Karl Edward Wagner's "Undertow." Many of these stories were collected in a series of *Whispers* paperback anthologies beginning in 1977. *Weirdbook* (1968–1997, revived in 2015) offered a wide variety of weird fiction including sword-and-sorcery and dark fantasy by the likes of Robert E. Howard, Joseph Payne Brennan, Darrell Schweitzer, Charles Saunders, L. Sprague de Camp, and Jessica Amanda Salmonson. Beneath this layer of professionally published magazines was a vibrant community of "fanzines," small-run, mimeographed labors of love serving the fan community and supporting sword-and-sorcery. These included titles like *Witchcraft & Sorcery, Chacal, Dark Phantasms,* and *Escape!,* with the venerable *Amra* enjoying higher and higher circulation with each issue.[1]

With demand for sword-and-sorcery outstripping production, a common strategy was to republish works by the old masters alongside talented newcomers in anthologized paperback editions. In 1963 Pyramid Books released the first of four noteworthy de L. Sprague de Camp-edited anthologies, *Swords and Sorcery,* followed by *The Spell of Seven* (1965), *The Fantastic Swordsmen* (1967), and *Warlocks and Warriors* (1970). For the first time a major, mass-market print work bore the name "swords and sorcery" on its cover, ensuring immortality for Fritz Leiber's moniker. The series opened up the brittle pages of the defunct *Weird Tales* to a new generation, introducing Robert E. Howard, Clark Ashton Smith, Fritz Leiber, and C.L. Moore to a mass-market paperback audience, while showcasing the talents of emerging post-pulp writers like Poul Anderson, Jack Vance, Moorcock, and Roger Zelazny. Readers were treated to solid representative examples of the old masters (Howard's "Shadows in the Moonlight," Leiber's "Thieves' House", Moore's "Black God's Kiss") alongside then-newcomers like Anderson, whose "The Valor of Cappen Varra" is now regarded as a classic of the genre.

When the Pyramid series concluded in 1970 with *Warlocks and Warriors*, de Camp's protégé Lin Carter filled the void with the five-volume *Flashing Swords* anthologies (Dell Books), published from 1973 through 1981. *Flashing Swords* was followed by *Swords Against Darkness* (Zebra Books), another five-volume anthology that ran from 1977–1979. Edited by Andrew Offutt, *Swords Against Darkness* featured a greater proportion of new authors than the de Camp/Carter anthologies, including the likes of Charles Saunders,

---

[1] The importance of these paying magazines on the fostering of sword-and-sorcery cannot be underestimated. Leiber credited a sale to *Unknown* and an unexpected sale to *Fantastic* for buoying his spirits and encouraging him to continue the Fafhrd and the Gray Mouser series (Amra, Vol. 2, No. 16).

noted horror authors Brian Lumley and Ramsay Campbell, Darrell Schweitzer, and a young Orson Scott Card, who would later gain acclaim as the author of the science-fiction novel *Ender's Game*. Other notable anthologies published during this renaissance era included *The Mighty Barbarians* (1969) and its follow-up *The Mighty Swordsmen* (1970), *Swords Against Tomorrow* (1970), and *Savage Heroes: Tales of Sorcery and Black Magic* (1977). *Realms of Wizardry* (1976), edited by Lin Carter, contained some sword-and-sorcery stories alongside dark fantasy and high fantasy selections.

Carter had by now firmly established himself in the burgeoning subgenre with his efforts contributing to the Lancer Conan Saga and his original tales of Thongor the Barbarian. The first of these, *The Wizard of Lemuria*, was published in 1965. Six more followed in succession. Carter was not just an author, editor, and burgeoning scholar, but a fan, possessed of a contagious enthusiasm for fantasy fiction and in particular sword-and-sorcery. In 1968 he co-founded the Swordsmen and Sorcerer's Guild of America, or S.A.G.A. Joining him in the effort were L. Sprague de Camp and John Jakes (Carter, *Imaginary Worlds* 149). With S.A.G.A., Carter sought to create a like-minded guild of sword-and-sorcery enthusiasts. Jakes was a natural to complete this sword-and-sorcery power trio. He had written a handful of stories of the blond-haired barbarian hero Brak, who first appeared in the magazine *Fantastic Stories* in 1965. After the advent of the paperback boom and the revival of sword-and-sorcery, Avon Books picked up the Brak stories, and padded with some additional original material published them as the anthology *Brak the Barbarian* (1968). Carter soon broadened S.A.G.A's ranks, inviting Fritz Leiber, Andre Norton, Jack Vance, Michael Moorcock, and Poul Anderson into the now eight-member club (Carter, *Flashing Swords #1* 13).

Carter described the charter and activities of the colorful group in his typical enthusiastic manner:

> Unlike other writer's associations, S.A.G.A. is strictly forbidden by its constitution, the Sacred Articulorum, to engage in any activity whatsoever of an official nature, including (paradoxically) the drawing-up of constitutions. No meetings, bulletins, conventions, assemblies, publications, banquets, awards, blacklists, campaigns, crusades, ballots, elections, officers, and like that. The SAGAmen pay no dues, fees, expenses, charges, tithes or weregild. About the only thing the Sacred Articulorum permit the eight members to do is get together in the bar at science fiction conventions and hoist a couple in honor of Absent Friends. We also bestow titles and honorifics on each other at every conceivable occasion, usually for no particular reason at all. De Camp, for instance, is Supreme Sadist of the Reptile Men of Yag, Moorcock is Veiled Thaumaturge of the Mauve Barbarians of Ningg, Jakes is Heredity Guardian of the Sacred Ruby-Studded Elephant Goad to the Court of Ubbo the Unmerciful, and the present writer

enjoys the prerogatives of Exalted Grand Booleywag, to say nothing
of the honor of Purple Druid of the Slithering Horde of the Slime
Pits of Zugthakya. (Carter, *Imaginary Worlds* 149–150)

S.A.G.A was more style than substance, and myth than fact. Jakes
confirmed the highly informal nature of the group, which never met
in any official capacity. "While I knew both Lin Carter and Sprague
de Camp because of our mutual interest in S&S, I don't recall any
'official' meetings of SAGA. Lin created this largely on his own but
I hastened to endorse that, and signed up" (Interview with John
Jakes). But Carter and S.A.G.A. did develop and sponsor the Gandalf
Awards to honor achievement in fantasy literature. The Gandalfs
were conferred at the World Science Fiction Convention, but proved
short-lived, lasting just eight years (1974-81). If collectively its
efforts were minor, the individual works of the S.A.G.A. authors
were an important chapter in the sword-and-sorcery renaissance.
Carter used his *Flashing Swords* anthology to showcase their work.
Flashing Swords #1 (Dell, 1973) included original novella-length
short stories by Leiber, Anderson, Vance, and Carter. It also contained one of the first definitions of the subgenre, a useful if lightly
sketched introduction to sword-and-sorcery, codifying it as a genre
begun by Robert E. Howard and broadly comprised of the amalgamation of adventure story, imaginary world fantasy, and supernatural
horror. *Flashing Swords #2-5* included additional original works by
the aforementioned authors as well as the likes of Avram Davidson,
Andre Norton, L. Sprague de Camp, Katherine Kurtz, Roger Zelazny,
C.J. Cherryh, Diane Duane, Craig Shaw Gardner, and Tanith Lee.
Dell agreed to publish two volumes of *Flashing Swords* prior to
seeing any sales figures for the first volume (Carter, *Flashing Swords
#1* 13) and the series ultimately spanned five anthologies, with its
last, *Demons and Daggers*, appearing in 1981. Several of its authors
including Zelazny, Norton, Lee, and Cherryh went on to become
successful authors of science fiction and mainstream fantasy, and
their inclusion in *Flashing Swords* is indicative of the marketplace
opportunity presented by sword-and-sorcery at this time. Authors
of all stripes were trying their hand at sword-and-sorcery and had
little trouble finding paying markets.

The 1960s and 70s also saw the subgenre's first critical explorations with a chapter in Lin Carter's *Imaginary Worlds* (1973),
followed by de Camp's *Literary Swordsmen and Sorcerers: The Makers
of Heroic Fantasy* (1976). *Imaginary Worlds* is a wide-ranging work
cataloging the birth and development of fantasy fiction, with its
last three chapters providing a "how to" formula for aspiring fantasy
authors. It was the first of its kind, at the time the only book-length
work devoted to a critical exploration of fantasy. Chapter Three,

"Lost Cities, Forgotten Ages," provides a helpful summary of the origins of the pulp strain of fantasy as pioneered by the likes of Burroughs, Merritt, Lovecraft, Smith, and Howard. Chapter Seven, "Post-Howardian Heroica: The Swordsmen and Sorcerers' Guild of America, Ltd," contains much useful information on sword-and-sorcery fiction of the 1960s and early 70s, including a summary of the de Camp/Carter Lancer Conan Saga collaborations and the formation of S.A.G.A. *Literary Swordsmen and Sorcerers* is a series of biographical chapters on several seminal high fantasy and sword-and-sorcery authors, including the likes of Tolkien, T.H. White (author of *The Once and Future King*), Lord Dunsany, and William Morris, as well as Smith and Howard. The final chapter, "Conan's Compeers," provides helpful references on the further development of sword-and-sorcery.

Amra continued to add additional helpful commentary on sword-and-sorcery's roots and definition. In the October 1974 issue of the fanzine, Seth Glick's "A Tentative Bibliography of S&S" offered the following:

> The category, Swords & Sorcery, occupies a niche somewhere between classic fantasy and science fantasy. It is characterized by a central figure of exceptional physical prowess and a simple but noble nature who is pitted in a struggle (often a quest) against forces of evil who usually employ magic as their primary weapon. The setting is a grim, primitive, but exotic world with a flavor of imagery from the ARABIAN NIGHTS, Greek mythology, and medieval Europe. For a reader to consider a story to be S & S, he must feel the proper subjective response to the names and descriptions employed by the author. Thus, even though a tale may be set on "another world" (e.g., KOTHAR), if it lacks interplanetary, scientific, or technological overtones (e.g., Barsoom, GOR series, JANDAR), the S & S mystique is maintained. Also, there should be no continuity with our concept of historical reality (e.g., SOLOMON KANE), although some writers use the device of drawing the hero from the real, modern world into the imaginary one (a "frame"). With some reservations these lattermost are included if the stories are consistent with the forementioned standards. Certain works are closely related to S & S in having settings of similar surrealism. However, they lack the movement and action of a true S & S saga (e.g., THE DYING EARTH, ZOTHIQUE). Works of classic fantasy have also been excluded. Although several of these have a central figure in conflict with evil magic, their worlds have more of a fairy tale flavor, with elves, dragons, usw. (e.g., the Tolkien trilogy, WORM OUROBOROS, RED MOON & BLACK MOUNTAIN, BROKEN SWORD, 3 HEARTS & 3 LIONS, etc.). Finally, tales related to the Arthurian cycle have also been omitted (*Amra*, Vol. 2 No. 64).

Arguably the high-water mark of the sword-and-sorcery renaissance was 1970 when Fritz Leiber won both the Hugo and Nebula awards for "Ill Met in Lankhmar," the first and only time these awards were bestowed on a pure sword-and-sorcery story.[2] 1970 also saw the first mass-market publication of Karl Edward Wagner's immortal wanderer Kane in the short novel *Darkness Weaves*. L. Sprague de Camp released the fourth and final entry in his celebrated four-volume Pyramid anthology, *Warlocks and Warriors*, featuring deep cuts from the likes of Howard, Kuttner, and Moore, creative "stretch" material from Lord Dunsany and H.G. Wells, and a recent entry from talented newcomer Roger Zelazny, "The Bells of Shoredan." Perhaps most noteworthy of all, at least from a purely commercial sense, 1970 saw the debut of the four-color *Conan the Barbarian* #1 from Marvel Comics. Debuting on the racks in October 1970, *Conan the Barbarian* ran for 275 issues until it ceased publication in 1993. While uneven in quality over its long run, it produced many iconic issues and storylines adapted from Howard's original stories, and introduced a new generation of readers to Howard's creation. Its success paved the way for several other sword-and-sorcery-inspired comics including *Warlord* and *Arak: Son of Thunder*. The year 1970 was supposed to see the debut of a new magazine named after this now red-hot fantasy subgenre. *Sword and Sorcery* was to be edited by author Kenneth Bulmer, but failed to appear when financial backing was withdrawn by the publisher (Moorcock, *Elric: The Sleeping Sorceress* xv).

Of the S.A.G.A. authors not already covered in Chapter Five, the best were Jack Vance and Poul Anderson, two meteoric talents who continued to shape and innovate within the boundaries of the sword-and-sorcery subgenre. The third was Karl Edward Wagner.

Jack Vance (1916–2013)

More than a decade before the sword-and-sorcery renaissance, a curious volume called *The Dying Earth* (1950) appeared with little fanfare from Hillman Periodicals, known largely as a publisher of true crime, romance, war, and westerns. The relative indifference with which it was first received may have been due to genre confusion: not quite fantasy enough for Howard-heads, nor proper "hard" science fiction favored by readers of *Analog*, *The Dying Earth* did not fit neatly into any one genre. Its cover was suitably mysterious and opaque, featuring a well-proportioned female in a gauzy gown, foregrounded by a trio of vaguely menacing, conspiratorial, cowled men, against a backdrop of stars. Then and today *The Dying Earth* is often categorized as science fiction, and not inaccurately. The action takes

---

[2] "Ill Met in Lankhmar" was published in the April 1970 issue of *Fantasy and Science Fiction*; the actual awards were bestowed in 1971.

place on a literal "dying Earth" of a distant future. Our planet is in its final throes, its aging, decaying sun on the verge of burning out and plunging the world into darkness. Flying cars and anti-gravity elevators dot the landscape, but have fallen into disuse and decay. Cities are abandoned, mute testaments of mankind's past achievements before the apocalypse. Today, some credit its author, Jack Vance, for creating an entirely new "dying earth" subgenre ("Dying Earth," *The Encyclopedia of Science Fiction*).

But a closer look at *The Dying Earth* reveals a much closer affinity with fantasy, and in particular sword-and-sorcery. Duels are fought with swords instead of guns. Horses and sail have resumed ascendancy over manned flight and the automobile. Most critically, magic has replaced science. Though the backdrop is vast and an irrecoverable apocalypse looms, the aims of its cast of characters are refreshingly small, often involving petty quests for personal enrichment. And the stories—six in the first volume—are short, loosely connected only by the grim universe in which they are set.[3] Later post-Hillman editions made *The Dying Earth's* sword-and-sorcery heritage far more explicit. A 1977 Pocket Books edition for example featured a sword-wielding, heroically proportioned warrior with tunic and cape battling an ogre with a helpless female draped over one monstrous arm, with a dark castle looming in the background. Yet its cover blurb maintained a degree of ambivalence, declaring it "The classic science fantasy of the world on the eve of destruction."

More than 60 years after its publication, *The Dying Earth* retains a classic status in the genre due to its well-crafted prose. Vance's style is of the James Branch Cabell/Lord Dunsany/Clark Ashton Smith school—evocative and atmospheric, studded with strange names and references left enchantingly unexplained—though also highly readable, lucid, and modern. In *Flashing Swords* #1, Carter declared Vance "virtually the only genuine stylist the field has recently produced" (*Flashing Swords* #1 41). Here is a sample of his prose, from "Turjan of Miir":

> Turjan hesitated, then opened his eyes. It was night in white-walled Kaiin, and festival time. Orange lanterns floated in the air, moving as the breeze took them. From the balconies dangled flower chains and cages of blue fire-flies. The streets surged with the wine-flushed populace, costumed in a multitude of bizarre modes. Here was a Melantine bargeman, here a warrior of Valdaran's Green Legion, here another of ancient times wearing one of the old helmets. In a

---

[3] One editor who agreed with classifying *The Dying Earth* as sword-and-sorcery was Lin Carter, who recruited Vance into S.A.G.A. and commissioned an original Dying Earth story ("Morreion") for *Flashing Swords* #1. He also republished "Liane the Wayfarer" in *Realms of Wizardry* (1976).

little cleared space a garlanded courtesan of the Kauchique littoral danced the Dance of the Fourteen Silken Movements to the music of flutes. In the shadow of a balcony a girl barbarian of East Almery embraced a man blackened and in leather harness as a Deodand of the forest. They were gay, these people of waning Earth, feverishly merry, for infinite night was close at hand, when the red sun should finally flicker and go black. (Vance, "Turjan of Miir" 9)

Vance adopted the anti-heroic strain of sword-and-sorcery pioneered by Cabell and Smith. *The Dying Earth* contains no Howardian heroics, feats of strength, or over-the-top swordplay—and some of its latter stories contain no swordplay at all. Some of its characters meet untimely and unheroic ends. Yet the series is studded with recognizable hallmarks of classic sword-and-sorcery. "Ulan Dhor" features a fearless, skilled swordsman on a quest to steal ancient tablets of lore from a forgotten city, still ruled by a half-mad wizard-god. The hero pits his sword arm, clear vision, and relentless will against the forces of religious superstition, conformity, and autocracy—and manages to rescue a beautiful woman and ride off with her into the sunset. The protagonist of "Guyal of Sfere" is an outsider, "born one apart from his fellows and early proved a source of vexation for his sire" ("Guyal of Sfere" 89). Dissatisfied with his familial customs and traditions and frustrated at having his deeper questions met with deflection or pat answers ("it is thus because it has always been thus,"), Guyal seeks answers from the mysterious Curator, who guards the Museum of Man in the Land of the Falling Wall. He learns that the past was a far greater place than the present decay into which mankind and his creations have fallen. As in Howard, sorcery is a stand-in for civilized corruption; Guyal observes, "Nevermore will there be the like; now, in the last fleeting moments, humanity festers rich as rotten fruit. Rather than master and overpower our world, our highest aim is to cheat it through sorcery" ("Guyal of Sfere" 118). The stories of the Dying Earth are at once more hopeful than in Howard and also infinitely darker. Guyal promises the hopeful and beautiful Shierl that "when we win to peace, then our world will be of gladness," yet behind the smiles is the implacable decay of the sun, entropy, and eternal darkness, from which not even a new and vibrant barbaric race will arise from the ashes.

After the sword-and-sorcery renaissance began in earnest in the 1960s, Vance returned to the Dying Earth with the stories "The Overworld," "The Mountains of Magnatz," "The Sorcerer Pharesm," "The Pilgrims," "The Cave in the Forest," and "The Manse of Iucounu." These appeared in *The Magazine of Fantasy & Science Fiction* in 1965 and 1966, and in 1966 Ace Books republished them with some additional original material as the paperback anthology *Eyes of the Overworld*. Vance returned to his Dying Earth setting once more, this time as sword-and-sorcery itself was beginning to sunset. *Cugel's Saga* (1983) is a picaresque novel of the travels of Cugel the Clever, a rake and a rogue in search of coin for his purse and the next meal in his belly. Cugel is not of the heroic mold of a Conan or Elric, but the scurrilous rogue as seen in Leiber's Gray Mouser and Cabell's Jurgen. When he does engage in swordplay, such as when he cuts down the monstrous, half-insect, half sea-hag Nissifer, it comes almost as a shock. *Cugel's Saga* takes Cugel on a mission of personal vengeance. He believes Iucounu the Laughing Magician has done him a great wrong—though in truth, Iucounu inflicts his "unfair and cruel" punishment only after catching Cugel in an attempted robbery of his home. *Cugel's Saga* unfolds with amusing scrapes and escapes as Cugel scrabbles for coin, women, and food, a wandering outsider in strange lands. Aside from a few bouts of melancholy, the stories are largely comic and strange, as Cugel is forced to flee uncomfortable and awkward situations of his own making. He accidently eats a small, jellylike creature that has taken 500 years to summon; he "humbly" proclaims to the resident of a palace of which he has begged entrance: "My name is of no consequence. You may address me as 'Exalted'" ("Cil" 172). Cugel is utterly without honor or integrity but is nicknamed "the Clever" for good reason; he consistently escapes harrowing scrapes and near-death at the hands of wizards and beasts through pluck and quick-thinking. In a final encounter against Iucounu, he lays his blade on a table, standing swordless against a mighty sorcerer, but with a final act of superlative cunning manages to vanquish his opponent. Vance ends the story with a sentiment Conan might appreciate, toasting the celebration of the vanquished sorcerer in Howardian fashion:

> "Why make plans? The sun might well go out tomorrow."
>
> Cugel performed an extravagant gesture. "That thought must be banished from our minds! Tonight we sit here drinking purple wine! Let tonight last forever!" ("Cugel's Saga" 576).

Vance followed *Cugel's Saga* with *Rhialto the Marvellous* (1984). Almost utterly bereft of swords and martial heroics, this collection concerns the struggles and schemes of a group of powerful and great—but also bickering and petty—magicians in 21st century Aeon, "when Earth is old and the sun is about to go out." In "Fader's Waft," the magician Rhialto is stripped of his most potent sorcery, and he must overcome a great challenge with naught but his wits and persuasion (the story concludes with Rhialto, victorious, with a beautiful girl draped over his arm). The final story of the cycle, "Morreion" (first printing in Lin Carter's *Flashing Blades #1*), follows a group of wizards traveling to a far-flung planet on the edge of the universe in search of a lost wizard and his rumored horde of precious, magical IOUN stones. It is sword-and-sorcery stretched to its literal limits—wizardry without swords, high magic lacking a counter-balance of heroic grit, and with little connection to any familiar terrestrial reality—yet it keeps a toehold in the genre with its brevity, good humor, small(ish) scope, and mercenary motivations. The wizards outwardly agree to the mission for altruistic reasons—the recovery of the lost wizard Morreion—but are inwardly scheming for possession of the stones and their own selfish ends.

Like most of the sword-and-sorcery greats, Vance wrote across multiple genres, including mystery novels and Hugo- and Nebula award-winning science fiction. Today he is best known for his work in the latter, including stories like *The Dragon Masters* and *The Last Castle*. But his contributions to sword-and-sorcery are equally praiseworthy. At the outer fringes of our universe, in a distant apocalyptic future, Vance literally and figuratively stretched the subgenre into new and interesting directions.

Poul Anderson (1926–2001)

Poul Anderson is today perhaps best known as a writer of science fiction. A prolific writer with more than 100 novels and collections of short stories to his credit, Anderson won seven Hugo awards for his work in SF, including his best known stories "The Queen of Air and Darkness" and "No Truce with Kings." But his heart lay in fantasy. In addition to his membership in S.A.G.A., Anderson belonged to the Hyborian Legion, a group of Robert E. Howard fans who assembled under the banner of the sword-and-sorcery fanzine *Amra*, of which Anderson was a steady contributor. He was also a founding member of the Society of Creative Anachronism, a group known for its elaborate (and bone-jarring) reenactments of medieval combat (Carter, *The Broken Sword* ix). Anderson's skillful co-navigation of the worlds of fantasy and science fiction, and his ability to combine the best of both genres—science and magic in a kind of alchemy, merging rationality and romance—resulted in unique works of lasting power. Wrote author and literary analyst Sandra Miesel in an afterword to the 1981 Anderson anthology *Fantasy*, "He makes what is magical real and what is real magical. Of such power is poetry born" (317).

When Anderson began his writing career in the late 1940s, sword-and-sorcery was at its lowest ebb. For most of the ensuing decade it fared little better, Vance's *The Dying Earth* (1950) and L. Sprague de Camp's *The Tritonian Ring* (1953) the rare exceptions. Yet 1954 saw publication of one the most remarkable books of Anderson's long, decorated career. *The Broken Sword* (Abelard-Schuman, 1954) debuted to little acclaim and saw just one printing in hardcover. But it has since been revived in two separate editions, most recently as part of the Gollancz Fantasy Masterworks series in 2002. Anderson's short novel is a fantasy pioneer, published before *The Lord of the Rings* and the Lancer Conan Saga and the general fantasy boom of the mid-1960s, and not consciously written in the traditions of high fantasy or sword-and-sorcery.[4] In a sense it is pre-genre, and displays sensibilities of both ends of the fantasy spectrum. Like J.R.R. Tolkien, Anderson exalted a "northern theory of courage," described by Tolkien scholar Tom Shippey as "confronting certain and ultimate defeat, but regarding that neither as an excuse for giving up, nor as a logical refutation of one's position" (Shippey 27-28). Heroes convicted with this type of courage fight against truly hopeless odds, but often with a grim smile even while in the midst of *Götterdämmerung*. But while Tolkien offered his characters the chance of *eucatastrophe,* or the sudden joyous turn, Anderson did not. No Christian paradise opens its doors to greet fallen heroes. *The Broken Sword* strays outside of strict sword-and-sorcery definitions with its world-shaking events and liberal use of powerful gods who seem to manipulate its characters' strings, influencing their fate to such a degree that their agency and free will is very much in question. Its tragic arc and doom-laden overtones are perhaps too removed from sword-and-sorcery's pulp roots. At one point the story sails clear into high fantasy when the protagonist Skafloc joins forces with the Irish God Manannan mac Lir on a magic ship, sailing across an ensorcelled sea to the icy mountain home of the god Bolverk to reforge the eponymous broken sword.

But Anderson skillfully grounds these mythological elements in an earthy story, lending *The Broken Sword* a quasi-scientific plausibility and an authentic, even historical air that steers the story back into sword-and-sorcery. The land of Faerie exists parallel to historical England, invisible to mortal men who lack the necessary "witch sight." But these two worlds are not so different. In lockstep with Anglo-Saxons losing battles to the invading Danes, kingdom after kingdom of the fantastic land of Alfheim falls to the invading trolls, save in the north, where the elves of Scania remain free—just as the historical kingdom of Wessex fended off Viking invaders in

---

[4] Anderson was clearly a fan of Robert E. Howard and in all likelihood read Howard's Conan stories prior to writing *The Broken Sword*. His essay "The Art of Robert E. Howard" appeared in the first issue of *Amra* (Vol. 2, No. 1, January 1959), just five years after publication of *The Broken Sword*, and demonstrates a mature familiarity with Howard in general, and Conan in particular. His first published venture into Howard criticism was his essay "The Barbarian" which appeared in the May 1956 *Magazine of Fantasy and Science Fiction*.

Anglo-Saxon-held England. The fantastic battles of Alfheim lie just beyond mankind's vision, save as shadowy, flickering images occasionally glimpsed. "Men had some glimpse of these doings—distant fires, galloping shadows, storm-winds bearing a brazen clangor" (*The Broken Sword* 100, 113). The hero of the story, Skafloc, is taken in his infancy from his unknowing mother by the elf-earl Imric to be raised in Elrheugh. Imric replaces Skafloc with Valgard, a changeling with the blood of elves and trolls in his veins. Valgard and Skafloc are two halves of a broken whole, and can be viewed as the eponymous broken sword. Skafloc is more vital and passionate than the haughty and cold elves among which he is raised, and he is restless in their midst, while Valgard's troll blood renders him prone to black moods and fits of violence and cruelty. The pair share a ferocity and barbaric vitality familiar to readers of the Conan stories: Skafloc is by age 15 described as having a "leopard gait," not far removed from the "panther-ish thews" Howard often used to describe the Cimmerian (*The Broken Sword* 15). Valgard is not utterly amoral and suffers pangs of grief and occasional moments of awful clarity of his acts of kinslaying. He is a pawn caught up in a much larger game of gods, witchery, and the implacable will of the Norns—the same web in which Skafloc is emeshed. Encounters between the two matched enemies become more frequent as the book grinds on, until the final battle at Elfheugh, when the two foster-brothers are reunited in mortal combat.

Anderson was deeply versed in Norse saga and his writing is studded with references to Old Norse language and mythology. Characters mingle skaldic verse with common speech in conversation, interwoven with old Norse words like "fetch," "fey," and "weird" or "wyrd," the latter the fate from which no man escapes. In the pagan hierarchy of the North, the Norns outrank the towering Jotuns (giants), even the godlike Aesir. The gods themselves will die in the fires of Ragnarok at their appointed time. That grimness bleeds through into *The Broken Sword* as its protagonists are slowly crushed beneath the merciless wheel of fate. *The Broken Sword* offers a darker, bleaker alternative to the consolation offered in much of the high fantasy published during the 1970s and 1980s. A handful of like-minded authors disenchanted with unicorns, fair maidens, and pure- of-heart heroes followed the path beaten by its grim, bloody trail, including Michael Moorcock, who wrote that Anderson's novel —"a school of epic fantasy fundamentally at odds with inkling reassurances"—provided considerable inspiration for his Elric stories (Moorcock, "Tolkien Times Two"). Richard Morgan, author of the sword and sorcery/grimdark trilogy *A Land Fit For Heroes*, lists *The Broken Sword* as one of three works on the acknowledgements page of *The Steel Remains*. Even if it is not pure sword-and-sorcery by its strictest definitions, *The Broken Sword* is a blueprint for how s&s can succeed at novel length: a skillful combination of the "real" and fantastic, a story both far away but also savage and lusty and human, fantasy grounded in history, short and fast-paced, and shorn of the lofty "elevated style" that characterized the high fantasy of the late 19th and most of the 20th century. *The Broken Sword* was reprinted in 1971 at the height of the sword-and-sorcery renaissance as part of the Lin Carter edited Ballantine Books Adult Fantasy Series. Anderson used the opportunity to revise his early work and tone down its savagery (*The Broken Sword* xv), which blunted some of its force.

The Broken Sword was not a one-off venture into sword-and-sorcery for Anderson but the start of a northern saga of his own. After reading some of Anderson's translations of heroic verse from Old Norse published in *Amra,* Carter encouraged Anderson to submit his manuscript of *Hrolf Kraki's Saga*. Carter published it in 1973 as part of the Ballantine Adult Fantasy Series (Carter, *Hrolf Kraki's Saga* xiv). Hrolf Kraki was a historical figure shrouded in legend—a Danish equivalent of England's King Arthur. Anderson shifts the story squarely into the camp of fantasy by inserting trolls, werewolves, witches, shape-shifting berserkers, and other fantastic elements. In tone and feel *Hrolf Kraki's Saga* is far closer to sword-and-sorcery than high fantasy, and deliberately so. As Anderson states in the foreword:

> Here is no *Lord of the Rings*, work of a civilized, Christian author—though probably it was one of Tolkien's many wellsprings. Hrolf Kraki lived in the midnight of the Dark Ages. Slaughter, slavery, robbery, rape, torture, heathen rites bloody or obscene, were parts of daily life. ... Love, loyalty, honesty beyond the most niggling technicalities, were only for one's kindred, chieftain, and closest friends. The rest of mankind were foemen or prey. And often anger or treachery broke what bonds there had been.

Hrolf Kraki's Saga won Best Novel from the British Fantasy Society in 1975. Anderson would publish several other sword-and-sorcery tales set during a mythical Viking age, including "The Tale of Hauk" (*Swords Against Darkness*), "The Valor of Cappen Varra" (*Fantastic Universe*), and *War of the Gods*. These are among the finest tales sword-and-sorcery has to offer, part of a lengthy, wide-ranging career that never saw Anderson abandon his sword-and-sorcery roots, despite lengthy stints in science fiction. In 1980 Zebra books published the first of his *The Last Viking* trilogy, *The Golden Horn*. A tale of the Viking king Hardrede, whom the back cover trumpets as "the real life CONAN" (the book also sports a "heroic fantasy" label on its spine, even though Harderde was historical, and Anderson's principal source for the work the 13th-century *Heimskingla*), *The*

Golden Horn was followed by *The Road of the Sea Horse* (1980) and *The Sign of the Raven* (1981). In 1980 Anderson tried his own hand at a tale of Conan with the authorized pastiche *Conan the Rebel*. Four years prior to his death, Anderson returned to the mythology of the north with *War of the Gods* (1997), a story of the legendary/quasi-historical Danish King Hadding. Like *Hrolf Kraki's Saga*, the story is a winning combination of gritty historical realism interspersed with gods, giants, and Valkyries.

Karl Edward Wagner (1945–1994)

Even as it sold beyond the wildest hopes of L. Sprague de Camp and ignited the sword-and-sorcery boom, by the 1970s the Lancer Conan Saga had begun to face criticism. Among its most vocal detractors was Karl Edward Wagner (1945–1994). Wagner edited a three-volume Conan series by Berkley/Putnam—*The Hour of the Dragon, The People of the Black Circle,* and *Red Nails*—which in rapid succession in 1977 gave readers a first look at unadulterated Robert E. Howard in mass-market paperback form. The Berkley/Putnam Conans reprinted the original tales exactly as they were published in their original *Weird Tales* run, without editorial emendations (Wagner, *Conan: The People of the Black Circle* 5). Their introductions were forthright and uncompromising, treating Howard's stories as the work of an artist worthy of preservation, not as a commodity or a rough palate upon which finishing touches needed to be applied. Wagner pulled no punches in his assessment of the Lancer Conans and the Gnome Press editions before them:

> Previous editions have been marred by the work of overzealous editors, too concerned with usage of commas, spelling variants, and apparent "inconsistencies." In an effort to fill in portions of Conan's sage not chronicled by Howard, there have been numerous "posthumous collaborations" in the form of completed fragments, revisions of non-Conan stories, and outright pastiches. It is this editor's feeling that the Conan stories should be presented exactly as Howard wrote them, and that examples of pastiche writing have no place in a collection of the original author's own stories (*Conan: The People of the Black Circle* 5)

Though guilty of writing the same Howard pastiche for which he criticized de Camp, Carter, et. al.—Conan with his novel *The Road of Kings* (1979), and Bran Mak Morn with *Legion from the Shadows* (1976)—Wagner did not claim that these were anything other than derivative works, and was careful to draw a bright line between posthumous pastiche "collaborations" and the texts of an original artist:

> I have written Howard pastiches myself, so I can speak both as a reader and an author: Every author leaves his personal mark on

whatever he writes; the only man who could write a Robert E. Howard story was Robert E. Howard. Read Howard pastiches as you will—but don't let anyone kid you that you're reading Robert E. Howard (*Conan: The Hour of the Dragon* 10)

The Berkley/Putnam Conans surpassed even the Lancers for presentation, with beautifully illustrated covers by talented artist Ken Kelly and their cover art reproduced as full-color, fold-out posters in the interior of each volume. De Camp put a stop to the series before Wagner could complete his stated goal of publishing all 21 original Conan stories (Breakiron, *The Nemedian Chroniclers #5*), but they played an important role in reversing the narrative that Howard, and sword-and-sorcery by extension, was lightweight entertainment suitable for exploitation.

Wagner was a bold, colorful personage. Outwardly he resembled a barbarian with his heavy frame, long hair, and thick beard. He partied hard and drank heavily, which contributed to his untimely death (Straub). But Wagner's outward appearance belied a rich inner intellectual life. Wagner earned an MD from the University of North Carolina School of Medicine in 1974. The following year he took his residency in psychiatry and participated in a Ph.D. program in neurobiology at the University of North Carolina. Ultimately he grew disenchanted with psychiatry and gave up the practice of medicine for a full-time writing career (Elliot). Wagner turned to sword-and-sorcery, creating one of the subgenre's iconic heroes in Kane, an immortal, world-weary mercenary doomed to wander the earth. The character proved popular. In addition to appearances in small press, Warner Books published a complete line of Kane stories at the height of the sword-and-sorcery renaissance, including the anthology *Death Angel's Shadow* (1973), the novels *Bloodstone* (1975), *Dark Crusade* (1976), and *Darkness Weaves* (1978), and the anthologies *Night Winds* (1978) and *The Book of Kane* (1985).

As with Clark Ashton Smith, Fritz Leiber, and Henry Kuttner, Wagner was equally adept and prolific working in horror. He edited the annual *Year's Best Horror Stories* over a storied 14 year run (1980–1994) and contributed several heavily anthologized short stories to the genre, including "Sticks" and ".220 Swift." Some of the Kane stories are horror masquerading as sword-and-sorcery. In "Sing a Song of Valdese" (originally published in *Chacal* #1, reprinted in *Night Winds*), Kane plays the role of dark avenger in a chilling night of vengeance 50 years in the making. "Reflections for the Winter of my Soul" (*Death Angel's Shadow*, 1973) is an atmospheric and chilling "whodunit" murder mystery with a werewolf stalking its victims. Wagner distilled the essence of Kane from his favorite literary and cinema villains, including the biblical Cain of whom he is a deliberate echo (Owston), as well as the restless and brooding King Kull, with whom Wagner felt a personal affinity:

> Howard takes great care to develop mood and atmosphere in his best stories, and in so doing makes the reader feel the dark, desperate undercurrent of his character's schemes and struggles. It is in this that I feel closest to Howard, and it is something that his conscious imitators have never captured. The disparity of writing styles aside, the mood immediately sets pastiche-Howard apart from the real article. Pseudo-Conan is out having just the best time, 'cause he's the biggest, toughest, mightiest-thewed barbarian on the block, and he's gonna have a swell time of brawling and chopping monsters and rescuing princesses and offing wizards and drinking and brawling and ... and... etc... etc.... But in Howard's fiction the underlying black mood of pessimism is always there, and even Conan, who enjoys a binge or a good fight, is not having a good time of it at all. This is particularly true of Solomon Kane and King Kull—driven men whom not even a desperate battle can exorcise their black mood, while Conan at times can find brief surcease in excesses of pleasure or violence. I think Solomon Kane and King Kull were closer to Howard's true mood, while Conan represented the ability to escape briefly from black reality that Howard wished he could emulate. He failed. Of all Howard's characters I most prefer King Kull, and it is Kull who is closest to my own Kane. ("The Once and Future Kane")

Kane's appearance in 1970 heralded the darkest sword-and-sorcery protagonist published to date, though a case could be made for Michael Moorcock's Elric. A world-weary mercenary, Kane sides with whomever offers the most coin. In *Dark Crusade*, the world is devolving into chaos, violence, and anarchy seething beneath a façade of order. The bandit leader Orted Ak-Ceddi touches flame to powder by reviving the cruel cult of Sataki, drawing thousands of converts to his dark crusade. After suffering a crushing military defeat to the forces of order (hordes of undisciplined, poorly armed foot soldiers, though committed cultists, are no match for disciplined cavalry), Orted enlists Kane to his cause. Kane throws his wartime generalship and savvy in with the cultists solely to line his pockets and further his own ambitions, heedless to the threat to humanity. But mankind is not worth saving. When a city is overrun its attackers return to a state of bestiality, reveling in rape and slaughter. Heroism is tired and bankrupt, the "poor old heroes of legend ... gone out and died for their lady's love." In *Darkness Weaves*, Kane is reduced to working for Efrel, a monstrously deformed and sex-starved sorceress, and resorts to heavy drinking and opium smoking to stomach the work. Yet for all his immoral behavior, mercenary selfishness, and nihilistic tendencies, Kane is not an outright villain, nor is he entirely without conscience: After leading Efrel's rebel forces to rapine and slaughter in the city of Prisarte, he admits that "black sorcery and wholesale massacre sicken me. ... I sold her my sword as her general, not wizard—and I fight with weapons of steel, not inhuman magic" (249).

Wagner famously rejected the adjective "anti-hero" for Kane, preferring the term "hero/villain" (Sinor). He also disavowed the term "sword-and-sorcery," preferring Moorcock's appellation "epic fantasy," or his own moniker "dark fantasy." "Sword and sorcery," Wagner said, "conjures an image of yarns about girls in brass bras who are in constant danger of losing them, and mighty warriors with eighteen-foot-long swords killing wizards and monsters faster than thought. A sword fight every other page, kill a monster every other chapter, and rescue a girl at the end—there's your sword and sorcery yarn" (Elliot). Wagner riffed off sword-and-sorcery's old guard, borrowing elements that he liked while also subverting the genre. In *Bloodstone*, the cynical Ossvalt undercuts one of Howard's beliefs that barbarians are generally more principled/courteous than their civilized counterparts, declaring barbaric moral virtue "a lie" and the "revered illusion of peasants" (88). A character chuckles at the ill luck that follows heroes who wield magic blades, a playful, metafictional jab at the likes of Elric/Stormbringer and Skafloc of *The Broken Sword*. "I've heard the legends of your magic swords, and they seem to serve their masters ill enough by the saga's end!" (*Bloodstone* 241). The brash young barbarian Dragar of "Undertow" is naive and dangerously overconfident—an obvious allusion to Conan circa "The Tower of the Elephant." But Wagner has a much darker fate in store for his would-be hero and lover.

Though not the best of the Kane stories, *Bloodstone* is a Rosetta Stone of sorts for the sword-and-sorcery subgenre. Wagner's glorious, over the top 1975 novel ("A grand and gory banquet of swordplay, sorcery, and super-science!" gushes a cover blurb by sword-and-sorcery author John Jakes) lays out the battle lines: science vs. sinew, reason vs. romance, and mankind's will and self-determination against the slavery and servitude of the machine. In this struggle sinew is not enough. Although sorcery is evil, a foul blight which sickens the land, deriving its power from the sacrifice of women upon its blood-drenched altars (286), unchecked science is worse—merciless, all consuming, intent on domination, and utterly inhuman. For all its horrors, sorcery is nevertheless preferable to a world ruled by science "in which man shall be a mindless slave to those devouring gods" (277). In a rare occurrence swords join forces with sorcery to defeat a common enemy.

The Bloodstone is a massive green and red-veined stone from beyond the stars, imbued with a pulsing intelligence. But it is inert and requires the hand of man to operate. It symbolizes unchecked progress which threatens to divest humanity of its agency. Once Kane has a taste of its power it takes a hypnotic hold, and it's not clear if he operates under his own agency or the stone's. "Kane's purpose was unswerving. His obsession to cleave through the barrier of centuries, to command the secrets of elder-world science, totally consumed him, drove from his thoughts all caution, all doubt. Before him lay the key to incalculable power; every atom of his energy must be directed toward unlocking it" (72). Wagner engages in what is likely a deliberate echo of Tolkien, whose One Ring was a visible symbol of the problem of unchecked power. A scene in *Bloodstone* in which Kane scrambles on hands and knees in the midst of a swirling, life-or-death combat, desperately seeking the ring which has slipped off his finger into brackish swamp water, is a nod to Isildur grasping for the One Ring after it slips off his finger into the river Anduin during an ambush by orcs.

Kane eventually discovers that he is a pawn of the ring, and that the former "masters" of the Bloodstone were its slaves. The story paints a struggle of mankind affirming its humanity—with all its maddening contradictions and imperfections—in the face of soulless technology. As the last remnants of a battle-torn, depleted group of warriors ride out for a seemingly hopeless final battle against the Bloodstone, an aged warrior reflects that "a man ought to attempt the illogical, if there's fire in his heart" (289). The desperate and seemingly hopeless battle turns when the Bloodstone realizes it too is imperfect, the creation of a sentient being of flesh. The shattering revelation is too great to comprehend. "Its alien mind was structured on the logic of symmetry, the fulfillment of geometric perfection. In the shattering realization that it stood alone, incomplete, imperfect, the inconceivable rationale of the crystal entity fell into chaos. ... For all its malevolent soul, it had been designed as a machine by its creators" (295-299). Technology is impotent in isolation; purposeless without life to wield it. The ancient gods and nature triumph, drowning the Bloodstone and its city of soulless modernity beneath cleansing waves.

Wagner, Vance, and Anderson were the best authors to emerge during the sword-and-sorcery renaissance but several other talented authors added significant contributions. Ramsey Campbell (b. 1946) wrote a series of stories of Ryre the swordsman, published in the five-volume *Swords Against Darkness* anthologies (1977–1979) and later collected and reprinted in *Far Away and Never* (1996). Among readers and fans, Campbell's "The Sustenance of Hoak" was the most well-received entry in the first *Swords Against Darkness* anthology (Offutt, *Swords Against Darkness II* 59). Campbell followed that with "The Changer of Names" (*Swords Against Darkness II*), "The Pit of Wings" (*Swords Against Darkness III*), and "The Mouths of Light" (*Swords Against Darkness V*). A devotee of H.P. Lovecraft, Campbell wrote "Cthulhu Mythos" stories and Lovecraft pastiche early in his career, and his sword-and-sorcery retains the same weird influences. Told with a sharp realism and a moody, unsettling style, his stories surprise with irruptions of grotesque horrors. Lovecraft and weird fiction scholar S.T. Joshi describes Campbell as possessing a simultaneous clarity and dreamlike nebulousness (Joshi, *The Modern Weird Tale* 166). Campbell's foray into sword-and-sorcery was unfortunately short-lived, likely due to a burgeoning horror career that got underway in earnest with the success of his acclaimed first novel *The Doll Who Ate His Mother* (1976). That same year Campbell completed three unfinished Robert E. Howard Solomon Kane stories published as *Hawk of Basti*, *The Castle of the Devil*, and *The Children of Asshur*. Campbell eventually returned to the character for a novelization of the film *Solomon Kane* (2009).

Aspiring African-American author Charles Saunders (b. 1946) experienced success in the mid-late 1970s with sword-and-sorcery credits in a handful of small magazines, including *Night Voyages, Dragonbane, Phantasy Digest, Dark Fantasy*, and *The Year's Best Fantasy Stories*. But the mass-market publication of *Imaro* (Daw Books, 1981) seemed to portend a change in his fortunes. Saunders grew up reading Edgar Rice Burroughs and Howard, to whom he was introduced via the Lancer Conan Saga (Harlib). With a prodigious strength and barbaric outsider mien, Imaro is Conan-esque, but differs in important ways. Whereas Conan fights his way to the crown of Aquilonia in a headlong charge for kingship, Imaro relentlessly searches for meaning in his past. We meet Imaro as a youth. His mother is banished after birthing Imaro out of wedlock outside the Ilyassi tribe, an irredeemable taboo. Imaro finds himself a despised outsider, unwelcome among the fierce warriors despite his unmatched strength and warrior prowess. The experience haunts him throughout his adventures. "Imaro's greatest foe during his formative years was the self-doubt implanted by his early experiences. As he fulfills the destiny for which he was honed like a weapon, the enemies that lurk within him prove to be as formidable as the human and supernatural ones that seek to bring him down" (Saunders, *Factoring Fear*). Although the stories in *Imaro* stand alone and can be read in isolation, each reveals a bit more of Imaro's heritage and his hard outer shell begins to chip away.

One of Saunders' chief motivations for writing the character was to introduce sword-and-sorcery readers to a protagonist of color, and a setting more culturally diverse than the default medieval (Saunders, "Chocolate Covered Conan"). To accomplish this,

Saunders borrowed Howard's Hyborian Age conceit of mythologizing the real world. Imaro's world, Nyumbani, is an alternate/fantasy version of Africa. By placing the stories on a fictitious yet familiar continent, Saunders spares the reader from tedious world-building. "Nyumbani was constructed in the appropriate Howardian manner: take the best and most interesting of a variety of cultures and civilizations, mix 'em together, full speed ahead, and damn the chronological contradictions!" Saunders followed *Imaro* with *Imaro II: The Quest for Cush* (1984) and *Imaro III: The Trail of Bohu* (1985). Additional volumes in the Imaro saga were planned, but Daw cancelled the series due to poor sales. Saunders recently returned to the character with a fourth volume, *Imaro: The Naama War* (2009).

In March 1977, Ballantine Books republished *The Tritonian Ring*, first released in 1951 in abridged format for the magazine *Two Complete Science Adventure Books*. The Ballantine edition emphasized its place in the newly formed subgenre with the tagline "An irresistible sword-and-sorcery adventure, set in fabled Atlantis" (far more helpfully than a 1968 edition which declared it "thrilling sword and sorcery for the fans of Tolkien's "The Lord of the Rings"). Author L. Sprague de Camp dedicated the book to Fritz Leiber. Though by now he had begun to feel the weight of criticism for his Howard pastiche, *The Tritonian Ring* proved de Camp could write entertaining and original sword-and-sorcery. In typical de Camp fashion the story is tongue-in-cheek, written as a light parody of the genre with its handsome and rugged but thick-headed hero Vakar of Lorsk bumbling through a series of adventures. In one scene, Vakar hails a man in a group of dock workers as "You—with the nose!" It also indulges in reader titillation, with Vakar enjoying one lusty encounter after another. *The Tritonian Ring* is set in Poseidonis, a prehistoric land mass consisting of the conjoined masses of Europe, Asia, and Africa prior to continental drift. This is the fabled time of Atlantis, whose spires had not yet sunk beneath the sea. The weapons, gear, architecture, and technology in the novel are Bronze Age, lending the book an air of realism. Over a familiar backdrop of chariots and bronze-plated cuirasses, de Camp introduces gorgons, wizards, and gods.

Loosely based on the gods of ancient Greece, the gods of Poseidonis are ultra-powerful but not infallible, and exert their influence through visions and suggestion. At the outset of *The Tritonian Ring* their time is drawing to a close. "Events will take a deadly turn for us in the next century, unless we change this pattern," councils Drax, the Tritonian god of war. The principal threat is the northern kingdom of Lorsk, and Vakar, its young prince and heir to the throne. The gods urge the warlike gorgons to launch a surprise attack and destroy the Loskan Empire before the threat can materialize. The

Lorskan king learns of the impending attack, and on the advice of the witch Gra dispatches Vakar on a quest to "seek the thing the Gods most fear"—the fabled Tritonian Ring, a plain circlet of iron forged from a fallen star, against which the Gods' power is useless. Should Vakar recover the star the secrets of iron smelting will be revealed, and the reign of the gods and the age of magic ended. Vakar is a fitting protagonist chosen (or perhaps fated) to undertake the quest. He is a modern man in every sense, a pragmatist whose interests lie in books, philosophy, and history. He scorns ancient customs and is among the first wave of new men abandoning old traditions in favor of the new gods of science and progress.

Though not of the same stature of a Conan or a Kane, and a reluctant hero who relies as much on his luck as on his skill with a blade, in the end Vakar embraces a philosophy suitable for a Howardian hero: "Wait to be sure of anything and you will find yourself looking out through the sides of a funerary urn, your quest unaccomplished." But thematically *The Tritonian Ring* is very much in opposition to Howardian sword-and-sorcery and asserts that civilized progress, not barbarism, is mankind's inevitable path. As Vakar watches a mob of commoners rise up against their murderous and oppressive noble rulers in an orgy of revenge killing, he laments that which will be lost. "The only sad thing is that they will in their stupid fury have destroyed all the amenities of civilized life in Belem, so that there will remain nothing but wretched savages, unable to rise from their own filth."

The year 1974 saw the debut of the black-and-white illustrated magazine *The Savage Sword of Conan*. As Conan adaptations are concerned, *Savage Sword* was and arguably remains the best of the lot. Unlike the *Conan the Barbarian* comic book, *Savage Sword* did not publish the Conan stories in any chronological order, but rather how an older Conan might have told them—just as Howard intended. From one issue to the next, readers are as likely to encounter the middle-aged king of "The Scarlet Citadel" as they are the young, hot-blooded, just getting his thieving career underway Conan of "The Tower of the Elephant." Its classification as a magazine rather than comic book allowed publisher Curtis (an imprint of Marvel Comics) to skirt the "comics code" of the era and treat its readers to nudity, severed limbs, and decapitations. In addition to Conan, *Savage Sword* published supplemental stories of Bran Mak Morn, Solomon Kane, and others. Stunning artwork by the likes of John Buscema, Barry Windsor-Smith, and Alfredo Alcala graced its covers and interior. It also published articles and photo spreads of sword-and-sorcery-themed convention events and other items of interest to fans of the subgenre. Issue #24 (November 1977), for example, featured a review of the Howard fanzine *Amra* and an article on the Buffalo, NY, chapter of the Society for Creative Anachronism. Anecdotally, *Savage Sword* was responsible for introducing almost many readers to Howard, and sword-and-sorcery in general, as the Lancer Conan Saga.

In 1975, Donald A. Wollheim (aka DAW Books) released the first of its yellow-spined *Year's Best Fantasy* anthologies. Lin Carter served as editor of the series from 1975–1980, followed by Arthur W. Saha from 1981–1988. Under Carter's tenure, the series offered readers a heavy rotation of sword-and-sorcery, publishing stories by the likes of Howard, Smith, Leiber, Ramsey Campbell, Saunders, Wagner, Poul Anderson, and others. Although not strictly the "year's best" (many stories were published years, often decades, prior), *Year's Best Fantasy* championed sword-and-sorcery alongside more mainstream fantasy stories and authors including Lloyd Alexander and T.H. White. Zebra Books (a division of Kensington Publishing Corporation) entered the sword-and-sorcery fray in earnest the same year, cranking out 10 Howard titles in 1975 alone. Zebra published 15 more works by Howard the following year alongside Howard pastiche by the likes of Andrew Offutt and Karl Edward Wagner ("Publisher Zebra Books/Kensington Publishing Corp.: Books Published in 1975/1976").

The end of the 1970s saw the debut of an ambitious sword-and-sorcery series. Over several glasses of wine at a fantasy and science-fiction convention held in Boston in 1978, Robert Lynn Asprin, Lynn Abbey, and Gordon Dickson hit upon the idea of authors writing sword-and-sorcery stories set in the same universe. This would circumvent the need to create new Hyborian Ages and Lankmars with each tale, and allow readers to plunge straight into the action of a shared universe. "Imagine, I proposed, if our favorite sword-and-sorcery characters shared the same settings and timeframes. Imagine the story potentials. Imagine the tie-ins. What if…" (Asprin 296). From this conversation was born Sanctuary, a crime-ridden and corrupt city of "outlaws and adventurers in a world of war and wizardry."[5] *Thieves World* (1979) was followed quickly by *Tales from the Vulgar Unicorn* (1980), *Shadows of Sanctuary* (1981), and *Storm Season* (1982) in a series that eventually spanned 12 volumes. Each book saw numerous printings, and the series as a whole sold more than a million copies (per the cover of *Thieves' World*, twenty-second printing). The *Thieves' World* anthologies spawned several standalone novels, comics, and role-playing games. Notably, *Thieves' World* published the works of several female authors including

---

[5] Asprin's essay is a telling portrait of the ready market and publishers' demand for more sword-and-sorcery at this time. Publisher Jim Baen of Ace Books agreed to a second volume of stories before the first was completed, and Asprin had to recruit unpublished authors to fill the first volume.

Marion Zimmer Bradley, C.J. Cherryh, Diana Paxson, and Janet Morris, and many of its stories (including the debut short story "Sentences of Death" by John Brunner) featured female protagonists. While some of its stories stretch the definition of sword-and-sorcery, its gritty, street-level viewpoint and mercenary plotlines are firmly of the genre. Sanctuary is home to the Vulgar Unicorn, an inn where prostitutes, sell-swords, and thieves meet for illicit dealings, as well as the Maze, a tangle of foul streets where mercenaries ply their trade—the latter in the spirit of the Maul of Howard's "The Tower of the Elephant." Worshippers of the old gods of the city quarrel and jockey for power with new gods, an echo of Leiber's gods of Lankhmar. Poul Anderson makes an appearance in the first volume with "The Gate of the Flying Knives." The story features the return of Cappen Varra, the charismatic bard of "The Valor of Cappen Varra," whose beautiful paramour of-the-moment, Danlis, finds herself caught in the middle of one such religious power struggle.

Though a novel idea that experienced strong initial success, *Thieves' World* eventually petered out as its plotlines and intrigues grew too subtle and delicately interwoven, their initial sword-and-sorcery simplicity buried beneath a complex web of intrigue that proved too formidable an obstacle for new readers. Explained co-editor Lynn Abbey, "Politics is not "sword and sorcery" and *Thieves' World*, at its best, was down-and-dirty sword and sorcery. Sales were starting to drop off and, worse, with story-lines that had become more incestuous than shared, we were unable to attract new readers. Even if people could find all nine, ten, or eleven backlist volumes of the series, very few readers wanted to read them all in order to read the new volume" (Silver).

Thieves World helped pave the way for greater female involvement in sword and sorcery. *Amazons!*, an anthology of warrior women written principally though not exclusively by female authors, debuted in 1979. *Amazons!* was loud and proud in its rejection of the male hierarchy that largely dominated sword-and-sorcery. Edited by Jessica Amanda Salmonson, its back cover reads "Taking the challenge of the great fantasy heroes such as Elric and Conan that only men can be the sword-wielding masters of the worlds of fantasy, this is an original collection of new stories of warrior-women in combat against dragons and demons, devils and despots." Contributors included Andre Norton, C.J. Cherryh, Elizabeth, Lynn, Joanna Russ, and Tanith Lee, among others, with Charles Saunders of *Imaro* fame the sole male contributor to crack the lineup.

As the 1970s drew to a close, it seemed the market for sword and sorcery was healthier than ever. Several series were selling quite well. In 1967–1977 Daw Books republished the Elric series in a six-volume paperback edition with striking cover paintings by Michael Whelan. Ace books released the final book in the 12-volume Conan Saga begun by Lancer, *Conan of Aquilonia*. This sold well enough to earn reprintings in 1981 and 1982. *Darkness Weaves* and *Night Winds* appeared in 1978, delivering more popular stories of Wagner's Kane. *Swords Against Darkness III* hit the shelves in 1978, followed by volumes IV and V in 1979. *Flashing Swords #4: Barbarians and Black Magicians* debuted in 1977, and series editor Lin Carter had one more volume up his sleeve, *Flashing Swords #5: Demons and Daggers*, which appeared in 1981. The aforementioned *Thieves' World* series was underway. In 1978, Zebra books published *Oron* by newcomer David C. Smith. Zebra even applied a genre-specific label on the spine of *Oron*, "Zebra Sword & Sorcery."

But as the 1970s wore on, some troubling warning signs began to emerge. Even as Anderson, Vance, and Wagner put out quality work, the subgenre was awash in barbarian novels of dubious originality—and more unforgivingly, questionable quality. Some sword-and-sorcery authors and editors had begun to question the purpose of the genre, and whether empty bombast had replaced art. Evidence of genre fatigue can be seen in the anthology *Heroic Fantasy* (1979, Daw Books). Although it proudly proclaimed itself of the genre ("all new stories of sword-and-sorcery," per its cover) the anthology's stories questioned the type of chest-thumping heroism that had become all too common by the late 1960s and 70s. "The Valley of the Sorrows" offered readers an uncomfortable portrait of a boisterous, death-dealing reaver haunted by the death of his friend, unable to recover from a moment of personal cowardice. "The Mistaken Oracle" flipped the sword-and-sorcery formula on its head by making a small, unassuming wizard the hero of the story, defying the expectations of a town who has hired a six-foot-six, muscular barbaric hero to slay a giant. "The Hero Who Returned" questions the very nature of heroism; its central hero is a dutiful ferryman who would rather live out his days in peace and uneventful domesticity (despite the objections of his starry-eyed wife, who dreams of heroic adventures in foreign lands with blue-eyed warriors). In an editorial, Gerald Page and Hank Reinhardt expressed open criticism of sword-swinging mercenaries and muscular "Mary Sue" barbarians, referencing "today's rather pale cardboard barbarians (whom we leave nameless, though their names sometimes resemble the raspberry they so richly deserve)" (Page and Reinhardt 206). Says Page in the introduction:

> The great cliché of modern heroic fantasy has been the muscular barbarian who seldom behaves as a human being, and whose muscles, as described in the stories, seldom seem to operate the way human muscles do. A few writers have tried to get around this by giving their

their hero powers that are godlike. To this we can only quote the old line … "What have the Deathless Gods … that can match Man's Courage?" Without the threat of failure, where is glory of success?

Sword-and-sorcery authors had not reckoned on the possibility that their meal ticket had an expiration date, and too many continued to push out the same, safe, clichéd stories of barbarians for which they had a paying market. But those certainties were about to encounter a sobering new reality and a swift change in fortunes as the 1980s got underway.

THE ART OF SWORD-AND-SORCERY

You can't judge a book by its cover—unless it's a sword-and-sorcery book, in which case, you probably can. Sword-and-sorcery artwork is polarizing: simultaneously beautiful and garish, empowering and sexist. At its best it soars and inspires; at its worst it is hackneyed and cliché, even offensive to some. But rarely is it ever dull. And it possesses a distinctive iconography that distinguishes its works as "of the genre." Sword-and-sorcery paperbacks published from the 1960s through the 1980s confront the reader with muscular, shirtless heroes locked in combat against monstrous denizens of the deep, or battling hordes of faceless opponents on choked battlefields. Corpses are often heaped under the hero's foot. Beautiful and scantily clad women in distress clutch desperately to a mighty leg, or cower, wide-eyed, in the rear.

The gold standard of sword-and-sorcery are the covers of the Lancer Conan Saga series, as painted by Frank Frazetta (1928–2010). The most iconic of his images is *Conan the Adventurer* (1966). Dark and brooding and heavily muscled, Conan lords over a mounded pyramid of corpses and shattered weapons, hand on the pommel of his downthrust sword. A curvaceous brunette clings to one of the Cimmerian's mighty legs, unperturbed by the carcass-strewn earth on which she reclines. In the background are lightly traced sinister images, including skulls, and a city, perhaps in flames. The barbarian is triumphant. Frazetta's cover of *Conan the Conqueror* is nearly as iconic. Here Conan is astride a mighty charger, bloody saber upraised as he rides like a titan, scattering enemies like tenpins on the battlefield. So powerful were Frazetta's dynamic images that they helped the Lancer Conan Saga to sell in excess of a million copies. Metallica guitarist Kirk Hammett was so taken by *Conan the Conqueror* that he paid $1M for the original painting at auction (Carlson).

Prior to Frazetta, sword-and-sorcery heroes were far less heroically exaggerated. The shirtless heroes of *Weird Tales* artists Virgil

Finlay and Hugh Rankin would scarcely turn heads on muscle beach. Jack Gaughan's cover of *The Fantastic Swordsmen* (1967) depicts Brak as athletic and strong, but smooth and lean. Jeffrey Catherine Jones' Kothar of *Kothar and the Wizard Slayer* (1970) is not even muscular, though the image is strikingly weird and very sword-and-sorcery. But post-Frazetta, sword-and-sorcery art was transformed. Subsequent artists repurposed and respun Frazetta's images, never straying too far from his template of a centrally placed, muscular hero dominating the action. This evolution is perhaps best demonstrated in the cover art of the L. Sprague de Camp-edited Pyramid Books/Berkley Medallion four-volume sword-and-sorcery series. Finlay's cover art on the first volume, *Swords & Sorcery* (1963), retains its *Weird Tales* heritage. The hero is placed at the corner of the image, his back to the reader. He wears a steel cuirass over his torso, and his one exposed arm is hardly heroically proportioned. *The Spell of Seven* (1965) offers more of the same. Its hero, a medieval knight, is small and completely subsumed by a giant leering lich with flaming eye sockets. But by the time the series concluded with *Warlocks and Warriors* (1970)—post-Frazetta and at the height of the sword-and-sorcery renaissance—a shirtless, unarmored, and hugely muscular hero prepares to deal an axe blow to a lizard man in the swell of a red sea, artwork courtesy of Jim Steranko.

An artistic arms race of brawn, reaching ridiculous proportions seen only on the steroid-infused Mr. Olympia bodybuilding stage, got underway during the heyday of sword-and-sorcery. Massive trapezius muscles, striated pectorals, and the neck of a full-grown bull are the focus of artist Melvyn Grant in the hero depicted on the cover art of 1977's *Shadow of the Wolf*. The ruggedly powerful but lean-ish, steel-cable and wire arms of the Conan depicted on *Conan the Adventurer* became bronzed and peaked 22-inch biceps by the time of *Echoes of Valor* (1987), whose Conan is a study in anatomy, complete with rippling pecs, rounded deltoids, six-pack abs, and bulging quadriceps. So powerful is this Conan that he's able to fight one-handed, the other busy clapping a flailing woman to his hip. Some publishers even borrowed this imagery to sell non-sword-and-sorcery books. Several "Lost World" books, including Edgar Rice Burroughs' *Back to the Stone Age* and *At the Earth's Core*, were re-released during this time period with covers intentionally mimicking sword-and-sorcery, including muscular broad-backed heroes and shapely, topless women in distress.

Sword-and-sorcery was far from unique in its use of scantily clad women. The action-oriented genre paperbacks of the era—often referred to broadly as "men's adventure" –featured women in every conceivable provocative pose and state of undress. Spy titles like *Have Nude, Will Travel* and *Bury Me Deep* render most sword-and-sorcery tame and light titillation in comparison (for a glorious look into the artistic abyss of the era, see the article "The Weirdest Spy Action Novels Ever Published"). But sword-and-sorcery joined in, gleefully and at times comically. A woman on the cover of *Kyrik: Warlock Warrior* is entirely nude, save for a dagger strapped to her pale thigh. She clings desperately to Kyrik's leg, even though this familiar tableaux places her in a rather precarious position—far out on the wing of a pterodactyl-like beast, rather than safely behind Kyrik's back in the saddle (which would, unforgivably, obscure her curves). The heroine of 1981's *Red Sonja* is strong and proud, with upraised sword freshly reddened with the corpse of a green-skinned humanoid at her feet. But her chain-mail bikini leaves little to the imagination. *Red Sonja's* artist, Boris Vallejo (b. 1941), become synonymous with sword-and-sorcery in the 1980s, illustrating hundreds of covers, calendars, movie posters, and the like, with a particular emphasis on the beauty of the female form.

Frazetta was a rare talent, in visual artistry the equal of the writing skill of Robert E. Howard or Fritz Leiber. But he was far from the only gifted artist working in sword-and-sorcery. Ken Kelly's (b. 1946) covers for the Karl Edward Wagner edited Berkley Medallion Conan trilogy rank among the finest examples of sword-and-sorcery art. While they lack a little of Frazetta's dynamism and savagery, Kelley's use of dark and light is stunning. Conan, sword ready to deliver an overhand strike to one of the wizards of "The People of the Black Circle" (1977), is a chief example. Kelly would go on to illustrate the album covers of sword-and-sorcery-inspired heavy metal band Manowar as well as the iconic album *Destroyer* for the rock band KISS. Jeffrey Catherine Jones (1944–2011) was so good that Frazetta once described her as "the greatest living painter" (Jones). Her work was more atmospheric than Frazetta and Kelly, evoking strangeness, wonder, and otherworldliness. Jones placed less emphasis on action and more on mood, her figures less sharply drawn and the emphasis on the whole of the image rather than a hero. She is perhaps best known in sword-and-sorcery circles for her covers of Fritz Leiber's Fafhrd and the Gray Mouser series, most notably *Swords Against Wizardry* (1968) and *Swords Against Death* (1970). Other notable artists with major contributions to sword-and-sorcery include the likes of Roy G. Krenkel, Tom Barber, Stephen Fabian, Michael Whelan, and Virgil Finlay.

CHAPTER SEVEN
Decline and Fall

"That was an age to live in!" he breathed hoarsely. "An age of heroes!"
Kane somberly rose to his feet. "A great race, a heroic age—it's true," he acknowl-
edged softly. "But I think the last of its heroes has passed."
                    —Karl Edward Wagner, "Two Suns Setting," *Night Winds*

Sword-and-sorcery reached a "weird" peak by the late 1960s/early 1970s. L. Sprague de Camp was in the midst of editing four classic sword-and-sorcery anthologies, starting with 1963's *Swords & Sorcery*. Talented newcomers Michael Moorcock and Karl Edward Wagner had arrived on the scene, while the classic works of older masters like Fritz Leiber and Jack Vance enjoyed new life in popular paperback editions. Lin Carter championed the genre with *Flashing Swords!*, a celebratory series of anthologies devoted unapologetically to sword-and-sorcery, and devoted a chapter to the subgenre in his groundbreaking fantasy study *Imaginary Worlds*. Magazines like *Fantastic Stories* and *Whispers* were publishing sword-and-sorcery alongside science fiction and horror. Off the beaten track but available to the hardcore fan were the "fanzines," led by *Amra*, a quasi-literary journal dedicated to the works of Robert E. Howard and swordplay-and-sorcery. In short, it was a healthy artistic and commercial time for sword-and-sorcery, with plenty to offer casual readers and die-hard fans.

But concurrent to this creative and commercial renaissance, sword-and-sorcery had begun to sow the seeds of its own destruction. The self-immolation began innocently enough from a group of well-meaning fans who loved Howard's stories and began to write homages. Howard's incredibly powerful template—muscular heroes in impossibly ancient ages of earth, besting their civilized and often sorcerous opponents with their natural physical advantages honed in harsh environments, clawing their way from base savagery to the gem-encrusted thrones of empires—was intoxicating, offering a ready formula that proved irresistible. Fans clamored for more. Just two years after Howard's death, *Weird Tales* reader Gene Risher of Johnstown, Pennsylvania, implored the magazine to relight Howard's extinguished lamp:

The loss of Howard and Lovecraft is irreparable. ... To my mind Howard was tops and I hope you will honor Mr. Robert J. Hoyer's request for reprints or a book of Mr. Howard's stories, especially the Conan series. I also propose that one of your other authors study Mr. Howard's style and characters and continue the Conan series. I don't think any Howard fan would be too harsh with criticism. After all, Conan was a strong character, and many weaker ones have out-lived their creators. So let's make Conan a monument to his creator. (*Weird Tales*, July 1938)

Weird Tales editor Farnsworth Wright dismissed the idea: Howard was a unique artist, he said, and his Conan stories were not mere formula that other writers could (or should) replicate:

Sorry to deny your request for some other author to carry on the Conan stories of the late Robert E. Howard. His work was touched with genius, and he had a distinctive style of writing that put the stamp of his personality on every story he wrote. It would hardly be fair to his memory if we allowed Conan to be recreated by another hand, no matter how skillfully. (*Weird Tales*, July 1938)

In the December 1937 *Weird Tales*, George W. Skora of Tucson, Arizona, expressed disbelief that anyone besides Howard could write convincingly of Conan:

No more will Conan the barbarian fight from one end to the other of those mysterious half-legendary lands, no more will he woo and win fair maidens in his inimitable fashion, no more will he defy warrior and king alike, for the master pen which created him is no more and with that passing Conan is likewise gone forever. I cannot conceive of his being recreated by anyone with the mastery of Robert E. Howard, and hence would rather see Conan dead as he had lived, a fighting-man who perished as he would have wished, sword in hand, the grim smile of desperate battle on his lips, in his ears the din of clashing blade and shouting men who felt its cunning edge. That world of his is gone. It would be blasphemy to attempt the rebuilding from dead ashes.

But many would try. John Jakes (b. 1932) was part of a new gener-ation that grew up in the heyday of the pulp fiction market, reading with pleasure the muscular tales of writers like Henry Kuttner, C.L. Moore, and in particular Howard. Jakes devoured the Conan stories, and wanted more than the 17 stories published in *Weird Tales*. To Jakes, Conan was an unforgettable, indomitable presence, and impossible to merely enjoy. He needed to tell his own stories. And so he did. Jakes created Brak, a blond-haired northern barbarian and an outcast from his tribe on colorful adventures as he makes his way south to the fabled golden land of Khurdisan. Brak first appeared in the May 1963 issue of *Fantastic*, but with the fantasy boom of the mid-late 1960s the Brak stories found a new home in the mass-mar-ket paperbacks. From 1968–1980 Jakes' byline appeared on five Brak softcovers, starting with *Brak the Barbarian* (1968), a collection of Brak's prior magazine appearances with some additional fleshing out/rewriting, followed by four sequels: *Brak the Barbarian Versus the Sorceress* (1969), *Brak the Barbarian Versus the Mark of the Demons* (1969), *When the Idols Walked* (1978), and *The Fortunes of Brak* (1980).

While not a Conan clone, Brak is an unmistakable homage to the Cimmerian. In a 1978 reprint, Simon and Shuster made sure potential readers were aware of the connection with a none-too-subtle back-cover quote from Lin Carter: "Crisp, vivid, exciting—the ghost of Robert E. Howard's Conan moves through the pages of John Jakes." Jakes has never been shy or unapologetic regarding his considerable debt to Howard, even in the face of criticism. From the introduction to *Brak the Barbarian*:

> When the first Brak tale saw print, its appearance was followed shortly by a letter to the magazine that had published it. I have lost my copy of the letter since, but I recall its inferences quite clearly—and painful ones they were for an author. That reader's letter expressed the opinion that Brak was but a pale ghost of the mighty Conan and, what was worse, had probably been conceived either out of an ignorance of Conan, or with full knowledge and therefore out of sheer cupidity. To the first part of the charge, I plead delightedly guilty. That teller of marvelous tales, Robert Howard, did indeed create a giant in whose shadow other "hero tales" must stand and, sometimes, admittedly, suffer. But be ignorant of all his work? Or believe that readers would be hoodwinked, and not feel the pulse of common blood which riots through all the warriors who inhabit the world of sword and sorcery? No. My motive for giving birth to Brak and his parallel universe on an old black iron Underwood was much simpler. There just are not enough stories of this kind to go around anymore; not enough, anyway, to please me. To help fill this dismal gap well or badly—I hope never indifferently—my barbarian, with the long yellow braid and the light of the south horizons glittering in his eyes, was born (7).

In an interview conducted later in his life, Jakes admitted to parroting Conan:

> I was reading a lot of fantasy and science-fiction when I was in high school, the 10 and 25 cent pulp paper specialties, and I just think I got hooked on the genre. I created Brak for the fantasy magazines. I was directly influenced by Robert Howard, by the fact that there weren't enough Conan stories to go around. ... I wanted to create a character much like Conan, put him in similar circumstances and have a good time writing it (Open Road Media).

Some of the Brak stories are serviceable sword-and-sorcery. Jakes cannot be accused of writing in an indifferent manner, and his passion for the genre was genuine. But as a whole the quality of the Brak stories are poor. Here is a representative sample of dialogue from *Brak vs. the Sorceress*, an exchange between Brak and the evil sorceress Nordica:

"I've decided I don't like you, barbarian."

"Nor I you, woman."

"I dislike anyone who stands against me."

His face remained sullen with defiance. Nordica laughed.

"But, as I said, there is a certain refreshing quality about your bold-ness" (34-35).

Brak the Barbarian (1968) follows a predictable formula. Brak defeats giant monsters with uninspired, rather ridiculous sounding names—Doomdog, Fanfish, and the Thing Which Crawls—typically by plunging his broadsword into their one vulnerable spot, foiling an evil plot, then making off with a nubile young girl slung over his shoulder. We are assured that Brak is a barbarian born:

> Tensely crouched, broadsword bared, Brak waited with the blood-hammer of danger running high in his veins. All pretense that he might be civilized had vanished from his face, which was ugly. Twilight scarlet glinted on his blade. He was a savage figure, a brawny animal like the very beasts he had hunted in the wild lands of the north that gave him birth. (*Brak the Barbarian* 128)

But Brak's barbarism is a thin, unconvincing veneer. He is no way savage, lion loincloth notwithstanding; indeed Brak is more caring and civil than almost anyone he encounters on his journeys. He refers to would-be princesses as "my lady" and refuses to pluck a jeweled sword from a battlefield corpse as it violates his sense of decency. The series contains some outright groaners, including a belief-defying dick joke at the crescendo of *Brak: When the Idols Walked*.

With Brak came a string of similar barbarians with guttural, disyllabic names like Kothar and Kyrik and Thongor. Gardener Fox (1911–1986) began writing sword-and-sorcery in the late 1960s with a series of stories of Kothar. As with Jakes, the Kothar stories rise to the level of serviceable entertainment. Fox is a very competent if not flashy writer, with a readable, entertaining style, and pens memora-ble monsters—the monstrous sea-beast Iormungar, the flame-eyed ancient lich Afgorkon—and fun fight scenes. But Kothar himself is dull and highly imitative. In the place of Conan, a Cimmerian, a barbarian from the north, Fox offers up … Kothar, a Cumberian, a barbarian from the north. Kothar even uses Howard's characters' affectations; Kull of Valusia oaths "By Valka," Kothar "By Dwalka" in moments of crisis. A scene in which he battles a web-slinging spider at the heart of a sorcerer's maze is suspiciously similar to Howard's "The Tower of the Elephant." And so on. Kothar is a rather dumb brute lacking any of Conan's subtlety of thought. He also lacks the Cimmerian's fierce agency, and wanders from place to place in aimless fashion. For much of *Kothar and the Wizard Slayer*, Kothar is a piece of meat in the grip of powers beyond his control; when not manipulated by the hypnotic powers of the beautiful, wicked sorceress Red Lori, he's in partial thrall to the lich Afgorkon, condemned to a life of poverty in exchange for the right to wield a magical sword.

Better is Fox's *Kyrik: Warlock Warrior* (1975). Although the cover of the Leisure Books edition declares itself "In the tradition of Conan," Kyrik is a more original creation than Kothar, a powerful barbaric king frozen by a sorcerer's spell and awoken after a thousand-year stasis. With the spell broken and blood coursing through his veins, Kyrik breathes deeply of the world and its pleasures. "He sniffed in the smells of human sweat and dusty road, the fragrance of the wildflowers bordering the highway. This was life! This was why a man was born, to drink at the wine of living, at the pleasures—aye, and even at the pains it brought. Otherwise, a man was a dead thing. As he had been dead, for a thousand years" (*Kyrik: Warlock Warrior* 74). Kyrik is the ultimate barbarian, enjoying the fiery embrace of willing women and slaying dozens of foes with ease with his powerful blade Blue Fang. By night he guzzles tankards of ale and gorges himself with slabs of beef. But while the story moves apace, Kyrik's world feels thin, undeveloped, and unconvincing.[1]

Around the same time that Brak made his first appearance, Lin Carter arrived on the scene with his first volume of the barbarian Thongor, *The Wizard of Lemuria* (1965). Carter wrote a total of six Thongor novels during the sword-and-sorcery renaissance including *Thongor of Lemuria* (1966), *Thongor Against the Gods* (1967), *Thongor in the City of Magicians* (1968), *Thongor at the End of Time* (1968), and *Thongor Fights the Pirates of Tarakus* (1970). The Thongor series is not Howard pastiche but a kaleidoscope of various influences; Carter borrowed elements from Edgar Rice Burroughs' Mars novels and the sword-and-planet stories of Otis Adelbert Kline, then layered on a dose of Howard. Carter seasoned the Thongor stories from high fantasy influences as well: the plot of *Thongor and the Wizard of Lemuria*, for example, concerns a race of anthropomorphic Dragon Kings plotting to overthrow the world and open a portal to allow the Gods of Evil to return to the earth. Thongor and his ally Sharajsha the wizard embark on a quest to reforge the Star Sword and foil the plot. The hybrid mishmash of high fantasy and sword-and-sorcery—with added sword-and-planet elements like Barsoomian airships—is a mess. As with Brak, Thongor is absent

---

[1] Fox's Kothar and Kyrik stories verge on parody and in places plunge headlong over the edge. The "Introduction" to *Kothar—Barbarian Swordsmen* is a scholarly examination of Kothar's world by "Donald MacIvers, Ph.D."—widely regarded as a pseudonym assumed by Fox. Viewing the subsequent stories through the deliberate humorous pretentiousness of the essay leads one to suspect that Fox was having some fun with the whole barbarian enterprise.

the darkness inherent in Conan's character. He operates under the same surface level barbaric mores, including an inherent distrust of sorcery and a disdain of the civilized city, but in Carter's hands these elements feel unconvincing and tacked on. Thongor lacks Conan's volatile temperament and instead is safe, civilized, and conservative. Moreover he's a lout, equal parts carelessness and cluelessness, but with enough manful strength, bravery, and luck to carry him through escape after escape ... after escape, until breezy encounters with carnivorous dinosaurs and vampiric plant-life begin to feel mundane. Despite their pedestrian quality, the Thongor series was popular enough to draw interest in a film adaptation, *Thongor in the Valley of the Demons*, which was scheduled to begin filming in 1978 for a slated 1979 release. It was later cancelled (Meyers).

The Wizard of Lemuria met with immediate criticism in the pages of *Amra*. Back-to-back reviews in the September 1965 issue demolished the work for its lack of originality:

> The only such distinguishing feature that I am able to discern in THE WIZARD OF LEMURIA is that it is entirely derivative of other works in the genre, with no obvious originality whatsoever. Add to this the absolute lifelessness of the characters—even at his very worst (which could, admittedly, be pretty abysmal at times), Edgar Rice Burroughs never created anybody quite this wooden. Add also for good measure a modicum of sleight-of-hand methods for getting people to the right place at the right time, somewhat reminiscent of the "with one bound, I was free" jokes.

> There is a plot, but the way it's presented makes it seem not much more than an accident. In order to further the cause of the goodies, a lump of meteoric metal has to be forged into a sword by means of volcanic fires, then tempered in lightning on a mountain-top. If this sequence was featured more prominently, with some sort of scientific or pseudo-scientific explanation a la Poul Anderson, it would go some way toward giving the book a basic motivation on more than the purely random level. However, the theme is played so halfheartedly that it might as well have been omitted altogether (Mercer).

> I had hoped that Lin Carter might be part of this vanguard, but I have been painfully—that is the only word for it—disappointed. He has done such an incompetent job that for a few moments there I thought he was writing a parody of swordplay-&-sorcery. But Ace has presented this novel as being in "... the Burroughs-Kline-Merritt tradition." I don't think they would attempt to slip a fast one over on their sword-&-sorcery fans and strong supporters. Instead, it appears that that able editor Don Wollheim had his blind eye to the telescope when he purchased this one.

> Why does this book offend me? Because there is not an ounce of originality in it. The people, machines, animals; names—everything has been assembled out of an old box of Burroughs and Howard fragments (Harrison).

Together these Conan clones earned the dubious nickname "Clonans" by sword-and-sorcery fandom. Their confluence speaks to Howard's omnipresence in the 1960s. Author Michael Drout in *Rings, Swords, and Monsters* described the plight of authors working in the long shadow of *The Lord of the Rings* and author J.R.R. Tolkien as suffering an "anxiety of influence." Tolkien had created such an influential, popular piece of art that ignoring him was impossible. Authors had no choice but to react to Tolkien, Drout theorizes, which meant either writing in imitation of or deliberately breaking away from his fiction. Carter felt the same acute "anxiety of influence" with Howard. In *Imaginary Worlds*, he describes the problem of working in Howard's considerable shadow as one of originality vs. fidelity: Why change a formula that brings its readers so much pleasure? "John Jakes has put his finger directly on the central ganglion of the whole question of tradition vs. imitation. He also brings up a point my readers may not, perhaps, be aware of: that is, we Sword & Sorcery chaps are generally looked down on as mere imitators of Howard, the implication being that we are wasting our time writing trivial and frivolous derring-do when we should be peeling back layers of character revelation and grappling with front-page problems like air-pollution" (145).

Carter chafed at accusations of being a Conan imitator and defended Thongor as a worthy successor, but simultaneously professed his loyalty to the Howardian formula and felt no need to alter it or extend its boundaries. The result was a kind of stasis, a barbaric stereotype that came to be associated with the broader subgenre. Critics began to take notice. An essay published in *Fantastic* by husband and wife duo Alexei and Cory Panshin derided the subgenre as "a frozen form, a ritual dance ... early Moore and Smith continue to have an influence on SF, but the sword and sorcery complex itself is a living fossil with no apparent ability to evolve." Carter objected to the claim but did not dispute its accuracy, writing, "Well, perhaps. But what of it? The stuff is fun to read, and fun to write, and the fossilization of the genre is, I suspect, largely in the eye of the beholder" (*Imaginary Worlds* 145). Carter described his work and that of his sword-and-sorcery contemporaries as a "gnomon," or "something added on to a pre-existing something which enlarges it without distorting or altering its essential proportions, shape or contour." "Sword & Sorcery is the smallest, tightest literary genre I can think of, and one that is *completely derivative*. We who write it all work within the narrow tradition whose parameters were set down by Howard in the 1930s" (145-147). He saw nothing wrong with this practice; he was merely writing that which he loved, in a genre that pleased him greatly:

The assertion made by the Panshins is, I think, built on a false premise, which is rendered even more shaky by their obvious inability to enjoy the genre. Must a school of writing evolve? I wonder why. Evolution implies change into something else. But mere change for the sake of change, experiment for the sake of experiment—the apparent aesthetic of the New Wave school of science fiction writing, to which I suppose Alexei Panshin belongs—seems to a rather backwards-looking conservative like myself a pointless exercise in futility. Must the sonnet sequence evolve into some form other than that of the sonnet sequence, or opera into something that is not opera? Must Sword & Sorcery turn itself into something radically different? Why on Xiccarph should it? (Imaginary Worlds 146).

Carter's pleas will elicit sympathy from die-hard sword-and-sorcery aficionados. There should be more Conan stories to enjoy. Where Carter errs, however, is his assertion that sword-and-sorcery is completely derivative. It has its conventions, as does any genre, but sword-and-sorcery is malleable enough to support experimentation and creative license. Poul Anderson's Cappen Varra and Michael Moorcock's Elric proved that a sword-and-sorcery hero need not be a brawny, loinclothed barbarian, while the likes of Clark Ashton Smith's Hyperborean cycle and Jack Vance's Dying Earth demonstrated that it need not even be heroic. Carter asserts that "there is absolutely no need for Sword & Sorcery to develop new maturities of style and theme and turn itself into sober, responsible 'adult fantasy'" (Imaginary Worlds 147), yet that is what Poul Anderson did with The Broken Sword (1954), a dark, brooding, Norse-myth-inspired sword-and-sorcery novel as different from the likes of Kothar, Barbarian Swordsman as H.P. Lovecraft is to Dean Koontz. Carter was guilty of conflating his own opinions with his peers' when he wrote that "most of us who write Sword & Sorcery do so out of a nostalgic affection for the genre and have no particular desire to change it" (Imaginary Worlds 148). One wonders how he overlooked Moorcock, who by the time of Imaginary Worlds had already unleashed onto the world Elric of Melnibone, a deliberate genre-bending foil to Conan.

Among Carter's critics were fellow sword-and-sorcery author Fritz Leiber and Carter's Lancer Conan Saga collaborator L. Sprague de Camp. In the Vol. 2, No. 50, issue of Amra (May 1969), Leiber disagrees with Carter's assessment of sword-and-sorcery as a genre defined by purple prose and comic-book action, and makes the case that original works were needed, not pastiche, in order to rescue it from ruin:

Beneath the words Lin Carter and I might find agreement, but contrary to his opinion voiced in Amra v2 #46, I think Corn and Comic Book Action and Purple Prose mean essentially Cliche, Unmotivated

Action, Bad Prose, and Contempt Of Subject In General, and are the
ruin of good sword and sorcery. Fine (not precious) and honest (not
lugubrious) writing are both very much needed. And new work is
needed rather than pastiches. The pure superman hero has become
a bore, whether he excels in brawn or brain.

Added de Camp in the April 1970 *Amra* column "Multiple Scrolls":

General comments: (1) Meseems the big, dumb, blundering, oafish
barbarian, who achieves wonders by sheer muscle, has been pretty
exhaustively exploited. They even sound alike: Jamnar, Kandar,
Kothar, Thongor.

Of course, it's fair to ask, what's the harm even of completely
derivative sword-and-sorcery? Aren't the likes of Brak, Thongor,
Kothar, and their ilk merely harmless fun? Much of it is simple
men's adventure, reflective of much of the contents of *Adventure*
and *Argosy* of the 1920s and 30s, and the war and spy paperbacks
of the late 1960s–1970s. In some respects the "Clonans" are to
sword-and-sorcery what bodice-rippers are to romance: escape
and wish-fulfillment, offering genre fans the pure stuff, mainlined
barbarian adventure.[2] But the signal-to-noise ratio became a major
problem for sword-and-sorcery in the 60s and 70s. The sheer glut
of sub-par product began to wear on an audience that, while loyal
and hungry for more heroic adventure, did not possess a limitless
patience. The cumulative deleterious effect took a toll as readers
began to tune out.

Just months after Carter's enthusiastic state of the industry letter
in the April 1970 issue of *Amra* (see chapter six), the September 1970
issue of the fanzine painted a very different portrait of the state of
barbarian fantasy. The flood of derivative material that Carter saw as
opportunity for authors would eventually spell doom for the genre,
according to Brian Hval in his "On the State of Heroic Fantasy":

I have been most tempted in the last few months to completely
give up reading heroic fantasy. It has become almost impossible to
separate the reasonable reading from the literary trash displayed
in the bookstore. Or perhaps I have finally been exhausted by the
same repetitious plots of half-naked barbarians chasing equally
naked women through numberless perils, the entire series of episodes menaced by some slimy Elder Evil (naked or half-naked?). All
fantasy stories appear to be identical. Broads and broad-swords,
brainless boozing barbarians! Despite repeated overdoses of
fortified vitamins, my system can stand only so much of this monotonous rubbish. Even some of the recent "classics" are archaeological
garbage. I pray that some god (benign or otherwise) will send these
unworthy tomes to their tombs!

---

[2] A few of the Brak series could be slipped into the romance section of a bookstore
without raising an eyebrow, so close to Fabio is the blonde-haired shirtless barbarian.

... But what is the worth of a single nugget if you have to toil through ten tons of literary dirt to find it? Readers may soon realize that it is not worth the effort. The Barbarian Bonanza may result in the Barbarian Bust!

The same sentiment was echoed by letter writer Douglas E Rice in the Vol. 2 No. 54 *Amra* (April 1971):

In truth, Sword & Sorcery is a very limited variation of Fantasy. It is quite natural for an author or publisher to capitalize on another author's works. Until a competent group of authors, editors, and publishers comes along and handles Sword & Sorcery stories to a point where people don't come up to a bookstand and read the repetitious yarns that are currently present, we can expect to go nowhere but down.

Carter stormed back against the critics with "In Defense of Heroes," but failed to score many points with his assertion that dialogue and characterization are unwelcome in sword-and-sorcery:

Any tale of Sword and Sorcery is by definition a pulp adventure with lots of action. An author of such who slows down the flow of action with either chit-chat or heavy description is ill-advised.

Several kinds of heroes, or central characters, anyway, are possible. There is the glib rogue who uses either his wits or his tongue—or both—to get out of trouble. The Gray Mouser is an example of this kind of character, as is Hamper the However in a recent novel by Robert Lory called MASTER OF THE ETRAX. The trouble with this sort of character is that he is given to lots of talk, which slows the novel to a standstill. The third or fourth time such a character fast-talks his way out of a fight the novel begins to take on a deadly, yawnsome quality.

... This is not to suggest, of course, that an author has no obligation to characterize his strong-jawed hero. Bulging thews do not a rounded character make. On the other hand, in an action story, depth and subtlety of characterization are out of place (*Amra* Vol. 2 No. 55, December 1971).

As noted in chapter six, much classic sword-and-sorcery art contains a particular iconography that some modern critics might term "problematic": a nude or scarcely clothed, recumbent female, at the feet of (or cowering behind) a centrally placed, muscular hero doing all the fighting. Margaret Brundage pioneered this now-familiar tableaux for *Weird Tales* in the 1920s and 30s, while Frank Frazetta perfected the formula for the cover of 1966's *Conan the Adventurer*. Images of this sort routinely adorned the covers of the Clonans and the anthologies of the era. The cover of *The Mighty Barbarians: Great Sword and Sorcery Heroes* (1969, Lancer Books) features a curvaceous, chained woman at the feet of a lean, muscular barbarian with outthrust hips, his dripping sword blade positioned just outside her waiting thighs. The expression on her face is one of orgasm. Many of these images are beautifully drawn. Moreover they serve a practical purpose—a visual shorthand for "this is a work of sword-and-sorcery." On a crowded wire-spinning rack, juxtaposed against competing western, spy, and war novels, these images of violence, titillation, and male wish-fulfillment could make a young reader open his wallet.

These images rarely matched the content of the better sword-and-sorcery authors. But many of the "Clonan" authors based entire plotlines around the barbarian-monster-helpless woman, spinning paint-by-number stories of barbarian heroes killing the monster, saving the girl, and collecting the treasure.[3] By the time of ubiquitous 1980s cover artist Boris Vallejo—a talented artist in the mold of Frazetta, but with a much more airbrushed and less savage, dynamic style—sword-and-sorcery art had assumed the worst clichés. Like the brightly clad super heroes of Stan Lee, or the tuxedoed super-spy archetype of Ian Fleming's James Bond series, the figure of the barbarian was born—muscular, shirtless, loincloth-appareled. And too often, shallow and dumb. This trend of rapidly staling cover art reached its nadir around the time of *Heroic Fantasy* (1979, DAW Books) released at the tail-end of the sword-and-sorcery renaissance. Its cover, proclaiming "All new stories of sword-and-sorcery," features a semi-muscular warrior in a loincloth, leaning casually upon an oversized sword even taller than he, phallic implications plain. A topless female wraps her arms around him, her well-placed arm and wisps of silk concealing her nudity as she gazes vacuously at the reader. Neither appear to take notice of the ghoulish horde closing in behind them. An editor's introduction to "The Valley of the Sorrows" by Galad Elflandsson refers to the sad state of the Clonan industry of the era: "The field of heroic fantasy abounds with Robert E. Howard imitations, which is to say it abounds in stories which present a series of predictable muscle-bound clichés that make you think not of Conan the Cimmerian, but of Steve Reeves in some of his lesser movies" (Page and Reinhardt 58).

Carter's gnomon theory bore out, in the end, to the detriment of the genre. Reluctant to stray from safe, lucrative formula, sword-and-sorcery gravitated toward a banal center and away from creative boundaries. It was becoming too self-aware, too proscriptive, and too rigorous in the applications of its definitions. The end result was hardening of the genre lines and creative stagnation. A few genuinely talented authors continued to break new ground, but their

---

[3] Frank Frazetta painted such a powerful image in his career ("Deathdealer," 1973) that he commissioned author James Silke to write a series of sword-and-sorcery novels based on the image, neatly inverting the typical author-artist relationship.

signal was drowned out by the noise. In the mid-1970s the cover of the Andrew Offutt-edited anthology *Swords Against Darkness* declared itself as "Heroic Fantasy in the Tradition of Robert E. Howard." The contents reveal some stiffening of the joints. Geo W. Proctor's "The Smile of Oisia" straddles and occasionally crosses the line between respectable homage and fawning pastiche. Its protagonists meet in The Silver Wolf (aka The Silver Eel, a favored watering hole of Leiber's Fafhrd and the Gray Mouser) before embarking on a raid of a wizard's tower and its fabled, monster-guarded riches (the exact plot of Robert E. Howard's "The Tower of the Elephant"). The opening paragraph echoes Henry Kuttner's Elak of Atlantis story "Thunder in the Dawn" in its cadence and structure. Richard L. Tierney's "The Ring of Set" is a more accomplished, skillful homage; it also borrows a motif from Howard (an evil ring wielded by the Stygian sorcerer Thoth-Amon, first appearance in Howard's "The Phoenix on the Sword"), but places it in the context of an original story. In the fourth volume of *Swords Against Darkness*, Offutt writes of a critique by a friend and fan who found the third volume "too dark" for his genre expectations; Offutt agreed and steered the series back toward a more acceptable, balanced center. Offutt made a few questionable decisions and outright editorial missteps in the series. The Andre Norton story "Sword of Unbelief" leading off volume two is unreadable; weak, listless, written in passive voice and flaccid prose, sharing none of the blood-pounding adventure and propulsive story that is a must for this type of fiction. David C. Smith's *Oron* (1978), though a relatively entertaining novel, reads as though Smith was obligated to apply a sword-and-sorcery template over a story he really wished to tell, that of a fate-destined, tragic hero. In an odd meta outburst, a couple of *Oron's* characters more or less declare themselves as "of genre" to the reader:

> Amrik scowled. "A man makes his own destiny, Kossuth. There are sorcerers and there are warriors, and to one is magic and to the other brawn and steel. A man makes his own destiny. I'm proof enough of that!" (102).

> "I bought my position and my authority by the sword, and now sorcery and madness are out to strangle it" (333).

Decades later, with pastiche glutting the industry, Moorcock condemned the folly of those who imitated Howard and lamented the damage they had wrought. "Sadly the vitality of the original Conan stories has not been reproduced in the imitations (including films) since done by a variety of hands and Howard's virtues (as a synthesist if nothing else) were threatened with burial as exploitive publishers encouraged further imitations and republished every piece of mediocre work Howard ever wrote" (*Wizardry & Wild*

Romance 58). But by the late 70s even Moorcock was guilty of churning out generic sword-and-sorcery material at such a rapid clip that quality was left by the wayside (Scroggins 60).

The Clonans were not solely responsible for the declining public and critical perception of sword-and-sorcery. A portion of the blame falls to de Camp and Carter. Almost all early sword-and-sorcery bears their stamp: they edited its first and most noteworthy anthologies, provided analysis of its works in the likes of *Amra*, wrote its early histories, and contributed to the sword-and-sorcery milieu with several stories of their own. Carter gave sword-and-sorcery its longest non-fiction treatment in his hallmark fantasy survey *Imaginary Worlds* (1973) which devotes two chapters to the birth and subsequent flowering of the subgenre. De Camp added to the conversation with the introductions to his four volume Pyramid anthologies, as well as *Literary Swordsmen and Sorcerers: The Makers of Heroic Fantasy* (1976), a collection of 10 biographical entries on key figures in the development of fantasy. *Literary Swordsmen and Sorcerers* includes chapters on Robert E. Howard and Clark Ashton Smith as well as a brief summation of the sword-and-sorcery authors that followed in Howard's wake ("Conan's Compeers"). And de Camp's entertaining columns are ubiquitous in the pages of the fanzine *Amra*.

De Camp and Carter deserve accolades for their role as pioneers, working largely without precedent in a field without codification or formal criticism. They were earnest in their efforts, and largely championed a genre ignored or dismissed outright by literary critics and academia. But theirs is no story of simple triumph. De Camp circumscribed and diminished sword-and-sorcery with superficial analysis in the introductions of his anthologies, marring them with personal biases and shallow analysis. Even as he shed some light on the historical foundations, form, and function of sword-and-sorcery, de Camp burdened the genre with an arbitrary set of limitations. Typically this took the form of a repeated assertion of sword-and-sorcery as a lightweight genre whose only purpose was to provide its readers with an escape from the real world. De Camp led off *Swords & Sorcery*, the first in the four volume Pyramid Books anthologies, with the following explanation:

> The tales collected under this name are adventure-fantasies, laid in imaginary prehistoric of medieval worlds, when (it's fun to imagine) all men were mighty, all women were beautiful, all problems were simple, and all life was adventurous. ... Heroic fantasy is escape reading in which you escape clear out of the real universe. (de Camp, *Swords and Sorcery* 7).

In the next volume, the *Spell of Seven*, de Camp criticized literary fiction for its dreary seriousness, but again limning

sword-and-sorcery as capable only of delivering shallow entertainment. "How would you like to escape to a world of wizards and
warlocks, warriors and wenches? ... Do you feel like saying: 'To hell
with the world's problems for a while! Let's read something for
fun'? Then you should read heroic fantasy" (7). The fourth and final
volume *Warlocks and Warriors* contains more of the same. "This is
pure escape literature and makes no bones about it. Reading for
serious purposes is fine, but even the most serious reader is better
off if he sometimes reads something for the hell of it. In these stories
one escapes clear out of the real world" (7).

This sort of reductionism allows little room for analysis or literary
criticism. De Camp effectively cut off sword-and-sorcery from the
fantastic literary traditions from which it sprung, and overlooked
the new aesthetic it introduced to traditional fantasy. Among de
Camp's critics was Karl Edward Wagner. Wagner stated that "epic
fantasy" (his preferred term for sword-and-sorcery) should not be
placed lower on the ladder of criticism than any other genre:

> When the universe is effectively envisioned and the characters
> are convincingly realized, epic fantasy can command the reader's
> attention on multiple levels of enjoyment. When the universe is
> a cardboard stage set and the characters comic book stereotypes,
> the result is cliché-ridden melodrama. While it would seem obvious
> that such holds true for *any* genre, there are some who insist that
> epic fantasy is no more than "swords and sorcery" hokum. It is a
> judgment comparable to dismissing the entire science fiction genre
> as "space opera" (*Conan: Red Nails* 1-2).

How much influence de Camp's introductions had is subjective, but
there is evidence they helped to perpetuate a perception of sword-and-
sorcery fiction as fluff entertainment. In an October 1970 Associated
Press review of *Warlocks and Warriors*, an AP reviewer regurgitated de
Camp's party line of sword-and-sorcery as escapist fare:

> Call them space opera or sword-play-and-sorcery stories, it makes
> little difference. Their purpose was to entertain. And this, most of
> them do. As the editor observes in his introduction, "This is pure
> escape literature and make no bones about it. Reading for serious
> purposes is fine, but even the most serious reader is better off if he
> sometimes reads something for the hell of it. In these stories one
> escapes clear out of the real world."
>
> One certainly does. Into the future, into the past. A variety of
> never-never lands, peopled by heroes with bulging muscles and
> singing swords, brilliant magicians, and really bad, bad-guys who
> never triumph but give the hero a terrible time before he finally
> puts them down.

De Camp was a professional cynic; little of the romantic blood of
Howard or the poetic soul of Smith flowed in his veins. He treated

Howard's eccentricities with suspicion, and at times, derision. His 1983 Howard biography, *Dark Valley Destiny: The Life of Robert E. Howard. Dark Valley Destiny*, contains copious and invaluable first-person research; de Camp traveled to Texas on five different occasions and interviewed dozens of sources who knew the Howard family first-hand. Unfortunately, the book is marred by dubious speculation on Howard's character, posthumous psychoanalysis of Howard conducted by co-author Jane Whittington Griffin, a psychologist specializing in child development (de Camp, *Dark Valley Destiny* 2).[4]

De Camp was also a pedant, and spent a great deal of real estate in *Amra* scrutinizing historical anachronisms that cropped up in Howard's fiction:

> Howard had some knowledge of the history of armor, as witness his story "Red Blades of Black Cathay" (Oriental Stories, Feb.-Mar., 1931). In this tale the hero, a European fighting in Central Asia against Jenghiz Khan, is described as wearing armor of the period of transition from mail to plate. Howard got his transition a century too early. And although one can find his various types of helmet in standard works on arms and armor, it would seem that Howard did not take these distinctions very seriously. Not only did he name types from +XV to +XVI, well into the gunpowder era, but he sometimes also referred to one single helmet by the names or two or three different types ("Hyborian Technology" 60)

Even the antediluvian Hyborian Age with its magic, monsters, and larger-than-life heroes did not escape de Camp's skeptical eye:

> Hyborian applied science is advanced enough to make a large magnet ("Shadows in Zamboula") strong enough to hold Conan's sword against his efforts to pull it free. I doubt if any piece of natural lodestone would have so dense a magnetic flux. On the other hand, it's hard to conceive of an electromagnet in such an environment. My guess is that our hero really took a whack at one of Baal-Pteor's spectral beasts, hit a heavy wooden table instead, and sank his sword so firmly into it that he could not pull it out ("Hyborian Technology" 61).

While demonstrative of de Camp's historical erudition, and perhaps written somewhat tongue-in-cheek to amuse readers, essays such as "Hyborian Technology" demonstrate that de Camp cared less about the spirit of a tale than its details and historical fidelity. Woe to the writer who used the wrong terminology or inadvertently placed an anachronism in a story; de Camp famously turned his back on Howard for 20 years after Howard mistakenly inserted a stirrup into the Bran Mak Morn story "Kings of the Night" (*Time and Chance* 216). As he obsessed over the nomenclature of a helmet

---

[4] De Camp later described *Dark Valley Destiny* as a "psycho-biography" of Howard (*Time and Chance* 391).

or the unlikelihood of a large magnet in an antediluvian era, he missed the deeper, mythical elements in Howard's stories, and failed to acknowledge the symbolic truths that fantasy can convey. In a biography written late in his life, *Time and Chance*, a self-effacing de Camp admitted to being "maddeningly literal minded" (246). He found story-germs in working out the mathematics of magic, creating "what if" scenarios based on the impact that magic would "really" have on a medieval world setting. While Howard's sorcerers summoned dark and mysterious demons from the netherworld, de Camp wrote an entire story about a wizard who starts a magic carpet business, and the subsequent angst arising from a powerful merchant guild fearful of the impact of this new form of horseless transportation on their lucrative business model ("The Rug and the Bull," *Flashing Swords!* #2). De Camp's "heroes" are very often unheroic—ordinary, flawed, and sometimes bumbling, such that a reader can feel superior to them—and he deliberately portrayed them that way, belonging as they did to a "benighted" ancient age. For example, his contribution to *Flashing Swords #3*, "Two Yards of Dragon," is a fun but decidedly detached, ironic story in which chivalry and knighthood are mocked, depicted as a misguided misadventure. De Camp was remorselessly cynical and even hostile of romanticism in his fiction. His essay "The Heroic Barbarian" uses the term "heroic" with tongue firmly in cheek. "The Romantic Illusion of a primitive Golden Age has, in fact, flourished right down to the present. Jack London, who much influenced Robert Howard and who incongruously combined Marxism, racism, and romanticism, was full of it." He summarized of the subgenre, "Hence the resemblance of so many heroes of ancient epics and modern sword-and-sorcery fiction to overgrown juvenile delinquents. Such liberated behavior, in the real world, does not make one a good life-insurance risk ("The Heroic Barbarian" 230-234).

De Camp could not identify with the feelings of alienation from society that fueled the writings of Howard and later sword-and-sorcery writers such as Leiber. He largely admitted as much later in life. "I suspect I have a pretty good estimate of my own abilities and limitations," he wrote. "For example, I cannot put into my stories the violent emotional intensity that Robert Howard did, because I do not suffer from his neuroses" (*Time and Chance* 323). To his credit he later admitted that he might not have been the optimal editor of the Lancer/Ace Conan line. "I daresay others could have done better as custodian of the saga and Howard's posthumous ghost writer. But I happened to be there at the time" (308).

Carter at times elevated the subgenre beyond de Camp's remorselessly literal view, but just as often parroted de Camp's patronizing views of sword-and-sorcery and mean-spirited appraisals of Howard. As a result, Carter's not-insubstantial critical writings frequently carry an air of the schizophrenic about them. Carter is everywhere sheepish and conflicted about Howard, whose works he both unabashedly devoured (and openly imitated in his own tales of Thongor) and at turns denigrated and belittled:

> He wrote two-fisted westerns, sport stories, gangster yarns, and an historical series about a dour Puritan adventurer named Solomon Kane who brawled his way through the black jungles of Africa, battering down blood-soaked altars armed with a huge iron-bound Bible. He secretly yearned to write yarns of magic and mystery in Tibet or stories about keen-eyed British espionage agents in India in the vein of Talbot Mundy, or swashbuckling pirate sagas like Rafael Sabatini, or the kind of romantic adventure fiction Edgar Rice Burroughs and Harold Lamb produced. But Howard's rather slapdash, derivative talents could not compete for the major pulps like *Argosy* or *All-Story* against writers like these, to say nothing of Jack London, James Oliver Curwood, and Max Brand, so he settled for *Weird Tales* (*Imaginary Worlds* 63).

In the same chapter of *Imaginary Worlds* in which he makes a claim that Howard lacked originality ("The Conan stories were really nothing new"), Carter also credits Howard with the creation of an entire subgenre of literature that he would defend and continue to write in until the end of his days. "The kind of story Howard created with his Conan yarns, and which C.L. Moore imitated with her tales of Jirel, we call 'Sword & Sorcery today'" (65-66). Exactly how a writer can both write stories that were "nothing new" but simultaneously birth a subgenre and a horde of imitators is not immediately apparent. Later in the same chapter Carter drew an unflattering comparison of Howard with sword-and-sorcery author Henry Kuttner (author of the serviceable, but hardly immortal Elak of Atlantis stories), building up Kuttner's versatility as an author at the expense of tearing down Howard: "[Kuttner] was, however, a superb craftsman—a born writer—a story-teller par excellence in much the same way that Howard had been; however, Kuttner was capable of a truly remarkable variety, unlike Howard" (67). This is a rather puzzling statement, coming on the heels of Carter's prior summation of Howard as a writer not only responsible for creating sword-and-sorcery, but also one who branched out to write westerns, historical fiction, and boxing stories.

Carter described Howard's Hyborian Age pre-historical setting as "slapdash," comparing them unfavorably with de Camp's air-tight secondary worlds. Of de Camp's collaboration with author Fletcher Pratt in the pages of the magazine *Unknown* ("The Castle of Iron," April 1941), Carter fawned, "The story opened with yet another display of what this incomparable team could do with rational, real-istic thinking as against the sloppy romanticism common to pulp writers" (*Imaginary Worlds* 79-80). Like de Camp, Carter saw only pure story in Howard, not his deeper philosophical ruminations or his commentary on modernity. He scoffed at the notion that speculative literature as a whole could have anything meaningful to say. "These days, science fiction takes itself awfully seriously and strives to pretend it is a Serious Literary Genre, hoping nobody will remember that its roots lie in a bunch of gaudy, horrendously vulgar thirty-year-old pulps. We Sword & Sorcery chaps, however, have few such pretensions" (158).

A Subgenre under Attack

Historically, sword-and-sorcery has fared poorly among critics. Reviewing the first published collection of Howard's stories, *Skull-Face and Others* (1946), a *New York Times* reviewer was so appalled by its violence that his review "was devoted to warning against the schizophrenic perils of heroic fiction and said little about the stories" (de Camp, "Skald in the Post Oaks" 23). Sword-and-sorcery author and essayist Samuel Delany describes the field as the "most despised sub-genre of paraliterary production" (*Silent Interviews: On Language, Race, Sex, Science Fiction, and Some Comics* 129). Essayist George Knight summed up of the field in its mid-80s nadir, "In such standard sources as *Fantasy Literature* (1979), edited by Marshall Tymn, Kenneth J. Zahorski, and Robert H. Boyer, Howard's fiction of Sword-and-Sorcery is redefined as "Sword and Sinew" and frowned upon. They admit that the 'style of sword and sinew work, like its rawboned superhero, is frequently muscular, energetic, and hard-driving, but is seldom elevated, sophisticated, or brilliantly polished'" ("Robert E. Howard: Hard-Boiled Heroic Fantasist" 128).

In his 1981 survey of horror and dark fantasy, *Danse Macabre*, popular horror author Stephen King unleashed one of the most infamous skewerings of the subgenre, categorizing it as a mediocre branch of fantasy that catered tales of power and wish-fulfillment for the powerless, "stories of strong-thewed barbarians whose extraordinary prowess at fighting is only excelled by their extraor-dinary prowess at fucking" (345). Added King:"This sort of fiction, commonly called 'sword and sorcery' by its fans, is not fantasy at its lowest, but it still has a pretty tacky feel; mostly it's the Hardy Boys dressed up in animal skins and rated R" (345).[5] King men-tions no individual works or authors of sword-and-sorcery in his

---

[5] For the curious, only comic book superheroes rank beneath sword-and-sorcery in King's hierarchy of bad literature.

savage broadside, save Howard, who he also praises as "the only writer who really got away with this stuff. ... Howard overcame the limitations of his puerile material by the force and fury of his writing and by his imagination." King's drive-by swipe shows little evidence of any knowledge of the genre outside of a superficial understanding of Howard, but he had ample support in de Camp; Conan's official editor was around this time describing Howard's fiction as "escapist entertainment," not a vehicle for the "revelation of profound truths") ("Editing Conan" 118). Later critics picked up the same "escapist" bat with which King beat the genre, painting sword-and-sorcery as a lowbrow form of entertainment kept afloat by the weekly allowances of otherwise powerless teenage boys. Wrote Robert Reginald in *Science Fiction and Fantasy Literature* (1992), "Conan has become established as an archetypal hero of the Sword-and-Sorcery subgenre. ... Like all superhero fantasies, this one appeals to readers (especially adolescent males) who feel that they are objects of scarcely viewed contempt in a world with whose complications they cannot cope" (Romeo, "Napoleon's Triumph?").

There is an element of boyishness in sword-and-sorcery, baked into its DNA from its creator. Howard was just entering manhood when he took his own life, and the weakness and infirmity that he associated with aging may have been a contributing factor in his suicide. In a May 9, 1936, letter to August Derleth he wrote, "When a man dies young he misses much suffering, but the old have only life as a possession, and somehow to me the tearing of a pitiful remnant from weak old fingers is more tragic than the looting of life in its rich full prime. I don't want to live to be old. I want to die when my time comes, quickly and suddenly, in the full tide of my strength and health" (Finn, *Blood and Thunder* 225). One month later Howard was dead from a self-inflicted gunshot wound. Howard opted not to confront the demons of aging and infirmity in his fiction, and most of his imitators followed suit. The mighty hero who can deal with impossible odds or any monstrous adversary, save his own age-in-duced infirmity, is a common sword-and-sorcery trope. Moorcock criticized sword-and-sorcery for its lack of adult characters. "Until relatively recently, very few adult central characters existed in pure 'sword and sorcery' stories—they are either permanent adolescents, like Conan, actual children like Ged in Ursula Le Guin's Wizard of Earth Sea, youths like Airar Alvarson in The Well of the Unicorn, or quasi-children like the hobbits in The Lord of the Rings" (*Wizardry & Wild Romance* 84). In the foreword to *Swords Against Darkness* editor Andrew Offutt acknowledged, "All of us who love to read it ... and those of us who can't help writing it are the very people Conan Doyle was referring to when he wrote:

> I have wrought my simple plan
> If I give one hour of joy
> To the boy who's half a man
> Or the man who's half a boy. (8)

Later sword-and-sorcery writers tackled aging. David Gemmell's *Legend* is about the aging warrior Druss battling foes on the battlefield along with increasingly creaky joints. Fafhrd and the Gray Mouser confront the weight of responsibility and the cooling of youthful ardor in *The Knight and Knave of Swords*. But Howard's sword-and-sorcery heroes never encountered the implacable foes that come with old age, and his shadow is formidable.

The late 1960s and early 70s were times of societal change, with the women's movement dominating news cycles. Sword-and-sorcery of the era was out-of-step. Often this took the form of helpless women in need of saving, but sometimes it surfaced as male chauvinism. In *Brak vs. the Sorceress* (1977), Brak accepts a mission to avenge the slaying of his pony, but also to teach a spirited woman a lesson in humility:

> To her, the life of a pony was a small thing, and therein lay her evil. To him, the pony's life mattered much. His choice was clear-cut. He would not slink away. He would punish her. He was Brak, a man.

Other works were more openly hostile. Fox did sword-and-sorcery no favors with the naked sexism and misogyny of *Kothar, Barbarian Swordsman* (1969). In "The Sword of the Sorcerer," the first published story of Kothar, the young barbarian casually contemplates rape:

> "He has told me you can save my throne for me. He did not tell me you would all but rape me at the same time."

> His barbaric blood was in a ferment. Elfa was a tease-body, as was Red Lori. Were all women? Kothar was a simple person, essentially. If a woman pleased him, he took her to bed with him. If she did not, he ignored her (29).

Again in Fox's *Kyrik: Warlock Warrior*:

> When she saw the way he stared, she flushed, then raised her chin defiantly. "I'm no roundheels to be tossed on the grass and enjoyed the way you did Myrnis!"

> Kyrik laughed, caught her by a bare arm, swung her in against him. He knew the softness of her body, its attraction. His green eyes stared down into her angry face.

> "Woman, if I wished, I could have you now, and well you know it. You want me, it's there in your black eyes"—the serpent on his sword hissed"—but I have other things to do" (106).

Female authors began to call out the worst of these clichés. In 1984, author and editor Marion Zimmer Bradley launched her own sword-and-sorcery anthology, *Sword and Sorceress*, countering the subgenre's sexism with an offering of strong feminine heroes:

The special sub-genre of fantasy known as "sword and sorcery" has been the last to be integrated between man and woman. Until recently, this bastion of male-dominated adventure fiction was the last stronghold of the brawny male hero; women were the reward or the incitement for his adventures, but never shared them. Women, in sword-and-sorcery fiction, when not a mere "screaming maiden" to be rescued from dragons, dangers and doom-laden Evil Wizards, remained strictly offstage, emerging now and again to reward the hero with her dower kingdom and a chaste kiss. But women read fantasy too, and we get tired of identifying with male heroes (9).

Jessica Amanda Salmonson took up the cause against sword-and-sorcery's objectification of women in *Amazons!* (1979), which won a World Fantasy Award for best collection in 1980:

A truly "good ol' boys" adventure preferably contains no bothersome wenches at all—merely a lewd reference or two in order to confirm the protagonist's and his friends' fundamental normalcy. By far the largest role women play in heroic fantasy or "sword and sorcery" is not in the text of the authors, but in illustrations rendered by artists of intriguing if limited ability. They habitually depict women of peculiar thigh and mammary proportions. ... In less romantic terms, it has been escape fantasy for the least mature aspects of the male ego: escape into worlds where simpletons are rewarded for unprovoked violence and undisguised misogyny. Even die-hard aficionados of the genre are wont to say, "It's bloody awful, but it's fun." But for readers (men or women) who cannot revel in warped attitudes toward women, it isn't even fun (14–15).

Sword-and-sorcery is far from uniformly sexist. From its earliest days it has not only been enjoyed by women, but practiced by female authors, and has featured the occasional strong female protagonist. In the 1930s, C.L. Moore (to whom Zimmer dedicated *Sword and Sorceress*) began writing her own tales of sword-and-sorcery featuring the heroine Jirel of Joiry. Howard sent a copy of his story "Sword Woman" featuring the strong female hero Dark Agnes to Moore, who praised both the character and Howard for his forward thinking (Finn, *Blood and Thunder* 186). The sword-and-sorcery renaissance of the 1960s and 70s saw the emergence of several female authors including Andre Norton, Tanith Lee, Jane Yolen, Salmonson, and Bradley. Many of these women contributed to its enduring anthologies. "Odds Against the Gods" by Tanith Lee in *Swords Against Darkness II* (1977) passes the pop-culture "Bechdel Test" on every level, featuring a female author writing about a female protagonist involved in a sexual relationship with another female. While containing its share of damsels in distress and occasionally distressing scenes of sexual assault, a deeper look beyond the titillation of its covers reveals sword-and-sorcery as home to strong female protagonists. Howard, for example, is described by biographer Mark Finn as a "proto-feminist" (Murphy) for his use of fiercely independent female characters, including "Dark Agnes" de Chastillon ("Sword Woman") and Red Sonya ("The Shadow of the Vulture"), as well as strong female supporting roles including Bêlit ("Queen of the Black Coast") and Valeria ("Red Nails"). In her essay "Tales from the Brass Bikini: Feminist Sword and Sorcery," author Paula R. Stiles—while acknowledging the subgenre's problematic depiction of women— writes that, starting in the late 70s and progressing through the 90s, the subgenre was an early haven for feminism:

> Decades before the tough, gun-toting vampire hunters with their sassy tats, navel-rings, and strange attractions to undead sexual partners from the other side of the fence, Sword and Sorcery (excuse me— "Heroic Fantasy," we're calling it, now) was the unapologetic ghetto of feminist fantasy. These heroines, who did not care one hoot whether they were drawn like men with tits or not, were powerful sorceresses, cold-blooded mercenaries with magical and Freudian blades, lusty queens, even lustier pirate captains, and female Conans who wore almost nothing into battle. If you wanted your feminism with a hefty dose of mindless, bloody action, S&S was your first stop. As a young tomboy growing up in the 70s and 80s, I ate it all up with a bronze dagger.

> Unsurprisingly, this subgenre is a morass of bad attitudes. Some of them have been progressive; Sword and Sorcery is one of the first genres to present lesbians as perfectly acceptable protagonists. Some of them have been anything but: rape, and its frequent use as an origin story for heroines, being an especially troubling subject (Stiles).

Howard's most famous female creation, Red Sonya of Rogatino, got her own fantasy series in the early 1980s. Authors David C. Smith and Richard Tierney teamed up to write a six volume series of the Hyrkanian swordswoman (earlier renamed Red Sonja by comic-book author Roy Thomas), consisting of *The Ring of Ikribu* (1981), *Demon Knight* (1982), *When Hell Laughs* (1982), *Endithor's Daughter* (1982), *Against the Prince of Hell* (1983), and *Star of Doom* (1983). Smith and Tierney followed the lead of Thomas, who took Howard's character out of her historical, 16th century Europe setting and placed her into the Hyborian Age of Conan. Although Sonja wears an oft-criticized chain-mail bikini in the series, she is portrayed not only as physically strong, but also fully three-dimensional—driven, flawed, and chaste. Her personal code dictates that only the man who bests her in combat is worthy of her affections. *The Ring of Ikribu* features a particularly effective sword duel with Lord Olin, a man whom she admires and for whom she possesses a physical attraction. Olin rashly challenges her to a duel to win her love. Sonja, the better swordsman, cannot bring herself to slay Olin in an implicitly sexualized scene whose strenuous cut and thrusts allude to ardent lovemaking.

Sword-and-sorcery has endured charges of racial stereotyping, with Howard a principal target. These criticisms are not entirely without merit. As with the charges of sexism, some sword-and-sorcery contains racist portrayals of people of color. Howard held ugly prejudices common to the early 20th century and these occasionally spill into his stories. These were far more prominent in his early Solomon Kane material and in particular his short story "The Last White Man," the latter of which makes for particularly uncomfortable reading material. But by the time of the Conan stories Howard had grown more enlightened, though some stories like "Shadows in Zamboula" and "Queen of the Black Coast" contain stereotyped depictions of blacks offensive today, if not uncommon in the 1930s. Today, most consider Howard racist by 21st century standards, but with beliefs largely mainstream in the early 20th. L. Sprague de Camp summed up in *Dark Valley Destiny*, "If a racist, Robert Howard was, by the standards of his time and place, a comparatively mild one" (176). Howard's second major biographer, Mark Finn, wrote in *Blood and Thunder*: "It is incredibly naive to throw a twenty-first-century value judgment onto people who were living a hundred years ago. For every instance of racism found in Howard's work, a compelling counterargument can be found elsewhere" (84).

Classic pulp-era sword and sorcery is the product of a different age, and a failure to apply historical context is not only unfair to the author, but intellectually lazy. Howard lived in an era in which Rudyard Kipling's "white man's burden"—a popular poem of the Anglo-Saxon "obligation" to civilize the dark races of the earth and lift them up from their barbaric squalor—scarcely raised an eyebrow, and when United States president Theodore Roosevelt referred to Africans as ape-like savages. Segregation was accepted and Jim Crow laws practiced. Stereotypical depictions of black cannibals such as those found in "Shadows in Zamboula" must be evaluated within this context. When you read A. Merritt's *The Ship of Ishtar* (1924), for example, you enter the world of the past—not only the figurative/fantastic past of the story, but also the historical realities of the 1920s in which it was written. Merritt engaged in the same racial stereotyping most writers of the pulp era employed: men of Nineveh and of Babylon are identified by their hook noses and ringleted beards; men of the Orient as "almond lidded, smiling yellow men."

But historical context does not lessen the pain of encountering bigotry in print. Charles Saunders, author of the *Imaro* stories, summed up his equivocal feelings of being a black sword-and-sorcery reader in his 1974 essay "Die, Black Dog!":

> For an avid reader of fantasy who also happens to be black, the exclamation in the title of this essay pops up far too often for comfort.

The genre-related problems of reader identification and suspension of disbelief become immeasurably magnified with these words, because the ethnic epithets that spew from the mouth of a Conan are all-too-well represented in the grim world of reality (Saunders, "Revisiting 'Die, Black Dog!'").

A few fringe critics accused sword-and-sorcery of perpetrating an underlying philosophy of hate. Hans Joachim Alpers (1943–2011), a German writer and editor of science fiction and fantasy, savaged sword-and-sorcery not only for its fixation and glorification of violence and sex ("like the Amen after the sermon: the genre gets its due—cool girls and hot deaths"), but its endorsement of a repellent brand of Nazi ideology. Alpers concluded that sword-and-sorcery not only glorified German fascism, but was in some sinister manner brainwashing its readers—teaching them fascist ideology under the guise of heroic escapism, and paving the way for a new Fourth Reich:

> The ideologies thereby propagated are: magic-mystic understanding of the world, i.e., mystification of relationships that could be grasped by the intellect; right of the stronger as the principle of societal organization; glorification of violence, particularly killing; oppression of women; emphasis on the racial superiority of the Nordic (Aryan) type; fatalism toward hierarchic structures and their consequences, such as wars; the fuehrerprinciple: the greatest butcher of them all shall determine our fate; imperialistic policy; and anti-intellectualism.

Although a far-fetched claim, Alpers is not alone in connecting the dots between sword-and-sorcery and fascism. Norman Spinrad's *The Iron Dream* (1972) pulls the neat metafictional trick of being a novel about a faux-novel, *Lord of the Swastika,* the latter "written" by Adolf Hitler in an alternative historical scenario (Hitler emigrates from Germany to the U.S. after World War I and becomes a successful science-fiction writer). *The Iron Dream* is satire and draws an explicit comparison between the underlying mythmaking of heroic fantasy/sword-and-sorcery and the ideologies of racial hierarchy and superiority promulgated by Nazi Germany. In a review of *The Iron Dream*, Hugo and Nebula award-winning author of the Earthsea series Ursula LeGuin took the opportunity to join Spinrad and Alpers and skewer sword-and-sorcery as crassly commercial, feeble-minded, and sexist:

> On the back cover Michael Moorcock compares the book with "the works of J.R.R. Tolkien, C.S. Lewis, G.K. Chesterton, and Sir Oswald Mosley. ... It is the very quintessence of sword and sorcery." None of the authors mentioned is relevant, except Mosley, but the reference to sword and sorcery is exact. The Iron Dream can be read as a tremendous parody of the subgenre represented by Moorcock's own Runestaff saga, and by Conan the Barbarian, and Brak the Barbarian, and those Gor books, and so on—"heroic fantasy" on the

sub-basement level, the writing of which seems to be motivated by a mixture of simple-minded escapism and money-minded cynicism.

Taken as a parody of S&S, the book hits all its targets. There is the Hero, the Alpha Male with his muscles of steel and his clear eyes and his manifest destiny; there are the Hero's Friends; there are the vile, subhuman enemies; there is the Hero's Sword, in this case a truncheon of interesting construction; there are the tests, quests, battles, victories, culminating in a final supernal super-victory of the Superman. There are no women at all, no dirty words, no sex of any kind: the book is a flawless example of clean obscenity. It will pass any censor, except the one that sits within the soul.

A parody of S&S, however, is self-doomed. You cannot exaggerate what is already witlessly exaggerated; you cannot distort for comic effect something that is already distorted out of all reality. All Spinrad can do is equal the crassest kind of S&S; no one could surpass it (LeGuin, "On Norman Spinrad's The Iron Dream").

LeGuin's criticisms exaggerate the worst characteristics of the "Clonans" to buttress their arguments. Thongor and Kothar wield pretentious magic swords and are possessed of manifest destiny, but these elements were previously unheard of in sword-and-sorcery, being far more common to high fantasy (exceptions like the Stormbringer-wielding Elric were often doomed to die at the point of their "hero's" sword). The Iron Dream is a more apt criticism of Arthurian fantasy, in which the magic sword Excalibur confers a divine right upon a king worthy enough to wield it, and the promised return of some mythical golden age. The Iron Dream cuts closer to home in its critique of sword-and-sorcery's frequent use of orgiastic battlefield violence, with its muscular heroes effortlessly slicing through faceless hordes of enemies.

But LeGuin's broader point stands. The sword-and-sorcery genre had grown distorted and exaggerated by self-imitation and self-parody, particularly by the late 1970s-80s. In the latter days of its renaissance, the critical noose continued to tighten. Even critics who recognized some of its authors' works as substantive were critical of the broader subgenre. In her 1978 survey of fantasy *The Hills of Faraway: A Guide to Fantasy*, Diana Waggoner states that Howard's stories "hold up remarkably well, in spite of his racism and machismo," and offers praise for his fantastic settings and worlds of "nightmare beauty." But she had little use for the rest of the subgenre. "Few adventure writers have written as well as he did, but all since have imitated him. ... Most of these imitations have been hackwork...although a few writers, notably Fritz Leiber in his Gray Mouser and Fafhrd stories, have achieved creditable work" (48). Her overall assessment of "adventure fantasy" (her stand-in phrase for sword-and-sorcery) is that it "remains what it always has been—escapist trash" (36). Waggoner takes aim at Lin Carter's and Andre Norton's fiction as particularly poor representatives, but reserves her most virulent venom for Moorcock's Elric stories, which she accuses of committing pseudo-intellectual butchery of its underlying mythic material, and sums up as "hack sword-and-sorcery" (64). The following year, the survey *Fantasy Literature* (1979) discarded the term sword-and-sorcery in favor of "sword and sinew," and characterized the subgenre as one defined by flat characterization, simple and linear storylines, a lack of thematic substance, a pedestrian and colloquial literary style, and finally "an extreme emphasis upon gratuitous and sensational violence. Of all the traits mentioned here, this is perhaps the most characteristic, and the most disturbing" (Tymn, Zahorski, and Boyer 23-24).

Sword-and-sorcery's poor critical reception tarnished the public's perception and contributed to the subgenre's commercial failures. Sums up Moorcock scholar Mark Scroggins:

> The popular imagination holds that sword and sorcery is the paradise of arrested male adolescence: broad-thewed and dim-witted barbarians stride across pseudo-medieval landscapes, fighting wizards and giant snakes, rescuing (and bedding) grateful but sketchily characterized young women—all for the entertainment and titillation of socially maladapted teenage boys (23).

Publishing Problems

A glut of derivative, uninspired material certainly contributed to the downfall of the sword-and-sorcery genre. But the exigencies of publishers and the publishing industry sped its destruction. These presumed gatekeepers of quality were in the 1960s through the early 1980s eager to publish anything with a barbarian on its cover. In the wake of the Lancers, the likes of Ace, Bantam, and Del Rey, along with small publishers and imprints like Zebra Books, Unibook, and Belmont Books, began to publish sword-and-sorcery in quantity, outstripping available talent and originality.

Founded in 1974 as an imprint of Kensington Publishing, Zebra over the next decade glutted the market with sword-and-sorcery and anything resembling it, including historical adventure and sword-and-planet, as well as romance and horror. Zebra was known for keeping a small staff, paying its authors low royalties and small advances (as little as 2% and $500, respectively), and paying late. By the early 1980s they had grown their sales to $10 million annually, but by 1993 were out of business. Founded by Walter Zacharius and Robert Grossman, who left Lancer after that publisher filed for bankruptcy in 1973, Zebra set the bar low, and "was open to talent from other publishers who'd been passed over for promotions or forced to retire" (Hendrix 184).

By the late 1970s Conan the Cimmerian had become an industry unto itself, and exhaustion of original Howard material proved no obstacle. Book 10 of the Lancer Conan Saga, *Conan the Avenger,* contained no Howard material save part 2 of his "Hyborian Age" essay; the rest of the book was devoted to the pastiche novel "The Return of Conan" by de Camp and Bjorn Nyberg. Book 11, *Conan of Aquilonia* (1977), was pure de Camp and Carter, as was the concluding volume *Conan of the Isles.* De Camp and Carter extended Conan's life and adventures far beyond anything Howard had hinted at in Conan's fictional biography: *Conan of Aquilonia* introduced a son for Conan, Conn, while *Conan of the Isles* depicted an aging Conan heading out on one final adventure before turning over the kingdom's reins to his son.

Conan may have sailed into the sunset in *Conan of the Isles,* but the pastiche ship was just leaving port under full steam. A de Camp/ Carter novelization of the film *Conan the Barbarian* hit the shelves in 1982. Publisher Tor Books continued the Conan line with a lengthy series published between 1982 and 2004, starting with *Conan the Invincible* by Robert Jordan, who would later go on to fame and fortune with his wildly popular high fantasy series *The Wheel of Time.* Sandwiched between the Tors and the Lancer/Ace Conans were additional Conan series by Bantam and Ace. These featured a limited amount of Howard material, and principally pastiche from the likes of de Camp (*Conan and the Spider God,* 1980), *Swords Against Darkness* editor Andrew Offutt (1979's *The Sword of Skelos*), and sword-and-sorcery stalwarts Karl Edward Wagner (1979's *Conan: The Road of Kings*) and Poul Anderson (*Conan the Rebel,* 1980). "Conan" glutted the shelves, and some of it was good, but very little of it original Howard.[6]

Sword-and-sorcery's own were turning against it. Though he had made a nice living with his stories of Elric, Moorcock came to dismiss the subgenre as a "compensatory fantasy of homicidal barbarians and grunting rapists" (*Wizardry & Wild Romance* 92). Poul Anderson wrote an infamous skewering for *Sword and Darkness III,* "On Thud and Blunder," (1978), which delivered a well-deserved critique of its sloppy, ill-researched, and implausible combat sequences, improbable feats of overland and overseas travel, and omission of religious and political elements. "While no one expects heroic fantasy to be of ultimate psychological profundity, it is often simple to the point

---

[6] This "boom-bust" sequence is not unique to sword and sorcery. In the 1990s the same phenomenon occurred with the horror genre. Stephen King—an author as influential to horror as Howard is to sword-and-sorcery—ignited a publishing frenzy in the 1970s–80s with the success of his novels *The Shining, The Stand,* and *Pet Sematary.* In a rush to feed voracious fans yearning for more horror, publishing companies opened the doors to a floodgate of second-rate writers churning out hastily-commissioned King clones. Readers eventually caught on, left in droves, and by the 1990s the horror genre was on life support.

of being simplistic. ...Worse, because it is still more obvious and still less excusable, is a frequent lack of elementary knowledge or plain common sense on the part of an author" ("On Thud and Blunder" 160). The subgenre had become a subject of justified self-parody. Terry Pratchett's *The Color of Magic* (1983) and its 1985 sequel *The Light Fantastic* lampooned a genre now saddled not only with bad books, but low-budget, cringe-worthy films (these will be explored in detail in chapter nine) with its toothless, aged "Cohen the Barbarian." Larry Niven painted a grim picture of a world in which barbarians triumphed over sorcery in the short story "Not Long Before the End." Each swordsman who dies in combat with a sorcerer causes "humanity's average intelligence (to rise) some trifling fraction." A clichéd barbarian warrior with the surname "Cononson" (Conan-son?) receives a lecture from a warlock that magic is a form of knowledge, and a non-renewing resource that generations of loutish barbarians are extinguishing at their peril.

Quality was at an all-time low and sword-and-sorcery became a genre for which some writers were willing to accept a royalty check, but not the shame of their name on the cover. "Chris Carlsen" authored the late 1970s Berserker trilogy *The Shadow of the Wolf*, *The Bull Chief*, and *The Horned Warrior*, but Carlsen was actually a pseudonym for Robert Holdstock. Holdstock, who would later go on to publish the World Fantasy Award winning *Mythago Wood* (1985), later described the Berserker series as "hackwork," written for money and to meet the genre expectations of publisher Sphere (Thompson). Of *The Bull Chief*, Holdstock said that it was "heavily influenced by commercial requirements, which accounts for many of the less tasteful ingredients within it," adding of a rape scene, "I was responding very much to instructions as I understood them from the commercial market. I think those instructions were a mistake for the commercial market. They were certainly a mistake for me to have obeyed, but I was young and innocent."

With sword-and-sorcery beginning to flag, publishers left for greener pastures, drawn by the promises of an alluring and lucrative new model: the fantasy series. Series (at first trilogies, but later five, seven, or more books) offered a more stable and profitable revenue model for publishers, a case made plain by the wild success of *The Lord of the Rings* "trilogy" (actually one book published in three volumes). Why publish a standalone sword-and-sorcery novel or short story collection when you can hook readers and their wallets on a multi-book series? Soon fantasy shelves became crowded with faux epics, starting with Terry Brooks' *Sword of Shannara* (1977) and its sequels *The Elfstones of Shannara* and *The Wishsong of Shannara* (Ballantine/Del Rey) and Stephen Donaldson's trilogy *The Chronicles* of *Thomas Covenant, the Unbeliever* (1977–1979). When sword-and-sorcery began its free-fall in the mid-1980s, high fantasy was just warming up with the likes of Dennis McKiernan's *Iron Tower* trilogy, Margaret Weiss and Tracy Hickman's *Dragonlance* Chronicles, and David Eddings' five book series *The Belgariad* (Del Rey). Short formats—historically the sweet spot for sword-and-sorcery—got lost in this new landscape of multi-page, multi-volume epics.

Karl Edward Wagner offered a semi-autographical vignette of the rapid transformation taking hold of fantasy publishing in the late 70s and early 80s in his short story "Neither Brute Nor Human." Damon Harrington is a sword-and-sorcery short story writer struggling to pay the bills in a market that has shifted to horror and high fantasy. His friend Trevor Nordgren (whose abrupt rise to fame and fortune and accompanying cocaine-fueled lifestyle has more than a few parallels to Stephen King), now enjoying six-figure advances for his latest horror novel *The Etching*, encourages Harrington to abandon sword-and-sorcery for greener pastures:

> "You ought to try to reach the greater audience, instead of catering to the cape-and-pimples set. You're getting labeled as a thud-and-blunder hack, and as long as publishers can buy you for a few grand a book, that's all they'll ever see in you" (*Why Not You and I?* 120).

Harrington's agent breaks the news to the struggling author that his publisher has cancelled his moderately successful Krystle Firewind sword-and-sorcery series, declaring it "sexist trash." She recommends he try a high fantasy trilogy:

> "Problem is that every paperback house that wants to already has one or two swords-and-sorcery series going. Do you think you could write high fantasy? That's getting to be big just now. You know—lighten up a little on the violence and bare tits, give your imaginary world more of a bunch of fairy-tale atmosphere, maybe link in a bunch of Celtic myths and that sort of thing."

> "I can try it." Harrington imagined Krystel Firewind stripped of sword and armor and a few inches of bustline, gowned in shimmering damask or maybe flowing priestess' robes (123–124).

The completed work, titled *Tallyssa's Quest: Book One of the Fall of the Golden Isles*, is published with a wraparound cover "depicting a billowingly berobed Tallyssa astride her flying unicorn and brandishing her Star of Life amulet to defend her elfin companions from a horde of bestial Kralkings." It earns Harrington his first five-figure advance and eventual fame and fortune—and it only requires his soul in return.

As the 1980s got underway, the decade brought with it, at least in America, a return to prosperity and material excess. The financial, societal, and political upheavals concurrent to sword-and-sorcery's birth in the 1930s, as well as its second renaissance in the mid-late 60s and 70s, had passed. An exploding stock market, coupled with suburban sprawl and the proliferation of new technologies competing for the entertainment dollar including personal computers and video game consoles, reversed the nation's zeitgeist from one that welcomed literary barbaric upheaval and overthrow to one that valued the fruits of civilization and industry. Peace and prosperity and faith in society's institutions are not a great breeding ground for sword-and-sorcery. It seemed that civilization was perhaps the natural state of mankind after all, at least in the U.S.

Blasted and reviled by the critics, groaning under a glut of poor Conan knock-offs, and unable to compete with elven princesses and epic quests, the sword-and-sorcery bubble burst, and the entire apparatus began falling to earth in the early to mid-1980s. Several authors were dragged down in its wake. Charles Saunders, for example, had just come onto the scene with the mass-market publication of *Imaro* (1981). The book met with a rough start after an unfortunately chosen cover blurb ("The Epic Novel of a Black Tarzan") led to a lawsuit from the estate of Edgar Rice Burroughs. A hastily redone cover and reprint may have contributed to poor initial sales, as well as a lukewarm reception for its two sequels *The Quest for Cush* (1984) and *The Trail of Bohu* (1985) (Lupoff 251). Michael Shea's *Nifft the Lean* was published in 1982 to rave critical reviews, winning Best Novel at the 1983 World Fantasy Awards, but commercial sales failed to match its critical reception. It remains an obscure novel to this day.

In July 1982 the venerable fanzine *Amra* ceased publication, ending its run with the Vol. 2, No. 71 issue. On the surface the magazine seemed healthier and more relevant than ever, in its final years boasting a higher page count and a professionally typeset, two-column format. Material was plentiful with the much hyped and anticipated *Conan the Barbarian* set to debut in movie theaters. But far less healthy was the sword-and-sorcery literary scene. For more than a decade prior its readers had decried the decline in quality of new stories and their adherence to stale formula, as in this letter by Jeffrey May:

> Lin Carter said that "in an action story, depth and subtlety of characterization are out of place." Here, I think, is the reason why heroic fantasy has been declining in the last several months. Too many writers have written stories without depth or subtlety of characterization, and the result has been a passel of thoroughly mediocre tales that left their readers thoroughly dissatisfied. Mr. Carter, depth and subtlety of characterization or description are never out of place in any story. I will not argue that Conan is subtlety characterized, but he is deeply characterized. Another heroic fantasy hero, the Gray Mouser, is both deeply and subtlety characterized, and to my mind

he is even better rounded out and better presented than Conan. And even if one portrays his hero in bold strokes, other characters need depth and subtlety in their portrayals, too. I believe that heroic fantasy, especially S&S, could well stand more and better characterization, most especially if one's hero is a barbarian. ... Until heroic fantasy writers shake off the idea that all heroic fantasy needs is a simple barbarian hero and a simple action plot, heroic fantasy is going to go absolutely nowhere, except maybe down" (*Amra* Vol. 2 No. 57).

In 1987, Karl Edward Wagner attempted a third sword-and-sorcery rejuvenation, launching the first of the short but memorable *Echoes of Valor* series for publisher Tor. *Echoes of Valor* is Wagner's love letter to sword-and-sorcery and a terrific introduction to its classic authors. In addition to leading off each volume with a Robert E. Howard story, Wagner introduced his readers to the likes of Henry Kuttner, C.L. Moore, Leigh Brackett, Manly Wade Wellman, and the little known but highly regarded Nictzin Dyalhis. *Echoes of Valor* published Howard's "The Black Stranger" for the first time in full, and followed that up with "The Frost-King's Daughter" and "The Shadow of the Vulture," the latter featuring Red Sonya of Rogatino. Wagner insisted on publishing the authors' stories as originally intended, including Leiber's "Adept's Gambit," in which he opted for the rare 1947 Arkham House edition rather than the more readily available version from the 1968 paperback collection *Swords in the Mist*. Unfortunately, *Echoes of Valor* was a commercial flop. In one of his final interviews, Wagner blamed a lack of promotion and poor sales for the death of the short-lived series, and the short memory of the sword-and-sorcery fan base. "No one cared about reading old stories," he concluded (Owston). *Echoes of Valor* lasted just three volumes before ceasing in 1991. Twenty years prior it would have been hard to conceive of it being anything but a smash hit.

Among the last true sword-and-sorcery novels to receive mass distribution were the "Death Dealer" novels by James Silke, based on a painting of the same name by legendary fantasy/sword and sorcery illustrator Frank Frazetta. These in some ways were the last gasp of the genre. Their striking cover art attempted to reclaim the magic of the Lancer/Ace Conan Saga, but the quality of the writing paled next to Howard. The Death Dealer series struck an unfavorable compromise between sword-and-sorcery and high fantasy, and as a result succeeded at neither. *Prisoner of the Horned Helmet* contains the most beefcake barbarian ever committed to paper, Gath of Baal, a murderous slab of beefcake and an overgrown teenager who just wants to be left alone. He battles a snake so large its tongue weighs 300 pounds, romances a sorceress named Cobra, Queen of Serpents, and spends most of the book awash in over the top gore, with corpses mounded on corpses...on corpses. Like this:

Gath of Baal stood on a pile of dead bodies working his axe. The surviving nomads surrounded him. Splattered with blood, they mindlessly charged up the bodies of the fallen into the Barbarian's slashing axe. Bodies and pieces of bodies tumbled in the air, tossed on fountains of blood, and still they charged. Gath was knee-deep in carnage, slipping on bloody chests and heads. Dying men clung to his legs, bit them, struggled with the last of their strength to pull him down into their mire of gore.

After four novels (*Prisoner of the Horned Helmet, Lords of Destruction, Tooth and Claw, Plague of Knives*) published quickly in succession from 1988–1990, the series vanished from the shelves.

So, too, it seemed, had sword-and-sorcery.

CHAPTER EIGHT

Underground, Resurgence, and New Directions

It's often argued that a good test of a writer is if he or she is able to make existing conventions seem completely fresh, as if you'd never read them before. So long as it attracts such writers, a genre never really perishes. It can be pronounced dead only to spring to life again, lusher than ever.
—Michael Moorcock, *Wizardry & Wild Romance*

By the mid-1980s, sword-and-sorcery was in serious decline. The demand for fantasy fiction had never been greater, but it was decidedly of the "high" variety. Terry Brooks was cranking out new titles in his wildly popular Shannara series. Margaret Weis and Tracy Hickman were in the midst of an incredible run with Dragonlance, a line of fiction set in the fantasy world of Krynn, a popular Dungeons & Dragons game supplement. Fresh off the success of *The Chronicles Thomas Covenant*, Stephen Donaldson was putting the finishing touches on a second popular trilogy featuring his leprous anti-hero.

In contrast, sword-and-sorcery was struggling to stay relevant—and failing. While many sword-and-sorcery titles were published in the 80s, much of it was of dubious quality and even more dubious originality, with publishers clinging to its most reliable franchise. The Lancer/Ace Conan Saga had run its course by 1977, ending with a trio of 100% pastiche works (*Conan of the Isles, Conan the Avenger, Conan of Aquilonia*). The commercial success of the series set the stage for additional pastiche efforts, starting with a run from Bantam from 1978–1982. The Bantam Conans ranged from well-written entertainment (*Conan the Rebel* by Poul Anderson, Karl Edward Wagner's *The Road of Kings*) to the atrocious (*Conan and the Spider God* by L. Sprague de Camp). *Conan the Liberator*, written by de Camp and Carter, is typical of the Bantam run. The book is serviceable entertainment for much of its page count, with Conan throwing his aid behind a rebel army to overthrow Numedides, the mad king of Aquilonia, and his evil sorcerer Thulandra Thuu. But it falls off the rails late when Conan enlists the help of a tribe of satyrs to help defeat his enemies on the battlefield. The Conan pastiche machine then got cranked up

in earnest with a line of Conan "originals" by publisher Tor. The Tor
Conan line spanned more than 20 years (1982–2004) and featured a
rotating cast of authors including Robert Jordan, Steve Perry, John
M. Roberts, Leonard Carpenter, and others. The Tor Conans are a
largely forgettable chapter in sword-and-sorcery, sometimes compe-
tently written and reasonably entertaining (John H. Hocking's *Conan
and the Emerald Lotus*), but in the main pale copies of Howard's red-
blooded creation. They are very much a commercial grab, an attempt
to replicate the profitable multi-volume "series" model adopted by
high fantasy. Even the better-written entries in the Tor series—John
Maddox Roberts' *Conan the Valorous* (1985), for example—are distorted amplifications of Howard's original, with Conan driven to
ever higher feats of strength and arms, including breaking the neck
of a bull the size of a young elephant in a pit duel. Had the Tor line
replaced "Conan" with original sword-and-sorcery heroes they likely
would have a much better reputation, but with authors desperately
filling every conceivable gap left in the P. Schuyler Miller/John D.
Clark essay "A Probable Outline of Conan's Career," they feel tired,
and exploitative. Cimmeria works best as a place "long ago and far
away," where "the axe and flint-tipped spear are like a dream," not
as a place where Conan engages in banal dialogue with goat herders
and takes a whack on the back of his head with an oat porridge ladle
(*Conan the Valorous*). By the 1980s Conan's continuing adventures in
paperback and comics were stretched beyond the point of credulity,
taking him on hundreds of adventures in every known country in
the Hyborian Age. These works moved units, but did no favors for the
plausibility of Howard's creation, nor sword-and-sorcery's reputation. Moreover, they paled compared to the best efforts high fantasy
was offering at the time, including Tad Williams' *Memory, Sorrow,
and Thorn* trilogy (published between 1988–1993) and George R.R.
Martin's ongoing series *A Song of Ice and Fire*, whose first volume, *A
Game of Thrones*, debuted in 1996.

On February 7, 1988, Lin Carter succumbed to a long, painful
battle with oral cancer. He was just 57 years old. Carter left behind
several unfinished projects, including a planned history of the origins
of the genre, *Robert E. Howard and the Rise of Sword and Sorcery*. Carter
would never finish a planned epic fantasy *Khymyrium*, of which only
fragments were published, nor add future stories to his long roll call
of heroes in faraway worlds under green stars including Thongor,
Kadji, and Ganelon Silvermane. While his fiction is, in hindsight,
largely pastiche, Carter was sword-and-sorcery's most visible, vocal
advocate. With his passing so, too, ended the Sword and Sorcerer's
Guild of America (SAGA), its showcase *Flashing Swords* anthology,
and the Gandalf Awards. Carter's work as editor of the Ballantine

Adult Fantasy Series (1969–1974), or the BAFS, was perhaps his greatest contribution. During his tenure the BAFS revived the works of talented but languishing fantasy authors, bringing to new life classics by Lord Dunsany, William Morris, David Lindsay, and others.[1]

In 1992 Fritz Leiber died, aged 81. The last collection of his incomparable Fafhrd and the Gray Mouser stories, *The Knight and Knave of Swords* (1988), appeared on the shelves just four years prior to his death, a testament to Leiber's lifelong commitment to the characters and the sword-and-sorcery subgenre. *The Knight and Knave of Swords* was nominated for the World Fantasy Awards Best Collection in 1989. Leiber left behind a formidable literary legacy in sword-and-sorcery, horror, and science fiction; H.P. Lovecraft scholar and biographer S.T. Joshi ranks Leiber as the only writer among Lovecraft's friends and colleagues who can be placed on an equal footing in regard to literary achievement: "Leiber's prodigally bountiful work, spanning and intermingling the genres of science fiction, fantasy, and horror, is of such depth and substance as to transcend the limitations of genre to become an authentic contribution to American and world literature" (*Fritz Leiber and H.P. Lovecraft: Writers of the Dark* 322).

In 1994 Karl Edward Wagner died from heart and liver failure, the result of long-term alcoholism. Like Leiber, Wagner left behind an impressive body of work, including a storied tenure as editor of *The Year's Best Horror Stories* from 1980 to 1994. His friend, horror author Peter Straub, though no sword-and-sorcery fan (he described Wagner's Kane stories as "so distant from what interested me as to be unapproachable. I didn't get it, and I still don't") was deeply taken with Wagner's horror stories, and in particular *In a Lonely Place*, for which Straub wrote the introduction. "By then, my respect for Karl was such that I would have agreed to do an introduction for a sword-and-sorcery collection from the point of view of a one-eyed cat and written in rhymed couplets if the stories had his name on them (come to think of it, as long as he could keep himself sufficiently entertained, Karl could probably have pulled it off!), but of course *In a Lonely Place* was nothing like that. Neither was it very much like anything else, either — I mean, the stories resembled no one else's" (Straub).

By the early to mid-1990s, a few exceptions aside, sword-and-sorcery seemed to have passed from the earth.[2] It was a death of natural

---

[1] According to one academic, the BAFS was chiefly responsible for codifying "fantasy" as a genre of literature and canonizing its greatest works (Jamie Williamson, *The Evolution of Modern Fantasy: From Antiquarianism to the Ballantine Adult Fantasy Series*).

[2] Publisher Baen, for example, issued the Robert E. Howard Library in 1995–96, which included collections of Kull, Solomon Kane, and Bran Mak Morn, among others.

causes—an excess of self-reference, repetition, stagnation, and tired formula—and the literal death of its core authors and champions. Its fall was expedited by the emergence of new publishing trends and markets unsuited to its native form, including the fantasy series. Changes were overdue, and necessary. And revolution was afoot. Starting in the early-mid 1980s, new voices and new perspectives began to alter its form and format. These included authors innovating on the classic formula, and the birth of new subgenres that drew their inspiration from sword-and-sorcery. Though in some ways markedly different, these new subgenres maintained elements of sword-and-sorcery, some vestigial, others vital.

Michael Shea (1946–2014) entered the sword-and-sorcery field in 1974 with *A Quest for Simbilis,* an authorized sequel to "The Eyes of the Overworld" set in Jack Vance's Dying Earth universe. Shea later added an original contribution to the genre with *Nifft the Lean* (1982), sword-and-sorcery in the style and sensibility of Vance and Leiber but also uniquely his own. *Nifft the Lean* collects four loosely connected novellas. Its narrative does not follow a linear timeline typical of most sword-and-sorcery, but is told as a series of (seemingly) posthumous reminisces by "Shag Margold," a friend of the roguish wanderer Nifft. Nifft is a traditional sword-and-sorcery hero—roguish, charismatic, mercenary, good with a blade, a thief and a fighter involved in high-stakes risks for treasure which he squanders in pleasures of the flesh as fast as he earns it. The novel's innovations are Shea's baroque style and its morphing of sword-and-sorcery with elements of high fantasy. Shea's fiendish imagination offers wonders on every page. "The Fishing of the Demon-Sea" opens with Nifft and his brawny sidekick Barnar the Chilite trussed up and ready to be executed for attempted thievery, before taking a sharp turn into a kaleidoscopic fever-dream. Nifft and Barnar are plucked from the execution stocks by lord Kamin, master of the town, only to be pressed into a suicidal rescue of Kamin's son Wimfort, who is imprisoned in an underground demon-realm. Shea's mingling of high fantasy and sword-and-sorcery includes a neat trick of intentional, metafictional play: Wimfort anticipates a cinematic, saga-worthy liberation as in E.R. Eddison or Tolkien, but his noble sensibilities are offended by a rescue like something out of Leiber. "What he wanted was rescue astride a golden griffon ... we offered mere escape—ignominious, bare-arse escape escorted by two scoundrels of unromantic appearance" (242). *Nifft the Lean* won the World Fantasy Award for Best Novel in 1983.

In the mid-1980s, female authors joined the ranks of sword-and-sorcery in large number. Marion Zimmer Bradley's *Sword and Sorceress* series debuted in 1984 and subsequent anthologies were published approximately annually in the subgenre's longest running series. After Zimmer Bradley died in 1999, the series continued under the editorship of author Diana Paxson, and of this writing has passed 30 volumes. *Sword and Sorceress* accepted submissions from male authors as well as female, but its emphasis was on centrally placed female protagonists, rather than those on the periphery or damsels in distress. Jessica Amanda Salmonson of *Amazons!* fame edited her third major anthology of sword-and-sorcery, *Heroic Visions* (1983). This featured a range of a more generic heroic fantasy, but also sword-and-sorcery, including four stories written by women. Salmonson used the platform as an opportunity to criticize the stale, pastiche-ridden state of the subgenre, and encourage new permutations:

> Heroic fantasy, in recent decades, has seemed too often to be epito-
> mized by Robert E. Howard's Conan the Barbarian, and this is a sad
> state of affairs. The millennia-old heritage of magical and heroic tales
> does not begin or culminate in the rather simplistic fictions of the
> pulp era or the current, slavish imitations thereof. Howard's work
> is admirable; he was surprisingly well-read, and invested his stories
> with the hodge-podge of an amateur historian or Harold Lamb fan,
> creating something primal, evocative, intriguing. Stylistically, he was
> weak. The dozen-score imitators of Howard have tended to capture the
> weakness of his style, but not the primal thread of his limited though
> worthwhile heroic vision—his, shall we say, pathos. Without denying
> Howard's genius or even qualifying it, it must yet be recognized that
> glorifying his rudimentary sword and sorcery as "ideal" heroic fantasy
> is akin to assuming Doc Smith's old-fashioned space opera is "ideal"
> science fiction. No area of fantasy should be so stagnant and devoid of
> stylistic and conceptual growth or variety (*Heroic Visions* 2).

Like most anthologies *Heroic Visions* contains a few clunkers, but its emphasis on the thematic concept of *strength*—regardless of what form that may take, be it physical, spiritual, or other-wise—demonstrated that one of the principal characteristics of sword-and-sorcery fiction—men (and women) of action—could take on new forms, and result in new stories beyond brawny, loin-cloth-wearing barbarians on crypt raids. Phyllis Ann Karr's "Tales Told to a Toymaker" introduces readers to Torin, a man who could have been a hero but opts to spend his days working in a toymaker's shop. When a classic sword-and-sorcery adventurer passes through and shares his tales of adventures in strange lands, Torin experi-ences a new sense of self-worth, allowing him a measure of victory over the haunting regret of his life choices. "Each of us climbs his own mountain," the adventurer tells the toymaker. Jane Yolen's violent and sensual "Sister Light, Sister Dark" is the highlight of *Heroic Visions*, featuring a skillful interplay of myth juxtaposed with the gritty truth that often lies behind mythological events.

In the mid-1980s, sword-and-sorcery received a much-needed infusion from a relative genre outsider. Young U.K. journalist David Gemmell had received a grim diagnosis: cancer. His physician estimated he had mere months to live (Priest). With death imminent, and facing the prospect of a likely hopeless struggle against a remorseless disease, Gemmell poured his fighting spirit into a work of heroic fantasy ultimately published as *Legend* (1984). *Legend* is an important evolution of sword-and-sorcery: Gemmell was not writing in the sword-and-sorcery tradition, but drew his principal influences from medieval and Dark Ages history, and the western. Gemmell was a Robert E. Howard admirer, though it is not clear when he first read Howard. According to sword-and-sorcery historian Steve Tompkins, Gemmell came to Howard's defense as early as 1988, in a published interview in the U.K. genre magazine *Fear*:

> Most of us have seen his blurbage for the Del Rey REH trade paperbacks: "I adore these books. Howard had a gritty, vibrant style—broadsword writing that cut its way to the heart, with heroes who are truly larger than life." Much earlier, in one of his first major interviews (for the U.K. genre magazine *Fear* in 1988), he bemoaned heroic fantasies in which it is a foregone conclusion that the hero "will kill 75 wizards, a couple of armies, several dragons, a few werebeasts...and end up crowned king of Lemuria or somewhere." The interviewer eagerly jumped in to ask if he meant characters "like Conan." "Conan's a bit different," Gemmell demurred. "It was done rather well. There was a pace and vitality about Howard's work that carried you through' ("Dog Brothers" 25-27).

Gemmell, who once stated that he wished he could have stood in the shield-wall at the Battle of Hastings ("Interview with David Gemmell"), had a knack for writing visceral battles and heroic last stands, and *Legend* feels more desperately vital than the Howard clones of the 1960s and 70s. *Legend* is frequently categorized as belonging to the amorphous "heroic fantasy" label, but with its muscular, martial action and historical fiction roots, it is far closer in spirit to sword-and-sorcery than high fantasy. The hero of *Legend* is Druss, an aging warrior and a veteran of innumerable battles. Like a once-great athlete coming out of retirement to prove he can still compete in his sport, Druss dusts off his axe Snaga and treks to the defense of the besieged fortress Dros Delnoch. The massively outnumbered Drenai (a mere 10,000, arrayed against an invading force of 500,000 Nadir) face either victory or death. On the eve of the final battle Druss admonishes his outnumbered and battle-weary forces to stand with him, one last time:

> "Some of you are probably thinking that you may panic and run. You won't! Others are worried about dying. Some of you will. But all men die. No ever gets out of this life alive.

> I fought at Skeln Pass when everyone said we were finished. They said the odds were too great, but I said be damned to them! For I am Druss, and I have never been beaten, not by Nadir, Sathuli, Ventrian, Vagrian, or Drenai.
>
> By all the gods and demons of this world, I will tell you now—I do not intend to be beaten here, either!" Druss was bellowing at the top of his voice as he dragged Snaga into the air. The ax blade caught the sun and the chant began.
>
> "Druss the Legend! Druss the Legend!"

Dros Delnoch is a keep ringed by six walls with names that resemble the stages of a man staring down the inevitability of his own death: Eldibar (exultation), Musif (despair), Kania (renewed hope), Sumitos (desperation), Valteri (serenity), and Geddon (death). These sword-and-sorcery equivalents of the Kubler-Ross stages of grief mirror Gemmell's experiences with confronting his own mortality. More than the details of battles or tactics of siege, *Legend* is a lesson in living one's life to the fullest. It's a celebration of the now: its heroes' lives are all the brighter because they are being bled out, day by day, on the walls of Dros Delnoch. Gemmell's own prognosis proved to be a mis-diagnosis, and he would go on to write more than 30 novels, including *The First Chronicles of Druss the Legend* (1993), a prequel to *Legend*.

Sword-and-sorcery has always held a kinship with horror, a legacy of its *Weird Tales* heritage and in particular the works of Clark Ashton Smith and H.P. Lovecraft. This dark thread continued in the works of Michael Moorcock in the 1960s and the eldritch-horror-infused sword-and-sorcery of Karl Edward Wagner and Ramsey Campbell in the 1970s. Campbell's world-weary hero Ryre is an early prototype of a type of protagonist who would come to characterize a new strain of dark fantasy that began to take hold the late 1990s, characterized by world-weary "heroes" and settings that evoked the worst clichés of Dark Ages Europe:

> Already Ryre disliked the port of Lipe. The wharf had been crowded with women who gazed at the disembarking men, expertly and hungrily. They hadn't been whores, simply women of the town. The men of Lipe would be even less fond of mercenaries than was generally the case with townsmen. Ignoring the women, Ryre had shouldered his way from the wharf. He'd had enough of battle for one year. The holes in his flesh had not been closed for long ("The Changer of Names" 31).

Glen Cook amped up this anti-heroic strain in his hybrid military fantasy/sword-and-sorcery series the Black Company. Cook worked in auto assembly and was an avid reader of Fritz Leiber, Jack Vance, and hard-boiled detective and mystery novelists Raymond Chandler and R.S. Prather. A chance encounter with a nameless, low-quality Lin Carter novel finally got him to set pen to paper. "While I was at work, I was reading a fantasy book by Lin Carter, and I threw it across the room and swore I could do better. I started working right away, using the company's typewriter and paper. I found out it's harder than I thought it would be" ("The Glen Cook Interview").

The Black Company (1984) retained some of sword-and-sorcery's aesthetics, including its use of morally compromised swords for hire, but made some important innovations. Cook deepened the limited characterization that defined much sword-and-sorcery with a first-person, foot soldier's viewpoint, as told by the mercenary soldier Croaker. The plot is driven by dialogue, with Cook offering minimal description. There are no heroes in the Black Company, a troupe of mercenaries for whom ethics and principle rank a distant second place to contractual obligations. Honorable behavior is defined as doing the job for which you have been paid:

> "We aren't heroes," the captain continued. "We're tough. We're stubborn. We try to honor our commitments. But we don't die for lost causes.
>
> I protested, the voice of tradition questioning his unspoken proposition.
>
> "The question on the table is the survival of the Company, Croaker."
>
> "We have taken the gold, Captain. Honor is the question on the table" (Cook 23-24).

The Black Company greatly amplified the latent cynicism and pessimism in the works of Howard and Wagner. Surveying an ocean after leaving a city swamped by corruption and violence, Croaker observes its serenity, but with a jaundiced eye. "We looked at a world never defiled by Man. Sometimes I suspect it would be better for our absence" (Cook 40). History is written by the victors, and can be rewritten, casting doubt on the veracity of the heroic stories. The Black Company operates in a world where heroism is futile and discretion the better part of valor, where "Dead heroes don't get a second chance." It's a world of moral relativism; "evil" is merely the other side you happen to be fighting against that day:

> "Evil is relative, Annalist. You can't hang a sign on it. You can't touch it or taste it or cut it with a sword. Evil depends on where you are standing, pointing your indicting finger. Where you stand now, because of your oath, is opposite the Dominator. For you he is where your Evil lies."
>
> She paced a moment, perhaps anticipating a response. I made none. She had encapsulated my own philosophy (281).

The "rebels" against which the Black Company fight, though only lightly developed by Cook and depicted as cannon fodder, are alluded to as the forces of good, the side that would be considered a rooting interest in a typical work of high fantasy:

> The Sons of the White Rose are everywhere. ... If one chooses sides on emotion, then the Rebel is the guy to go with. He is fighting for everything men claim to honor: freedom, independence, truth, the right. ... All the subjective illusions, all the eternal trigger-words. We are minions of the villain of the piece. We confuse the illusion and deny the substance.
>
> There are no self-proclaimed villains, only regiments of self-proclaimed saints. Victorious historians rule where good or evil lies.
>
> We abjure labels. We fight for money and an indefinite pride. The politics, the ethics, the moralities, are irrelevant (107).

The Black Company is an important transitional work in the development of fantasy fiction. A handful of authors borrowed its bleakness, gray morality, and grit, and blended it with elements of sword-and-sorcery and high fantasy to create a new subgenre. Popularly known today as grimdark, this subgenre often takes the form of lengthy novels or multi-book series featuring large casts of characters in high-stakes adventures, but grounds these high fantasy hallmarks in harsh, gritty environments, peopled with morally compromised protagonists. In many ways, grimdark is sword-and-sorcery wildly amplified—mercenary heroes become disillusioned, amoral beings, and the frequent but often stylized combat of sword-and-sorcery transformed into shocking scenes of graphically depicted carnage and suffering. Grimdark amplifies the pessimism that underlie Howard's cataclysmic Hyborian Age tales and often presents a nihilistic view of the world, in which heroes rarely make a difference and often don't live to fight another day.

Cook, Wagner, and Campbell inform and prefigure the dirty, gloomy, war-weary heroes and settings of Richard Morgan's A Land Fit for Heroes and George R.R. Martin's A Song of Ice and Fire. Martin, often credited as the originator of grimdark with his first A Song of Ice and Fire novel, *Game of Thrones*, was a fan of both J.R.R. Tolkien and Tad Williams (author of the high fantasy series *Memory, Sorrow, and Thorn*), but also Fritz Leiber, Jack Vance, and Robert E. Howard, as well as historical fiction (MacLaurin; Warner). Martin's stew of influences birthed a template that is at once broad of scope and complex, but also street-level visceral and gritty. In A Song of Ice and Fire, political machinations and the ebb and flow of lengthy wars operate alongside personal death-duels and shocking scenes of violence and suffering.

A Song of Ice and Fire kicked off a wave of new grimdark fiction led by the likes of Joe Abercrombie, Richard Morgan, and Mark Lawrence. Abercombie grew up on high fantasy including the likes of David Eddings, Margaret Weis and Tracy Hickman, J.R.R. Tolkien, and Ursula LeGuin, with a smattering of Michael Moorcock's Elric. But post-Martin he was transformed. Sword-and-sorcery was a

FLAME AND CRIMSON

second-hand influence, passed to Abercrombie through Martin as well as role playing games such as Dungeons and Dragons ("The New Sword and Sorcery"). The grimy, cynical worldview expressed by the likes of Martin's child-killing "nobleman" Jamie Lannister—himself a product of the likes of Croaker, Kane, and Ryre—prefigure and inform *The Heroes* (2011), a work whose title seethes with irony:

> "Who cares who's buried where?" muttered Craw, thinking about all the men he'd seen buried. "Once a man's in the ground he's just mud. Mud and stories. And the stories and the men don't often have much in common.

In *The Heroes*, almost anyone can be bought or sold, and "glory" and "honor" are the vocabulary of fools. When men die on the battlefield, at best they receive a few muttered words before their bodies are tipped into the mud, to themselves become mud:

> "They think when it comes to them there will be a lesson, a meaning, a story worth telling. That death will come to them as a dread scholar, a fell knight, a terrible emperor. He poked at the boy's corpse with a toe, rolled it onto its side, then let it flop back. Death is a bored clerk, with too many orders to fill. There is no reckoning. No profound moment. It creeps up on us from behind, and snatched us away while we shit."

Richard Morgan's war-torn trilogy A Land Fit for Heroes—consisting of *The Steel Remains* (2008), *The Cold Commands* (2012), and *The Dark Defiles* (2014)—owes a considerable debt to Cook, whom Morgan cites in the acknowledgments of the second volume, as well as Karl Edward Wagner.[3] An execution by man-eating squids in Wagner's *Darkness Weaves* is re-enacted in gruesome detail in *The Cold Commands*. The setting of A Land Fit for Heroes is earth in some impossibly distant future, post-cataclysm, in which advanced technology can be unearthed and employed with apparent "magical" effects, similar to Wagner's *Bloodstone* and Vance's Dying Earth.

On its surface A Land Fit for Heroes is high fantasy. A dark, sorcerous being of great power with a portentous name (the Ilwrack Changeling) has been discovered on an island far out to sea, and his awakening could mean the end of the world. A trio of heroes embarks on a mission to locate the island and dispatch the Ilwrack Changeling before he arises from his sorcerous slumber. But a deeper look reveals its debt to sword-and-sorcery. The series' principal protagonist, Ringil Eskiath, is a rakish mercenary whose sorcerous streak and healthy sexual appetite evoke the Gray Mouser, while his Fafhrd-esque sidekick is the boisterous, brawling Egar, a renowned warrior from the semi-barbaric Majak peoples. *The Cold Commands*

---

[3] Morgan also lists Moorcock and Leiber as influences.

is essentially a series of connected episodic encounters—a raid on a temple, a slave revolt, and a battle with a hostile alien humanoid race called the Dwenda—of which each could serve as a traditional sword-and-sorcery short story. In a sequence straight out of the Elric Saga, Ringil wanders into a shadowy parallel plane of existence called The Grey Planes, while the race of amoral Dwenda and their pale, sharply angular features evoke Moorcock's Melniboneans.

Today, grimdark is a vital subgenre. Mark Lawrence's three-book series The Broken Empire, Scott Lynch's three volume Gentleman Bastard series, and Steven Erikson's 10-volume Malazan Book of the Fallen rank among the bestselling works in fantasy. All owe a debt, direct or inherited, to Glen Cook—and behind him, sword-and-sorcery.

Even as sword-and-sorcery experienced a steep decline and morphed into new subgenres, fans and scholar-historians began to take a deeper interest in its origins and roots. Prior to the 80s there were no full-length, formal studies of sword-and-sorcery. The fanzine Amra (1959–1982) published some of its earliest criticism and occasional pieces of literary analysis and reviews, but much of it was "Hyborian scholarship"—interesting but rather esoteric and insular debates about weapons, ocean trade, and other Hyborian Age ephemera. The best of these articles were collected and republished in 1979 and 1980 as The Blade of Conan and The Spell of Conan, respectively.

In 1983, Bluejay Books published Dark Valley Destiny: The Life of Robert E. Howard, the first full-length biography of Howard. Written by L. Sprague de Camp, his wife Catherine Crook de Camp, and psychologist Jane Whittington Griffin, Dark Valley Destiny is an impressive monument of first-person research, conducted via five research trips to Texas by the authors over a period of five years. Dark Valley Destiny adds considerable depth and complexity to the creator of sword-and-sorcery, whose life had been previously covered in lightly sketched introductions, single chapters, or piecemeal in Glenn Lord's The Last Celt: A Bio-Bibliography of Robert Ervin Howard (1976), a mix of biographical and autobiographical material whose principal contribution is an exhaustive bibliography of Howard's works. Dark Valley Destiny traces the origins of Howard's family tree and the circuitous route that ultimately led the family to Cross Plains. It provides anecdotes from Howard's childhood and adolescence, his struggles in school, his friendships and personal interests, and his abortive romantic relationship with Novalyne Price Ellis. Dark Valley Destiny offers insight on the lasting appeal of Conan and, more broadly, sword-and-sorcery. According to the authors, the Conan stories are an expression of our deep-seated resistance to collectivism: "The great barbarian represents an ideal of masculine autonomy and a resistance to authority, which appeal to his predominately male readership" (288).

Unfortunately, *Dark Valley Destiny* is also a flawed work. It relies too heavily on speculation and opinion and the medical credentials of Griffin, who never met Howard but attempts a form of posthumous psychoanalysis based on outdated Freudian theory. For example, the authors claim that Howard's dark-haired, blue-eyed heroes were conscious or unconscious reflections of his father, Isaac, "the man his son would have liked to be" (258). Any evidence that contradicts Howard's Oedipal urges is dismissed: The authors conclude that a letter from Dr. Howard written to Lovecraft describing a loving father-son relationship "spent pleasantly on discussion of men, women, animals, out-door life, adventure, history of long-lived frontiersmen," is "roseate fancy" on the part of Dr. Howard (359). The book casts Howard's life as an inevitable dark march to suicide, placing him in the role of helpless victim unable to recover from a series of traumatic childhood influences, including a series of moves into unfamiliar country, a passive-aggressive and overly controlling mother, and a "godlike physician" of a father. The "dark valley" of Howard's youth—Dark Valley Creek, a region of Palo Pinto County, Texas—is used in a literal and figurative manner by the authors, who imbue it with supernatural force:

> Howard's fears are rooted in his very early childhood, in his Dark Valley days, where the encroaching woods brooded over his childish head and the creek, babbling beside his home, seemed a mighty river, whose swirling waters brought terror to his heart. Those fears were compounded by his mother's timidity in an isolated region, where her husband's practice took him so far from home, and by her constant ill health, often masked by a denial and false jollity. It was compounded, too, by the huge man who was his father. The doctor's authoritative air made him seem almost superhuman; his quick and frequent angers gave him the aura of a god or a demon who could not be gainsaid (287).

Howard was unable to escape the "dark valley destiny" of his past, the authors speculate, as he "was, despite his great talents and virtues, a fatally flawed personality. He suffered from pathological dependence on his mother, from delusions of persecution, from a fascination with suicide" (366).

Dark Valley Destiny remains a priceless collection of interviews and hard-gathered facts, but marred by dated psychoanalysis and overwrought speculation. It is an interpretation of Howard's life, the most detailed to date, and an important contribution to sword-and-sorcery. It is, however, absent any formal literary criticism, forsaking in-depth reviews of Howard's works to focus on biography.

The following year *The Dark Barbarian* (1984) broke new ground as the first collection of serious literary analysis of Howard's work. It includes essays by the likes of Fritz Leiber, Glenn Lord (then agent for the Robert E. Howard estate), and editor Don Herron, who contributed two essays, one under a pseudonym. *The Dark Barbarian* surveys Howard's fantasy stories but also his westerns, poetry, and supernatural horror stories, as well as details of his writing career in the pulps. It makes a convincing case for the influence of the western and the American frontier on Howard's writings. Perhaps its most important contribution is the George Knight/Don Herron essay "Robert E. Howard: Hard-Boiled Heroic Fantasist," which removes Howard from the tradition of Lord Dunsany, William Morris, E.R. Eddison, and J.R.R. Tolkien, making a compelling case for Howard as a writer whose heritage and birthright was not high fantasy, but historical adventure, his unique environment, and the geopolitics of the 1920s and 30s. The book's cornerstone essay, Herron's "The Dark Barbarian," credits Howard for introducing an entirely new archetype to American fiction: the Dark Barbarian. "The inherent appeal of this character has created a major sub-genre of the fantastic, the Sword-and-Sorcery or heroic fantasy tale, and put Howard in the select ranks of the literary legend-makers: Ned Buntline, Alexander Dumas, Mary Shelley, Sir Arthur Conan Doyle, Bram Stoker, Edgar Rice Burroughs, Dashiell Hammett, H.P. Lovecraft, J.R.R. Tolkien, and Ian Fleming" (149). According to Herron, Howard's Dark Barbarian archetype added a bleak counterweight to the roseate fantasy of the late 19th and early 20th century, and anticipates the anti-hero, now ubiquitous in popular culture. Its appendices include "Robert E. Howard's Library," a listing of the volumes Howard had in his possession at the time of his death in June 1936, an important tool for scholars researching the wide swath of fiction, non-fiction, and poetry that informed Howard's writings. The following year saw the appearance of *Cromlech*, a short-lived literary journal that lasted just three issues, but contained essays like Charles Hoffman's "Conan the Existential" that continued to make the case for Howard as an author of literary merit.

Howard's life and literary legacy has received additional entries and updates in the ensuing decades. The 21st century has given rise to a new Howard renaissance, but importantly one focused on literary excavation and preservation rather than exploitative pastiche. Publisher Gollancz as part of its Fantasy Masterworks series issued the *Conan Chronicles; Volume 1* in 2000 followed by a second volume the following year. Describing itself as "a library of some of the greatest, most influential fantasy ever written ... books which, along with Tolkien, Peake, and others, shaped modern fantasy" (back cover, *The Conan Chronicles Volume 1: The People of the Black Circle*), the *Conan Chronicles* placed Howard shoulder-to-shoulder with fantasy's greatest authors.[4] In 2003, small U.K. publisher Wandering Star issued *Conan of Cimmeria: Volume One*, followed by a second volume in 2004. Though limited to a small print run and today rare and expensive, these were published in the U.S. by Del Rey in affordable, widely printed trade paperbacks as *The Coming of Conan the Cimmerian*, *The Bloody Crown of Conan*, and *The Conquering Sword of Conan*. The Wandering Star/Del Rey collections added unfinished drafts, notes, and other miscellanea, and today are considered the "definitive" Conan texts. With the publication of the Gollancz and Wandering Star/Del Rey texts, Conan went from disposable mass market entertainment to literary canonization.

In 2009, Howard scholar Mark Finn wrote a self-described "corrective" to *Dark Valley Destiny* with *Blood & Thunder: The Life & Art of Robert E. Howard*. The second full-length biographical study of Howard refutes many of the former's claims regarding Howard's character. Finn posits that the interview questions de Camp posed to his subjects were leading in nature, evoking negative responses about Howard for which de Camp had come looking, and already believed to be true. Finn claims that Howard—a noted teller of "tall rales" who routinely mixed fact with fiction, and myth with reality, in casual conversation, a cultural affectation shared by many Texas natives then and today—succeeded in pulling the wool over de Camp's eyes, from beyond the grave. "All of de Camp's questions to Robert's friends, acquaintances, and the general populace of Cross Plains who deigned to speak to him were tinged with that sort of bias. De Camp went looking specifically for the pieces of Robert's life that would validate his thesis. All other extraneous information was not used or, worse, not followed up on. Worst of all, de Camp, who had so long worked in the shadow of Robert's genius, allowed himself to be fooled by the man he thought he knew better than anyone else" (243-244).

While not as exhaustive or meticulously-researched as *Dark Valley Destiny*, *Blood & Thunder* offers a convincing argument that Howard was very much a product of his environment. *Blood & Thunder* provides a colorful look into early 20th century Texas, one of the last vestiges of American frontier life. It describes how Howard's father Isaac moved Robert and his mother Hester from small town to small town, following medical work that resulted from the boom-and-bust cycles of oil speculation. These small towns were wild and violent places, Finn writes, and Isaac's services as a physician were needed to stitch

---

[4] The Gollancz Fantasy Masterworks series also republished Vance's *The Dying Earth*, Moorcock's Elric, and Leiber's Fafhrd and the Gray Mouser stories.

men back together. Into this potent mix of brawling, wealth-chasing men, towns that knew untapped wealth and crushing poverty in a span of days, and the wide-open plains of sand and scrub of rural Texas, Howard's career as a writer was born. It is from historical Texas that Howard drew his inspiration for his fantasy tales. Finn's insights in these chapters are a refreshing corrective to the idea that Howard's "weird tales" were entirely products of his own imagination, and sprang, fully formed, from the recesses of his mind. Writes Finn, "To ignore the presence of the Lone Star State in Robert E. Howard's life and writing invites, at the very least, a few wrongheaded conclusions, and at worst, abject character assassination" (249).

With new insights and new critical interest, Howard scholarship underwent a renaissance at the turn of the 21st century. Journals including the peer-reviewed *The Dark Man, REH: Two-Gun Raconteur,* and the outstanding *The Cimmerian* published close textual literary analysis, new research into Howard's life and works, and essays on Howard's literary legacy and influence. REHupa (The Robert E. Howard United Press Association) provided a platform for Howard fans and scholars to write and circulate fanzines of thoughtful analysis and commentary amongst each other. These began as newsletters printed and mailed among REHupa members, but were later published online. The Robert E. Howard Foundation, a nonprofit organization devoted to preserving Howard and supporting research and scholarly efforts, was founded in November of 2006. The foundation provides support for Robert E. Howard Days, a gathering of die-hard "Howard heads" held each year in Cross Plains, Texas. David C. Smith, author of *Oron,* wrote a new biography of Howard, *Robert E. Howard: A Literary Biography* (2018, Pulp Hero Press) that shifts the focus from the facts of Howard's life to his artistic contributions as a writer. It's an incisive look from Smith, who credited Howard for launching his own career in sword-and-sorcery some 40 years prior.

Most recently, Conan has been the subject of cultural analysis in works that demonstrate how he made the leap from obscure character in the yellowed pages of *Weird Tales* to ubiquitous cultural icon. Paul Sammon's *Conan the Phenomenon* (2007) traces Conan from the pulps to 1960s pop phenomenon, to his various stage, screen, and television appearances, and finally his reappearance in new graphic novel interpretations, collectible figurines and busts, and video-game avatars. Sammon's book features lavish, full-color reproductions of Conan artwork from the 1930s to the present day. Michael Moorcock's introductory essay "Conan: American Phenomenon" places Howard's most famous creation in a select group of America's greatest literary and mythological heroes. "For all his roots in our earliest fables, Conan the Cimmerian is a thoroughly American creation. Like Natty Bumpo, Ahab, Tarzan, Hopalong Cassidy, Sam Spade or Superman, he is as much a product of his culture and landscape as Gandalf or Maigret are of theirs" (xi).

Conan Meets the Academy (2013, MacFarland & Company, Inc.) is a collection of academic essays of the sort typically reserved for mainstream literary fiction. Like *Conan the Phenomenon*, its subject is not just Robert E. Howard's Conan, but the 21st century pop culture "Conan the Barbarian" of films, pastiche, and video games. *Conan Meets the Academy* embraces Conan with a pop culture awareness, celebrating the later permutations of Howard's barbaric archetype as much as the original stories. Explains editor Jonas Prida, "Although there is vigor in purity, seeing only Howard's Conan as Conan misses opportunities for interesting and productive discussions. ... They can be studied and analyzed based on their own merits without the constant meta-analytic struggle about original intent" (6-7). The essays employ analytical techniques from various disciplines including archaeology, cultural studies, stylometry (the study of word usage, with a particular focus on word distribution and quantification, to determine style and authorship), folklore studies, and literary history. The broader field of sword-and-sorcery is ripe for similar studies.

Although Conan is its most recognizable and enduring figure, the larger subgenre which Howard spawned has also proven durable. Blogger and historian Steve Tompkins noted that even in the mid-1980s, when sword-and-sorcery was down, it was never out. Many lesser-known sword-and-sorcery titles were published in the 1980s and into the 1990s, according to Tompkins, including Keith Taylor's five-volume *Bard* series, Darryl Schweitzer's *The White Isle* (1989), Andrew Whitmore's *The Fortress of Eternity* (1990), Simon Green's *Down Among the Dead Men* (1993), David C. Smith's *Engor's Sword Arm* (1997), Brian McNaughton's *Throne of Bones* (1997), Matthew Woodring's Stover's *Iron Dawn* (1997), *Jericho Moon* (1998), and *Heroes Die* (1999), and the novels of Paul Kearney ("After Aquilonia and Having Left Lankhmar"). At the turn of the new millennium Lynn Abbey relaunched the Thieves World universe, defunct since 1989, with the novel *Sanctuary* (2002), followed by a pair of anthologies: *Turning Points* (2002) and *Enemies of Fortune* (2004). These may not have enjoyed the same critical reception or commercial success as comparable works of grimdark or high fantasy, but they kept sword-and-sorcery alive with a slow, steady pulse of output.

Classic sword-and-sorcery works have recently received new life in collector's editions as well as affordable, popular trade paperbacks. Gollancz as part of its Fantasy Masterworks series published

The First and Second Books of Lankhmar in 2001, bringing all of
Fritz Leiber's Fafhrd and the Gray Mouser stories to a new reading
audience at the turn of the century. The series also reprinted Michael
Moorcock's Elric Saga as well as Poul Anderson's *The Broken Sword*
(2002), the latter restoring Anderson's original text from 1954. The
Elric stories were reprinted in expansive volumes by Del Rey starting
in 2008, followed by "definitive editions" by Gollancz in 2013–2014.
Paizo Publishing's Planet Stories line brought back to print a large
number of classic sword-and -planet stories, but also a handful of
sword-and-sorcery authors including the collected Jirel of Joiry
(*Black God's Kiss*, C.L. Moore), Henry Kuttner (*Elak of Atlantis*), and A.
Merritt's *The Ship of Ishtar*. The series ran from 2007 through 2012.

The second decade of the new millennium saw the appearance of
two important sword-and-sorcery anthologies. *Swords & Dark Magic:
The New Sword and Sorcery* features 17 original stories by classic
authors as well as new talents. It also contains a highly useful and
readable introduction to sword-and-sorcery. "Check Your Dark Lord
at the Door" by editors Lou Anders and Jonathan Strahan adds some
helpful critical rigor to the oft-misunderstood subgenre:

> Sword and sorcery. The name says it all. Action meets magic. If
> high fantasy is about vast armies divided along the lines of obvious
> good versus ultimate evil, epic struggles to vanquish dark lords
> bent on world domination, then sword and sorcery is its antithesis.
> Smaller-scale character pieces, often starring morally compromised
> protagonists, whose heroism involves little more than trying to
> save their own skins from a trap they themselves blundered into in
> search of spoils. Sword and sorcery is where fantasy fiction meets the
> western, with its emphasis on traveling swordsmen wandering into an
> exotic setting and finding themselves thrust into unanticipated con-
> flicts there. As high fantasy concerns itself with warring nations and
> final battles, sword and sorcery focuses on personal battles, fought
> in the back alleys of exotic cities, in the secret chambers of strange
> temples, in the depths of dark dungeons. If high fantasy is a child of
> *The Iliad*, then sword and sorcery is a product of *The Odyssey* (xi).

As for the contents, three classic authors return to familiar
grounds: Michael Moorcock delivers an original Elric story, "Red
Pearls"; Glen Cook returns to the Black Company with "Tides Elba";
and Michael Shea to the world of the Dying Earth with "Hew the
Tintmaster." Tanith Lee and C.J. Cherryh, veterans of classic sword-
and-sorcery renaissance-era anthologies *Amazons!* and *Swords
Against Darkness*, make appearances, along with Gene Wolfe and
Steven Erikson, veteran authors better known for their works of
science fantasy and high fantasy. In general, *Swords & Dark Magic*
is on the dark end of the scale with graphic depictions of violence,
sword-and-sorcery sliding into grimdark.

FLAME AND CRIMSON

Tachyon Publishing's *Sword & Sorcery: An Anthology* (2012) is an unabashed callback to the early days of the genre, reprinting stories by Howard, Leiber, Anderson, Moore, and Moorcock. It also includes "Path of the Dragon," an excerpt from *A Storm of Swords*, the third book in George R.R. Martin's popular A Song of Ice and Fire series. Its presence in the anthology feels slightly calculated and opportunistic, but also demonstrates the sword-and-sorcery grit and realism underpinning what is ostensibly a work of high fantasy:

> "There was no higher honor than to receive your knighthood from the Prince of Dragonstone."
>
> "Tell me, then—when he touched a man on the shoulder with his sword, what did he say? 'Go forth and kill the weak'? Or go forth and defend them? At the Trident, those brave men Viserys spoke of who died beneath our dragon banners—did they give their lives because they believed in Rhaegar's cause, or because they had been bought and paid for?" Dany turned to Mormont, crossed her arms, and waited for an answer.
>
> "My queen," the big man said slowly," all you say is true. But Rhaegar lost on the Trident. He lost the battle, he lost the war, he lost the kingdom, and he lost his life. His blood swirled downriver with the rubies from his breastplate, and Robert the Usurper rode over his corpse to steal the Iron Throne. Rhaegar fought valiantly, Rhaegar fought nobly, Rhaegar fought honorably. And Rhaegar died.

Martin teamed up with co-editor Gardner Dozois for *Warriors* (2010), an anthology of warriors depicted across time and genre. The eclectic nature of *Warriors* is an homage to the liberal literary mixing of Martin's youth; Martin commissioned the anthology as a nod to his pleasant days as a youth combing through drugstore wire spinner racks, leading to many happy finds. In these racks one could discover science fiction sandwiched alongside westerns, or a bodice-ripping romance next to a John Carter of Mars novel. Most of *Warriors'* contents are not sword-and-sorcery, but the last in the anthology, Martin's own "The Mystery Knight," is much closer in spirit to the subgenre than A Song of Ice and Fire, even though it is set in the same universe and serves as a prequel. "The Mystery Knight" features the characters Dunk and Egg, whom Martin featured in another pair of novellas, "The Hedge Knight" and "The Sworn Sword." Its tight focus on two heroes, rather than the sprawling cast of characters of A Song of Ice and Fire, lends to its sword-and-sorcery feel.

Sword-and-sorcery received an infusion in 2007 from a "literary novelist" with Michael Chabon's *Gentlemen of the Road*. Chabon, who prior had written slice-of-life realist works *The Mysteries of Pittsburgh* and *Wonder Boys* (though had begun to nudge into genre fiction with 2007's *The Yiddish Policemen's Union*, which won the Hugo and Nebula

Awards), penned a story of two rogues embroiled in a series of color-ful picaresque episodes. While technically historical adventure—the story is set in the medieval kingdom of Arran west of the Caspian Sea circa 950 A.D.—and bereft of magic or horror, Chabon drew his chief inspiration from the likes of Howard, Moorcock, and Leiber, whom he re-read in anticipation of starting work on the novel. The work's principal concern are the fortunes of Amram, a massive axe-wielding African, and Zelikman, a rapier-wielding physician. Its emphasis on swashbuckling adventure over historical fidelity pushes the work firmly into sword-and-sorcery territory:

> I also, maybe more importantly, re-read some of my lifelong favorite writers of historical swashbuckling romance: Alexander Dumas, Rafael Sabatini, Robert E. Howard, Fritz Leiber, Michael Moorcock (to whom the story is dedicated), George MacDonald Fraser. The tone of the writing, the style, the approach to the idea of heroic swords-men and their personalities (of which I favor the ironic variety found in the last three authors named and perhaps in Dumas, as well), all that was in many ways more of a challenge than the details of period, which are just a matter ultimately of reading and using the imagination ("Questions for Michael Chabon").

Further adding to the novel's sword-and-sorcery/picaresque her-itage, *Gentlemen of the Road* was initially published in serial form in the *New York Times* in 2007.

In recent years, sword-and-sorcery has been revived in its classic form, with authors hammering its notched and bent blade back into shape and introducing new readers to the joy of rediscovery. Perhaps the best example of the modern revival is Howard Andrew Jones' *The Desert of Souls*. Jones' novel features a likeable pair of adven-turers, Dabir and Captain Asim, who recall a bit of Fafhrd and the Gray Mouser. Against its backdrop of quasi-historical eighth century Baghdad, the pair spend much of the book in pursuit of the wizard Fifouz, who plots to visit an ancient curse on the city. Its trappings of classic sword-and-sorcery—magic, undead monsters, godlike snakes, paired with an Arabian Nights feel—imbue the work with a sense of nostalgia. But Jones adds an interesting new dimension to the story by overlaying a meta-narrative about the larger concept of storytelling. Through his characters' dialogue, Jones—himself a first-time novelist—comments on the courage it takes to tell stories, which open up an author to inevitable criticism. "I have seldom met a man who so feared taking up a pen," says an old fortune teller to Asim, who finds it easier to wade into combat with a blade than to tell a tale.

Rogue Blades Entertainment (whose website boasts "putting the HERO back into HEROICS) made a recent foray into the genre with a trio of anthologies: *Return of the Sword* (2008), *Rage of the Behemoth* (2009), and *Demons: A Clash of Steel Anthology* (2010). Of the handful of sword-and-sorcery publishers today, Rogue Blades is perhaps the most unabashedly pro-genre. Its website includes a helpful definition of sword-and-sorcery alongside a constellation of other genres, including explanations of lesser-known niches "sword and soul" and "swashbuckling adventure":

> Sword & sorcery is fiction set in a land different from our own, where technology is relatively primitive, allowing the protagonists to overcome their martial obstacles face-to-face. Magic works, but seldom at the behest of the genre's heroes. More often sorcery is just one more obstacle used against them and is usually wielded by villains or monsters. The landscape is exotic; either a different world, or far corners of our own. S&S heroes live by their cunning or brawn, frequently both. They are strangers or outcasts, rebels imposing their own justice on the wilds or the strange and decadent civilizations which they encounter. They are usually commoners or barbarians; should they hail from the higher ranks of society, they are discredited, disinherited, or from the lowest rungs of nobility. The protagonists of S&S must best fantastic dangers, monstrous horrors, and dark sorcery to earn riches, astonishing treasure, the love of dazzling members of the opposite sex, or the right to live another day. Most important of all, S&S moves at a headlong pace and overflows with action and thrilling adventure. Robert E. Howard's Conan is the most famous of the S&S protagonists ("About RBE Genres").

DMR Books is another new publisher embracing the roots of the subgenre with new authors, new stories, and a stable of authors unlike any other. For his *Swords of Steel* anthologies, editor D.M. Ritzlin contracted heavy metal musicians with a love of sword-and-sorcery and dark fantasy to write the stories. The contents are suitably dark, violent, and moody. From the back cover of *Swords of Steel* (2015):

> Modern fantasy has been plagued with convoluted plots and series without end. Who better to return traditional fantasy to its former glory than the heavy metal bards? Members of such bands as Bal-Sagoth, Manilla Road, Twister Tower Dire, Cauldron Born, Solstice, and more—proving their talent for the written word as well as song—cut through the modern wasteland, wielding literary Swords of Steel.

Swords of Steel ("Not for Wimps!") is a call to arms for a return to traditional sword-and- sorcery, straddling the lines of homage and pastiche. Another example of this style of fiction is the jointly authored short novel *King of the Bastards* (2015) by Brian Keene and Steven Shrewsbury. An aging Rogan, barbaric king of Albion, finds palace life a bore. As with Conan, kingship is a wearying exercise in which daggers are poised at his back, and his wine cups laced with poison:

> I wanted to be a ruler, a king, to have what I always wanted—ultimate power. Once I took the crown of Albion, even more fighting went on. There was always a bastard around to try to take my crown. On a tower of skulls, I built my throne and knew peace at last.

Rogan turns over his crown to his son, Rohain, and sets off on new adventures. His ship is waylaid and capsized; following a bloody, pyrrhic victory in which he and a companion barely reach shore alive, he learns that his kingdom has been overthrown. Rogan has to make his way off the demon-haunted island and return home to free his captive son and subjects. Keene and Shrewsbury deliberately harken back to the barbarian-centric sword-and-sorcery of the 1960s and 70s, but infuse *King of the Bastards* with elements of zombie fiction (Keene is a Bram Stoker-winning author of the zombie novel *The Rising*) and splatterpunk horror to create a sword-and-sorcery novel modern in feel, if uneven in execution.

The Mighty Warriors (2018, Ulthar Press) is perhaps the most transparent appeal to fans of pulp and renaissance age sword-and-sorcery. Editor Robert M. Price offers tribute to the Hans Stefan Santesson-edited Lancer collections *The Mighty Barbarians* (1969) and *The Mighty Swordsmen* (1970) in its introduction. "I loved [Santesson's] approach, combining pulp-era tales of heroic fantasy with new stories continuing the same tradition. The result is this book" (4). *The Mighty Warriors* features new stories of classic heroes of sword-and-sorcery, some by their original authors. Charles Saunders has an excellent tale of Imaro in the volume, "Amudu's Bargain," while Adrian Cole (author of numerous sword-and-sorcery stories including *The Dream Lords*) contributes a fun Elak of Atlantis pastiche, "Spawn of the Sea God." David C. Smith offers up another tale of Oron, "The Shadow of Dia-Sust."

Other notable recent sword-and-sorcery/sword-and-sorcery-influenced authors and stories include James Enge's Morlock the Maker series, including *Blood of Ambrose* (2009), *This Crooked Way* (2009), and *The Wolf Age* (2010), and Paul Kemp's Egil and Nix stories including *The Hammer and the Blade* (2012), *A Discourse in Steel* (2013), and *A Conversation in Blood* (2017). Enge's Morlock stories appear to owe much to Michael Shea, along with Leiber, Vance, and a few trappings borrowed from Moorcock.[5] Dialogue-driven, *This Crooked Way* exhibits the clear influence of the likes of Joe Abercrombie. Magic is far more ubiquitous than is found in traditional sword-and-sorcery, and the presence of dwarves, dragons, and the occasional use of multiple viewpoint storytelling at times pushes *Blood of Ambrose* toward the high fantasy end of the spectrum. But the episodic, street-level adventures of the outsider Moorlock—a spellcaster and black-blade wielder harkening back to

---

[5] Among sword-and-sorcery authors, Enge claims Vance, Leiber, and Charles Saunders as influences, along with the likes of Lord Dunsany, James Branch Cabell, Ursula LeGuin, Leigh Brackett, and Joe Abercrombie, among others (Wanchoo).

Elric, albeit with more heart and humor—returns it to its sword-and-sorcery roots. Kemp is perhaps best known for his work writing fictional tie-ins to the Dungeons & Dragons campaign setting the Forgotten Realms. The Forgotten Realms also served as the springboard for the career of R.A. Salvatore, whose stories of the dark elf ranger Drzzt Do'Urden, though perhaps closer to high fantasy, borrow elements of classic sword-and-sorcery including an outsider as its central character. Salvatore is by far the most commercially successful modern author whose works can be loosely classified as sword-and-sorcery with more than 10,000,000 copies of his works sold ("Biography"). Saladin Ahmed's *Throne of the Crescent Moon* (2012) won a Locus Award for Best First Novel and was nominated for the 2013 Hugo Award for Best Novel. Ahmed's novel drew the attention and praise of genre critics for its use of sword-and-sorcery traditions in a non-traditional, Middle Eastern setting, as written by a non-white author (Farabee).

Sword-and-sorcery fiction also maintains a small web presence. Heroic Fantasy Quarterly has been publishing heroic fantasy/sword-and-sorcery fiction and poetry since 2009 in an online format, and recently republished the best of these in *The Best of Heroic Fantasy Quarterly*, volumes 1 and 2. Swords and Sorcery Magazine has been publishing stories on its website on a monthly basis since 2012. Black Gate, which once published a print journal but is now a website only, publishes articles, essays, and reviews of modern and classic sword-and-sorcery, as well as occasional pieces of fiction, amidst extensive coverage of other fantasy and science fiction genres.

New technologies and platforms have assisted with a recent sword-and-sorcery revival. Print-on-demand services can fulfill books, journals, and magazines as orders are placed, allowing publishers to bypass the expense of printing and maintaining a large inventory of books. As a result, niche genres like sword-and-sorcery can exist on the periphery of publishing. *Tales from the Magician's Skull* is the result of a successful Kickstarter campaign that raised more than $36,000 from 808 backers, smashing its modest goal of $5,000. Issue one includes 72 pages of sword-and-sorcery, including seven stories by James Enge, John C. Hocking, Howard Andrew Jones, Aeryn Rudel, Bill Ward, C. L. Werner, and Chris Willrich. The magazine is a deliberate return to the pulp era —having exceeded its stretch goals, the publishers printed issue #1 on textured, tan-colored paper stock that evokes a "weathered pulp feel." "If you're a collector who owns pulp magazines from the classic era, you'll know the effect we're going for" ("Tales from the Magician's Skull"). Edited by Howard Andrew Jones, the magazine is published by Goodman Games, a role playing game company, and alongside the fiction offers a translation of the creatures, spells, and magic items featured in the stories into the game mechanics of Goodman Games' Dungeon Crawl Classics. This adds additional utility for the magazine as a role-playing aid.

Skelos: The Journal of Weird Fiction and Dark Fantasy is the result of another successful kickstarter. Issue #1 debuted in 2016 and two additional issues have appeared since. A blend of fiction, poetry, and non-fiction, *Skelos* publishes weird fiction, dark fantasy, horror, sword-and-sorcery, new eeird, and slipstream. Editors Mark Finn, Chris Gruber and Jeffrey Shanks have a vision of bridging the gap between classic weird fiction and new weird fiction (Finn, "Skull Session" 6). Skelos has added critical illumination to sword-and-sorcery: Nicole Emmelhainz' essay "A Sword-Edge Beauty as Keen as Blades: C.L. Moore and the Gender Dynamics of Sword and Sorcery" in volume 1 makes a strong case that the subgenre is more female-friendly than previously acknowledged and can even be considered proto-feminist.

Sword-and-sorcery has fallen from its heyday of widespread mass-market penetration, but is still being written by artists blending its traditional forms and tropes with new techniques and influences. The genre has grown more diverse, offering exotic but culturally respectful settings, and fuller, deeper characterization. Its shape has morphed from its original pulp magazine roots—short, linear stories of adventure suited to newsstand magazines—to novels and multi-volume series. Classic sword-and-sorcery continues to be produced in peripheral, fan-driven magazines like *Tales from the Magician's Skull* and by specialty publishers. In the likes of grimdark and urban fantasy, sword-and-sorcery can be felt beneath the surface, a transformative force from the past exerting its influence on a handful of the most popular fantasy works of the modern age. While it may have fallen from its former seat of glory and has been pushed to the margins of publishing, its influence enjoys a healthy presence in the broader popular culture. Sword-and-sorcery has moved beyond the pages of pulps and paperbacks, and permeated music, gaming, and movies, where it continues to be consumed in far greater quantities than ever before.

CHAPTER NINE
The Cultural Impact of Sword-and-Sorcery

In the crypts of Atlantean kings, I found what I was looking for.
—Manilla Road, "Necropolis"

In the years of its renaissance and subsequent fall from grace, sword-and-sorcery slipped its literary bonds and permeated the broader culture. In the 1970s, the side panels of custom vans sported air-brushed warriors and wizards straight out of the Hyborian Age. In the 1980s, colorful coin-operated video arcade games like *Rastan, Hercules*, and *Gauntlet* took players on 8-bit quests, battling hordes of attackers in underground dungeons while in search of treasures. Popular cartoons *He-Man* and *Thundaar the Barbarian* exposed millions of children to a PG-helping of sword-and-sorcery tropes every Saturday morning. Though it lasted just a single season, for a time sword-and-sorcery cracked prime-time television. *Son of Zorn* (September 2016 to February 2017) featured an animated barbarian lead that made an incongruous intrusion into the lives of a modern family. A simultaneous homage to *He-Man* and *Thundaar*, with cartoonishly "adult" violent and sexual urges, *Son of Zorn* was a mashup of sword-and-sorcery's worst stereotypes, but was unmistakably of the subgenre.

Today you can't swing an Atlantean blade without severing one of sword-and-sorcery's far-flung tentacles. Rather than embark on a vain attempt to track down every spin-off comic, artwork image, or television show referencing the genre, this chapter focuses on three major areas of clear influence: gaming, music, and movies. In the once wildly popular and still influential and widely played *Dungeons and Dragons* role-playing game, the thunder and bombast of heavy metal music, and in a barbarous horde of films featuring muscular sword-wielding heroes and bikini-clad heroines, the imagery and themes of sword-and-sorcery literature are evident, and today remain vibrantly alive.

A Game Phenomenon's
Sword-and-Sorcery Roots

In 1974, two diehard wargamers from Lake Geneva, Wisconsin, revolutionized the tabletop game industry by asking a series of simple "what if" questions. The turn-based wargames they played involved a high level of abstraction, with one figurine representing 50, 100, or 1,000 or more soldiers. These simulated large-scale battles well, but could not re-create the stories they truly enjoyed: the weird pulp fantasy of Jack Vance, Fritz Leiber, and Robert E. Howard. So, the two men wondered: what if these pieces of painted metal were 1:1 representations? What if instead of following a rigidly defined set of turn-based rules, players could assume an imaginary role, and play the part of Cugel the Clever, the Gray Mouser, or Conan the Cimmerian? What if these imaginary characters, instead of re-enacting military engagements from the past, instead participated in freewheeling adventures from popular fantasy fiction, limited only by the imaginations of the minds gathered around the game table?

With this simple stroke of out-of-the-box thinking, Gary Gygax and Dave Arneson spurred a revolution in game design. Soon the pair began to assemble and playtest the first rough-hewn rules that would be published under the name *Chainmail* (1971). Over the next three years their game would increase in sophistication and complexity, eventually codified and published as *Dungeons and Dragons*, or *D&D*, in 1974. *D&D* was the first in a new breed of tabletop gaming called role playing games, or RPGs, which today have evolved and expanded to include simulations of nearly every corner of genre fiction, from westerns, to space opera, to vampires.

When Gygax and Arneson began to flesh out their ideas and create a coherent set of rules—for example, how magic worked, how character classes functioned, how combat was conducted—in short, how the laws of the universe of this new fictitious game world would operate within codified game rules—they turned to fantasy literature for inspiration. The two men wanted to provide players with an approximate simulation of the adventures of the heroes from the fantasy fiction boom of the 1960s and 1970s. Avid readers both, Gygax and Arneson were faced with a variety of choices, from William Morris to J.R.R. Tolkien, to Jack Vance and Robert E. Howard. Ultimately, they turned to sword-and-sorcery.

A common misconception is that *D&D* owes its principal debt to the high fantasy of J.R.R. Tolkien. It's an easy mistake to make: *D&D*'s halfling (aka hobbit) and woodland ranger (aka Aragorn) character classes, its distinctive fantasy races and classes (elves, dwarves, wizards, fighters) banded together into adventuring "parties," and a handful of its iconic monsters (orcs, demon-like Balrogs, ents/treants, etc.) are lifted directly from Tolkien's fictional realm of Middle-Earth. But these are largely surface elements. While *D&D* includes trappings from *The Lord of the Rings*, its heart and soul, and guts and spirit, are derived from sword-and-sorcery:

> Somewhere I came across a story by Robert E. Howard, an early taste of the elixir of fantasy to which I rapidly became addicted. Even now I vividly recall my first perusal of *Conan the Conqueror*, Howard's only full-length novel. After I finished reading that piece of sword & sorcery literature for the first time, my concepts of adventure were never quite the same again. From these literary fruits came the seeds which grew into today's most popular roleplaying games. ... A careful examination of the games will quickly reveal that the major influences are Robert E. Howard, L. Sprague de Camp and Fletcher Pratt, Fritz Leiber, Poul Anderson, A. Merritt, and H. P. Lovecraft. Only slightly lesser influence came from Roger Zelazny, E. R. Burroughs, Michael Moorcock, Philip Jose Farmer, and many others. Though I thoroughly enjoyed *The Hobbit*, I found the Ring Trilogy ... well, tedious (Gygax, "The influence of J.R.R. Tolkien on the *D&D* and *AD&D* games" 12).

D&D adventuring parties may outwardly resemble the collection of dwarves, elves, hobbits, and men that comprise the Fellowship of the Ring, but they have very different aims and objectives. Rather than the altruism of an Aragorn, or the hearth-and-home concerns of Frodo, *D&D* parties embrace the mercenary motivations of the likes of Conan and Fafhrd and the Gray Mouser, particularly in the game's first edition. *D&D* at its roots is a game in which player-characters explore dark and dangerous dungeons in search of gold and gems and magic items and in pursuit of self-enrichment, power, and prestige. *D&D* adventures can include saving the world, and later iterations of the game would allow player-characters to advance all the way to the ranks of immortals. But the early iterations of the game provided an experience very familiar to readers of sword-and-sorcery, that "money, and acquiring it, is real power," and that life is greed in action (Leiber, "Ill Met in Lankhmar" 153). Looting dungeons and killing monsters is the prime occupation of *D&D* characters. The early iterations of *D&D* rewarded such behavior by awarding "experience points" not only for monsters killed, but for each gold piece looted from ancient crypts.

Gygax greatly downplayed Tolkien's influence on *D&D*:

> A frequently asked question—or assertion, in the case of those who don't bother to ask—deals with the amount of influence of J.R.R. Tolkien on the creation of the DUNGEONS & DRAGONS and ADVANCED DUNGEONS & DRAGONS role-playing games. The answer to the inquiry is complex, for there are two parts. The popularity of Professor Tolkien's fantasy works did encourage me

to develop my own. But while there are bits and pieces of his words reflected hazily in mine, I believe that his influence, as a whole, is quite minimal (Gygax, "The influence of J.R.R. Tolkien on the *D&D* and *AD&D* games 12).

Residual legal bitterness may have played a part in Gygax' dismissal: *D&D* publisher Tactical Studies Rules (TSR) enterprises was threatened with a lawsuit by Tolkien Enterprises for borrowing some of Tolkien's creations without obtaining permission and settled the matter out of court. Later iterations of the game replaced Tolkien-specific nomenclature, for example swapping out "hobbit" with "halfling," "ent" with "treant," and "balrog" with "type VI demon." But in truth *D&D* owes comparatively little to high fantasy. In fact, it actively promoted sword-and-sorcery literature. The premier issue of *The Dragon* featured the article "Fritz Leiber: A Conversation with Fafhrd and the Mouser," in which Leiber offered readers suggestions on how to port over the arms and armaments of the peoples of his fictional world of Nehwon into their games. The second issue proclaimed *The Dragon* "The magazine of Fantasy, Swords & Sorcery and Science Fiction Gaming" on its cover, and included the Gardner Fox story "Shadow of a Demon," featuring Niall of the Far Travels, "a mercenary, a sell-sword, a barbarian out of the forested mountains of Norumbria." Fox would write a total of 10 stories of Niall for *Dragon Magazine* between 1976 and 1981.

Years later, former *Dragon* magazine editor/publisher Jake Jaquet reconfirmed the link of sword-and-sorcery and fantasy gaming. "Certainly you can't disassociate the influence that earlier sword and sorcery literature, novels, and short stories had on the development of the *Dungeons and Dragons* game. ... Gary Gygax would have been first to say that the game of *Dungeons and Dragons* was certainly influenced by what he had read, from Howard to Tolkien and everyone in between" (Smith, Jaquet, Bonadonna).

D&D's distinctive game mechanics—alignment, character levels, and its magic system—are all derived from sword-and-sorcery, with exact parallels in the literature. *D&D* characters operate under alignments of law and chaos, behavioral and moral coordinates borrowed from the Poul Anderson novel *Three Hearts and Three Lions* and expanded on and popularized in Michael Moorcock's Elric series. Magic-users cast spells governed by a magic system lifted directly from Jack Vance's Dying Earth stories, or wield magic items like Vance's Ioun stones. The thief character class is taken from Fritz Leiber's world of Nehwon and the Fafhrd and the Gray Mouser series; the hierarchical Mafia-like thieves' guilds in which player-character thieves participate and advance within are straight out of stories like "Ill Met in Lankhmar." *D&D* thief "levels" are all but spelled out in the text of Leiber's story where we meet "tall, tight-lipped Slevyas, *master thief* candidate, and fat, darting eyed Fissif thief *second class*" (108). Some of *D&D*'s iconic creatures are lifted from the pages of sword-and-sorcery. *D&D*'s undead magic-using lich, for example, appears in the story "Sword of the Sorcerer" in Gardner Fox's *Kothar: Barbarian Swordsman*, in which the lich Afgorkon gives Kothar his magic sword Frostfire. The ancient, evil sorcerer Thulsa Doom, described as "the greatest of all wizards" with a face "a bare white skull, in whose eye sockets flamed livid fire" (Howard, "The Cat and the Skull" 114) is also a near-identical match of the description provided in the *Advanced Dungeons and Dragons Monster Manual*.[1]

In 1977, TSR released an advanced version of *D&D*. *Advanced Dungeons and Dragons*, or *AD&D*, was a substantial expansion of the basic rules and an attempt to standardize game play, which was previously characterized by a sparse, loose style with rules adjudicated on the fly by the gamemaster. It also reconfirmed the central influence of sword-and-sorcery. The introduction to the *AD&D Dungeon Master's Guide*—a reference book designed to help the gamemaster develop adventures and adjudicate game play with references, rules, and tables—notes that the game "presupposes ... an adventurer in a world of swords & sorcery":

> Keep such individuality in perspective by developing a unique and detailed world based on the rules of *Advanced D&D*. No two campaigns will ever be the same, but all will have the common ground necessary to maintaining the whole as a viable entity about which you and your players can communicate with the many thousands of others who also find swords & sorcery role playing gaming as an amusing and enjoyable pastime (Gygax, *Dungeon Master's Guide* 7–8).

Many players were content to play *AD&D*'s rules as written, but others, seeking to enrich their gaming experience through an understanding of the source material underpinning the game mechanics, sought out the books listed in Appendix N. This now widely referenced resource includes several sword-and-sorcery titles, including Gardner Fox's Kothar and Kyrik series, Robert E. Howard's Conan, Andrew Offutt's *Swords Against Darkness* anthology, Fritz Leiber's Fafhrd and the Gray Mouser series, Michael Moorcock's Elric stories, and Jack Vance's *The Dying Earth,* as well as sword-and-sorcery precursors H.P. Lovecraft, Lord Dunsany, and A. Merritt. A popular *AD&D* game supplement released the following year, *Deities and Demigods* (1980), contained information on pantheons of heroes, gods, and monsters from Michael Moorcock's Melnibone and Fritz

---

[1] Interested readers can find extensive online listings correlating D&D's character classes, monsters, magic weapons, and more to the literature. See DeVarque, "Literary Sources of D&D."

Leiber's Nehwon, translated into *D&D* game mechanics. TSR also published the board game *Lankhmar* in 1976. Originally conceived by Leiber and his friend Otto Fischer in the 1930s, *Lankhmar* is a game in which 2-4 players assume control of one of the factions of Leiber's restless city and go to war against the others.

D&D was not the only role-playing game inspired by sword-and-sorcery, but merely the first and most popular. Subsequent game companies went directly to the source material and licensed sword-and-sorcery titles for supplements or stand-alone games. In 1981 Chaosium published *Thieves' World*, a game based on the series of novels and anthologies of the same name. The game's gimmick was establishing compatibility across multiple role playing game systems. The same year Chaosium debuted the *Stormbringer* role-playing game, based on Michael Moorcock's world of Elric of Melnibone. *Stormbringer* used the Basic Roleplaying game engine introduced in its flagship game *Runequest*, but with modifications to simulate the feel of Moorcock's invented world. These included demon-summoning magic, and an alignment system requiring characters to side with either law, chaos, or the balance. *Stormbringer* proved popular enough to warrant five revisions, with the last appearing in 2001.

Not to be outdone by a rival publisher TSR landed the largest and most recognizable sword-and-sorcery property. In 1984 the publisher released two game modules set in the Hyborian Age of Conan. *Conan Unchained!* and *Conan Against Darkness!* gave D&D players the option of assuming the role of Conan or one of his compatriots in battles against the Stygian sorcerer Thoth-Amon. After receiving critiques that the D&D's game mechanics did not sufficiently model Howard's stories, TSR released a stand-alone boxed set with original rules, *Conan Role Playing Game*, in 1985.

These efforts were just the start for Conan roleplaying. The following year Steve Jackson Games, publisher of the Generic Universal Role Playing System, or GURPS, published the *GURPS Conan* game supplement (1986). L. Sprague de Camp wrote the introduction. In 2004 Mongoose Publishing released *Conan: The Roleplaying Game*, with a second edition appearing in 2007. The most recent entry in Hyborian Age roleplaying is *Conan: Adventures in an Age Undreamed Of* (2017, Modiphius Entertainment). Game designers consulted Howard scholars and scholarship in the game's design with the goal of establishing the ultimate in Hyborian Age fidelity and playability.

Conan: Adventures in an Age Undreamed of has helped ensure sword-and-sorcery's footprint in role-playing into the 21st century, but other classic sword-and-sorcery-based games remain available as well. Mongoose Publishing, under an open game license from the holders of the *Runequest* property, in the same year released *Runequest: Lankhar* (2007) and *Elric of Melnibone* (2007). Several additional supplements followed. *Savage Worlds* (2003) is a rules-light game designed to replicate the feel of old pulp literature. Designed with flexibility in mind, the system has spawned supplements for weird western, science fiction, and zombie game play. Pinnacle Entertainment in 2015 published *Lankhmar: City of Thieves*, a supplement for game play in Nehwon and Lankhmar, with gaming information adapted from Leiber's stories. *Barbarians of Lemuria* (2008, new edition in 2015) is a sword-and-sorcery role-playing game inspired by the Thongor stories of Lin Carter. The game mechanics, less cumbersome than the likes of *D&D* and *Runequest*, have drawn praise for their ability to replicate the freewheeling action of sword-and-sorcery. In 2012 North Wind Adventures published *Astonishing Swordsmen and Sorcerers of Hyperborea*, a role-playing game of swords, sorcery, and weird fantasy. Now in its second edition, the game's creators describe it as "the premier sword-and-sorcery RPG" inspired by the works of Robert E. Howard, H.P. Lovecraft, and Clark Ashton Smith. It offers a free game aid on its website, Drunken Debauchery!, a "random generator designed just for those special times when the adventurers are *between* adventures, and they have returned to civilization to carouse and spend their hard-won gold" (Chapman). *Astonishing Swordsmen and Sorcerers of Hyberborea* is aligned with the Old School Renaissance, or OSR, a loose collection of publishers, authors, and fans dedicated to reviving, reimagining, and celebrating the classic editions of *D&D*.

D&D's popularity surged through the late 1970s and into the early 80s, then peaked in the mid-1980s, after which mismanagement and over-expansion at TSR resulted in serious financial troubles (a bell-curve that, perhaps not coincidentally, closely mirrors sword-and-sorcery's rise and fall). Driven out of the company, Gygax went on to design his own role-playing game, *Dangerous Journeys*, in 1992. TSR began a slow decline and eventually was sold to Wizards of the Coast in 1997. There it experienced a revival with the launch of a third edition in 2000 that returned the game to its sword-and-sorcery roots. *D&D* 3.0 took a "back to the dungeon" approach, away from the direction in which it had begun to drift with the publication of high-magic, nation-shaking campaign worlds like Dragonlance and SpellJammer, the latter of which allowed player-characters to adventure beyond the stars.

Today, traditional tabletop role-playing games remain a viable and healthy industry. *D&D*, which recently underwent a 5th edition, continues to attract thousands of new players, some of whom go on to discover its literary ancestry. The podcast *Appendix N*, which debuted in July 2017, introduces listeners to *D&D*'s source material, principally focusing on the plot and theme of the stories but also their application to dungeon masters seeking to return the game its sword-and-sorcery roots. Arguably *D&D*'s most profound and lasting legacy is its influence on the video-game industry. Personal computing by the late 1970s was beginning to take root, and designers capitalized with electronic role playing games like *Ultima*, *Wizardry*, and *Wizard's Crown*. While these early video RPGs were relatively crude, game designers innovated at a rapid rate. Today's video games including *Final Fantasy* and *World of Warcraft* are sophisticated, detailed, and immersive, but retain the influence of *D&D* and its sword-and-sorcery heritage.

Heavy Metal: Soundtrack of Sword-and-Sorcery

With harsh riffs blasted out of amplified electric guitars, chest-compressing drum beats, and vocals ranging from guttural growls to soaring operatics, heavy metal music is the sound of a battlefield. Its listeners pump their fists, headbang, or engage in a form of ritualistic, violent, but controlled dancing called "moshing." In her sociological study *Heavy Metal: The Music and its Culture*, Deena Weinstein claims that heavy metal's adherents embrace metal music for the sense of power it engenders. "The essential song element in heavy metal is power, expressed as sheer volume. Loudness is meant to overwhelm, to sweep the listener into the sound, and then to lend the listener the sense of power that the sound provides" (23). With page-turning stories of visceral life-and-death combat, and protagonists living lives "turned up to 11," sword-and-sorcery is a natural source of inspiration. Many heavy metal acts co-opted its thematic and aesthetic content for their lyrics, and its imagery for their album art or stage props. Some hired artists to paint idealized, muscular depictions of themselves in the tradition of Frank Frazetta or Boris Vallejo, or donned armor, furs, and swords for album cover photographs.

Heavy metal's birth is generally correlated with the release of *Black Sabbath* (1970), the self-titled debut album of a British quartet of the same name. Black Sabbath is known for the haunting wails of lead singer Ozzy Osbourne, and the gloomy, dark, heavy guitar tone of Tony Iommi, but also for establishing the sorcerous, demonic imagery for which heavy metal has become widely associated. While Sabbath's debut is not as overtly sword-and-sorcery as later metal acts, songs like "The Wizard" and "Black Sabbath" reference a wandering wizard, an encounter with the devil, and black magic. By the late 1970s and early 1980s, rock and metal acts were liberally

dipping into sword-and-sorcery source material. Hard rock/proto
metal band Molly Hatchet commissioned a trio of works from Frank
Frazetta for their album covers, including his iconic Death Dealer
image on their 1978 self-titled album. A decade later the same image
appeared on a sword-and-sorcery book series by James Silke. The
album cover of Judas Priest's "Hero, Hero" (1981) featured a painting by artist Mel Grant which originally appeared on the Andrew
Offutt sword-and-sorcery novel *Sword of the Gael*.

Perhaps the most openly sword-and-sorcery band of the early
days of heavy metal was Manilla Road. Formed in 1977, Manilla
Road wrote Robert E. Howard homages and borrowed Howardian
names and imagery for its songs, including "Queen of the Black
Coast" (*Metal*, 1982) and "Road of Kings" and "Hour of the Dragon"
(*Open the Gates*, 1986). Manilla Road's lyrics are straight out of
Howard, as here in "Queen of the Black Coast":

> Take me back, across the sea
> Of Vilayet, to my queen
> No kingdom hers, but for the sea
> A coastal curse, a pirate's dream
>
> Scourge of the west coast
> Hellcat of my dreams
>
> The *Tigress* sailed, The south so vast
> The queen was hung from her own mast
> From winged death she did save
> My hardened soul, from the grave
>
> Funeral pyre forever
> Burning out to sea
>
> Queen of the black coast
> Watch as the heads roll

In an interview published on the Cimmerian Shadows website,
Manilla Road founder/ vocalist/guitarist/songwriter Mark Shelton
acknowledged sword-and-sorcery as a chief influence, along with the
likes of H.P. Lovecraft and Edgar Allan Poe:

> (Question): I can't let the phrase "Sword & Sorcery" pass by without
> further comment, so why not ruminate a bit on this particular breed
> of fantasy? In my view, fantasy in general – but particularly S&S –
> is something that either chimes deep within one's core, or passes
> by utterly unheeded. Personally, I can't imagine not being moved
> into shuddering awe by the thought of forbidden jewels smoulder-
> ing behind darksome draperies; of the clatter of unearthly armour
> across snow-clad wastes; or of toppled empresses pining in exile for
> their sundered, exotic thrones. You?
>
> (Answer): Hell, that is why Robert E. Howard is my favourite author.
> He gives you all of that in his stories. Man, the Conan stuff is so just
> what you said. And yes it is an incredibly cool genre of authorship.

> I can't get enough when it is well done. Whether it be cinematic or written or musical, adventure fantasy always tugs at my soul.

Michael Moorcock forged a direct early link between sword-and-sorcery and hard rock by collaborating with "space rock" act Hawkwind, with whom he wrote lyrics and performed as a vocalist on *Warrior on the Edge of Time* (1975) and *Sonic Attack* (1981), with additional writing credits on 1985's *The Chronicle of the Black Sword*. Moorcock also wrote the lyrics for the song "Black Blade" for proto-metal act Blue Oyster Cult (off 1980's *Cultosaurus Erectus*). Elric proved to be a fecund source of inspiration for several heavy metal and hard rock acts of the 1970s and 1980s.[2] Early proto-metal act Deep Purple borrowed the name of their album *Stormbringer* (1974) from the albino emperor, while New Wave of British Heavy Metal artist Tygers of Pan Tang are named after an island nation in Melnibone. Moorcock later returned the favor to heavy metal, dedicating *Elric at the End of Time* (1984) to Lemmy Kilmister, the hard-partying, gravelly voiced lead singer of the heavy metal band Motorhead. Italian power metal band Domine have written concept albums based on Moorcock's works, including the likes of "Champion Eternal" and "Stormbringer Ruler."

As heavy metal took center stage in the 1980s, a handful of bands took sword-and-sorcery's thematic material "up to 11." The muscular members of the band Manowar donned loincloths and furs and brandished broadswords for the cover of *Into Glory Ride* (1983), which featured tracks called "Secret of Steel," "Warlord," and "Gloves of Metal." Manowar matched its barbaric look with powerful songs of battlefield mayhem and conquest, including the likes of "Hail and Kill" and "Black Wind, Fire and Steel." Manowar readily acknowledges a considerable debt to sword-and-sorcery; the band's website proudly proclaims it is "The first metal band to include sword & sorcery imagery in both their lyrics and on their album covers." The band Cirith Ungol, which took its name from a mountain pass in J.R.R. Tolkien's *The Lord of the Rings*, nevertheless claimed a greater influence from sword-and-sorcery. Said drummer Robert Garven in a 2000 interview, "Everyone in the band was a big "Sword and Sorcery" literature fan, especially Greg [Lindstrom, guitars] and I. He would always turn us on to the great writers who gave us inspiration for our music. We read all the books ... Conan, Bran Mak Morn, etcetera, but the books that stood out in my mind are Michael Moorcock's masterpieces: Elric, Hawkmoon, Corum among others"

---

[2] For a comprehensive listing of hard rock and metal acts inspired by Moorcock's works (and they are legion), seek out "Chronicle of the Black Sword: Rock and Metal Inspired by Michael Moorcock's Multiverse" on the Ride into Glory website.

("Cirith Ungol Interview with Robert Garvin"). Moorcock's influence was plainly evident from the band's album covers, which featured classic Elric artwork from Michael Whelan.

Today sword-and-sorcery continues to find expression in the works of heavy metal musicians. Howie Bentley, guitarist and songwriter for the band Cauldron Born, credits Howard's Bran Mak Morn and his battles against the Roman legions for the concepts behind the band's album ...*And Rome Shall Fall* (Bentley). Bentley's record label Echoes of Crom Records caters to bands using sword-and-sorcery and weird fiction in their lyrics. This includes the Russian metal band Blacksword, whose influences include Moorcock, Clark Ashton Smith, and David C. Smith. The latter's short story "Engor's Sword Arm" figures prominently in "Sword Arm," a song about a woman taken by force by the wizard Bilitu, and her rescue by the one-armed, mighty warrior Engor (Stevens). The popular German power metal band Blind Guardian based its song "Tanelorn" (*At the Edge of Time*, 2011) on the mythical, El Dorado-like city of Moorcock's Elric series. Austin, Texas- based Eternal Champion is unabashedly Howardian and Moorcockian, from the cover art of its album *The Armor of Fire* (2016), featuring a curvaceous blonde clinging to the knee of a muscular warrior, to songs like "The Last King of Pictdom." Arkham Witch, though principally known for songs inspired by the works of H.P. Lovecraft, dipped deeply into Howard's Kull for "The Mirrors of Tuzun Thune," off the album *Demos from the Deep* (2014).

Some heavy metal musicians have come full circle, paying homage to the source material by writing sword-and-sorcery fiction of their own. In 2015 DMR published *Swords of Steel* (DMR Books), an anthology of horror/adventure stories "in the tradition of Robert E. Howard, Michael Moorcock, George R.R. Martin, and H.P. Lovecraft." The authors are all members of metal bands, including Manilla Road, Bal-Sagoth, Cauldron Born, Twisted Tower Dire, Solstice, Borrowed Time, Eternal Champion, and Gatekeeper. Sword-and-sorcery author David C. Smith confirmed the mutual attraction between sword-and-sorcery and heavy metal in an introduction to the anthology. "The attraction of sword-and-sorcery and weird adventure stories for heavy metal musicians is natural and self-fulfilling. The raw sensibilities of the dark, inner landscape of the heart, so essential to this fiction, is the same territory explored by heavy metal musicians—dangerous, confrontational, brutally honest" (*Swords of Steel* 7). DMR Books has since published two more volumes of heavy metal musician-authored sword-and-sorcery, *Swords of Steel* 2 and *Swords of Steel* 3.

Heavy metal and sword-and-sorcery possess an apparent contradiction at their core—an anti-establishment ethos coupled with a conservative streak. Both cater to outsiders and non-conformists, but also draw borders around themselves, often sharply and rigidly. Heavy metal subculture is noted for being culturally conservative; its fans engage in heated discussions about who is and is not metal, saving their harshest criticisms for metal bands that break ranks and take to playing radio-friendly rock.[3] Metal bands must never "sell out"; they must conform to the genre's broad but finite codes of acceptable sound, content, and visuals. "This conservatism, rooted in romantic preservationism, creates an ongoing subculture, sharply distinguished from the mass culture of pop music" (Weinstein 137). Manowar in particular is known for drawing battle lines between true metal and false metal, as on the song "Black Arrows" (*Hail to England*, 1984):

> Let each note I now play
> be a black arrow of death
> sent straight to the hearts
> of all those who play false metal

Alex Avdeev of the band Blacksword says of heavy metal's insular tendencies, "There's nothing better than to be among the people you love to be encompassed with, a company of individuals sharing your thoughts and approving your decisions. The same is with Echoes of Crom, a label run by Howie Bentley, where only true metal bands are signed. You can talk to the label representatives without unpleasantness of being deigned upon and without having even the slightest chance of derided with being called 'closed-minded' (which is actually a synonym for 'focused,' whilst 'open-minded' equalizes to 'absent-minded,' so people don't really take offense in that)" (Stevens). As with heavy metal, sword-and-sorcery fans have a habit of circling the wagons. Quarrels occasionally erupt over the finer points of the subgenre, while the ethereal, princess-and-pixie style of fantasy championed on the covers of magazines like *Realms of Fantasy* are treated with disdain.

Perhaps due to their harsh subject matter, over-the-top manner of expression, and position on the periphery of music and literature, heavy metal and sword-and-sorcery have endured similar patterns of criticism. Critics often correlate heavy metal's garish imagery and violent, aggressive expression with an absence of artistry or subtlety. Rock critic Robert Duncan declared heavy metal "pimply, prole, putrid, unchic, unsophisticated, anti-intellectual (but impossibly preten-tious) ... the dance of defeat and decay ... music made by slack-jawed, alpaca-chrome for slack-jawed, alpaca-haired, downy-mustachioed

---

[3] Most notably Metallica, which in 1991 was pilloried by many fans following the release of its radio friendly "black" album.

imbeciles in cheap, too large T-shirts with pictures of comic-book Armageddon ironed on the front" (Weinstein 1). Likewise, sword-and-sorcery's critics often point to its muscular heroes and frequent bouts of swordplay as evidence of an inherent crudity and shallowness. It is high fantasy's less respectable cousin; boorish and loud.

But while they may not always practice the art of subtlety, sword-and-sorcery and heavy metal's loudness and bombast should not be mistaken for an absence of thought, or as lesser art. The harsh cries of the buzzard critics are drowned out by the powerful voice of Manowar's Joey Demaio ("Metal Warriors"):

> Every one of us has heard the call
> Brothers of true metal, proud and standing tall
> We know the power within us has brought us to this hall
> There's magic in the metal, there's magic in us all
> Heavy metal, or no metal at all, whimps and poseurs leave the hall

Sword-and-Sorcery Meets the Silver Screen

Sword-and-sorcery's 1960's resurgence began in paperback books and magazines, but soon spread beyond the printed page. Over the next two decades the genre made its way into comics, role-playing games, video games, music, and ultimately the motion picture industry. In the wake of the literary renaissance, a colorful, uncouth horde of sword-and-sorcery films featuring muscular, loinclothed heroes, scheming wizards, and scantily clad women flooded the movie theaters. Sword-and-sorcery had met the silver screen, and for a brief time rivaled and even surpassed the ubiquitous westerns that dominated the first six-plus decades of the 20th century.

While it was not the first of its kind, today the most well-known and enduring sword-and-sorcery film is *Conan the Barbarian* (1982). Securing budgeting for a film is notoriously difficult, but *Conan the Barbarian* had the benefit of a convincing series of recent related commercial successes—the Lancer/Ace Conan Saga, a popular spinoff comic book, and the big box office take of *Star Wars* (1977), which demonstrated the film-going public's appetite for epic adventure. The idea for the film was conceived by filmmaker Edward Summer and producer Edward Pressman, who in 1977 did the hard work of uniting various and splintered Conan factions and stakeholders, including Glenn Lord and an increasingly litigious L. Sprague de Camp. Summer and Pressman founded Conan Properties, Inc. in 1977, through which they secured the rights to produce a Howard-inspired screenplay. Summer and Pressman next landed charismatic bodybuilding champion and budding film star Arnold Schwarzenegger to play the lead (Sammon, *Conan the Phenomenon* 100). The final piece of the puzzle was maverick filmmaker John

Milius, recruited to rewrite an ambitious but untenable first-draft script treatment by Oliver Stone, then direct the film. With these building blocks in place, and a $19.5 million budget secured, principal shooting began in January of 1981. *Conan the Barbarian* was released on May 21, 1982, and went on to gross over $100 million. It also proved to have staying power, grossing more than $300 million including DVD and other media sales (107). Currently it sits at a 70% "fresh" rating on review aggregate website *rottentomatoes.com*.

Although he did not base the film on any single Conan story, Milius borrowed Howardian themes, imagery, and in some places Howard's words. As a result *Conan the Barbarian* feels far more Howardian than its numerous sequels and spinoffs. For example its opening lines, spoken by the actor Mako against an utterly black screen, paraphrase the opening lines of the first Conan story (in order of publication), "The Phoenix on the Sword":

> Know, O prince, that between the years when the oceans drank Atlantis and the gleaming cities, and the years of the rise of the Sons of Aryas, there was an Age undreamed of, when shining kingdoms lay spread across the world like blue mantles beneath the stars—Nemedia, Ophir, Brythunia, Hyperborea, Zamora with its dark-haired women and towers of spider-haunted mystery, Zingara with its chivalry, Koth that bordered on the pastoral lands of Shem, Stygia with its shadow-guarded tombs, Hyrkania whose riders wore steel and silk and gold. But the proudest kingdom of the world was Aquilonia, reigning supreme in the dreaming west. Hither came Conan the Cimmerian, black-haired, sullen-eyed, sword in hand, a thief, a reaver, a slayer, with gigantic melancholies and gigantic mirth, to tread the jeweled thrones of the Earth under his sandaled feet. ("The Phoenix on the Sword")

> Between the time when the oceans drank Atlantis, and the Rise of Sons of Aryas, there was an age undreamed of. And unto this, Conan, destined to wear the jeweled crown of Aquilonia upon a troubled brow. (*Conan the Barbarian*)

Conan the Barbarian opens with a quote from German philosopher Friedrich Nietzsche, "That which does not kill us makes us stronger," and sets out to prove the veracity of that claim in a single-minded pursuit. The first visual in the film is the forging of a sword, shot in epic fashion: molten steel poured into a mold, hammered into shape, and thrust into cold snow in a plume of steam to harden. Over this sequence plays "Anvil of Crom," perhaps the most iconic track in an unforgettable Basil Poldedouris score. Conan's father tells his young son that he must discover the deeper meaning behind its polished steel. "The secret of steel has always carried with it a mystery. You must learn its riddle, Conan. You must learn its discipline. For no one, no one in this world can you trust. Not men, not women, not beasts. This (pointing to sword) you can trust."

But the film's focus on the blade is a bait and switch. Viewers expecting an Excalibur-like divine right to kingship via transference of a sword find something very different in *Conan the Barbarian*. The Riddle of Steel is an enigma which takes the next two hours to unravel, and remains open to viewer interpretation. Conan, still a child, is taken captive in a raid of Vanir led by the mesmeric Thulsa Doom (James Earl Jones). Doom beheads Conan's mother in front of the boy with the hallowed blade, plucked from his father's still warm corpse. In captivity Conan is forced to push a revolving "wheel of pain" over years, hard labor which forges his body into heroic proportions. In the gladiator pits he learns how to fight and emerges as an unpolished but merciless killer. Realizing his potential his captors enlist him in weapons training with the finest eastern sword masters, honing his rough material to a fine edge. At the culmination of his training a captor asks, "What is best in life?" Conan replies, "To crush your enemies, see them driven before you, and to hear the lamentation of the women." His training is complete.

Conan is eventually set free by a captor who recognizes in him the soul of a wolf, ill-suited to a life of slavery. Conan befriends a pair of thieves, the beautiful blonde warrior Valeria and the roguish archer Subotai. The trio raid a temple of Set, slay a giant man-eating snake, and make off with a pile of jewels. Wild celebrations follow, during which the trio fall into a drunken stupor and are captured by city guards. Brought before King Osric (Max Von Sydow), they are offered wealth beyond imagining for the rescue of Osric's daughter, who has fallen under the spell of the cult of Thulsa Doom. Says a grieving Osric, "There comes a time, thief, when the jewels cease to sparkle, and the gold loses its luster, when the throne room becomes a prison, and all that is left is a father's love for his child." Osric's words echo the thoughts of King Kull, who in an hour of weariness muses, "There comes, even to kings, the time of great weariness. Then the gold of the throne is brass, the silk of the palace becomes drab. The gems in the diadem and upon the fingers of the women sparkle drearily like the ice of the white seas" (Howard, "The Mirrors of Tuzun Thune" 55).

Doom's cult of followers resemble the followers of Jim Jones, blindly loyal and ready to commit suicide at his command. *Conan the Barbarian* can be viewed as a critique of eastern mysticism and transcendentalism, and the widespread but ultimately failed "love and peace" hippie philosophy of the 1960s, whose lofty ambitions of world peace and equal sharing of resources and capital did not square with human nature. Doom's cult attempts to recruit Conan, but he has no use for the "peace" they are selling: "They told him to throw down his sword and return to the earth. Ha! Time enough for the earth in the grave." Conan attempts to infiltrate Doom's cult but is outed as a spy, and punished to death via crucifixion on the Tree of Woe, a scene lifted from Howard's "A Witch Shall be Born."

Before he orders Conan put to death, Doom offers Conan an answer to the Riddle of Steel. He beckons to a beautiful female follower on a nearby cliff, who leaps to her death without hesitation. Reflecting on her suicidal plunge, Doom observes:

> "Steel isn't strong, boy. Flesh is stronger. What is steel compared to the hand that wields it? Look at the strength of your body, the desire in your heart. I gave you this."

Doom is both right, and wrong—just as Conan's father is both right, and wrong. The answer to the Riddle of Steel (appears) to be the melding of man and steel, or perhaps the forging of a man's spirit and will into steel. Enflamed with the bright blade of vengeance, Conan survives his crucifixion and makes good on his vow to avenge his slain parents, beheading Doom with his father's shattered blade—the same one that Doom used to behead his mother. Conan has proven to be stronger than steel, his iron will carrying him to victory when steel breaks under the strain of use. But by slaying Doom with his father's blade, steel triumphs over the all-too-human flesh of the demi-god-like cult leader. Doom had grand ambitions to cleanse the world with fire, but finds his cult and his life ended by the naked ambition of a single-minded barbarian.

The film ends with barbarism ascendant: rather than a bearer of Promethean enlightenment to a benighted people, Conan brings destruction, wheeling a flaming chain-pendant lamp in mighty circles before tossing it into Doom's temple of Set, which crashes into ruin. At the end of the film we are left with an enigmatic figure: a barbarian on a throne, a being of muscular power and force, but contemplative, chin in hand, still seeking the answers.

Milius had a moderate appreciation of Howard's writings, but was firmly in alignment with his belief that civilization was corrupt and transitory:

> Howard is not a writer that I would say was going to be influential on my work for the rest of my life—he's not Melville or Conrad—but he had some great images and visions. I enjoyed his knowledge of history, too. Howard drew from almost every imaginable culture. Most importantly, Howard and I share the same view of civilization. Which is, to put it mildly, a highly skeptical one (Sammon, "Nine Days in Cimmeria").

In the 30+ years following its release, *Conan the Barbarian* has attained cult-like status and a loyal following of fans. But the film is not without its critics. Chief among them are Howard purists, who fault the film for its use of an original screenplay rather than adapting an authentic Howard story. Their loudest criticisms are reserved for the portrayal of Conan's character. In many respects

Schwarzenegger's Conan is not an accurate depiction of Howard's Conan—the former is less subtle, not as intelligent, and only half as savage, easily captured and occasionally duped. Certainly the film would be more fondly remembered in Howard circles had it not taken such liberties.[4] But the "purist argument" is a separate issue, independent from any evaluation of the artistic merits of *Conan the Barbarian* as a standalone film. Time has proven it to be stirringly well-made, surprisingly substantial from a thematic perspective, and beautiful to look at—and in particular to listen to. Poledouris' score is often mentioned as one of the best of all time, across all cinema ("Official Ballot: AFI's 100 Years of Film Scores"). It is far more ambitious thematically than most sword-and-sorcery litera-ture. Milius' use of Neitzschean existentialism, strongly implied in Howard's writings but given far more explicit treatment in *Conan the Barbarian*, proves that sword-and-sorcery is sturdy enough to support philosophical elements on its brutish frame. The film also serves as an accessible gateway to the original Howard stories and the broader sword-and-sorcery genre. *Conan the Barbarian* spawned a sequel, *Conan the Destroyer*, in 1984, as well as a spinoff, *Red Sonja*, in 1985. Karl Edward Wagner of Kane fame wrote three screenplays for producer De Laurentiis for a rumored third installment which failed to materialize (Owston). A loose remake with a new storyline and lead actor was released in 2011.

The box office success of *Conan the Barbarian* led to a wave of imita-tive sword-and-sorcery films throughout the 1980s. Although some qualify as passable, light-weight entertainment, none include its underlying depth or complexity, earnestness, or attention to detail. The loinclothed, brutish barbarian stereotype, birthed in the sword-and-sorcery literature of the late 1960s and reinforced by some elements of *Conan the Barbarian* (though dispelled and redeemed by the latter's muted ending and moody philosophy), very quickly became a tired cliché. Sturgeon's law ("ninety percent of everything is crap") is too generous of a hit-miss ratio for the crude horde of derivative films that poured out of the decade in a loincloth-clad flood of stupidity. Most display a total ignorance of the source mate-rial. Ostensibly "sword and sorcery," many of these films are high fantasy with barbarians: babies born with great destinies to save kingdoms, wielding magic swords and bows of unlimited potency, on ponderous quests to rid lands of evil. Most are mindless and crass spectacle, fixated on muscled lead actors, scantily clad women,

---

[4] Although Schwarzenegger's Conan is not wholly unlike Howard's Conan: When Conan is told that the gods will not help their cause in a pitched final battle, he barks (in Howardian fashion), "Then tell them to stay out of the way!"

and gratuitous violence. Michael Moorcock lamented of the pitiful scene: "The people who make the movies seem to have no genuine instinct for the form (as Ford had, for instance, for the Western) and cannot convince an increasingly sophisticated audience. The old Conan movies were both derivative of bad action movies and of bad books derived and debased from Howard's originals! They very rapidly degenerated into complete meaninglessness—and the public, it seems, objected. After *Red Sonja* (1985) was released in the US and Britain it was scarcely in the theatres long enough for anyone to see it all the way through" (*Wizardry and Wild Romance* 144–145).

Perhaps the best remembered of these films is 1982's *The Sword and the Sorcerer*. A mishmash of the worst high fantasy clichés and the trappings of sword-and-sorcery, *The Sword and the Sorcerer* owes more to the swashbuckling films of Errol Flynn than Howard or Leiber. The wise and strong King Richard rules over the kingdom of Ehdan, "once a haven for barbaric plunder, now transformed into a prosperous and civilized nation." But the peace is about to end: Richard's mortal enemy, the tyrant Cromwell, summons a demon to help him in his plan to usurp the kingdom. Richard's son, Talon (played in wooden fashion by Lee Horsley), survives the butchery of a coup, and after earning his stripes abroad as a Conan-esque "buccaneer, slave, rogue, and a general," returns as a fur-garbed mercenary to reclaim the crown. Talon wields a three-bladed sword that can launch its blades like a medieval firearm; this stroke of creative genius evidently earned directly Albert Pyun the leeway to forgo acting and plot.

The Sword and the Sorcerer debuted in theatres a month prior to *Conan the Barbarian* but somehow manages to feel like a cheap imitation, including a scene in which Talon suffers a crucifixion, a palace raid that includes an intrusion into an orgy, and a battle with a large serpent. Though murkily filmed, a mess of shouted cliché dialogue, and marred by a cloyingly generic "heroic" soundtrack, B-grade soap opera acting, bad dick jokes, and clumsy swordplay, *The Sword and the Sorcerer* was a commercial success, grossing $39 million at the box office on a budget of $4 million. Its success, coupled with that of *Conan the Barbarian*, ensured that more sword-and-sorcery films would follow.

Like *The Sword and the Sorcerer*, *Deathstalker* (1983) features a barbarian hero with too-handsome looks and well-coiffed hair, named (entirely non-ironically) Deathstalker. The film opens with the worst clichés imaginable: Deathstalker rescues a beautiful woman from her abductor, and although she has endured brutality and implied rape, upon rescue immediately falls into the arms of her rescuer with willing lust. The film is marred by plodding action, abysmal monster effects and makeup, gratuitous rape scenes, a low-budget soundtrack plundered from the westerns of Sergio Leone, and awful-beyond-be-lief acting. So much screen time is allotted to exposed female breasts and buttocks that one wonders what the running time of the film would be were they excised. *Deathstalker* vacillates between slap-stick comedy and plodding seriousness, unsure what it wants to be and failing at both. Nevertheless, the film manages to hew closer to sword-and-sorcery than *The Sword and the Sorcerer*, particularly in the mercenary outlook of its main hero, an outsider. "Heroes and fools, are the same thing," Deathstalker says. "An outlaw is free. I steal and kill to stay alive, not for the luxury of glory." For the flimsiest of reasons, Deathstalker embarks on a quest to recover a sword, chalice, and an amulet. His path ultimately leads him to the palace of an evil sorcerer hosting a gladiator-style, winner-kill-all competition to determine a champion. The ensuing "combat" sequences are straight out of a professional wrestling circuit, with less believability. With a budget of just $450,000 (and it shows), *Deathstalker* managed to gross more than $11 million and spawned four sequels, with the last, *Deathstalker IV: Match of the Titans*, going straight to video in 1991.

Noteworthy if only for its visuals is the 1983 animated film *Fire and Ice*. Directed by Ralph Bakshi and co-produced by Frank Frazetta, *Fire and Ice* has some effective scenes and sequences, and its rotoscoped animation—though used with greater impact in the Bakshi-directed *The Lord of the Rings* (1978)—is reasonably well-done for the time period. But it's deeply flawed, with no characterization and a thin plot that relies too heavily on extended and repetitive sequences of capture/escape/recapture. A barbarian warrior, Larn—again the only survivor of a village raid, in an already tired plot device—pursues the string-bikini-clad Princess Teegra, attempting to liberate her from the forces of the evil sorcerer Nekron. Larn teams up with Darkwolf, a fierce, mysterious warrior who wears a wolfish headpiece. Darkwolf's only apparent *raison d'etre* is to pander to Frazetta fans, as he greatly resembles the subject of Frazetta's memorable *Death Dealer* painting. The film spends considerable time on lingering views of Teegra's cur-vaceous body and offers up plenty of violence, as Larn and Darkwolf mow through hordes of grunting semi-Neanderthals, slaughtering them with great facility. Sword and axe ultimately best sorcery.

Sword-and-sorcery may have reached its filmic nadir with the nigh-incomprehensible Italian film *Conquest* (1983). Directed by Lucio Fulci of ultra-graphic *Zombie!* fame, *Conquest* opens with a shocking scene of dismemberment and cannibalism of a helpless female at the hands of a horde of ravening dog-men. That might be the highlight. The main protagonist, Ilias, undertakes a quest in a strange and dangerous land, and ultimately finds himself opposing the evil sorceress Ocron. Ilias befriends Mace, a barbaric, outsider hero who looks and reasonably plays the part of a sword-and-sorcery protagonist. After Orcon kills Ilias, Mace smears his face with his friend's ashes and embarks on a mission of revenge. Fans of camp film will likely enjoy *Conquest's* incredibly poor monster costumes, clumsy fight scenes, a magic bow that can summon unending magic arrows of unerring accuracy, buckets of blood, and ample decapitations and dismemberment. From incomprehensible costuming (topless women wearing expressionless steel masks?) to an incomprehensible plot, it has nothing else to recommend it.

Italy continued to crank out sword-and-sorcery films throughout the 1980s, including the likes of *Ator, the Fighting Eagle* (1982), *Sword of the Barbarians* (1982), and *The Throne of Fire* (1983). *Ator* would go on to spawn three sequels. *Ator, the Fighting Eagle* is perhaps the most unapologetic ripoff of *Conan the Barbarian* of all the films of the era—no small feat. The film opens with darkness and flame, a dull echo of the sword-forging sequence of *Conan the Barbarian*. Ator's mother and clan are slain in a raid of their village by evil cultists (though in a blazing flash of originality they worship spiders rather than snakes!). Ator's bride-to-be is captured and his foster parents slain. Ator embarks on a mission of revenge which takes him on a temple raid. First he trains his muscular frame to learn the art of combat under a strict Oriental teacher. In the wilderness he encounters an evil shape-shifting sorceress and befriends a beautiful and ferocious blonde warrior, Rune, who claims to desire only wealth, but also desires Ator. The high "spider priest" is a poor man's James Earl Jones. Perhaps the most incongruous and original element in the film is a bear cub that accompanies Ator and Rune on their journey. This relatively minor detail formed the basis for perhaps the most widely known of the post-*Conan the Barbarian* sword and sorcery films, *The Beastmaster* (1982). A moderate box office success, *The Beastmaster* enjoyed a long second life on cable television and spawned two sequels, as well as a syndicated television series that ran from 1999 to 2002.

Conan the Barbarian spawned a sequel which unfortunately has almost nothing to recommend it. *Conan the Destroyer* (1984) removed the philosophy, grit, and grimness of its predecessor in favor of slapstick comedy and mindless action sequences. Schwarzenegger, who returned to reprise his role, and director Richard Fleischer later admitted that the film deliberately spurned complexity in favor of more stunts, special effects, and lingering shots of the physiques of its leading actors. Unlike Milius, Fleischer failed to do any homework on Howard, and instead focused purely on the visuals established in the Marvel Conan comic books (Sammon, *Conan the Phenomenon* 110–111). These crass, mercenary decisions helped the film achieve a coveted PG rating and reach a broader audience, but the results were predictably disastrous. Conan is given a comic relief sidekick, a weasely thief named Malak who spends half the movie swallowing gems and shying away from danger while Conan does all the fighting. The supporting cast is poor: in place of the tough and charismatic Valeria, *Conan the Destroyer* offers Jehnna, a whiny teenage blonde princess, as a potential love interest. Other actors and roles were added for pure novelty's sake. Grace Jones plays Zhula, a staff-wielding warrior-woman with a perpetual scowl on her face. Towering ex-NBA star Wilt Chamberlain, as wooden an actor as they come, plays the warrior Bombatta. The film was a commercial success, earning $31M domestically on a budget of $16.5M and paving the way for a spin-off, 1985's *Red Sonja*. If possible, *Red Sonja* is even worse than its predecessor, with a woeful rating of 15% on Rotten Tomatoes.

The sword-and-sorcery film mill continued to grind on through the 1980s. The likes of *The Warrior and the Sorceress* (1984) and *The Barbarians* (1987) kept local video rental stores awash in VHS tapes whose shell cases depicted airbrushed paintings of muscled men in loincloths. Perhaps a few reasonably entertained viewers went on to read Howard, Leiber, or Moorcock, which is about the best that can be hoped of this era. Today the sword-and-sorcery film phenomenon remains a 1980s oddity, and a reminder of the former cultural ubiquity of the subgenre.

After giving filmgoers a well-deserved break, sword-and-sorcery experienced a comeback in the 1990s with a pair of successful television series that opened the door for additional films. *Hercules: The Legendary Journeys* (1995–1999) and its spinoff, *Xena: Warrior Princess* (1995–2001), convinced the studios that sword-and-sorcery had a viable and ready television audience. Subsequent films like *Kull the Conqueror* (1997) and *The Scorpion King* (2002), though of mediocre quality, provide reasonable entertainment. The latter film dropped the ponderous seriousness of some of the genre's previous efforts, placing Dwayne "The Rock" Johnson in the lead role as a lighthearted and oft-shirtless assassin who embarks on a mission to rescue a dangerous but beautiful sorceress.

The current decade has seen the revival of the Conan franchise with *Conan the Barbarian* (2011), directed by Marcus Nispel and starring Jason Mamoa as Conan. The film had a difficult birth: after some seven years in development, Nispel was brought in to replace original director Brett Ratner, and multiple writers were hired to salvage the script (Goldstein, Rainey). The result, unsurprisingly, is a mess. While it borrows names and scattered bits of dialogue from Howard's stories, the plot owes more to a low-budget *The Lord of the Rings*. In the opening minutes we're introduced to Conan as a "prophesized" child with a portentous destiny: he and the barbarian tribes will help save the Hyborian Age from a world-shaking evil. Conan's Cimmerian village is a bucolic Shire, complete with flute music and a slow-turning waterwheel. Conan and his young playmates encounter a group of ferocious Picts that may as well be Uruk-Hai, complete with painted faces and exaggerated and toothy mouths issuing monstrous roars. The boy Conan kills them all with little difficulty and much savagery. The plot of the film is murky, ponderous, and ludicrous: evil warlord Khalar Zym is attempting to reassemble a shattered mask worn by the powerful and evil god Acheron (more shades of Sauron and the One Ring), and season it with the "pure blood" of one of Acheron's descendants. This effort will bring Zym's wife back from the dead, and provide the added side-bonus of drenching the world with rivers of blood. A piece of the mask is hidden in Conan's Cimmerian village, and so we get the same tired, overworn sword-and-sorcery plot device—a village raid that leaves Conan's father dead, and his people slain. Conan embarks on a mission of revenge, with a predictable ending.

Conan the Barbarian (2011) has no idea what it wants to be: Sword-and-sorcery? High fantasy? Homage to the 1982 original (we get a blade-forging sequence and a serious discussion between young Conan and his father about the "mystery" of steel)? Nod to the Howard stories, of which there are allusions to "Queen of the Black Coast" and "The Tower of the Elephant"? In seeking to be all things, it manages to be none. The film's sizeable budget ($90M) is woefully underutilized, as the CGI already looks flimsy, flat, and dated. Not surprisingly, Conan the Barbarian was a box office bomb and made back only half its costs, grossing $21M in the U.S., and another $27M internationally. It presently sits at a 23% "Rotten" rating on rottentomatoes.com. The entire exercise leaves one wondering, why go to such lengths to secure the Conan property only to ignore Howard's themes and stories, and any of the elements that make for good sword-and-sorcery? Barely qualifying as a forgettable action flick, Conan the Barbarian (2011) has left genre fans wondering if they will ever see another sword-and-sorcery film as good as the 1982 original, or anything resembling the classic Howard, Leiber, Vance, and Moorcock stories.

Some day, perhaps. As of the publication of this book there are rumors of a new Conan television series, teasing fans with the hopes of seeing Howard's original stories retold with the same skill, art, and attention to detail as HBO's acclaimed A Game of Thrones. Reportedly Elric has been optioned for television, with reports that New Republic Pictures have acquired the rights to Moorcock's stories. This story shall also be told...but for now, the printed page must suffice.

CHAPTER TEN
Why Sword-and-Sorcery?

The time has come for sorcery and swords!
　　—Fritz Leiber, "The Lords of Quarmall," *Swords Against Wizardry*

Edgar Rice Burroughs, forefather of the genre and creator of Tarzan and John Carter of Mars, summed up in a 1930 essay for *Reader's Digest*, "Entertainment is fiction's purpose" (Sellers). Art requires no further purpose than being, and the colorful, bold form of storytelling known as sword-and-sorcery very much *is*. It is Conan in "The Tower of the Elephant," matching his speed and sinew against a giant, implacable spider. It is the bard Cappen Varra and the northern hero Jamie, enjoying the attentions of women whom they have fought to rescue—including the wife of a powerful magnate, whose ardent embrace is as hazardous as any sword duel ("Uh, have a care milady," he said. "Pressing against ringmail, all bloody and sweaty too, can't be good for a complexion."). It is adventure and strangeness, horror and battle, and magic, might, and mirth. And the best of it makes for incredibly fun, page-turning reading. As Lester del Rey stated in *The World of Science Fiction, 1926–1976*, "If fiction has any major function, that function is to entertain the reader ... certainly the purpose of science fiction has always been to entertain, and while it can only entertain a certain portion of the public, that is true of most other fiction" (349).

Sword-and-sorcery's rousing entertainment comes without the time commitment required of most literary forays into fantasy. You can read "Bazaar of the Bizarre" and "The Tale of Satampra Zeiros" in short order, visiting strange worlds and experiencing vicarious adventure without wading through tedious info-dumps of culture and politics. Sword-and-sorcery cuts to the chase (literally and figuratively) and plunges the reader headlong into the action. Most of its classic adventures are anthologized short stories, and if a story is poor the disappointment fades quickly as you turn the page to the next adventure. It is the fantasy equivalent of Tinder, but (largely) without the guilt.

That sword-and-sorcery is, and entertains, should be enough. But the subgenre has been dismissed by some critics with a vitriol

beyond any justifiable critique of crude art. It remains largely misunderstood, the aesthetic it offers to the wider fantasy genre largely
unprobed. So the question, "Why sword-and-sorcery?" perhaps
warrants a deeper look.

On July 28, 1914, millions of young men enflamed with national
pride responded to the call of duty and marched onto the battlefields
of France. Theirs was no romantic ride into battle on horseback,
rose-wreathed sabers aloft, but a methodical, suicidal advance
across muddy fields and into machine-gun fire at places like the
Somme and Belleau Wood. In four years of warfare, more than nine
million combatants were killed.

On October 29, 1929, a stock market crash known as Black Tuesday
ushered in the Great Depression, sending hundreds of thousands of
young men to the unemployment line. In the United Kingdom unemployment reached as high as 20%; in the U.S. it peaked at 25%.

In 1965 American men as young as 18 were drafted to fight a war
many considered unjust, and thrust into jungle combat in Vietnam
against an enemy that often wore no uniforms. There was no clear
objective, no exit strategy. More than 58,000 were killed in action.

In 1997 an IBM supercomputer named Deep Blue became the first
computer to defeat a world champion chess player in a tournament.
Garry Kasparov was so shaken by the loss that he cried foul and
insisted that the computer must have been controlled by a human
grand master. It was not.

Mankind has been pushed from its former place at the center
of the universe. Where there were once battles of sword vs. sword,
with chance of quarter and ransom, today soldiers at computers
dispatch unmanned drones to bomb distant targets. Where once we
believed we had free will, behavioral psychology and neuroscience
has brought our motivations into doubt. Impossibly large, powerful,
and complex institutions can cause economic free-fall overnight in
our modern economy. Where once most believed in a benevolent,
all-knowing god who offered the consolation of an afterlife, that
certainty is gone. Today many consider mankind a higher order of
animal, and human "consciousness" merely another form of consciousness alongside animal and increasingly, artificial intelligence.
We face an uncertain dawn of genetic conformity and machine-as-
sisted immortality—or extinction.

Where there was once certainty, we are now assailed with doubt,
and worse—mechanical existence in a cynical, barren world devoid
of magic, wonder, and heroism. These are the unfortunate side-ef-
fects of progress and modern civilization. As German philosopher
Max Weber concluded in a lecture delivered at the end of the

Edwardian Era, in the midst of the savagery of World War I and at the dawning of the modern age:

> The fate of our times is characterized by rationalization and intellectualization and, above all, by the disenchantment of the world. Precisely the ultimate and most sublime values have retreated from public life either into the transcendental realm of mystic life or into the brotherliness of direct and personal human relations. It is not accidental that our greatest art is intimate and not monumental ("Science as a Vocation").

The precursors and first wave of sword-and-sorcery authors in the early 20ᵗʰ century experienced acute feelings of disenchantment wrought by the atomization of human emotion, not unlike the far more well-known post-World War I "Lost Generation" authors, and created art in reaction. As H.P. Lovecraft explained in "Lord Dunsany and his Work" (1922):

> Modern Science has, in the end, proved an enemy to art and pleasure; for by revealing to us the whole sordid and prosaic basis of our thoughts, motives, and acts, it has stripped the world of glamour, wonder, and all those illusions of heroism, nobility, and sacrifice which used to sound so impressive when romantically treated. Indeed, it is not too much to say that psychological discovery, and chemical, physical, and psychological research have largely destroyed the element of emotion among informed and sophisticated people by resolving it into its component parts (175).

Howard wrote of the modern industrial state into which he had the perceived misfortune of being born:

> As just as I have struggled for a maximum amount of freedom in my own life, I look back with envy at the greater freedom known by my ancestors on the frontier. Hard work? Certainly they worked hard. But they were building something; making the most of opportunities; working for themselves, not merely cogs grinding in a soulless machine, as is the modern working man, whose life is a constant round of barren toil infinitely more monotonous and crushing than the toil on the frontier (*A Means to Freedom* 698).

Few fates are more enervating than an inability to change one's circumstances, and being a cog in an uncaring mechanical universe. Sword-and-sorcery rages against this machine. It offers the modern reader an alternative, posing the question: Which is the superior? The old barbaric ways, in which life was nasty, brutish, and short, but men and women were at least masters of their own fate, operating with a heightened awareness borne of daily struggles for survival? Or the modern industrialized state, in which we accept security and civility and predictability in exchange for hyper-specialized, disconnected jobs, purposelessness, and widespread anxiety and depression?

Sword-and-sorcery recognizes the importance of emotion and instinct, without which humans are mere automatons. Howard reacted with revulsion against the purely scientific mind and modern civilization's pressure to suppress emotion. In a December 1930 letter to Lovecraft he wrote:

> Yet the trend of so many materialists to suppress all primitive emotions is against my every instinct. Civilization, no doubt, requires it, and peace of mind demands it, yet for myself I had rather be dead than to live in an emotionless world. The clear white lamp of science and the passionless pursuit of knowledge are not enough for me; I must live deeply and listen to the call of the common clay in me, if I am to live at all. Without emotion and instinct, I would be a dead, stagnant thing.

In sword-and-sorcery the warrior with a sharp sword and an iron will is exalted. It is the ultimate expression of anthropocentrism, and the ultimate rejection of pessimism, cynicism, and powerlessness:

> We live in a day when a malaise chokes the land and its pitiful people. Americans and Europeans have succumbed to what Nietzsche called the slave morality, the slave mentality. We scorn heroes, binding them to the ground like the once-towering Gulliver because we do not want to be reminded that we, too, could tower, could rise, could bear the burden of greatness. Conan, Thongor, Elak, Imaro, and their fellows remind us of the heroic possibility (Price 6)

Conan, a wild-haired barbarian from the horde, rises from savage to thief, to mercenary to war-chief, and eventually to King of Aquilonia. He is a paragon of human achievement—not born into power or prestige, but a man who carves a bloody path to the top with his sword-arm, cunning, and naked will.

Sword-and-sorcery fills an aesthetic void left by high fantasy. It brings to center stage the outsider, the hero on the periphery. Instead of the king-in-waiting Aragorn, or the conservative, lover of hearth-and-home Bilbo, sword-and-sorcery offers the likes of Gray Mouser and Elric of Melnibone—lusty nonconformists, disaffected political anarchists, wanderers, and wayfarers. Its heroes offer a voice for the disaffected. They enjoy life and its basic pleasures; they reject positions of authority because they know the dreadful ethical and spiritual compromises these positions often require.

Sword-and-sorcery acknowledges our species' fascination with and predilection for violence. It exalts strength, and skill in battle. Its images of carnage-swept battlefields, strewn with corpses, shattered shields, and reddened sword and axe, lorded over by a muscular champion, have been appropriated by heavy metal bands and role-playing and video-game designers, who have tapped into its power and repurposed it for new audiences hungry for such vicarious visceral experience.

Much sword-and-sorcery is pure entertainment, and entertainment only, but at its best it offers thoughtful commentary on the human condition. Between its brightly painted Frank Frazetta covers, it presents the reader with the contrast of civilization and barbarism, and fate vs. free will. Are nations at their strongest when they are young and possess a warlike spirit, and are they ultimately doomed to collapse when they become wealthy, secure, and civilized? Are the strong dragged down by hordes of the needy and weak, or is it the responsibility of the strong to lift up their brethren and throw off the yoke of corrupt authority? Is barbarism an atavistic instinct that must be guarded against, lest it come rising, red-handed and roaring, back to the surface? Or are its nobler manifestations—a willingness to grapple with fate, cast off safety and security, and explore new frontiers and conquer new worlds—worthy of preservation? And do we even have a choice, or will the rule of barbarism return, despite our best efforts to keep it in check, making mockery of our institutions and dooming humanity's efforts toward moral and social progress? These themes are played out, again and again, and the answers sword-and-sorcery offers are often equivocal. As Fafhrd breaks away from the oppressive society of "The Snow Women" in a deadly race on skis, culminating in a breathtaking leap to freedom, a boy becomes a man, and a barbarian constrained by a suffocating, parochial culture chooses the wider civilized world. As we encounter the unexpected strangeness and wonder of being introduced to an inhuman (but all too human) race, whose culture has fallen into decadence and amorality, we are provided a sobering glimpse into the fate of nations, possibly our own (Michael Moorcock's "The Dreaming City").

For all their romance, Howard's writings offered a cyclical view of human history with a deep underlying bleakness: the overthrow of established order by barbarians, who would themselves be overthrown by stronger, more committed barbarians. And, finally, worlds ending in cataclysm, with the cycle repeated again and again throughout the ages. But as Howard told his once girlfriend Novalyne Price-Ellis, Conan's grim struggles for survival are cheery compared to fruitless battles against the modern machine:

> I don't think you're going to like ol' Conan. His struggle is big, uncomplicated with civilized standards. The people who read my stuff want to get away from this modern, complicated world with its hypocrisy, its cruelty, its dog-eat-dog life. They want to go back to the origin of the human race. The civilization we live in is a hell of a lot more sinister than the time I write about. In those days, girl, men were men and women were women. They struggled to stay alive, but the struggle was worth it (Price Ellis 63).

Sword-and-sorcery does not re-create ancient history or offer up post-Roman, Dark Age barbarism as a human ideal. This is a

mistaken analysis that has led some to label the subgenre as misguided and dangerous romanticism, or equate its frequent use of
bronze-skinned and blonde-headed barbarian heroes to Hitlerian
fascism. The barbaric template offered by sword-and-sorcery fiction
is a myth. In almost all instances it ignores historical barbarism's
gross inequalities and abhorrent traditions. But historical fidelity is
not its intent. Its heroes are a facet of our humanity, a reminder of
the potency of individual sovereignty and human agency.

Fantasy is the literature of escape, and sword-and-sorcery falls
squarely into this tradition. It offers a glimpse at existence beyond
our ordinary round, awakening world-weary hearts to the possibilities of productive disruption and rebellion. J.R.R. Tolkien identified
this unique power of fantasy in his "On Fairy Stories":

> At no time can I remember that the enjoyment of a story was depen-
> dent on belief that such things could happen, or had happened, in
> "real life." Fairy-stories were plainly not primarily concerned with
> possibility, but with desirability. If they awakened desire, satisfying
> it while often whetting it unbearably, they succeeded. ... Fantasy, the
> making or glimpsing of Other-worlds, was the heart of the desire of
> Faërie. I desired dragons with a profound desire. Of course, I in my
> timid body did not wish to have them in the neighbourhood, intrud-
> ing into my relatively safe world, in which it was, for instance, possible
> to read stories in peace of mind, free from fear. But the world that
> contained even the imagination of Fáfnir was richer and more beauti-
> ful, at whatever cost of peril. The dweller in the quiet and fertile plains
> may hear of the tormented hills and the unharvested sea and long for
> them in his heart. For the heart is hard though the body be soft.

Sword-and-sorcery breaks the spell of despondency cast by an
unsatisfying reality, and the suffocation of economic and social
forms of control. Readers returning from its pages look upon the
world with a new perspective and a restored vision. Howard felt an
urge for renewal after his exchanges with Lovecraft, who though
a well-mannered gentleman who cared for his correspondents,
slashed at the hamstrings of Howard's romanticism with a grinding
materialism. Howard needed re-enchantment—even if that meant
creating worlds of mortal peril, populated with wicked sorcerers and
foul monsters, and great empires that rise from chaos and savagery,
only to fall and be ground to the dust of eternity.

As with Howard, Fritz Leiber began writing his stories in the
throes of the Great Depression, when the excesses and promises of
the Roaring Twenties came to a crashing end for millions. His city of
Lankhmar, though crime-ridden and dangerous, offers wealth and
opportunity for the brave. The unshakeable friendship of his two
heroes are a reminder that salvation lies in people, not institutions.
Michael Moorcock penned his stories of Elric at the height of the

1960s, offering a disaffected hero who questions the decadence, moral decay, and wasteful consumption of his bankrupt kingdom. In so doing he invited his readers living in one of the most tumultuous periods in human history to do the same. It is no coincidence that sword-and-sorcery was born in the turbulent years between two world wars, then returned to prominence as civilization again appeared on the brink of ruin following the Cuban missile crisis and the Vietnam War. Or that it experienced a second resurgence during the rapid growth of the computer age.

Fantasy fiction transports us beyond the boundaries of our normal lives—including our biases and convictions—and upon returning enables us to see the world from a new perspective, through a process called re-enchantment. Re-enchantment is not false optimism, but is a stroke of lightning on the printed page, awakening readers to new possibilities and potentialities. As Ursula LeGuin wrote in "The Critics, the Monsters, and the Fantasists," fantasy offers somewhere else, a vision of other worlds that dispel despondency. "The literature of imagination, even when tragic, is reassuring, not necessarily in the sense of offering nostalgic comfort, but because it offers a world large enough to contain alternatives, and therefore offers hope."

The best fantasy allows us to both enjoy the view — to read for sheer enjoyment and pleasure's sake—while consciously or subconsciously providing a mechanism for examining our own beliefs and prejudices, and reframing our social, cultural, and political structures.

> Fantasy IS escapism, but wait ... why is this wrong? What are you escaping from, and where are you escaping to? Is the story opening windows or slamming doors? The British author G. K. Chesterton summarized the role of fantasy very well. He said its purpose was to take the everyday, commonplace world and lift it up and turn it around and show it to us from a different perspective, so that once again we see it for the first time and realize how marvelous it is. Fantasy—the ability to envisage this world in many different ways—is one of the skills that makes us human (Peschel).

The long look back from our own 21st century existence to the worlds of sword-and-sorcery, seen through the lens of ocean-washed Atlantis and the passage of millennia, brings the world we've left behind into sharper view. When we join authors like Howard, Leiber, Moorcock, and Wagner in their best tales of escape, we take the journey with our eyes and our minds open, and return with a clearer appreciation of what is right and good in the world—and what is wrong, or has been distorted, or lost.

And of course, above all else, we return entertained.

A Probable Timeline of Sword-and-Sorcery

1886: H. Rider Haggard's *She* introduces a mass audience to lost cities and a dark sorceress

1890: Haggard's *Eric Brighteyes* updates the Icelandic Sagas for modern readers

1908: Lord Dunsany writes sword-and-sorcery without the fanfare with "The Fortress Unvanquishable, Save for Sacnoth"

1912: Sword-slinging interplanetary adventurer John Carter appears like a comet with Edgar Rice Burroughs' "Under the Moons of Mars" (*The All-Story* magazine)

1912: Burroughs' provides an influential template of the noble savage with "Tarzan of the Apes"

1919: James Branch Cabell's sardonic, cynical "hero" of *Jurgen: A Comedy of Justice* provides an unlikely source of inspiration for Robert E. Howard, Fritz Leiber, Michael Moorcock, and Karl Edward Wagner, among others

1923: *Weird Tales* publishes its first issue in March, providing the platform for sword-and-sorcery to take root.

1924: A. Merritt delivers rousing, sorcerous adventure with *The Ship of Ishtar* (*Argosy All-Story* magazine)

1928: H.P. Lovecraft's "The Call of Cthulhu" (*Weird Tales*) delivers a new brand of cosmic, tentacled horror

1928: Howard's Puritanical adventurer Solomon Kane delivers bright vengeance and proto-sword-and-sorcery in "Red Shadows"

1929: The first appearance of Howard's "The Shadow Kingdom" (*Weird Tales*), widely regarded as the first sword-and-sorcery story

1931: Clark Ashton Smith's story of a temple raid gone bad, "The Tale of Satampra Zeiros," offers up a sardonic, dark strain of sword-and-sorcery

1932: Merritt's *Dwellers in the Mirage* (*Argosy*) provides likely inspiration for...

1932: "The Phoenix on the Sword," the first published story of Conan of Cimmeria

1934: C.L. Moore's "Black God's Kiss" introduces readers to Jirel of Joiry, the first female sword-and-sorcery protagonist

1936: Published posthumously, "Red Nails" is Howard's last story featuring Conan

1938: Henry Kuttner's "Thunder in the Dawn," the first published story of Elak of Atlantis, cements the template for post-Howardian heroica

1939: Fritz Leiber's "Two Sought Adventure" the first published story of Fafhrd and the Gray Mouser, appears in *Unknown*

1946: Arkham Press collects the likes of Bran Mak Morn, Kull, and Conan in the hardcover *Skull-Face and Others*

1950: *Conan the Conqueror*, the first of seven Conan volumes by Gnome Press, keeps the Cimmerian in print in a world gone mad for science fiction

1950: Jack Vance cloaks sword-and-sorcery in the guise of SF with *The Dying Earth*

1953: The "Ace Double" *Conan the Conqueror/The Sword of Rhiannon* brings Howard and Leigh Brackett, respectively, to a mass audience on the opposite sides of the same book

1954: Poul Anderson's *The Broken Sword* should have been a thunderbolt, but is overshadowed by *The Lord of the Rings*.

1959: *Amra* Vol. 2, No. 1, journal of the "Hyborian Legion" published by George Scithers, starts a pen-and-pencil messageboard and forum for sword-and-sorcery fans

1961: Michael Moorcock's "The Dreaming City," the first published story of Elric of Melnibone, appears in *Science Fantasy*.

1961: Leiber first suggests the term "sword-and-sorcery" in the pages of *Ancalagon,* and later cements it in response to an inquiry from Moorcock in the pages of *Amra*

1963: *Swords and Sorcery*, first in an influential four-volume Pyramid sword-and-sorcery anthology edited by L. Sprague de Camp, puts the genre's name on the cover of a paperback

1965: Debut of Lin Carter's *The Wizard of Lemuria*, the first stand-alone sword-and-sorcery novel ever published. At least seven more volumes of Carter's oafish barbarian Thongor follow.

1966: *Conan the Adventurer*, the first volume in the Conan Saga by publisher Lancer, with striking cover art by Frank Frazetta, hits the wire-spinners

1968: Leiber delivers an outstanding short novel of sword-and-sorcery with *The Swords of Lankhmar*

1968: *Brak the Barbarian* collects and brings to a mass audience John Jakes' homage to Conan

1969: *The Mighty Barbarians*, edited by Hans Stefan Santesson, delivers a mighty collection of sword-and-sorcery

1969: Gardner F. Fox offers up a tongue-in-cheek barbaric hero with *Kothar—Barbarian Swordsman*

1970: Leiber's "Ill Met in Lankhmar" is published in the *Magazine of Fantasy and Science Fiction,* and also wins the Nebula Award for Best Novella

1970: Publication of Karl Edward Wagner's *Darkness Weaves With Many Shades*, the first appearance of the immortal Kane

1970: *Conan the Barbarian* #1 (Marvel), with the mighty tag team of writer Roy Thomas and artist Barry Smith, brings Conan to full-color life

1972: Publication of *Elric of Melnibone,* Moorcock's first full-length novel of the doomed albino prince

1973: Publication of Lin Carter's love letter to sword-and-sorcery and his S.A.G.A drinking buddies, *Flashing Swords! #1*

1973: Carter's *Imaginary Worlds* adds some critical rigor to sword-and-sorcery

1974: *Savage Sword of Conan* (Curtis Magazine, an imprint of Marvel Comics) skirts the Comics Code and brings nudity and bloodshed to a horde of grateful teenage boys

1975: More barbaric blunder from Fox with *Kyrik: Warlock Warrior*

1975: Wagner goes batshit crazy (in a good way) with *Bloodstone*

1977: Wagner extends a middle finger to posthumous Howard collaborations and pastiche with *The Hour of the Dragon* (Berkley)

1977: *Swords Against Darkness*, the start of a fine five-volume series of anthologies edited by Andrew Offutt

1979: The Robert Asprin-edited *Thieves' World* provides a shared sword-and-sorcery universe for authors to tell their stories.

1979: Jessica Amanda Salmonson serves up some powerful female-centric stories with the anthology *Amazons!*

1979: Gary Gygax delivers unto geekdom the Advanced Dungeons and Dragons *Dungeon Master's Guide*, with its iconic fantasy literature signpost Appendix N

1980: *Thundarr the Barbarian* introduces a generation of young viewers to a sword-and-sorcery ethos on Saturday mornings

1981: Charles Saunders' *Imaro* is the first sword-and-sorcery hero of color

1981: The debut of Keith Taylor's underrated series featuring the Celtic hero Bard. Five volumes are eventually published, the last in 1991.

1982: The first Conan pastiche by Tor, *Conan the Defender*, hits the shelves. Author Robert Jordan would later hit it much bigger with his multi-volume high fantasy series *The Wheel of Time*.

1982: Michael Shea's *Nifft the Lean* reinvigorates sword-and-sorcery, but for a dwindling audience

1982: The arresting and well-made *Conan the Barbarian*, directed by John Milius and starring Arnold Schwarzenegger, begins a tidal wave of subsequent junk celluloid sword-and-sorcery knockoffs

1982: The venerable fanzine *Amra* ceases publication with Vol. 2, No. 71

1983: L. Sprague de Camp, Catherine Crook de Camp, and Jane Whittington Griffin collaborate on *Dark Valley Destiny*, an important but flawed biography of Howard

1983: Heavy metal band Manowar dons fur codpieces and wields broadswords for the cover of *Into Glory Ride*

1984: David Gemmell gives sword-and-sorcery a much-needed infusion of heroism with *Legend*

1984: Editor Marion Zimmer Bradley proves sword-and-sorcery is not just for men with *Sword and Sorceress*. Thirty volumes (and counting) are eventually published.

1984: Don Herron sets the record straight on Howard as a writer of substance with *The Dark Barbarian: The Writings of Robert E. Howard: A Critical Anthology*

1985: Terry Pratchett's *The Light Fantastic* and its geriatric hero Cohen the Barbarian effectively parodies the subgenre

1987: Wagner's *Echoes of Valor* reminds readers of what once was, as sword-and-sorcery rapidly fades into yesteryear

1988: *The Knight and Knave of Swords*, Leiber's last published collection of Fafhrd and the Gray Mouser, brings to a close sword-and-sorcery's most iconic duo

1988: James Silke's *Prisoner of the Horned Helmet* draws the curtain on the sword-and-sorcery renaissance … until it rises again

Works Cited

Abercrombie, Joe. *The Heroes*. New York, NY: Orbit, 2011. Print.

Abercrombie, Joe. "The New Sword and Sorcery." Joe Abercrombie. com. January 14, 2010. https://joeabercrombie.com/the-new-sword-and-sorcery/. Retrieved April 10, 2018. Web.

"About RBE Genres." Rogue Blades Entertainment. http://roguebladesentertain.wixsite.com/roguebladespresents/genre. Retrieved April 11, 2018. Web.

Alpers, Hans Joachim. "Loincloth, Double Ax, and Magic: 'Heroic Fantasy' and Related Genres." *Science Fiction Studies* #14, March 1978. DePauw University website. http://www.depauw.edu/sfs/backissues/14/alpers14art.htm. Retrieved April 6, 2016. Web.

Anderson, Poul. *The Broken Sword*. New York, NY: Ballantine Books, 1971. Print.

Anderson, Poul. *The Broken Sword*. Ashland, OR, Blackstone Publishing, 2011. CD.

Anderson, Poul. "On Thud and Blunder." *Fantasy*. New York, NY: Tor, 1981. Print.

Asprin, Robert Lynn. "Essay: The Making of Thieves' World." *Thieves' World Book 1: Thieves' World*. Edited by Asprin and Lynn Abbey. New York, NY: Ace Fantasy, 1986. Print.

Ator, the Fighting Eagle. Directed by Joe D'Amato. Filmirage, 1982. DVD.

Bentley, Howie. "From Hell's Heart—Robert E. Howard and Heavy Metal Music: A History of Inspiration." Metal-Rules.com. September 16, 2011. https://www.metal-rules.com/2011/09/16/from-hells-heart-robert-e-howard-and-heavy-metal-music-a-history-of-inspiration/. Retrieved April 23, 2018. Web.

"Biography." Manowar. http://manowar.com/biography/. Retrieved September 19, 2016. Web.

"Biography." R.A. Salvatore. http://rasalvatore.com/biography.aspx. Retrieved April 8, 2018. Web.

"Blunders." *Amra*, Vol. 2, No. 7. Stanford, CA: George H. Scithers, Nov. 1959. p. 3. Print.

Boucher, Anthony and J. Francis McComas. "Recommended Reading." *The Magazine of Fantasy and Science Fiction.* Sept. 1953, p. 99. Print.

Boyer, Robert H. and Kenneth J. Zahorski. "Introduction." *The Fantastic Imagination: An Anthology of High Fantasy.* Edited by Boyer and Zahorski. New York, NY; Avon Books, 1977. Print.

Bradley, Marion Zimmer. *Sword and Sorceress.* New York, NY: Daw Books, 1984. Print.

Breakiron, Lee. "Arrested Development." The Nemedian Chroniclers #5. *Robert-E-Howard Electronic Amateur Press Association.* Vernal Equinox 2010. http://robert-e-howard.org/NemedianChroniclers5.pdf. Retrieved Jan. 27, 2018. Web.

Breakiron, Lee. "A Lion Among Fanzines." The Nemedian Chroniclers #2. *Robert-E-Howard Electronic Amateur Press Association.* Vernal Equinox 2009. http://robert-e-howard.org/NemedianChroniclers2REV.pdf. Retrieved Dec. 10, 2017. Web.

Burroughs, Edgar Rice. *The Gods of Mars: The Collected John Carter of Mars, Vol. 1.* New York, NY: Disney Editions, 2012. Print.

Burroughs, Edgar Rice. *Tarzan of the Apes.* New York, NY: Ballantine Books, 1972. Print.

Cabell, James Branch. *Jurgen: A Comedy of Justice.* Project Gutenberg. http://www.gutenberg.org/ebooks/8771. Web.

Campbell, John W. "Heroes are Out of Date." *Amra*, Vol. 2, No. 2. Stanford, CA: George H. Scithers, 1959. p. 7. Print.

Campbell, Ramsey. *Far Away & Never.* West Warwick, RI: Necronomicon Press, 1996. Print.

Capella, Ray. "Hyborians, Be Seated." *The Blade of Conan.* Edited by L. Sprague de Camp. New York, NY: Ace Books, 1979. Print.

Carlsen, Chris. *Berserker: Shadow of the Wolf.* London: Sphere Books, 1977. Print.

Carlson, Michael. "Obituaries: Frank Frazetta: Influential artist who worked on the "Conan the Barbarian, Tarzan, and Lil' Abner Comics." *The Independent.* July 20, 2010. https://www.independent.co.uk/news/obituaries/frank-frazetta-influential-artist-who-worked-on-the-lsquoconan-the-barbarianrsquo-lsquotarzanrsquo-2030288.html. Retrieved Feb. 4, 2019. Web.

Carpenter, Humphrey. *J.R.R. Tolkien: A Biography.* New York, NY: Houghton Mifflin, 2000. Print.

Carter, Lin. "A Changeling in Elfland."*in* Anderson, Poul. *The Broken Sword.* New York, NY: Ballantine Books, 1971. Print.

Carter, Lin. "The Doom of the Skjoldungs," *in* Anderson, Poul. *Hrolf Kraki's Saga.* New York, NY: Ballantine Books, 1973. Print.

Carter, Lin. *Imaginary Worlds*. New York, NY: Ballantine Books, 1973. Print.

Carter, Lin. "In Defense of Heroes." *Amra*, Vol. 2 No. 55. Philadelphia, PA: Terminus, Owlswick, & Ft. Mudge Electric St. Railway Gazette, December 1971. pp. 14–16. Print.

Carter, Lin. "Introduction: Of Swordsmen and Sorcerers." *Flashing Swords! #1*. Edited by Carter. New York, NY: Dell Publishing Co., Inc., 1973. Print.

Carter, Lin. "Jack Vance." *Flashing Swords! #1*. Edited by Carter. New York, NY: Dell Publishing Co., Inc., 1973. Print.

Carter, Lin. *Realms of Wizardry*. Garden City, NY: Doubleday, 1976. Print.

Carter, Lin. "S&S Scrolls (review of *The Players of Hell*)." *Amra*, Vol. 2 No. 52. Chicago, IL: Terminus, Owlswick, & Ft. Mudge Electric St. Railway Gazette, April 1970. p. 22. Print.

Carter, Lin. "Swordsmen and Sorcerers at Play." *The Spell of Conan*. Edited by L. Sprague de Camp. New York, NY: Ace Books, 1980. Print.

Carter, Lin. *Thongor and the Wizard of Lemuria*. New York, NY: Berkley Medallion Books, 1976. Print.

Chabon, Michael. *Gentlemen of the Road*. New York, NY: Del Rey Books, 2008. Print.

Chapman, Colin. "Drunken Debauchery!" Astonishing Swordsmen and Sorcerers of Hyperborea. 2013. https://www.hyperborea.tv/resources.html. Retrieved May 1, 2018. Web.

Charnas, Suzy McKee. "Where No Man Had Gone Before" *in* Moore, CL. *Black God's Kiss*. Bellevue, WA: Planet Stories, 2007. Print.

"Cirith Ungol (Interview with Robert Garvin)." Metal Nightmare Magazine. February 23, 2005. https://web.archive.org/web/20050223140041/http:/www.geocities.com/metalnightmarezine/cirithungol.html. Retrieved September 21, 2016. Web.

"Clark Ashton Smith." Eldritch Dark. September 19, 2006. http://www.eldritchdark.com/articles/biographies/3/clark-ashton-smith. Retrieved April 9, 2017. Web.

Conan the Barbarian. Directed by John Milius. Universal Pictures, 1982. DVD.

Conan the Barbarian. Directed by Marcus Nispel. Lionsgate, 2011. DVD.

"Conan the Barbarian (2011)." Box Office Mojo. https://www.boxofficemojo.com/movies/?page=main&id=conan3d.htm. Retrieved September 21, 2018. Web.

Conan the Destroyer. Directed by Richard Fleischer. Universal Pictures, 1984. DVD.

Connors, Scott. "Pegasus Unbridled: Clark Ashton Smith and the Ghettoization of the Fantastic." *The Unique Legacy of Weird Tales: The Evolution of Modern Fantasy and Horror.* Edited by Justin Everett and Jeffrey H. Shanks. Lanham, MD: Rowman & Littlefield, 2015. Print.

Connors, Scott. "Twilight of the Gods: Howard and the *Volkstumbewegung.*" *The Barbaric Triumph.* Edited by Don Herron. Gillette, NJ: Wildside Press, 2004. Print.

Connors, Scott and Ron Hilger. "A Note on the Texts." *in* Smith, Clark Ashton. *A Vintage from Atlantis: The Collected Fantasies of Clark Ashton Smith, Vol. 3.* New York, NY: Night Shade Books, 2016. Print.

Conquest. Directed by Lucio Fulci. Clemi Cinematografica, 1983. DVD.

"Contents." *Amra*, Vol. 2 No. 46. Chicago, IL: Terminus, Owlswick, & Ft. Mudge Electric St. Railway Gazette, April 1968. p. 2. Print.

Cook, Glen. *The Black Company.* New York, NY: Tor Books, 1984. Print.

Deathstalker. Directed by James Sbardellati. New World Pictures, 1983. DVD.

De Camp, L. Sprague, Catherine Crook De Camp, Jane Whittington Griffin. *Dark Valley Destiny: The Life of Robert E. Howard.* New York, NY: Bluejay Books, 1983. Print.

De Camp, L. Sprague and Lin Carter. *Conan the Liberator.* New York, NY: Bantam Books, 1979. Print.

De Camp, L. Sprague and Lin Carter. "Introduction." *Conan of the Isles.* New York, NY: Ace Books, 1979. Print.

De Camp, L. Sprague. "Editing Conan." *The Blade of Conan.* Edited by de Camp. New York, NY: Ace Books, 1979. Print.

De Camp, L. Sprague. "The Heroic Barbarian." *The Spell of Conan.* Edited by de Camp. New York, NY: Ace Books, 1980. Print.

De Camp, L. Sprague. "Hyborian Technology." *The Blade of Conan.* Edited by de Camp. New York, NY: Ace Books, 1979. Print.

De Camp, L. Sprague. "Introduction." *in* Howard, Robert E., de Camp, and Lin Carter. *Conan.* New York, NY: Ace Books, 1979. Print.

De Camp, L. Sprague. "Introduction." *The Fantastic Swordsmen.* Edited by de Camp. New York, NY: Pyramid Books, 1967. Print.

De Camp, L. Sprague. "Introduction: Heroic Fantasy." *Swords & Sorcery.* Edited by de Camp. New York, NY: Pyramid Books, 1963. Print.

De Camp, L. Sprague. "Introduction." *Warlocks and Warriors.* Edited by de Camp. New York, NY: Berkley Medallion Books, 1970. Print.

De Camp, L. Sprague. *Literary Swordsman and Sorcerers: The Makers of Heroic Fantasy.* Sauk City, WI: Arkham House, 1976. Print.

De Camp, L. Sprague. "Multiple Scrolls." *Amra*, Vol. 2 No. 52. Philadelphia, PA: Terminus, Owlswick, & Ft. Mudge Electric St. Railway Gazette, April 1970. p. 15. Print.

De Camp, L. Sprague. "Mundy's Vendhya." *The Blade of Conan*. Edited by de Camp. New York, NY: Ace Books, 1979. Print.

De Camp, L. Sprague. "Robert E. Howard's Fiction." *The Robert E. Howard Reader*. Edited by Darrell Schweitzer. Rockville, MD: Borgo Press, 2010. Print.

De Camp, L. Sprague. "The Rug and the Bull." Carter, Lin. *Flashing Swords* #2. Garden City, NY: Nelson Doubleday, 1973. Print.

De Camp, L. Sprague. "Scroll" (review of Poul Anderson's *The Last Viking*, Books 1-3). *Amra*, Vol. 2 No. 71, Philadelphia, PA: Terminus, Owlswick, & Ft. Mudge Electric St. Railway Gazette, July 1982. p. 3. Print.

De Camp, L. Sprague. "Skald in the Post Oaks." *The Spell of Conan*. Edited by de Camp. New York, NY: Ace Books, 1980. Print.

De Camp, L. Sprague. *The Spell of Seven*. New York, NY: Pyramid Books, 1965. Print.

De Camp, L. Sprague. *Time & Chance*. Hampton Falls, NH: Donald M. Grant, 1996. Print.

De Camp. L. Sprague. *The Tritonian Ring*. New York, NY: Del Rey, 1977. Print.

Delany, Samuel. "Sword & Sorcery, S/M, and the Economics of Inadequation: The Camera Obscura Interview." *Silent Interviews: On Language, Race, Sex, Science Fiction, and Some Comics.* Hanover, NH: Wesleyan University Press, 1994. Print.

Del Rey, Lester. "Forty Years of C.L. Moore." in Moore, C.L. *The Magic of C.L. Moore*. Edited by Del Rey. New York, NY: Del Rey, 1975. Print.

Del Rey, Lester. *The World of Science Fiction, 1926–1976: The History of a Subculture*. New York, NY: Ballantine Books, 1979. Print.

DeMaio, Joey. (1984). Black Arrows [Recorded by Manowar]. On *Hail to England* [CD]. London: Music for Nations.

DeMaio, Joey. (1992). Metal Warriors [Recorded by Manowar]. On *The Triumph of Steel* [CD]. New York, NY: Atlantic.

DeVarque, Aardy. R. "Literary Sources of D&D." Aardy's RPG Page. http://www.hahnlibrary.net/rpgs/sources.html. Web.

Dirda, Michael. "Introduction." *in* Smith, Clark Ashton. *A Vintage from Atlantis: The Collected Fantasies of Clark Ashton Smith, Vol. 3.* New York, NY: Night Shade Books, 2016. Print.

Doyle, Arthur Conan. *The Lost World*. Project Gutenberg. http://www.gutenberg.org/ebooks/139. Web.

Drake, David. "The Barrow Troll." *Night & Demons*. Riverside, NJ: Baen, 2012. eBook.

The Dragon, Vol. 1, No. 1. Lake Geneva, WI: TSR Periodicals, June 1976. Print.

The Dragon, Vol. 1, No. 2. Lake Geneva, WI: TSR Periodicals, August 1976. Print.

Drew, Steve. "Talking Community with r/Fantasy." The Grim Tidings Podcast. thegrimtidingspodcast.com. Podcast.

Drout, Michael. *Rings, Swords, and Monsters: Exploring Fantasy Literature*. Prince Frederick, MD: Recorded Books, 2008. CD.

Dunsany, Lord. "The Bride of the Man-Horse." *In the Land of Time and Other Fantasy Tales*. Edited by S.T. Joshi. New York, NY: Penguin Books, 2004. Print.

Dunsany, Lord. "The Fortress Unvanquishable, Save for Sacnoth." *In the Land of Time and Other Fantasy Tales*. Edited by S.T. Joshi. New York, NY: Penguin Books, 2004. Print.

"Dying Earth." The Encyclopedia of Science Fiction. Gollancz. September 17, 2013. http://www.sf-encyclopedia.com/entry/dying_earth. Retrieved Dec. 31, 2018. Web.

Eddison, E.R. "Foreword to Egil's Saga" *in* Carter, Lin. "The Doom of the Skjoldungs," *in* Anderson, Poul. *Hrolf Kraki's Saga*. New York, NY: Ballantine Books, 1973. Print.

Eddison, E.R. *Styrbiorn the Strong*. Minneapolis, MN: University of Minnesota Press, 2011. Print.

Eddison, E.R. *The Worm Ouroboros*. New York, NY: Ballantine Books, 1967. Print.

Elliot, Jeffrey. "Interview with Karl Wagner." East of Eden. July 1981. http://karledwardwagner.org/Karl.html. Retrieved January 29, 2018. Web.

Emmelhainz, Nicole. "Strange Collaborations: *Weird Tales*'s Discourse Community as a Site of Collaborative Writing." *Skelos: The Journal of Weird Fiction and Dark Fantasy*, Vol. 1, No. 1. Edited by Mark Finn, Chris Gruber, and Jeffrey Shanks. Tallahassee, FL: Skelos Press, 2016. Print.

Emmelhainz, Nicole. "A Sword-Edge Beauty as Keen as Blades: C.L. Moore and the Gender Dynamics of Sword and Sorcery." *Skelos: The Journal of Weird Fiction and Dark Fantasy*, Vol. 1, No. 1. Edited by Mark Finn, Chris Gruber, and Jeffrey Shanks. Tallahassee, FL: Skelos Press, 2016. Print.

Eng, Steve. "The Poetry of Robert E. Howard." *The Dark Barbarian*. Edited by Don Herron. Gillette, NJ: Wildside Press, 2000. Print.

Everett, Justin and Jeffrey Shanks. "Introduction: *Weird Tales*—Discourse Community and Genre Nexus." *The Unique Legacy of Weird Tales: The Evolution of Modern Fantasy and Horror*. Edited by Everett and Shanks. Lanham, MD: Rowman & Littlefield, 2015. Print.

"The Eyrie." *Weird Tales*, December 1937. p. 762. Print.

"The Eyrie." *Weird Tales*, July 1937. p. 128. Print.

"The Eyrie." Weird Tales, July 1938. p. 124. Print.

Farabee, Mindy. "Beyond 'Game of Thrones': Exploring diversity in speculative fiction." June 9, 2013. *LA Times*. http://herocomplex.latimes.com/books/beyond-game-of-thrones-exploring-diversity-in-speculative-fiction/#/0 Accessed April 8, 2018. Web.

Finn, Mark. *Blood & Thunder: The Life & Art of Robert E. Howard*. Austin, TX: MonkeyBrain Books, 2006. Print.

Finn, Mark. "Skull Session." *Skelos: The Journal of Weird Fiction and Dark Fantasy*, Vol. 1, No. 1. Tallahassee, FL: Skelos Press, Summer 2016. pp. 4-6. Print.

Fire and Ice. Directed by Ralph Bakshi. 20th Century Fox, 1983. DVD.

Fox, Gardner F. *Kothar and the Wizard Slayer*. New York, NY: Unibook, 1970. Print.

Fox, Gardner F. *Kothar—Barbarian Swordsman*. New York, NY: Belmont Books, 1969. Print.

Fox, Gardner F. *Kyrik: Warlock Warrior*. New York, NY: Leisure Books, 1975. Print.

Frye, Northrop. *Anatomy of Criticism: Four Essays*. Princeton, NJ: Princeton University Press, 1990. Print.

Garth, John. *Tolkien and the Great War*. New York, NY: Houghton Mifflin Company, 2003. Print.

Gemmell, David. *Legend*. New York, NY: Del Rey, 1984. Print.

"The Glen Cook Interview." *Quantum Muse*. https://www.quantummuse.com/glen_cook_interview.html. Retrieved April 7, 2018. Web.

Glick, Seth. "A Tentative Bibliography of S&S." *Amra*, Vol. 2 No. 64. Philadelphia, PA: Terminus, Owlswick, & Ft. Mudge Electric St. Railway Gazette, October 1974. p. 7. Print.

Goldstein, Patrick and James Rainey. "Brett Ratner and 'Conan': Premature Exhilaration? *LA Times*. November 12, 2008. https://latimesblogs.latimes.com/the_big_picture/2008/11/brett-ratner-an.html. Retrieved June 2, 2019. Web.

Grin, Leo. "The Fortress Unvanquishable, Even for Sacnoth." The Cimmerian. February 19, 2007. http://leogrin.com/

CimmerianBlog/the-fortress-unvanquishable-even-for-sacnoth/. Retrieved March 15, 2019. Web.

Grin, Leo. "The Reign of Blood." *The Barbaric Triumph*. Edited by Don Herron. Gillette, NJ: Wildside Press, 2004. Print.

Guran, Paula. "Karl Edward Wagner." *DarkEcho Horror*. http://www.darkecho.com/darkecho/features/kew.html. Retrieved Jan. 22, 2017. Web.

Gygax, Gary. "The influence of J.R.R. Tolkien on the D&D and AD&D games: Why Middle Earth is not part of the game world." *Dragon* #95. Lake Geneva, WI: TSR, Inc., March 1985. p. 12. Print.

Gygax, Gary. *Dungeon Master's Guide*. Lake Geneva, WI; TSR, Inc., 1979. Print.

Haggard, H. Rider. *Eric Brighteyes*. New York, NY: Zebra Books, 1978. Print.

Haggard, H. Rider. "King Solomon's Mines." *Three Complete Novels: H. Rider Haggard*. Avenel, NJ: Gramercy, 1996.

Haggard, H. Rider. *She*. New York, NY: Lancer Books, 1965. Print.

Harlib, Amy. "Adding to the Gumbo Mix: Charles R. Saunders." The Zone. https://web.archive.org/web/20110607105724/http://www.zone-sf.com/crsaunders.html. Retrieved Feb. 4, 2018. Web.

Harrison, Harry. "Chopped Vigorously." *Amra*, Vol. 2, No. 36. Chicago, IL: Terminus, Owlswick, & Ft. Mudge Electric St. Railway Gazette, September 1965. p. 18. Print.

Hartwell, David. G. "Introduction." *Masterpieces of Fantasy and Enchantment*. Edited by D. Hartwell. Garden City, NY: Doubleday Book & Music Clubs, Inc., 1988. Print.

Hartwell, David G. and Jacob Weisman. *The Sword & Sorcery Anthology*. San Francisco, CA: Tachyon Publications, 2012. Print.

Harvey, Ryan. "The Fantasy Cycles of Clark Ashton Smith PART I: The Averoigne Chronicles." 2007. *Black Gate*. Retrieved January 17, 2016. Web.

Helland, Jonathan. "C.L. Moore, M. Brundage, and Jiriel of Joiry: Women and Gender in the October 1934 *Weird Tales*." *The Unique Legacy of Weird Tales: The Evolution of Modern Fantasy and Horror*. Edited by Justin Everett and Jeffrey H. Shanks. Lanham, MD: Rowman & Littlefield, 2015. Print.

Hendrix, Grady. *Paperbacks from Hell: The Twisted History of '70s and '80s Horror Fiction*. Philadelphia, PA: Quirk Books, 2017. Print.

Herron, Don. "The Dark Barbarian." *The Dark Barbarian*. Gillette, NJ: Wildside Press, 2000. Print.

Hester, Patrick. "Sword & Sorcery Panel, Parts 1, 2, 3." *The SF Signal Podcast*. Sfsignal.com, 2011. Podcast.

Holmes, Morgan T. "Gothic to Cosmic: Sword-and-Sorcery Fiction in *Weird Tales*." *The Unique Legacy of Weird Tales: The Evolution of Modern Fantasy and Horror*. Edited by Justin Everett and Jeffrey H. Shanks. Lanham, MD: Rowman & Littlefield, 2015. Print.

Holmes, Morgan T. "RE: "Smith-ian" or Gothic sword-and-sorcery." Message to Brian Murphy. September 2, 2019. E-mail.

Howard, Robert E. "By this Axe I Rule." *Kull: Exile of Atlantis*. Edited by Rusty Burke and Patrice Louinet. New York, NY: Del Rey, 2006. Print.

Howard, Robert E. "The Cat and the Skull." *Kull: Exile of Atlantis*. Edited by Rusty Burke and Patrice Louinet. New York, NY: Del Rey, 2006. Print.

Howard, Robert E. *The Collected Letters of Robert E. Howard* (3 vols.). Edited by Rob Roehm. Sugar Land, TX: The Robert E. Howard Foundation Press, 2007. Print.

Howard, Robert E. *The Conan Chronicles, Volume 1: The People of the Black Circle*. London: Millennium, 2000. Print.

Howard, Robert E. *Conan the Conqueror*. Edited by L. Sprague de Camp. New York, NY: Lancer Books, 1967. Print.

Howard, Robert E. "The Cat and the Skull." *Kull: Exile of Atlantis*. Edited by Rusty Burke and Patrice Louinet. New York, NY: Del Rey, 2006. Print.

Howard, Robert E. "The Devil in Iron." *The Coming of Conan the Cimmerian*. Edited by Rusty Burke and Patrice Louinet. New York, NY: Del Rey, 2003. Print.

Howard, Robert E. "Kings of the Night." *Kull: Exile of Atlantis*. Edited by Rusty Burke and Patrice Louinet. New York, NY: Del Rey, 2006. Print.

Howard, Robert E. "Letter to Clark Ashton Smith." Dec. 14, 1933. *in* Howard, Robert E. *The Hour of the Dragon*. Edited by Karl Edward Wagner. New York, NY: Berkley Medallion Books, 1977. Print.

Howard, Robert E. "The Mirrors of Tuzun Thune." *Kull: Exile of Atlantis*. Edited by Rusty Burke and Patrice Louinet. New York, NY: Del Rey, 2006. Print.

Howard, Robert E. "The People of the Black Circle." *The Bloody Crown of Conan*. Edited by Rusty Burke and Patrice Louinet. New York, NY: Del Rey, 2003. Print.

Howard, Robert E. "The Phoenix on the Sword." *The Coming of Conan the Cimmerian*. Edited by Rusty Burke and Patrice Louinet. New York, NY: Del Rey, 2003. Print.

Howard, Robert E. "Queen of the Black Coast." *The Coming of Conan the Cimmerian*. Edited by Rusty Burke and Patrice Louinet. New York, NY: Del Rey, 2003. Print.

Howard, Robert. E. "The Shadow Kingdom." *Kull: Exile of Atlantis*. Edited by Rusty Burke and Patrice Louinet. New York, NY: Del Rey, 2006. Print.

Howard, Robert E. "Swords of the Purple Kingdom." *Kull: Exile of Atlantis*. Edited by Rusty Burke and Patrice Louinet. New York, NY: Del Rey, 2006. Print.

Howard, Robert. E. "Untitled Fragment." *Kull: Exile of Atlantis*. Edited by Rusty Burke and Patrice Louinet. New York, NY: Del Rey, 2006. Print.

Howard, Robert E., and L. Sprague de Camp. *Conan the Adventurer*. Edited by De Camp. New York, NY: Lancer Books, 1966. Print.

Hval, Brian. "On the State of Heroic Fantasy." *Amra*, Vol. 2 No. 53. Philadelphia, PA: Terminus, Owlswick, & Ft. Mudge Electric St. Railway Gazette, September 1970. p. 24. Print.

"Interview with David Gemmell." SFFWorld (reprinted with permission of *Orbit*). August 1, 1998. https://www.sffworld.com/1998/08/scifiint_23/. Retrieved March 3, 2018. Web.

Jackson, Gordon M. "The Weirdest Spy Action Novels Ever Published." Gizmodo. February 11, 2015. https://io9.gizmodo.com/the-weirdest-spy-action-novels-ever-published-1685259336. Retrieved January 13, 2018. Web.

Jakes, John. *Brak the Barbarian*. New York, NY: Avon Books, 1968. Print.

Jakes, John. *Brak vs. the Sorceress*. New York, NY: Pocket Books, 1977. Print.

Jakes, John. "Re: Some Answers to your Brak Questions." Message to Brian Murphy. October 31, 2017. E-mail.

Jones, Howard Andrew. *The Desert of Souls*. New York, NY: Thomas Dunne Books, 2011. Print.

Jones, Jeffrey. Official Website. https://web.archive.org/web/20080113011329/http:/ulster.net/~jonesart/welcome.html. Retrieved Feb. 10, 2019. Web.

Joshi, S.T. "Afterword." *Fritz Leiber and H.P. Lovecraft: Writers of the Dark*. Edited by Ben J. Szumskyj and Joshi. Holicong, NJ: Wildside Press, 2003. Print.

Joshi, S.T. "Introduction." *Lord Dunsany: In the Land of Time and Other Fantasy Tales*. In the Land of Time and Other Fantasy Tales. Edited by Joshi. New York, NY: Penguin Books, 2004. Print.

Joshi, S.T. *The Modern Weird Tale: A Critique of Horror Fiction.* Cited from "Ramsey Campbell." Wikipedia. April 10, 2019. https://en.wikipedia.org/wiki/Ramsey_Campbell#cite_note–17. Retrieved July 10, 2019. Web.

Joshi, S.T. "Science and Superstition: Fritz Leiber's Modernization of Gothic." *Fritz Leiber: Critical Essays.* Edited by Benjamin Szumskyj. Jefferson, NC: McFarland & Company, 2008. Print.

Keene, Brian and Steven Shrewsbury. *King of the Bastards.* Lexington, KY: Apex Publications: 2014. Print.

Kellogg, Robert. "Introduction." *The Sagas of Icelanders."* New York, NY: Penguin Books, 2001. Print.

King, Stephen. *Danse Macabre.* New York, NY: Berkley Books, 1983. Print.

Kline, Otis Adelbert. "Why *Weird Tales*?" *Weird Tales.* Edited by Marvin Kaye. Garden City, NY: Nelson Doubleday, 1988. Print.

Knight, George. "Robert E. Howard: Hard-Boiled Heroic Fantasist." *The Dark Barbarian.* Edited by Don Herron. Gillette, NJ: Wildside Press, 2000. Print.

Kuttner, Henry. "Dragon Moon." *Elak of Atlantis.* Bellevue, WA: Planet Stories, 2007. Print.

Kuttner, Henry. "Thunder in the Dawn." *Elak of Atlantis.* Bellevue, WA: Planet Stories, 2007. Print.

Lai, Rick. "Conan Versus Tsathoggua." The Lovecraft ezine. September 17, 2013. https://lovecraftzine.com/2013/09/17/conan-versus-tsathoggua-by-rick-lai/. Retrieved September 3, 2019. Web.

Lamb, Harold. *Hannibal.* New York, NY: Bantam Books, 1958. Print.

Lamb, Harold. "The Three Palladins." *Swords from the East.* Edited by Howard Andrew Jones. Lincoln, NE: Bison Books, 2010. Print.

Lansdale, Joe. "Introduction: Kuttner Sharpens His Literary Sword." *Elak of Atlantis.* Bellevue, WA: Planet Stories, 2007. Print.

"Leading book genres worldwide as of January 2014, by revenue (in million U.S. dollars)." Statista. http://www.statista.com/statistics/322187/book-genres-revenue/. Retrieved Dec. 29, 2015. Web.

Le Guin, Ursula K. "The Critics, the Monsters, and the Fantasists." *in* Beagle, Peter. S. *The Secret History of Fantasy.* San Francisco, CA: Tachyon Publications, 2010. Print.

Le Guin, Ursula K. "On Norman Spinrad's *The Iron Dream.*" *Science Fiction Studies #1,* Spring 1973. DePauw University website. https://www.depauw.edu/sfs/backissues/1/leguin1art.htm. Retrieved April 8, 2016. Web.

Le Guin, Ursula K. *A Wizard of Earthsea*. New York, NY: Bantam Books, 1968. Print.

Leiber, Fritz. "Author's Note." *The Swords of Lankhmar*. New York, NY; Ace Books, 1968. Print.

Leiber, Fritz. "Bazaar of the Bizarre." *Fantasy Masterworks 18: The First Book of Lankhmar*. London: Gollancz. 2001. Print.

Leiber, Fritz. "The Circle Curse." *Swords Against Death*. New York, NY: Ace Books, 1981. Print.

Leiber, Fritz. "The Cloud of Hate." *Fantasy Masterworks 18: The First Book of Lankhmar*. London: Gollancz. 2001. Print.

Leiber, Fritz. "Fafhrd and Me." *The Spell of Conan*. Edited by L. Sprague de Camp. New York, NY: Ace Books, 1980. Print.

Leiber, Fritz. "Howard's Style." *The Spell of Conan*. Edited by L. Sprague de Camp. New York, NY: Ace Books, 1980. Print.

Leiber, Fritz. "Ill Met in Lankhmar." *Fantasy Masterworks 18: The First Book of Lankhmar*. London: Gollancz. 2001. Print.

Leiber, Fritz. "Letter." *Amra,* Vol. 2 No. 16. Arlington, VA: George H. Scithers, July 1961. pp. 21-23. Print.

Leiber, Fritz. "Letter." *Ancalagon* #2. Philadelphia, PA: George R. Heap, Philadelphia Science Fiction Society, April 1961. pp. 6-7. Print.

Leiber, Fritz. "The Lords of Quarmall." *Swords Against Wizardry*. New York, NY: Ace Books, 1968. Print.

Leiber, Fritz. "The Mouser Goes Below." *Fantasy Masterworks 24: The Second Book of Lankhmar*. London: Gollancz. 2001. Print.

Leiber, Fritz. "On the New World Tarzan." *Amra*, Vol. 2, No. 50. Chicago, IL: Terminus, Owlswick, & Ft. Mudge Electric St. Railway Gazette, May 1969. p. 18. Print.

Leiber, Fritz. "The Seven Black Priests." *Swords Against Death*. New York, NY: Ace Books, 1981. Print.

Leiber, Fritz. "The Snow Women." *Swords and Deviltry*. New York, NY: iBooks, 2003. Print.

Leiber, Fritz. "Stardock." *Swords Against Wizardry*. New York, NY: Ace Books, 1968. Print.

Leiber, Fritz. "Titivated Romance." *The Blade of Conan*. Edited by L. Sprague de Camp. New York, NY: Ace Books, 1979. Print.

Leiber, Fritz. "The Unholy Grail." *Fantasy Masterworks 18: The First Book of Lankhmar*. London: Gollancz. 2001. Print.

Lewis, C.S. "Tolkien's *The Lord of the Rings*." *On Stories and Other Essays On Literature*. Orlando, FL: Harcourt, Inc., 1982. Print.

Liptak, Andrew. "Donald Wollheim and the Ace Double Novel." Kirkus. August 16, 2013. https://www.kirkusreviews.com/

features/donald-wollheim-and-ace-double-novel/. Retrieved May 1, 2016. Web.

Liptak, Andrew. "The Rise of the Paperback Novel." Kirkus. January 15, 2015. https://www.kirkusreviews.com/features/rise-paperback-novel/. Retrieved May 1, 2016. Web.

Liptak, Andrew. "The Unauthorized Lord of the Rings." Kirkus. December 5, 2013. https://www.kirkusreviews.com/features/unauthorized-lord-rings/. Retrieved January 13, 2018. Web.

Lochhead, Marion. *Renaissance of Wonder.* New York, NY: Harper & Row, Publishers, 1977. Print.

London, Jack. "The Call of the Wild." *Jack London Stories.* New York, NY: Platt & Munk, 1960. Print.

London, Jack. *The Jacket (or Star Rover).* Librivox. Read by Barry Eads. March 27, 2012. https://archive.org/details/jacket_1203_librivox. Audio.

Loucks, Donovan. "Written Works." The H.P. Lovecraft Archive. March 10, 2001. http://www.hplovecraft.com/internet/ahcfaq/written.aspx. Web.

Louinet, Patrice. "Atlantean Genesis," *in* Howard, Robert E. *Kull: Exile of Atlantis.* Edited by Rusty Burke and Patrice Louinet. New York, NY: Del Rey, 2003. Print.

Lovecraft, H.P. "The Doom that Came to Sarnath." *The Doom that Came to Sarnath.* New York, NY; Del Rey, 1991. Print.

Lovecraft, H.P. "The Haunter of the Dark." *Bloodcurdling Tales of Horror and the Macabre.* New York, NY: Del Rey, 1982. Print.

Lovecraft, H.P. Letter to Elizabeth Toldridge, March 8, 1929. *in* Carter, Lin. *Lovecraft: A Look Behind the Cthulhu Mythos.* New York, NY: Ballantine Books, 1972. Print.

Lovecraft, H.P. Letter to Fritz Leiber, Dec. 19, 1936. *in Fritz Leiber and H.P. Lovecraft: Writers of the Dark.* Edited by Ben J. Szumskyk and S.T. Joshi. Holicong, NJ: Wildside Press, 2003. Print.

Lovecraft, H.P. *Letters to C.L. Moore and Others.* Edited by David E. Schultz and S.T. Joshi. New York, NY: Hippocampus Press, 2017. Print.

Lovecraft, H.P. "Lord Dunsany and his Work." *in* Joshi, S.T. *A Dreamer and a Visionary: H.P. Lovecraft in His Time.* Liverpool: Liverpool University Press, 2001. Print.

Lovecraft, N.P. "Nemesis." The H.P. Lovecraft Archive. October 20, 2009. http://www.hplovecraft.com/writings/texts/poetry/p121.aspx. Web.

Lovecraft, H.P. "Supernatural Horror in Literature." The H.P. Lovecraft Archive. October 20, 2009. http://www.hplovecraft.com/writings/texts/essays/shil.aspx. Web.

Lovecraft, H.P., and Robert E. Howard. *A Means to Freedom: The Letters of Robert E. Howard and H.P. Lovecraft, 1930–1932; 1933–1936* (2 vols.). Edited by S.T. Joshi, David E. Schultz, and Rusty Burke. New York, NY: Hippocampus Press, 2011. Print.

Lupoff, Richard. *Master of Adventure: The Worlds of Edgar Rice Burroughs.* Lincoln, NE: Bison Books, 2005. Print.

MacLaurin, Wayne. "A Conversation with George R.R. Martin." SF Site. November 2000. https://www.sfsite.com/01a/gm95.htm. Retrieved March 24, 2018. Web.

Mandel, Paul. "Tarzan of the Paperbacks." Life Magazine. Nov. 1963. ERBzine. http://www.erbzine.com/mag14/1433.html. Retrieved March 21, 2019. Web.

"Mark Shelton." https://www.cimmerianshadows.co.uk/post/mark-shelton. Cimmerian Shadows. 2012. Retrieved May 15, 2019. Web.

Martin, George R.R. "Path of the Dragon." *The Sword & Sorcery Anthology*. Edited by David G. Hartwell and Jacob Weisman. San Francisco, CA: Tachyon Publications, 2012. Print.

Martin, George R.R. and Gardner Dozois. *Warriors.* Grand Haven, MI: Brilliance Audio, 2011. CD.

May, Jeffrey. "The Deeper Swordsman-Hero." *Amra*, Vol. 2 No. 57. Philadelphia, PA: Terminus, Owlswick, & Ft. Mudge Electric St. Railway Gazette, June 1972. p. 19. Print.

Mayer, John. "The Dark Muse of Karl Edward Wagner, part 1." Metro Pulse. October 28, 2009. https://web.archive.org/web/20120225121956/http://www.metropulse.com/news/2009/oct/28/dark-muse-karl-edward-wagner-part–1/. Retrieved April 1, 2017. Web.

Mercer, Archie. "Scroll, With Salt." *Amra*, Vol. 2, No. 36. Chicago, IL: Terminus, Owlswick, & Ft. Mudge Electric St. Railway Gazette, September 1965. p. 17. Print.

Merritt, A. *Dwellers in the Mirage.* New York, NY: Avon Books, 1967. Print.

Merritt, A. *The Ship of Ishtar.* Redmond, WA: Planet Stories, 2009. Print.

Meyers, Richard. "Thongor in the Valley of the Demons." *Starlog* #15. August 1978. pp. 32-33. Cited on *2 Warps to Neptune.* January 14, 2016. https://2warpstoneptune.com/2016/01/14/the-first-sword-and-sorcery-movie-was-almost-thongor-in-the-valley-of-the-demons/. Retrieved Sept. 22, 2018. Web.

Miesel, Sandra. "Afterword: An Invitation to Elfland." *in* Anderson, Poul. *Fantasy.* New York, NY: Tor, 1981. Print.

Moorcock, Michael. "The Bane of the Black Sword." *The Elric Saga: Part II*. Garden City, NY: Nelson Doubleday, 1984. Print.

Moorcock, Michael. "Conan: American Phenomenon." *in* Sammon, Paul M. *Conan the Phenomenon*. Milwaukie, OR: Dark Horse Books, 2007. Print.

Moorcock, Michael. "Elric." *Elric: The Stealer of Souls*. New York, NY: Del Rey, 2008. Print.

Moorcock, Michael. "Elric of Melnibone." *The Elric Saga: Part I*. Garden City, NY: Nelson Doubleday, 1984. Print.

Moorcock, Michael. "Introduction." *Duke Elric*. New York, NY: Del Rey, 2009. Print.

Moorcock, Michael. "Introduction." *Elric: The Sleeping Sorceress*. New York, NY: Del Rey, 2008. Print.

Moorcock, Michael. "Letter." *Amra*, Vol. 2, No. 3. Stanford, CA: George H. Scithers, May 1959. p. 4. Print.

Moorcock, Michael. "Moorcock's Miscellany Forums." Multiverse. August 6, 2004. https://web.archive.org/web/20090416042718/http://www.multiverse.org/fora/showthread.php?t=1102. Retrieved March 9, 2019. Web.

Moorcock, Michael. "Putting a Tag on it." *Amra*, Vol. 2, No. 15. Arlington, VA: George H. Scithers. pp. 15–18. Print.

Moorcock, Michael. "The Sailor on the Seas of Fate." *The Elric Saga: Part I*. Garden City, NY: Nelson Doubleday, 1984. Print.

Moorcock, Michael. "The Secret Life of Elric of Melnibone." *Elric: The Stealer of Souls*. New York, NY: Ballantine Books, 2008. Print.

Moorcock, Michael. "The Stealer of Souls." *Elric: The Stealer of Souls*. New York, NY: Ballantine Books, 2008. Print.

Moorcock, Michael. "Stormbringer." *The Elric Saga: Part II*. Garden City, NY: Nelson Doubleday, 1984. Print.

Moorcock, Michael. "Tolkien Times Two." *The Guardian*. January 25, 2003. https://www.theguardian.com/books/2003/jan/25/featuresreviews.guardianreview18. Retrieved Jan. 31, 2017. Web.

Moorcock, Michael. *Wizardry & Wild Romance: A Study of Epic Fantasy*. Austin, TX: MonkeyBrain, Inc., 2004. Print.

Moore, Alan. "Foreword." *Elric: The Stealer of Souls*. New York, NY: Ballantine Books, 2008. Print.

Moore, C.L. "Black God's Kiss." *Black God's Kiss*. Bellevue, WA: Planet Stories, 2007. Print.

Moore, C.L. "Hellsgarde." *Black God's Kiss*. Bellevue, WA: Planet Stories, 2007. Print.

Moore, C.L. Letter to HP Lovecraft, January 30, 1936, in *In the Land of Time and Other Fantasy Tales*. Edited by S.T. Joshi. New York, NY: Penguin Books, 2004. Print.

Morgan, Richard. *The Steel Remains*. London: Gollancz, 2008. Print.

Morgan, Richard. *The Cold Commands*. New York, NY: Ballantine Books, 2011. Print.

Mundy, Talbot. *Tros of Samothrace: Tros*. New York, NY: Avon Books, 1967. Print.

Murphy, Brian. "Updated Blood and Thunder Portends Good Start to 2012 for Robert E. Howard Fans." Black Gate. Dec. 22, 2011. https://www.blackgate.com/2011/12/22/updated-blood-and-thunder-portends-good-start-to-2012-for-robert-e-howard-fans/. Retrieved February 23, 2018. Web.

Murray, Will. "Introduction to 'The Book of Hyperborea.'" Eldritch Dark. December 2006. http://www.eldritchdark.com/articles/reviews/67/introduction-to-'the-book-of-hyperborea'. Retrieved September 3, 2019. Web.

Newsinger, John. "Fantasy and Revolution: An Interview with China Mieville." Marxists Internet Archive. Autumn 2000. https://www.marxists.org/history/etol/writers/newsinger/2000/xx/mieville.htm. Retrieved Oct. 8, 2018. Web.

Niven, Larry. "Not Long Before the End." *Barbarians*. Edited by Robert Adams, Martin H. Greenberg, and Charles H. Waugh. New York, NY: Signet, 1986. Print.

Nyberg, Bjorn, and L. Sprague de Camp. "The Return of Conan." *in* Howard, Robert E., Nyberg, and de Camp. *Conan the Avenger*. New York, NY: Lancer Books, 1968. Print.

Nyikos, Daniel. "The Lovecraft Circle and the 'Weird Class': 'Against the Complacency of an Orthodox Sun-Dweller." *The Unique Legacy of Weird Tales: The Evolution of Modern Fantasy and Horror*. Edited by Justin Everett and Jeffrey H. Shanks. Lanham, MD: Rowman & Littlefield, 2015. Print.

"Official Ballot: AFI's 100 Years of Film Scores." American Film Institute. September 23, 2005. http://www.afi.com/Docs/100Years/scores250.pdf. Retrieved May 10, 2019. Web.

Offutt, Andrew J. *Swords Against Darkness*. New York, NY: Zebra Books, 1977. Print.

Offutt, Andrew J. *Swords Against Darkness II*. New York, NY: Zebra Books, 1977. Print.

Open Road Media. "Brak the Barbarian, a classic Sword and Sorcery Tale by John Jakes." Youtube. July 12, 2012. https://www.youtube.com/watch?v=AqA_ydQhWSs. Retrieved Jan. 7, 2019. Web.

Owston, Chuck. "Karl Edward Wagner: An Interview for Dark Troubadour." The British Fantasy Society. Nov. 15, 2011 (original appearance *Dark Troubadour* #1, Autumn 1994). http://www.britishfantasysociety.org/reviews/karl-edward-wagner-an-interview-for-dark-troubadour/. Retrieved on Oct. 18, 2017. Web.

Page, Gerald W. and Hank Reinhardt. *Heroic Fantasy*. Edited by Page and Reinhardt. New York, NY: Daw Books, 1979. Print.

Peschel, Bill. "Interview With Terry Pratchett." Planetpeschel. September 14, 2006. https://planetpeschel.com/2006/09/interview-with-terry-pratchett/. Retrieved Oct. 9, 2018. Web.

Pendragon, Eric. "Introduction." *Savage Heroes: Tales of Sorcery & Black Magic*. Edited by Pendragon. London: Star Books, 1975. Print.

Prescott, Orville. "Introduction." *The Worm Ouroboros*. New York, NY: Ballantine Books, 1967. Print.

Price Ellis, Novalyne. *One Who Walked Alone*. Hampton Falls, NH: Donald M. Grant Publisher, Inc., 1986. Print.

Price, Robert M. "Know O Prince: An Introduction." *The Mighty Warriors*. Edited by Price. Warren, RI: Ulthar Press, 2018. Print.

Prida, Jonas. "Introduction." *Conan Meets the Academy*. Edited by Prida. Jefferson, NC: McFarland & Company, 2013. Print.

Priest, Christopher. "David Gemmell (obituary)." *The Guardian*. Aug. 2, 2006. https://www.theguardian.com/news/2006/aug/02/guardianobituaries.booksobituaries. Retrieved March 3, 2018. Web.

Proctor, Geo. W. "The Smile of Oisia." *Swords Against Darkness*. Edited by Andrew J. Offutt. New York, NY: Zebra Books, 1977. Print.

"Publisher Zebra Books/Kensington Publishing Corp.: Books Published in 1975/1976." Internet Speculative Fiction Database. http://www.isfdb.org/cgi-bin/publisheryear.cgi?132+1975; http://www.isfdb.org/cgi-bin/publisheryear.cgi?132+1976. Web.

"Questions for Michael Chabon." *The New York Times Magazine*. Feb. 8, 2007. https://www.nytimes.com/2007/02/08/magazine/11chabon-questions.html. Retrieved Sept. 1, 2019. Web.

Reginald, Robert. *Science-Fiction and Fantasy Literature 1975–1991*. Detroit, MI: Gale Research, Inc, 1992. Print. *Cited in* Romeo, Gary. "Napoleon's Triumph?" *The Cimmerian*, Vol. 1, No. 1. Edited by Leo Grin. Downey, CA. April 2004. Print.

Reiter, Geoffrey. "'A Round Cipher': Word-Building and World-Building in the Weird Works of Clark Ashton Smith." *The Unique Legacy of Weird Tales: The Evolution of Modern Fantasy and Horror*. Edited by Justin Everett and Jeffrey H. Shanks. Lanham, MD: Rowman & Littlefield, 2015. Print.

Rice, Douglas E. "On Opilla's Opinion." *Amra*, Vol. 2 No. 54. Philadelphia, PA: Terminus, Owlswick, & Ft. Mudge Electric St. Railway Gazette, April 1971. p. 24. Print.

Richardson, Deuce. "Forefathers of Sword and Sorcery: A. Merritt." DMR Books. Aug. 21, 2018. https://dmrbooks.com/test-blog/2018/8/21/forefathers-of-sword-and-sorcery-a-merritt. Retrieved August 25, 2019. Web.

Richardson, Deuce. "Forefathers of Sword and Sorcery: H. Rider Haggard." DMR Books. June 24, 2018. https://dmrbooks.com/test-blog/2018/6/24/forefathers-of-sword-and-sorcery-h-rider-haggard. Retrieved August 25, 2019. Web.

Richardson, Deuce. "The Sword and Sorcery Legacy of Donald A. Wollheim: Part Two." DMR Books. November 4, 2018. https://dmrbooks.com/test-blog/2018/11/4/the-sword-and-sorcery-legacy-of-donald-a-wollheim-part-two. Retrieved Jan. 1, 2019. Web.

Rickard, Dennis. "Through Black Boughs: The Supernatural in Howard's Fiction." *The Dark Barbarian*. Edited by Don Herron. Gillette, NJ: Wildside Press, 2000. Print.

Roberts, John Maddox. *Conan the Valorous*. New York, NY; Tor Books, 1985. Print.

Roehm, Rob. "'New' Howard Letter." Howard History. September 6, 2019. https://howardhistory.com/2019/09/06/new-howard-letter/. Retrieved Sept. 7, 2019. Web.

Salmonson, Jessica Amanda. *Amazons!* Edited by Salmonson. New York, NY: Daw Books, 1979. Print.

Salmonson, Jessica Amanda. *Heroic Visions*. Edited by Salmonson. New York, NY; Ace Books, 1983. Print.

Sammon, Paul M. *Conan the Phenomenon*. Milwaukie, OR: Dark Horse Books, 2007. Print.

Sammon, Paul M. "Nine Days in Cimmeria." *Cinefantastique*, Vol. 11, #3. Oak Park, IL: Frederick S. Clarke, September 1981. pp. 17-37. Print.

Sargent, Pamela. "Introduction," *in Women of Wonder: The Classic Years: Science Fiction by Women from the 1940s to the 1970s*. Cited in Helland, Jonathan. "C.L. Moore, M. Brundage, and Jiriel of Joiry: Women and Gender in the October 1934 *Weird Tales*." *The Unique Legacy of Weird Tales: The Evolution of Modern Fantasy and Horror*. Edited by Justin Everett and Jeffrey H. Shanks. Lanham, MD: Rowman & Littlefield, 2015. Print.

Saunders, Charles. "Factoring Fear: Imaro, Conan and Kane." Charles R. Saunders. September 19, 2015. http://www.reindeermotel.com/CHARLES/charles_blog68_factoring.html. Retrieved February 4, 2018. Web.

Saunders, Charles. *Imaro*. New York, NY: Daw Books, 1981. Print.

Saunders, Charles. "Of Chocolate Covered Conans and Pompous Pygmies." Charles R. Saunders. September 7, 2010. http://www.reindeermotel.com/CHARLES/charles_blog37_chocolateconan.html. Retrieved Feb. 5, 2018. Web.

Saunders, Charles. "Revisiting 'Die, Black Dog!'" Charles R. Saunders. Feb. 12, 2011. http://www.reindeermotel.com/CHARLES/charles_blog42_dieblackdog.html. Retrieved Feb. 24, 2018. Web.

The Savage Sword of Conan #16. Edited by Roy Thomas. New York, NY: Magazine Management Co., 1976. Print.

The Savage Sword of Conan #24. Edited by Roy Thomas. New York, NY: Magazine Management Co., 1977. Print.

Schweitzer, Darrell. "Fritz Leiber, Critical Essays (review)." *Mythopoeic Society*. www.mythsoc.org. Retrieved March 11, 2019. Web.

Schweitzer, Darrell. "King Kull as a Prototype of Conan." *The Robert E. Howard Reader*. Edited by Schweitzer. Rockville, MD: Borgo Press, 2010. Print.

Scroggins, Mark. *Michael Moorcock: Fiction, Fantasy and the World's Pain*. Jefferson, NC: McFarland & Company, 2016. Print.

Scudders, Bernard (*trans.*). "Egil's Saga." *The Sagas of Icelanders*." New York, NY, Penguin Books, 2001. Print.

Sellers, Michael. "Edgar Rice Burroughs in 1930 on 'The Purpose of Entertainment Fiction.'" The John Carter Files. May 3, 2012. https://thejohncarterfiles.com/2012/05/edgar-rice-burroughs-in–1930-on-the-purpose-of-entertainment-fiction/. Retrieved August 26, 2019. Web.

Shanks, Jeffrey. "History, Horror, and Heroic Fantasy: Robert E. Howard and the Creation of the Sword-and-Sorcery Subgenre." *Critical Insights: Pulp Fiction of the '20s and '30s*. Edited by Gary Hoppenstand. Amenia, NY: Salem Press, 2013. Print.

Shanks, Jeffrey. "Hyborian Age Archaeology: Unearthing Historical and Anthropological Foundations." *Conan Meets the Academy*. Edited by Jonas Prida. Jefferson, NC: McFarland & Company, 2013. Print.

Shea, Michael. *Nifft the Lean*. London; Panther Books, 1985. Print.

Shelton, Mark. (1982). Queen of the Black Coast [Recorded by Manilla Road]. On *Metal* [CD]. Wichita, KS: Roadster Records.

Shippey, Tom. "Tolkien and the Appeal of the Pagan: Edda and Kalevala." *Roots and Branches*. Switzerland, Walking Tree Publishers, 2007. Print.

Shovlin, Paul W. "Psycho-ology 101: Incipient Madness in the Weird Tales of Robert Bloch." *The Unique Legacy of Weird Tales: The Evolution of Modern Fantasy and Horror*. Edited by Everett and Shanks. Lanham, MD: Rowman & Littlefield, 2015. Print.

Silver, Steven H. "A Conversation With Lynn Abbey." SF Site. October 2002. https://www.sfsite.com/11a/la139.htm. Retrieved Feb. 10, 2018. Web.

Sinor, Bradley H. "Excellence Demanded, Whiners Piss Off: The Last Interview of Karl Edward Wagner." East of Eden. http://karledwardwagner.org/Karl.html. Retrieved Feb. 3, 2018. Web.

Smiley, Jane. "Preface." *The Sagas of Icelanders.*" New York, NY, Penguin Books, 2001. Print.

Smith, Clark Ashton. "The Beast of Averoigne." *The Return of the Sorcerer.* Gaithersburg, MD: Prime Books, 2009. Print.

Smith, Clark Ashton. "The Dark Eidolon." *The Return of the Sorcerer.* Gaithersburg, MD: Prime Books, 2009. Print.

Smith, Clark Ashton. "The Empire of the Necromancers." *The Return of the Sorcerer.* Gaithersburg, MD: Prime Books, 2009. Print.

Smith, Clark Ashton. "The Isle of the Torturers." *The Return of the Sorcerer.* Gaithersburg, MD: Prime Books, 2009. Print.

Smith, Clark Ashton. "The Seven Geases." *The Return of the Sorcerer.* Gaithersburg, MD: Prime Books, 2009. Print.

Smith, Clark Ashton. "The Testament of Athammaus." *Swords & Sorcery.* Edited by L. Sprague de Camp. New York, NY: Pyramid Books, 1963. Print.

Smith, David C. "Introduction." *Swords of Steel.* Edited by D.M. Ritzlin. DMR Books, 2015. Print.

Smith, David C. *Oron.* New York, NY: Zebra Books, 1978. Print.

Smith, David C., Jake Jaquet, and Joe Bonadonna. "Sword and Sorcery, Part 1." Youtube. August 19, 2008. https://www.youtube.com/watch?v=1WX1iiISUkY. Retrieved Sept. 24, 2016. Web.

Smith, David C. and Richard L. Tierney. *Red Sonja: The Ring of Ikribu.* New York, NY: Ace Books, 1981. Print.

Solon, Ben. "Howard's Cthuloid Tales." *The Blade of Conan.* Edited by L. Sprague de Camp. New York, NY: Ace Books, 1979. Print.

Spinrad, Norman. *The Iron Dream.* New York, NY: Avon, 1972. Print.

Stevens, Eric. "A Taste of Siberian Steel...Interview with Alex Avdeev of Russian Metal Band, 'Blacksword.'" Metal Underground. April 22, 2010. https://xmetalundergroundx.wordpress.com/2010/04/22/blacksword_interview/. Retrieved June 27, 2018. Web.

Stiles, Paula R. "Tales from the Brass Bikini: Feminist Sword and Sorcery." Broad Universe. Nov. 2011. https://web.archive.org/web/20111228100610/http://broaduniverse.org/broadsheet-archive/tales-from-the-brass-bikini-feminist-sword-and-sorcery-november-2011-bs-r. Retrieved February 23, 2018. Web.

Strahan, Jonathan and Lou Anders. *Swords & Dark Magic: The New Sword and Sorcery*. New York, NY: Harper Voyager, 2010. Print.

Straub, Peter. "Various Encounters with Karl: Remembering Karl Edward Wagner." Weird Fiction Review. July 2, 2012. http://weirdfictionreview.com/2012/07/various-encounters-with-karl/. Retrieved Jan. 31, 2018. Web.

The Sword and the Sorcerer. Directed by Albert Pyun. Group 1 International Distribution Organization Ltd., 1982. DVD.

"Sword and Sorcery." The Encyclopedia of Science Fiction. Gollancz. Dec. 19, 2017. http://www.sf-encyclopedia.com/entry/sword_and_sorcery. Retrieved Nov. 11, 2018. Web.

Swords of Steel. DMR Books. Edited by D.M. Ritzlin. 2015. Print.

"Tales from the Magician's Skull." Kickstarter, Goodman Games. https://www.kickstarter.com/projects/1409961192/tales-from-the-magicians-skull. Retrieved April 14, 2018. Web.

Thomas, G.W. "A Reader's Guide to Sword and Sorcery Magazines." http://www.gwthomas.org/ssrgmags.htm. Retrieved Nov. 6, 2016. Web.

Thomas, Paul Edmund. "Afterword: The Writing of Styrbiorn the Strong," in Eddison, E.R. *Styrbiorn the Strong*. Minneapolis, MN: University of Minnesota Press, 2011. Print.

Thompson, Raymond H. "Interview with Robert Holdstock." The Camelot Project. 1999. http://d.lib.rochester.edu/camelot/text/thompson-interview-robert-holdstock. Accessed Nov. 25, 2018. Web.

Tierney, Richard L. "Introduction." *in* Howard, Robert E. *Tigers of the Sea*. New York, NY: Zebra Books, 1975. Print.

Tolkien, J.R.R. "On Fairy Stories." *The Tolkien Reader*. New York, NY: Ballantine Books, 1982. Print.

Tompkins, Steve. "After Aquilonia and Having Left Lankhmar: Sword-and-Sorcery Since the 1980s." The Cimmerian. http://leogrin.com/CimmerianBlog/after-aquilonia-and-having-left-lankhmar-sword-and-sorcery-since-the–1980s/. Retrieved February 18, 2016. Web.

Tompkins, Steve. "Dog Brothers." *The Cimmerian*, vol. 3, no. 10. Edited by Leo Grin. Downey, CA, October 2006. Print.

Tompkins, Steve. "Introduction." *Kull: Exile of Atlantis*. Edited by Rusty Burke and Patrice Louinet. New York, NY: Del Rey, 2006. Print.

Tymn, Marshall B., Kenneth J. Zahorski, Robert H. Boyer. *Fantasy Literature: A Core Collection and Reference Guide*. New York, NY: R.R. Bowker Company, 1979. Print.

Vance, Jack. "Cugel's Saga." *Tales of the Dying Earth*. New York, NY: Orb Books, 2000. Print.

Vance, Jack. "The Dying Earth." *Tales of the Dying Earth*. New York, NY: Orb Books, 2000. Print.

Vance, Jack. "Rhialto the Marvellous." *Tales of the Dying Earth*. New York, NY: Orb Books, 2000. Print.

Vick, Todd. B. "The Mirror of E'ch-Pi-El: Robert E. Howard in the Letters of H. P. Lovecraft (Part 3) by Bobby Derie." September 13, 2015. On An Underwood No. 5. http://onanunderwood5.blogspot.com/2015/09/the-mirror-of-ech-pi-el-robert-e-howard_13.html. Retrieved February 18, 2016. Web.

Virginia Commonwealth Library. "Jurgen." James Branch Cabell: Man of Letters and Libraries. https://gallery.library.vcu.edu/exhibits/show/jamesbranchcabell/cabellswriting/jurgen. Retrieved March 15, 2019. Web.

Waggoner, Diane. *The Hills of Faraway: A Guide to Fantasy*. New York, NY: Atheneum, 1978. Print.

Wagner, Karl Edward. *Bloodstone*. New York, NY: Warner Books, 1975. Print.

Wagner, Karl Edward. "Cold Light." *Death Angel's Shadow*. New York, NY: Warner Books, 1973. Print.

Wagner, Karl Edward. *Dark Crusade*. New York, NY: Warner Books, 1976. Print.

Wagner, Karl Edward. *Darkness Weaves*. New York, NY: Warner Books, 1978. Print.

Wagner, Karl Edward. "Editor's Introduction to 'Adept's Gambit.'" *Echoes of Valor*. Edited by Wagner. New York, NY: Tor Books, 1987. Print.

Wagner, Karl Edward. "Editor's Introduction to 'The Black Stranger.'" *Echoes of Valor*. Edited by Wagner. New York, NY: Tor Books, 1987. Print.

Wagner, Karl Edward. "Foreword." *in* Howard, Robert E. *The Hour of the Dragon*. New York, NY: Berkley Medallion Books, 1977. Print.

Wagner, Karl Edward. "Foreword." *in* Howard, Robert E. *The People of the Black Circle*. New York, NY: Berkley Medallion Books, 1977. Print.

Wagner, Karl Edward. "Foreword." in Howard, Robert E. *Red Nails*. New York, NY: Berkley Medallion Books, 1977. Print.

Wagner, Karl Edward. "Henry Kuttner: Introduction." *Echoes of Valor III*. Edited by Wagner. New York, NY: Tor Books, 1991. Print.

Wagner, Karl Edward. "The Once and Future Kane." *Midnight Sun: The Complete Stories of Kane*. New York, NY: Night Shade Books, 2003. Print.

Wagner, Karl Edward. "Neither Brute Nor Human." *Why Not You and I?* New York, NY: Tor, 1987. Print.

Wagner, Karl Edward. *Night Winds*. New York, NY: Warner Books, 1978. Print.

Wanchoo, Mihir. "Interview with James Enge." *Fantasy Book Critic*. May 28, 2009. http://fantasybookcritic.blogspot.com/2009/05/interview-with-james-enge-interviewed.html. Retrieved August 27, 2019. Web.

Warner, Andrea. "George R.R. Martin: Fantasy for Non-Fantasy People." AbeBooks.com. 2006. https://www.abebooks.com/docs/Fantasy/george-martin.shtml. Retrieved March 24, 2018. Web.

Weber, Max. "Science as a Vocation." Anthropological Research on the Contemporary. Dec. 2011. http://anthropos-lab.net/wp/wp-content/uploads/2011/12/Weber-Science-as-a-Vocation.pdf. Retrieved Oct. 8, 2018. Web.

Weinstein, Deena. *Heavy Metal: The Music and its Culture*. Boston, MA: Da Capo Press, 2000. Print.

Williamson, Jamie. *The Evolution of Modern Fantasy: From Antiquarianism to the Ballantine Adult Fantasy Series*. New York, NY: Palgrave Macmillan, 2015. Print.

Acknowledgments

I would like to thank Lee Breakiron for providing me with access to the entire run of *Amra* and the issue of *Ancalagon* in which the term "sword-and-sorcery" was born; Deuce Richardson for his helpful comments, erudition, and critique; Morgan Holmes for his ideas and encouragement; Steve Tompkins, who showed me the art of criticism, and if not for his untimely passing would have written the definitive history of sword-and-sorcery; and most of all my wife, for her patience and support.

About the Author

Brian Murphy (born 1973) discovered Robert E. Howard in the pages of *Savage Sword of Conan* in the early 1980s, sparking a lifelong love of fantasy. He went on to read widely in fantasy and science fiction before discovering his true passion lay in sword-and-sorcery fiction.

Murphy started writing about fantasy on the web in 2007 and was recruited to join a group of bloggers at The Cimmerian, a website dedicated to Howard, J.R.R. Tolkien, and heroic fantasy. Since then he has been published in numerous print publications and online venues, including The Cimmerian, Black Gate, Mythprint, *REH: Two-Gun Raconteur*, *The Dark Man*, DMR blog, *Skelos*, and SFFaudio.com.

Murphy's essay "The Unnatural City" (from the Cimmerian, Vol. 5 No. 2) was nominated for Outstanding Achievement—Essay at the first annual Robert E. Howard Foundation awards in 2009, as was his "Unmasking 'The Shadow Kingdom': Kull and Howard as Outsiders" (from *REH: Two-Gun Raconteur* #14) in 2011.

By day Murphy works for a healthcare publishing company. He enjoys heavy metal music and is an on-again/off-again player of *Dungeons & Dragons* and other role-playing games. He is married and lives with his wife and two daughters in Massachusetts. To learn more about his interests and writings please visit *The Silver Key*: http://thesilverkey.blogspot.com/.

About the Artist

Tom Barber (born 1946) illustrated the covers of many iconic sword-and-sorcery, historical adventure, weird horror, and science fiction paperbacks and magazines in the late 1970s and early 1980s. These include the cover art for *Black Vulmea's Vengeance*, a collection of pirate stories written by Robert E. Howard; four covers for a series of Talbot Mundy reprints; and three covers in a revival of *Weird Tales* edited by Lin Carter. He also did work for *Heavy Metal* magazine and *Galileo Magazine of Science & Fiction*.

A graduate of the Art Institute of Boston, Barber served as an Army medic in Germany in the late 1960s during the Vietnam War. Upon his return to the U.S. he embarked on a career in art and was named Best Professional Artist of the year by the New England Science Fiction Convention in 1976.

After moving to Arizona where he spent time panning for gold and other pursuits, Barber returned east and to general painting in 1988. *Sword-and-Sorcery Reanimated* (2019) marks a return to classic sword-and-sorcery.

Barber lives in New Hampshire with his significant other, Terri. To view his art or inquire about purchasing his work please visit http://tombarberart.com/.

Printed in Great Britain
by Amazon